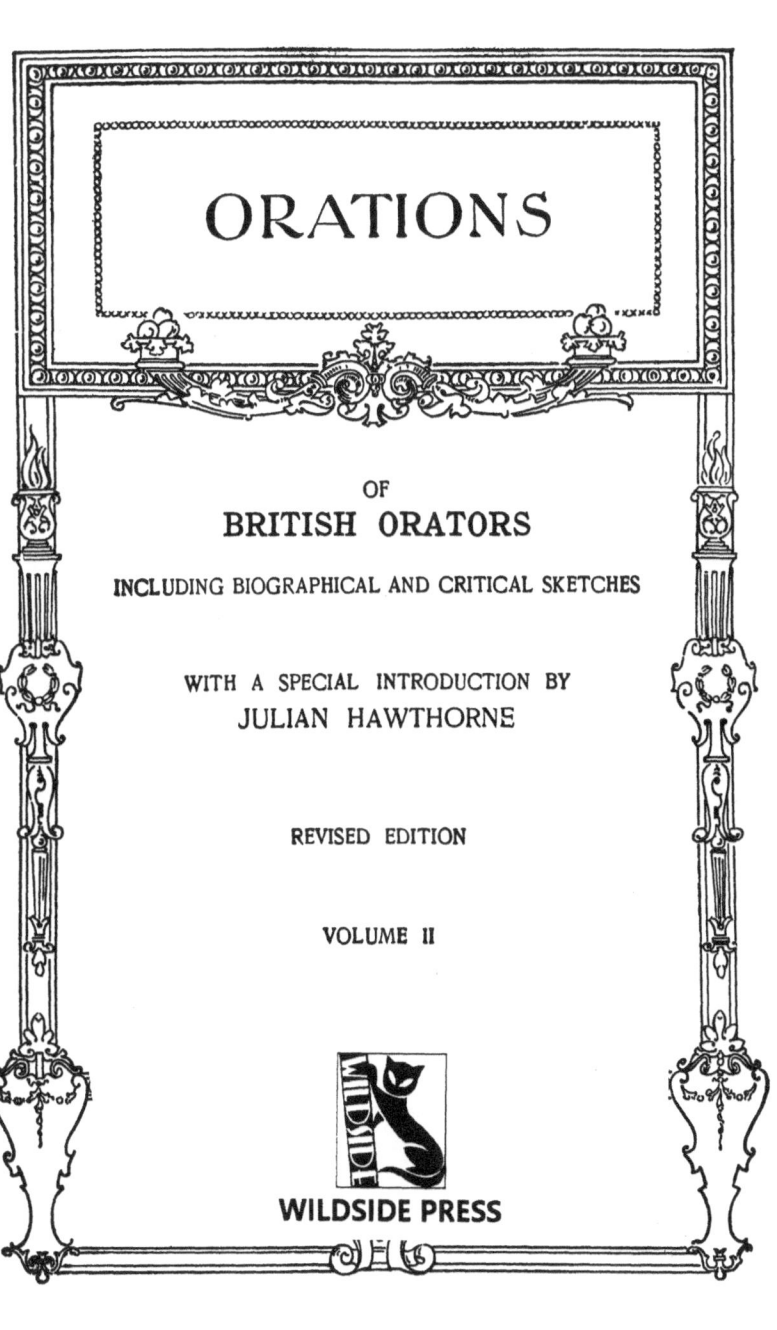

ORATIONS

OF

BRITISH ORATORS

INCLUDING BIOGRAPHICAL AND CRITICAL SKETCHES

WITH A SPECIAL INTRODUCTION BY
JULIAN HAWTHORNE

REVISED EDITION

VOLUME II

WILDSIDE PRESS

CONTENTS

iv CONTENTS

ILLUSTRATIONS

ON HIS REFUSAL TO NEGOTIATE
WITH BONAPARTE

—

BY

WILLIAM PITT

WILLIAM PITT

1759—1806

William Pitt the younger was remarkable for the precocity of his powers, as well as for the superiority of the powers themselves. His life lasted but forty-seven years, yet he was for some twenty-three years practically the ruler of England, and died in the harness; the interregnum of the Addington ministry, 1801 to 1804, was made up of his supporters. His career did not begin until the American Revolution was practically over; but had he been able to deal with it, it is probable that the example of his great father, as well as his sympathy with Burke, not to speak of his own generous and magnanimous character, would have prompted him to favor the contentions of the colonists But as it was, his life was passed in the struggle with Napoleon, and his death was thought to have been hastened by his grief at the victories of the latter over the combined armies, culminating with the rout of Austerlitz. In addition to his foreign policy, however, Pitt gave vigorous attention to internal affairs; and was severe in repressing the Jacobins; while his effort to remove some of the Roman Catholic disabilities, being opposed by the King, led to his resignation from office in 1801.

For a man thoroughly honorable, and devoted to the public weal; pure in life, public and private; and endowed with signal abilities, Pitt incurred more and bitterer enmities than any contemporary public man. He was hated on the Continent with a virulence which could not be surpassed; and his political opponents in England were hardly less unmeasured in their abuse of him. The cause of this is probably to be sought in the austerity of his personal bearing, the lack of lightness and sunshine in his nature, his preoccupation with affairs, to the exclusion of all those relaxations and common human sympathies which make men acquainted with one another, and form the real basis of their friendly communion with one another Pitt was solitary, dry, forbidding, proud, and uncongenial, he took everything seriously, and felt to the full his own enormous responsibilities The formality and loftiness of his manners, his impatience of opposition, his indifference to the sensibilities of others, and the secrecy with which he hedged about most of his acts, combined to raise up foes and to give plausibility to slanders. Probably no man who has attained equal eminence, and whose deeds have been so consistently honorable and patriotic, has met during his lifetime with so much misrepresentation and obloquy. But history has done him justice as one of the great men of England.

A great orator he could hardly be termed, especially when compared with the mighty genius of some of his contemporaries and immediate predecessors. But all that he said had weight and point, and tended to the making of history One of his most interesting speeches was delivered in the House of Commons on February 3, 1800, defending his refusal to negotiate with Bonaparte for a peace with France.

ON HIS REFUSAL TO NEGOTIATE WITH BONAPARTE

S IR: I am induced, at this period of the debate, to offer my sentiments to the House, both from an apprehension that at a later hour the attention of the House must necessarily be exhausted, and because the sentiment with which the honorable and learned gentleman [Mr. Erskine] began his speech, and with which he has thought proper to conclude it, places the question precisely on that ground on which I am most desirous of discussing it. The learned gentleman seems to assume as the foundation of his reasoning, and as the great argument for immediate treaty, that every effort to overturn the system of the French Revolution must be unavailing; and that it would be not only imprudent, but almost impious, to struggle longer against that order of things which, on I know not what principle of predestination, he appears to consider as immortal. Little as I am inclined to accede to this opinion, I am not sorry that the honorable gentleman has contemplated the subject in this serious view. I do, indeed, consider the French Revolution as the severest trial which the visitation of Providence has ever yet inflicted upon the nations of the earth; but I cannot help reflecting, with satisfaction, that this country, even under such a trial, has not only been exempted from those calamities which have covered almost every other part of Europe, but appears to have been reserved as a refuge and asylum to thóse who fled from its persecution, as a barrier to oppose its progress, and perhaps ultimately as an instrument to deliver the world from the crimes and miseries which have attended it.

Under this impression, I trust the House will forgive me, if I endeavor, as far as I am able, to take a large and comprehensive view of this important question. In doing so, I agree with my honorable friend [Mr. Canning] that it would, in any case, be impossible to separate the present discussion from the former

3

crimes and atrocities of the French Revolution; because both
the papers now on the table, and the whole of the learned gentleman's argument, force upon our consideration the origin of
the war, and all the material facts which have occurred during
its continuance. The learned gentleman [Mr. Erskine] has
revived and retailed all those arguments from his own pamphlet, which had before passed through thirty-seven or thirty-
eight editions in print, and now gives them to the House em-
bellished by the graces of his personal delivery. The First
Consul has also thought fit to revive and retail the chief arguments used by all the opposition speakers and all the opposition
publishers in this country during the last seven years. And
(what is still more material) the question itself, which is now
immediately at issue—the question whether, under the present
circumstances, there is such a prospect of security from any
treaty with France as ought to induce us to negotiate—cannot
be properly decided upon without retracing, both from our own
experience and from that of other nations, the nature, the causes,
and the magnitude of the danger against which we have to
guard, in order to judge of the security which we ought to
accept.

I say, then, that before any man can concur in opinion with
that learned gentleman; before any man can think that the substance of His Majesty's answer is any other than the safety of
the country required; before any man can be of opinion that, to
the overtures made by the enemy, at such a time and under
such circumstances, it would have been safe to return an
answer concurring in the negotiation—he must come within one
of the three following descriptions: He must either believe that
the French Revolution neither does now exhibit nor has at any
time exhibited such circumstances of danger, arising out of the
very nature of the system, and the internal state and condition
of France, as to leave to foreign powers no adequate ground of
security in negotiation; or, secondly, he must be of opinion
that the change which has recently taken place has given that
security which, in the former stages of the Revolution, was
wanting; or, thirdly, he must be one who, believing that the
danger exists, not undervaluing its extent nor mistaking its
nature, nevertheless thinks, from his view of the present pressure on the country, from his view of its situation and its pros-

pects, compared with the situation and prospects of its enemies, that we are, with our eyes open, bound to accept of
inadequate security for everything that is valuable and sacred,
rather than endure the pressure, or incur the risk, which would
result from a further prolongation of the contest.

In discussing the last of these questions, we shall be led to
consider what inference is to be drawn from the circumstances
and the result of our own negotiations in former periods of the
war; whether, in the comparative state of this country and
France, we now see the same reason for repeating our then
unsuccessful experiments; or whether we have not thence derived the lessons of experience, added to the deductions of reason, marking the inefficacy and danger of the very measures
which are quoted to us as precedents for our adoption.

Unwilling, sir, as I am to go into much detail on ground which
has been so often trodden before; yet, when I find the learned
gentleman, after all the information which he must have received, if he has read any of the answers to his work (however
ignorant he might be when he wrote it), still giving the sanction of his authority to the supposition that the order to M.
Chauvelin [French minister] to depart from this kingdom was
the cause of the war between this country and France, I do
feel it necessary to say a few words on that part of the subject.

Inaccuracy in dates seems to be a sort of fatality common
to all who have written on that side of the question; for even
the writer of the note to His Majesty is not more correct, in
this respect, than if he had taken his information only from the
pamphlet of the learned gentleman. The House will recollect
the first professions of the French Republic, which are enumerated, and enumerated truly, in that note. They are tests
of everything which would best recommend a government to
the esteem and confidence of foreign powers, and the reverse of
everything which has been the system and practice of France
now for near ten years. It is there stated that their first principles were love of peace, aversion to conquest, and respect for
the independence of other countries. In the same note it seems,
indeed, admitted that they since have violated all those principles; but it is alleged that they have done so only in consequence of the provocation of other powers. One of the first of
those provocations is stated to have consisted in the various out-

rages offered to their ministers, of which the example is said to have been set by the King of Great Britain in his conduct to M. Chauvelin. In answer to this supposition, it is only necessary to remark that before the example was given, before Austria and Prussia are supposed to have been thus encouraged to combine in a plan for the partition of France, that plan, if it ever existed at all, had existed and been acted upon for above eight months. France and Prussia had been at war eight months before the dismissal of M. Chauvelin. So much for the accuracy of the statement.

I have been hitherto commenting on the arguments contained in the notes. I come now to those of the learned gentleman. I understand him to say that the dismissal of M. Chauvelin was the real cause, I do not say of the general war, but of the rupture between France and England; and the learned gentleman states particularly that this dismissal rendered all discussion of the points in dispute impossible. Now I desire to meet distinctly every part of this assertion. I maintain, on the contrary, that an opportunity was given for discussing every matter in dispute between France and Great Britain as fully as if a regular and accredited French minister had been resident here; that the causes of war which existed at the beginning, or arose during the course of this discussion, were such as would have justified, twenty times over, a declaration of war on the part of this country; that all the explanations on the part of France were evidently unsatisfactory and inadmissible, and that M. Chauvelin had given in a peremptory ultimatum, declaring that if these explanations were not received as sufficient, and if we did not immediately disarm, our refusal would be considered as a declaration of war. After this followed that scene which no man can even now speak of without horror, or think of without indignation; that murder and regicide from which I was sorry to hear the learned gentleman date the beginning of the legal government of France.

Having thus given in their ultimatum, they added, as a further demand (while we were smarting under accumulated injuries, for which all satisfaction was denied) that we should instantly receive M. Chauvelin as their ambassador, with new credentials, representing them in the character which they had just derived from the murder of their sovereign. We replied, " He came here as the representative of a sovereign whom you have put to a cruel and illegal death; we have no satisfaction for the injuries we have received, no security from the danger with which we are threatened. Under these circumstances we will not receive your new credentials. The former credentials you have yourself recalled by the sacrifice of your king."

What, from that moment, was the situation of M. Chauvelin? He was reduced to the situation of a private individual, and was required to quit the kingdom under the provisions of the Alien Act, which, for the purpose of securing domestic tranquillity, had recently invested His Majesty with the power of removing out of this kingdom all foreigners suspected of revolutionary principles. Is it contended that he was then less liable to the provisions of that act than any other individual foreigner, whose conduct afforded to government just ground of objection or suspicion? Did his conduct and connections here afford no such ground? or will it be pretended that the bare act of refusing to receive fresh credentials from an infant republic, not then acknowledged by any one power of Europe, and in the very act of heaping upon us injuries and insults, was of itself a cause of war? So far from it, that even the very nations of Europe whose wisdom and moderation have been repeatedly extolled for maintaining neutrality, and preserving friendship with the French Republic, remained for years subsequent to this period without receiving from it any accredited minister, or doing any one act to acknowledge its political existence.

In answer to a representation from the belligerent powers, in December, 1793, Count Bernstorff, the minister of Denmark, officially declared that " it was well known that the National Convention had appointed M. Grouville minister plenipotentiary at Denmark, but that it was also well known that he had neither been received nor acknowledged in that quality." And as late as February, 1796, when the same minister was at length, for the first time, received in his official capacity, Count Bernstorff, in a public note, assigned this reason for that change of conduct: " So long as no other than a revolutionary government existed in France, His Majesty could not acknowledge the minister of that government; but now that the French constitution is completely organized, and a regular government established in France, His Majesty's obligation ceases in that respect, and

M. Grouville will therefore be acknowledged in the usual form."
How far the Court of Denmark was justified in the opinion that
a revolutionary government then no longer existed in France
it is not now necessary to inquire; but whatever may have been
the fact in that respect, the principle on which they acted is clear
and intelligible, and is a decisive instance in favor of the proposition which I have maintained.

Is it, then, necessary to examine what were the terms of that
ultimatum with which we refused to comply? Acts of hostility
had been openly threatened against our allies; a hostility
founded upon the assumption of a right which would at once
supersede the whole law of nations. The pretended right to
open the Scheldt we discussed at the time, not so much on account of its immediate importance (though it was important
both in a maritime and commercial view) as on account of the
general principle on which it was founded. On the same arbitrary notion they soon afterward discovered that sacred law
of nature which made the Rhine and the Alps the legitimate
boundaries of France, and assumed the power, which they have
affected to exercise through the whole of the Revolution, of
superseding, by a new code of their own, all the recognized
principles of the law of nations. They were, in fact, actually
advancing towards the republic of Holland, by rapid strides,
after the victory of Jemappes, and they had ordered their generals to pursue the Austrian troops into any neutral country,
thereby explicitly avowing an intention of invading Holland.
They had already shown their moderation and self-denial by incorporating Belgium with the French Republic. These lovers
of peace, who set out with a sworn aversion to conquest, and
professions of respect for the independence of other nations;
who pretend that they departed from this system only in consequence of your aggression, themselves, in time of peace, while
you were still confessedly neutral, without the pretence or shadow of provocation, wrested Savoy from the King of Sardinia,
and had proceeded to incorporate it likewise with France.
These were their aggressions at this period, and more than these.
They had issued a universal declaration of war against all the
thrones of Europe, and they had, by their conduct, applied it
particularly and specifically to you. They had passed the decree
of November 19, 1792, proclaiming the promise of French suc-

cor to all nations who should manifest a wish to become free; they had, by all their language as well as their example, shown what they understood to be freedom; they had sealed their principles by the deposition of their sovereign; they had applied them to England by inviting and encouraging the addresses of those seditious and traitorous societies, who, from the beginning, favored their views, and who, encouraged by your forbearance, were even then publicly avowing French doctrines, and anticipating their success in this country—who were hailing the progress of those proceedings in France which led to the murder of its king; they were even then looking to the day when they should behold a National Convention in England formed upon similar principles.

And what were the explanations they offered on these different grounds of offence? As to Holland: they told you the Scheldt was too insignificant for you to trouble yourselves about, and therefore it was to be decided as they chose, in breach of positive treaty, which they had themselves guaranteed, and which we, by our alliance, were bound to support. If, however, after the war was over, Belgium should have consolidated its liberty (a term of which we now know the meaning, from the fate of every nation into which the arms of France have penetrated) then Belgium and Holland might, if they pleased, settle the question of the Scheldt by separate negotiation between themselves. With respect to aggrandizement, they assured us that they would retain possession of Belgium by arms no longer than they should find it necessary to the purpose already stated, of consolidating its liberty. And with respect to the decree of November 19, 1792, applied as it was pointedly to you, by all the intercourse I have stated with all the seditious and traitorous part of this country, and particularly by the speeches of every leading man among them, they contented themselves with asserting that the declaration conveyed no such meaning as was imputed to it, and that, so far from encouraging sedition, it could apply only to countries where a great majority of the people should have already declared itself in favor of a revolution: a supposition which, as they asserted, necessarily implied a total absence of all sedition.

What would have been the effect of admitting this explanation? to suffer a nation, and an armed nation, to preach to the inhabitants of all the countries in the world that they themselves were slaves and their rulers tyrants; to encourage and invite them to revolution by a previous promise of French support to whatever might call itself a majority, or to whatever France might declare to be so. This was their explanation; and this, they told you, was their ultimatum.

But was this all? Even at that very moment, when they were endeavoring to induce you to admit these explanations, to be contented with the avowal that France offered herself as a general guarantee for every successful revolution, and would interfere only to sanction and confirm whatever the free and uninfluenced choice of the people might have decided, what were their orders to their generals on the same subject? In the midst of these amicable explanations with you came forth a decree which I really believe must be effaced from the minds of gentlemen opposite to me, if they can prevail upon themselves for a moment to hint even a doubt upon the origin of this quarrel, not only as to this country, but as to all the nations of Europe with whom France has been subsequently engaged in hostility. I speak of the decree of December 15, 1792. This decree, more even than all the previous transactions, amounted to a universal declaration of war against all thrones, and against all civilized governments. It said, wherever the armies of France shall come (whether within countries then at war or at peace is not distinguished) in all those countries it shall be the first care of their generals to introduce the principles and the practice of the French Revolution; to demolish all privileged orders, and everything which obstructs the establishment of their new system.

If any doubt is entertained whither the armies of France were intended to come; if it is contended that they referred only to those nations with whom they were then at war, or with whom, in the course of this contest, they might be driven into war; let it be remembered that at this very moment they had actually given orders to their generals to pursue the Austrian army from the Netherlands into Holland, with whom they were at that time in peace. Or, even if the construction contended for is admitted, let us see what would have been its application, let us look at the list of their aggressions, which was read by my right honorable friend [Mr. Dundas] near me.

With whom have they been at war since the period of this declaration? With all the nations of Europe save two (Sweden and Denmark), and if not with these two, it is only because, with every provocation that could justify defensive war, those countries have hitherto acquiesced in repeated violations of their rights rather than recur to war for their vindication. Wherever their arms have been carried it will be a matter of short subsequent inquiry to trace whether they have faithfully applied these principles. If in terms this decree is a denunciation of war against all governments; if in practice it has been applied against every one with which France has come into contact; what is it but the deliberate code of the French Revolution, from the birth of the republic, which has never once been departed from, which has been enforced with unremitted rigor against all the nations that have come into their power?

If there could otherwise be any doubt whether the application of this decree was intended to be universal, whether it applied to all nations, and to England particularly; there is one circumstance which alone would be decisive—that nearly at the same period it was proposed [by M. Baraillon], in the National Convention, to declare expressly that the decree of November 19th was confined to the nations with whom they were then at war; and that proposal was rejected by a great majority, by that very Convention from whom we were desired to receive these explanations as satisfactory.

Such, sir, was the nature of the system. Let us examine a little farther, whether it was from the beginning intended to be acted upon in the extent which I have stated. At the very moment when their threats appeared to many little else than the ravings of madmen, they were digesting and methodizing the means of execution, as accurately as if they had actually foreseen the extent to which they have since been able to realize their criminal projects. They sat down coolly to devise the most regular and effectual mode of making the application of this system the current business of the day, and incorporating it with the general orders of their army; for (will the House believe it!) this confirmation of the decree of November 19th was accompanied by an exposition and commentary addressed to the general of every army of France, containing a schedule as coolly conceived, and as methodically reduced, as any by which the most quiet business of a justice of peace, or the most regular routine of any department of state in this country could be conducted. Each commander was furnished with one general blank formula of a letter for all the nations of the world! The people of France to the people of ——, Greeting, " We are come to expel your tyrants." Even this was not all; one of the articles of the decree of the fifteenth of December was expressly " that those who should show themselves so brutish and so enamored of their chains as to refuse the restoration of their rights, to renounce liberty and equality, or to preserve, recall, or treat with their prince or privileged orders, were not entitled to the distinction which France, in other cases, had justly established between government and people; and that such a people ought to be treated according to the rigor of war, and of conquest." Here is their love of peace; here is their aversion to conquest; here is their respect for the independence of other nations!

It was then, after receiving such explanations as these, after receiving the ultimatum of France, and after M. Chauvelin's credentials had ceased, that he was required to depart. Even at that period I am almost ashamed to record it, we did not on our part shut the door against other attempts to negotiate, but this transaction was immediately followed by the declaration of war, proceeding not from England in vindication of her rights, but from France, as the completion of the injuries and insults they had offered. And on a war thus originating, can it be doubted by an English House of Commons whether the aggression was on the part of this country or of France? or whether the manifest aggression on the part of France was the result of anything but the principles which characterize the French Revolution?

What, then, are the resources and subterfuges by which those who agree with the learned gentleman are prevented from sinking under the force of this simple statement of facts? None but what are found in the insinuation contained in the note from France, that this country had, previous to the transactions to which I have referred, encouraged and supported the combination of other powers directed against them.

Upon this part of the subject, the proofs which contradict such an insinuation are innumerable. In the first place, the evidence of dates; in the second place, the admission of all the

different parties in France; of the friends of Brissot, charging
on Robespierre the war with this country, and of the friends
of Robespierre charging it on Brissot, but both acquitting England; the testimonies of the French government during the
whole interval, since the declaration of Pilnitz and the pretended
treaty of Pavia; the first of which had not the slightest relation to any project of partition or dismemberment; the second
of which I firmly believe to be an absolute fabrication and
forgery, and in neither of which, even as they are represented,
any reason has been assigned for believing that this country had
any share. Even M. Talleyrand himself was sent by the constitutional king of the French, after the period when that concert which is now charged must have existed, if it existed at
all, with a letter from the King of France, expressly thanking
His Majesty for the neutrality which he had uniformly observed. The same fact is confirmed by the concurring evidence
of every person who knew anything of the plans of the King
of Sweden in 1791; the only sovereign who, I believe, at that
time meditated any hostile measures against France, and whose
utmost hopes were expressly stated to be, that England would
not oppose his intended expedition; by all those, also, who knew
anything of the conduct of the Emperor or the King of Prussia;
by the clear and decisive testimony of M. Chauvelin himself in
his despatches from hence to the French government, since published by their authority; by everything which has occurred
since the war; by the publications of Dumourier; by the publications of Brissot; by the facts that have since come to light
in America, with respect to the mission of M. Genet, which
show that hostility against this country was decided on by
France long before the period when M. Chauvelin was sent
from hence, besides this, the reduction of our peace establishment in the year 1791, and continued to the subsequent year,
is a fact from which the inference is indisputable; a fact which,
I am afraid, shows not only that we were not waiting for the
occasion of war, but that, in our partiality for a pacific system,
we had indulged ourselves in a fond and credulous security,
which wisdom and discretion would not have dictated. In addition to every other proof, it is singular enough that, in a
decree, on the eve of a declaration of war on the part of France,
it is expressly stated, as for the first time, that England was

then departing from that system of neutrality which she had hitherto observed.

But, sir, I will not rest merely on these testimonies or arguments, however strong and decisive. I assert distinctly and positively, and I have the documents in my hand to prove it, that from the middle of the year 1791, upon the first rumor of any measure taken by the Emperor of Germany, and till late in the year 1792, we not only were no parties to any of the projects imputed to the Emperor, but, from the political circumstances in which we stood with relation to that court, we wholly declined all communications with him on the subject of France. To Prussia, with whom we were in connection, and still more decisively to Holland, with whom we were in close and intimate correspondence, we uniformly stated our unalterable resolution to maintain neutrality, and avoid interference in the internal affairs of France, as long as France should refrain from hostile measures against us and our allies. No minister of England had any authority to treat with foreign states, even provisionally, for any warlike concert, till after the battle of Jemappes; till a period subsequent to the repeated provocations which had been offered to us, and subsequent particularly to the decree of fraternity of the nineteenth of November; even then, to what object was it that the concert which we wished to establish, was to be directed? If we had then rightly cast the true character of the French Revolution, I cannot now deny that we should have been better justified in a very different conduct. But it is material to the present argument to declare what that conduct actually was, because it is of itself sufficient to confute all the pretexts by which the advocates of France have so long labored to perplex the question of aggression.

At that period Russia had at length conceived, as well as ourselves, a natural and just alarm for the balance of Europe, and applied to us to learn our sentiments on the subject. In our answer to this application we imparted to Russia the principles upon which we then acted, and we communicated this answer to Prussia, with whom we were connected in defensive alliance. I will state shortly the leading part of those principles. A despatch was sent from Lord Grenville to His Majesty's minister in Russia, dated the twenty-ninth of December, 1792, stating a desire to have an explanation set on foot on the subject of the war with France. I will read the material parts of it.

" The two leading points on which such explanation will naturally turn are the line of conduct to be followed previous to the commencement of hostilities, and with a view, if possible, to avert them; and the nature and amount of the forces which the powers engaged in this concert might be enabled to use, supposing such extremities to be unavoidable.

" With respect to the first, it appears, on the whole, subject, however, to future consideration and discussion with the other powers, that the most advisable step to be taken would be, that sufficient explanation should be had with the powers at war with France, in order to enable those not hitherto engaged in the war to propose to that country terms of peace. That these terms should be the withdrawing their arms within the limits of the French territory; the abandoning their conquests, the rescinding any acts injurious to the sovereignty or rights of any other nations, and the giving, in some public and unequivocal manner, a pledge of their intention no longer to foment troubles or to excite disturbances against other governments. In return for these stipulations, the different powers of Europe who should be parties to this measure might engage to abandon all measures, or views of hostility against France, or interference in their internal affairs, and to maintain a correspondence and intercourse of amity with the existing powers in that country, with whom such a treaty may be concluded. If, as the result of this proposal so made by the powers acting in concert, these terms should not be accepted by France, or being accepted, should not be satisfactorily performed, the different powers might then engage themselves to each other to enter into active measures for the purpose of obtaining the ends in view; and it may be considered whether, in such case, they might not reasonably look to some indemnity for the expenses and hazards to which they would necessarily be exposed."

The despatch then proceeded to the second point, that of the forces to be employed, on which it is unnecessary now to speak.

Now, sir, I would really ask any person who has been from the beginning the most desirous of avoiding hostilities, whether it is possible to conceive any measure to be adopted in the situation in which we then stood which could more evidently demonstrate our desire, after repeated provocations, to preserve peace, on any terms consistent with our safety; or whether any sentiment could now be suggested which would have more plainly marked our moderation, forbearance, and sincerity? In saying this I am not challenging the applause and approbation of my country, because I must now confess that we were too slow in anticipating that danger of which we had, perhaps, even then sufficient experience, though far short, indeed, of that which we now possess, and that we might even then have seen, what facts have since but too incontestably proved, that nothing but vigorous and open hostility can afford complete and adequate security against revolutionary principles, while they retain a proportion of power sufficient to furnish the means of war.

I will enlarge no farther on the origin of the war. I have read and detailed to you a system which was in itself a declaration of war against all nations, which was so intended, and which has been so applied, which has been exemplified in the extreme peril and hazard of almost all who for a moment have trusted to treaty, and which has not at this hour overwhelmed Europe in one indiscriminate mass of ruin, only because we have not indulged, to a fatal extremity, that disposition which we have, however, indulged too far; because we have not consented to trust to profession and compromise, rather than to our own valor and exertion, for security against a system from which we never shall be delivered till either the principle is extinguished, or till its strength is exhausted.

I might, sir, if I found it necessary, enter into much detail upon this part of the subject; but at present I only beg leave to express my readiness at any time to enter upon it, when either my own strength or the patience of the House will admit of it; but I say, without distinction, against every nation in Europe, and against some out of Europe, the principle has been faithfully applied. You cannot look at the map of Europe, and lay your hand upon that country against which France has not either declared an open and aggressive war, or violated some positive treaty, or broken some recognized principle of the law of nations.

This subject may be divided into various periods. There were some acts of hostility committed previous to the war with this country, and very little, indeed, subsequent to that declaration, which abjured the love of conquest. The attack upon the Papal State, by the seizure of Avignon, in 1791, was accompanied with specimens of all the vile arts and perfidy that ever disgraced a revolution. Avignon was separated from its lawful sovereign, with whom not even the pretence of quarrel existed, and forcibly incorporated in the tyranny of one and indivisible France. The same system led, in the same year, to an aggression against the whole German Empire, by the seizure of Porentrui, part of the dominions of the Bishop of Basle. Afterwards, in 1792, unpreceded by any declaration of war, or any cause of hostility, and in direct violation of the solemn pledge to abstain from conquest, they made war against the King of Sardinia, by the seizure of Savoy, for the purpose of incorporating it, in like manner, with France. In the same year, they had proceeded to the declaration of war against Austria, against Prussia, and against the German Empire, in which they have been justified only on the ground of a 'rooted hostility, combination, and league of sovereigns, for the dismemberment of France. I say that some of the documents brought to support this pretence are spurious and false. I say that even in those that are not so, there is not one word to prove the charge principally relied upon, that of an intention to effect the dismemberment of France, or to impose upon it, by force, any particular constitution. I say that, as far as we have been able to trace what passed at Pilnitz, the declaration there signed referred to the imprisonment of Louis XVI; its immediate view was to effect his deliverance, if a concert sufficiently extensive could be formed with other sovereigns for that purpose. It left the internal state of France to be decided by the king restored to his liberty, with the free consent of the states of his kingdom, and it did not contain one word relative to the dismemberment of France.

In the subsequent discussions, which took place in 1792, and which embraced at the same time all the other points of jealousy which had arisen between the two countries, the Declaration of Pilnitz was referred to, and explained on the part of Austria in a manner precisely conformable to what I have now stated. The amicable explanations which took place, both on this subject and on all the matters in dispute, will be found in the official correspondence between the two Courts which has been made public; and it will be found, also, that as long as the negotiation continued to be conducted through M. Delessart, then Minister for Foreign Affairs, there was a great prospect that those discussions would be amicably terminated; but it is notorious, and has since been clearly proved on the authority of Brissot himself, that the violent party in France considered such an issue of the negotiation as likely to be fatal to their projects, and thought, to use his own words, that " war was necessary to consolidate the Revolution." For the express purpose of producing the war they excited a popular tumult in Paris; they insisted upon and obtained the dismissal of M. Delessart. A new minister was appointed in his room, the tone of the negotiation was immediately changed, and an ultimatum was sent to the Emperor, similar to that which was afterwards sent to this country, affording him no satisfaction on his just grounds of complaint, and requiring him, under those circumstances, to disarm. The first events of the contest proved how much more France was prepared for war than Austria, and afford a strong confirmation of the proposition which I maintain, that no offensive intention was entertained on the part of the latter power.

War was then declared against Austria, a war which I state to be a war of aggression on the part of France. The King of Prussia had declared that he should consider war against the Emperor or empire as war against himself. He had declared that, as a coestate of the empire, he was determined to defend their rights; that, as an ally of the Emperor, he would support him to the utmost against any attack; and that, for the sake of his own dominions, he felt himself called upon to resist the progress of French principles, and to maintain the balance of power in Europe. With this notice before them, France declared war upon the Emperor, and the war with Prussia was the necessary consequence of this aggression, both against the Emperor and the empire.

The war against the King of Sardinia follows next. The declaration of that war was the seizure of Savoy by an invading army—and on what ground? On that which has been stated already. They had found out, by some light of nature, that the Rhine and the Alps were the natural limits of France. Upon that ground Savoy was seized; and Savoy was also incorporated with France.

Here finishes the history of the wars in which France was

engaged antecedent to the war with Great Britain, with Holland, and with Spain. With respect to Spain, we have seen nothing which leads us to suspect that either attachment to religion, or the ties of consanguinity, or regard to the ancient system of Europe, was likely to induce that Court to connect itself in offensive war against France. The war was evidently and incontestably begun by France against Spain.

The case of Holland is so fresh in every man's recollection, and so connected with the immediate causes of the war with this country, that it cannot require one word of observation. What shall I say, then, on the case of Portugal? I cannot, indeed, say that France ever declared war against that country. I can hardly say even that she ever made war, but she required them to make a treaty of peace, as if they had been at war; she obliged them to purchase that treaty; she broke it as soon as it was purchased; and she had originally no other ground of complaint than this, that Portugal had performed, though inadequately, the engagements of its ancient defensive alliance with this country in the character of an auxiliary—a conduct which cannot of itself make any power a principal in a war.

I have now enumerated all the nations at war at that period, with the exception only of Naples. It can hardly be necessary to call to the recollection of the House the characteristic feature of revolutionary principles which was shown, even at this early period, in the personal insult offered to the King of Naples by the commander of a French squadron riding uncontrolled in the Mediterranean, and (while our fleets were yet unarmed) threatening destruction to all the coast of Italy.

It was not till a considerably later period that almost all the other nations of Europe found themselves equally involved in actual hostility; but it is not a little material to the whole of my argument, compared with the statement of the learned gentleman, and with that contained in the French note, to examine at what period this hostility extended itself. It extended itself, in the course of 1796, to the states of Italy which had hitherto been exempted from it. In 1797 it had ended in the destruction of most of them; it had ended in the virtual deposition of the King of Sardinia; it had ended in the conversion of Genoa and Tuscany into democratic republics; it had ended in the revolution of Venice, in the violation of treaties with the new Venetian

Republic; and, finally, in transferring that very republic, the creature and vassal of France, to the dominion of Austria.

I observe from the gestures of some honorable gentlemen that they think we are precluded from the use of any argument founded on this last transaction. I already hear them saying that it was as criminal in Austria to receive as it was in France to give. I am far from defending or palliating the conduct of Austria upon this occasion. But because Austria, unable at last to contend with the arms of France, was forced to accept an unjust and insufficient indemnification for the conquests France had made from it, are we to be debarred from stating what, on the part of France, was not merely an unjust acquisition, but an act of the grossest and most aggravated perfidy and cruelty, and one of the most striking specimens of that system which has been uniformly and indiscriminately applied to all the countries which France has had within its grasp? This only can be said in vindication of France (and it is still more a vindication of Austria) that, practically speaking, if there is any part of this transaction for which Venice itself has reason to be grateful, it can only be for the permission to exchange the embraces of French fraternity for what is called the despotism of Vienna.

Let these facts and these dates be compared with what we have heard. The honorable gentleman has told us, and the author of the note from France has told us also, that all the French conquests were produced by the operations of the allies. It was, when they were pressed on all sides, when their own territory was in danger, when their own independence was in question, when the confederacy appeared too strong, it was then they used the means with which their power and their courage furnished them, and, "attacked upon all sides, they carried everywhere their defensive arms."

I do not wish to misrepresent the learned gentleman, but I understood him to speak of this sentiment with approbation. The sentiment itself is this, that if a nation is unjustly attacked in any one quarter by others, she cannot stop to consider by whom, but must find means of strength in other quarters, no matter where; and is justified in attacking, in her turn, those with whom she is at peace, and from whom she has received no species of provocation. Sir, I hope I have already proved, in a great measure, that no such attack was made upon France; but, if it was made, I maintain that the whole ground on which that argument is founded cannot be tolerated.   In the name of the laws of nature and nations, in the name of everything that is sacred and honorable, I demur to that plea; and I tell that honorable and learned gentleman that he would do well to look again into the law of nations before he ventures to come to this House to give the sanction of his authority to so dreadful and execrable a system.

I certainly understood this to be distinctly the tenor of the learned gentleman's argument, but as he tells me he did not use it, I take it for granted he did not intend to use it.   I rejoice that he did not; but at least, then, I have a right to expect that the learned gentleman should now transfer to the French note some of the indignation which he has hitherto lavished upon the declarations of this country.   This principle, which the learned gentleman disclaims, the French note avows; and I contend, without the fear of contradiction, it is the principle upon which France has uniformly acted.   But while the learned gentleman disclaims this proposition, he certainly will admit that he has himself asserted, and maintained in the whole course of his argument, that the pressure of the war upon France imposed upon her the necessity of those exertions which produced most of the enormities of the Revolution, and most of the enormities practised against the other countries of Europe.   The House will recollect that, in the year 1796, when all these horrors in Italy were beginning, which are the strongest illustrations of the general character of the French Revolution, we had begun that negotiation to which the learned gentleman has referred   England then possessed numerous conquests. England, though not having at that time had the advantage of three of her most splendid victories, England even then appeared undisputed mistress of the sea.   England, having then engrossed the whole wealth of the colonial world; England, having lost nothing of its original possessions; England then comes forward, proposing a general peace, and offering—what? offering the surrender of all that it had acquired, in order to obtain—what?   Not the dismemberment, not the partition of ancient France, but the return of a part of those conquests, no one of which could be retained, but in direct contradiction to that original and solemn pledge which is now referred to as the proof of the just and moderate disposition of the French Republic. Yet even this offer was not sufficient to procure peace, or to arrest the progress of France in her defensive operations against other unoffending countries!

From the pages, however, of the learned gentleman's pamphlet (which, after all its editions, is now fresher in his memory than in that of any other person in this House or in the country), he is furnished with an argument, on the result of the negotiation, on which he appears confidently to rely. He maintains that the single point on which the negotiation was broken off was the question of the possession of the Austrian Netherlands, and that it is, therefore, on that ground only that the war has, since that time, been continued. When this subject was before under discussion, I stated, and I shall state again (notwithstanding the learned gentleman's accusation of my having endeavored to shift the question from its true point), that the question then at issue was not whether the Netherlands should in fact be restored; though even on that question I am not (like the learned gentleman) unprepared to give any opinion. I am ready to say, that to leave that territory in the possession of France would be obviously dangerous to the interests of this country, and is inconsistent with the policy which it has uniformly pursued at every period in which it has concerned itself in the general system of the Continent. But it was not on the decision of this question of expediency and policy that the issue of the negotiation then turned. What was required of us by France was, not merely that we should acquiesce in her retaining the Netherlands, but that, as a preliminary to all treaty, and before entering upon the discussion of terms, we should recognize the principle that whatever France, in time of war, had annexed to the republic, must remain inseparable forever and could not become the subject of negotiation. I say that, in refusing such a preliminary, we were only resisting the claim of France to arrogate to itself the power of controlling, by its own separate and municipal acts, the rights and interests of other countries, and moulding, at its discretion, a new and general code of the law of nations.

In reviewing the issue of this negotiation, it is important to observe that France, who began by abjuring a love of conquest, was desired to give up nothing of her own, not even to give up all that she had conquered; that it was offered to her to receive back all that had been conquered from her; and when she rejected the negotiation for peace upon these grounds, are we then to be told of the unrelenting hostility of the combined powers, for which France was to revenge itself upon other countries, and which is to justify the subversion of every established government, and the destruction of property, religion, and domestic comfort, from one end of Italy to the other? Such was the effect of the war against Modena, against Genoa, against Tuscany, against Venice, against Rome, and against Naples, all of which she engaged in, or prosecuted, subsequent to this very period.

After this, in the year 1797, Austria had made peace; England and its ally, Portugal (from whom we could expect little active assistance, but whom we felt it our duty to defend), alone remained in the war. In that situation, under the pressure of necessity, which I shall not disguise, we made another attempt to negotiate. In 1797, Prussia, Spain, Austria, Naples, having successively made peace, the princes of Italy having been destroyed, France having surrounded itself, in almost every part in which it is not surrounded by the sea, with revolutionary republics, England made another offer of a different nature. It was not now a demand that France should restore anything. Austria having made a peace upon her own terms, England had nothing to require with regard to her allies, she asked no restitution of the dominions added to France in Europe. So far from retaining anything French out of Europe, we freely offered them all, demanding only, as a poor compensation, to retain a part of what we had acquired by arms from Holland, then identified with France. This proposal also, sir, was proudly refused, in a way which the learned gentleman himself has not attempted to justify, indeed of which he has spoken with detestation. I wish, since he has not finally abjured his duty in this House, that that detestation had been stated earlier; that he had mixed his own voice with the general voice of his country on the result of that negotiation.

Let us look at the conduct of France immediately subsequent to this period. She had spurned at the offers of Great Britain; she had reduced her Continental enemies to the necessity of accepting a precarious peace; she had (in spite of those pledges repeatedly made and uniformly violated) surrounded herself by new conquests on every part of her frontier but one. That one was Switzerland. The first effect of being relieved from the war with Austria, of being secured against all fears of Continental invasion on the ancient territory of France, was their unprovoked attack against this unoffending and devoted country. This was one of the scenes which satisfied even those who were the most incredulous that France had thrown off the mask, " if indeed she had ever worn it." It collected, in one view, many of the characteristic features of that revolutionary system which I have endeavored to trace—the perfidy which alone rendered their arms successful—the pretexts of which they availed themselves to produce division and prepare the entrance of Jacobinism in that country—the proposal of armistice, one of the known and regular engines of the Revolution, which was, as usual, the immediate prelude to military execution, attended with cruelty and barbarity, of which there are few examples. All these are known to the world. The country they attacked was one which had long been the faithful ally of France, which, instead of giving cause of jealousy to any other power, had been for ages proverbial for the simplicity and innocence of its manners, and which had acquired and preserved the esteem of all the nations of Europe; which had almost, by the common consent of mankind, been exempted from the sound of war, and marked out as a land of Goshen, safe and untouched in the midst of surrounding calamities.

Look, then, at the fate of Switzerland, at the circumstances which led to its destruction. Add this instance to the catalogue of aggression against all Europe, and then tell me whether the system I have described has not been prosecuted with an unrelenting spirit, which cannot be subdued in adversity, which cannot be appeased in prosperity, which neither solemn professions, nor the general law of nations, nor the obligation of treaties (whether previous to the Revolution or subsequent to it) could restrain from the subversion of every state into which, either by force or fraud, their arms could penetrate. Then tell me, whether the disasters of Europe are to be charged upon the provocation of this country and its allies, or on the inherent principles of the French Revolution, of which the natural result produced so much misery and carnage in France, and carried desolation and terror over so large a portion of the world.

Sir, much as I have now stated, I have not finished the catalogue. America, almost as much as Switzerland, perhaps, contributed to that change which has taken place in the minds of
those who were originally partial to the principles of the French
Government. The hostility against America followed a long
course of neutrality adhered to under the strongest provocations, or rather of repeated compliances to France, with which
we might well have been dissatisfied. It was on the face of it
unjust and wanton; and it was accompanied by those instances
of sordid corruption which shocked and disgusted even the
enthusiastic admirers of revolutionary purity, and threw a new
light on the genius of revolutionary government.

After this, it remains only shortly to remind gentlemen of the
aggression against Egypt, not o. nitting, however, to notice the
capture of Malta in the way to Egypt. Inconsiderable as that
island may be thought, compared with the scenes we have witnessed, let it be remembered that it is an island of which the government had long been recognized by every state of Europe,
against which France pretended no cause of war, and whose
independence was as dear to itself and as sacred as that of any
country in Europe. It was in fact not unimportant, from its
local situation to the other powers of Europe; but in proportion
as any man may diminish its importance, the instance will only
serve the more to illustrate and confirm the proposition which
I have maintained. The all-searching eye of the French Revolution looks to every part of Europe, and every quarter of the
world, in which can be found an object either of acquisition or
plunder. Nothing is too great for the temerity of its ambition,
nothing too small or insignificant for the grasp of its rapacity.
From hence Bonaparte and his army proceeded to Egypt. The
attack was made, pretences were held out to the natives of that
country in the name of the French King, whom they had murdered. They pretended to have the approbation of the Grand
Seignior, whose territories they were violating; their project
was carried on under the profession of a zeal for Mohammedan-
ism; it was carried on by proclaiming that France had been
reconciled to the Mussulman faith, had abjured that of Christianity, or, as he in his impious language termed it, of the sect
of the Messiah.

The only plea which they have since held out to color this

atrocious invasion of a neutral and friendly territory, is that it was the road to attack the English power in India. It is most unquestionably true that this was one and a principal cause of this unparalleled outrage; but another, and an equally substantial, cause (as appears by their own statements) was the division and partition of the territories of what they thought a falling power. It is impossible to dismiss this subject without observing that this attack against Egypt was accompanied by an attack upon the British possessions in India, made on true revolutionary principles. In Europe the propagation of the principles of France had uniformly prepared the way for the progress of its arms. To India the lovers of peace had sent the messengers of Jacobinism, for the purpose of inculcating war in those distant regions on Jacobin principles, and of forming Jacobin clubs, which they actually succeeded in establishing; and which in most respects resembled the European model, but which were distinguished by this peculiarity, that they were required to swear in one breath hatred to tyranny, the love of liberty, and the destruction of all kings and sovereigns, except the good and faithful ally of the French Republic, Citizen Tippoo!

What, then, was the nature of this system? Was it anything but what I have stated it to be? an insatiable love of aggrandizement, an implacable spirit of destruction against all the civil and religious institutions of every country? This is the first moving and acting spirit of the French Revolution; this is the spirit which animated it at its birth, and this is the spirit which will not desert it till the moment of its dissolution, " which grew with its growth, which strengthened with its strength," but which has not abated under its misfortunes, nor declined in its decay. It has been invariably the same in every period, operating more or less, according as accident or circumstances might assist it; but it has been inherent in the Revolution in all its stages; it has equally belonged to Brissot, to Robespierre, to Tallien, to Reubel, to Barras, and to every one of the leaders of the Directory, but to none more than to Bonaparte, in whom now all their powers are united. What are its characters? Can it be accident that produced them? No, it is only from the alliance of the most horrid principles, with the most horrid means, that such miseries could have been brought upon Europe. It is this paradox which we must always keep in mind when we are discussing any question relative to the effects of the French Revolution. Groaning under every degree of misery, the victim of its own crimes, and as I once before expressed in this House, asking pardon of God and of man for the miseries which it has brought upon itself and others, France still retains (while it has neither left means of comfort nor almost of subsistence to its own inhabitants) new and unexampled means of annoyance and destruction against all the other powers of Europe.

Its first fundamental principle was to bribe the poor against the rich by proposing to transfer into new hands, on the delusive notion of equality, and in breach of every principle of justice, the whole property of the country. The practical application of this principle was to devote the whole of that property to indiscriminate plunder, and to make it the foundation of a revolutionary system of finance, productive in proportion to the misery and desolation which it created. It has been accompanied by an unwearied spirit of proselytism, diffusing itself over all the nations of the earth; a spirit which can apply itself to all circumstances and all situations, which can furnish a list of grievances and hold out a promise of redress equally to all nations; which inspired the teachers of French liberty with the hope of alike recommending themselves to those who live under the feudal code of the German Empire; to the various states of Italy, under all their different institutions; to the old republicans of Holland, and to the new republicans of America; to the Catholic of Ireland, whom it was to deliver from Protestant usurpation; to the Protestant of Switzerland, whom it was to deliver from popish superstition; and to the Mussulman of Egypt, whom it was to deliver from Christian persecution; to the remote Indian, blindly bigoted to his ancient institutions; and to the natives of Great Britain, enjoying the perfection of practical freedom, and justly attac.ed to their constitution, from the joint result of habit, of reason, and of experience. The last and distinguishing feature is a perfidy which nothing can bind, which no tie of treaty, no sense of the principles generally received among nations, no obligation, human or divine, can restrain. Thus qualified, thus armed for destruction, the genius of the French Revolution marched forth, the terror and dismay of the world. Every nation has in its turn been the witness, many have been the victims of its principles; and it is left for us to decide whether we will compromise with such a danger, while we have yet resources to supply the sinews of war, while the heart and spirit of the country is yet unbroken, and while we have the means of calling forth and supporting a powerful co-operation in Europe.

Much more might be said on this part of the subject; but if what I have said already is a faithful, though only an imperfect, sketch of those excesses and outrages which even history itself will hereafter be unable fully to represent and record, and a just representation of the principle and source from which they originated, will any man say that we ought to accept a precarious security against so tremendous a danger? Much more—will he pretend, after the experience of all that has passed in the different stages of the French Revolution, that we ought to be deterred from probing this great question to the bottom, and from examining, without ceremony or disguise, whether the change which has recently taken place in France is sufficient now to give security, not against a common danger, but against such a danger as that which I have described?

In examining this part of the subject, let it be remembered that there is one other characteristic of the French Revolution as striking as its dreadful and destructive principles: I mean the instability of its government, which has been of itself sufficient to destroy all reliance, if any such reliance could at any time have been placed on the good faith of any of its rulers. Such has been the incredible rapidity with which the revolutions in France have succeeded each other that I believe the names of those who have successively exercised absolute power, under the pretence of liberty, are to be numbered by the years of the Revolution, and by each of the new constitutions, which, under the same pretence, has in its turn been imposed by force on France, all of which alike wer founded upon principles which professed to be universal, and were intended to be established and perpetuated among all the nations of the earth. Each of these will be found, upon an average to have had about two years as the period of its duration.

Under this revolutionary system, accompanied with this perpetual fluctuation and change, both in the form of the government and in the persons of the rulers, what is the security which has hitherto existed, and what new security is now offered? Before an answer is given to this question, let me sum up the history of all the revolutionary governments of France, and of their characters in relation to other powers, in words more emphatical than any which I could use—the memorable words pronounced, on the eve of this last constitution, by the orator who was selected to report to an Assembly, surrounded by a file of grenadiers, the new form of liberty which it was destined to enjoy under the auspices of General Bonaparte. From this reporter, the mouth and organ of the new government, we learn this important lesson:

" It is easy to conceive why peace was not concluded before the establishment of the constitutional government. The only government which then existed described itself as revolutionary; it was, in fact, only the tyranny of a few men who were soon overthrown by others, and it consequently presented no stability of principles or of views, no security either with respect to men or with respect to things.

" It should seem that that stability and that security ought to have existed from the establishment, and as the effect of the constitutional system; and yet they did not exist more, perhaps even less, than they had done before. In truth, we did make some partial treaties; we signed a Continental peace, and a general congress was held to confirm it; but these treaties, these diplomatic conferences, appear to have been the source of a new war, more inveterate and more bloody than before

" Before the eighteenth Fructidor (fourth September) of the fifth year, the French Government exhibited to foreign nations so uncertain an existence that they refused to treat with it. After this great event, the whole power was absorbed in the Directory; the legislative body can hardly be said to have existed; treaties of peace were broken, and war carried everywhere, without that body having any share in those measures. The same Directory, after having intimidated all Europe, and destroyed, at its pleasure, several governments, neither knowing how to make peace or war, or how even to establish itself, was overturned by a breath, on the thirteenth Prairial (eighteenth June), to make room for other men, influenced perhaps by different views, or who might be governed by different principles.

" Judging, then, only from notorious facts, the French Government must be considered as exhibiting nothing fixed, neither in respect to men nor to things."

Here, then, is the picture, down to the period of the last
revolution, of the state of France under all its successive governments!

Having taken a view of what it was, let us now examine
what it is. In the first place, we see, as has been truly stated,
a change in the description and form of the sovereign authority. A supreme power is placed at the head of this nominal
republic, with a more open avowal of military despotism than
at any former period; with a more open and undisguised abandonment of the names and pretences under which that despotism long attempted to conceal itself. The different institutions,
republican in their form and appearance, which were before
the instruments of that despotism, are now annihilated; they
have given way to the absolute power of one man, concentrat-
ing in himself all the authority of the state, and differing from
other monarchs only in this, that (as my honorable friend [Mr.
Canning] truly stated it) he wields a sword instead of a sceptre.
What, then, is the confidence we are to derive either from the
frame of the government, or from the character and past conduct of the person who is now the absolute ruler of France?

Had we seen a man of whom we had no previous knowledge
suddenly invested with the sovereign authority of the country;
invested with the power of taxation, with the power of the
sword, the power of war and peace, the unlimited power of
commanding the resources, of disposing of the lives and fortunes, of every man in France; if we had seen at the same
moment all the inferior machinery of the Revolution, which,
under the variety of successive shocks, had kept the system
in motion, still remaining entire—all that, by requisition and
plunder, had given activity to the revolutionary system of
finance, and had furnished the means of creating an army, by
converting every man who was of age to bear arms into a
soldier, not for the defence of his own country, but for the
sake of carrying the war into the country of the enemy; if we
had seen all the subordinate instruments of Jacobin power subsisting in their full force, and retaining (to use the French
phrase) all their original organization; and had then observed
this single change in the conduct of their affairs, that there
was now one man with no rival to thwart his measures, no colleague to divide his powers, no council to control his operations,

no liberty of speaking or writing, no expression of public opinion to check or influence his conduct; under such circumstances, should we be wrong to pause, or wait for the evidence of facts and experience, before we consented to trust our safety to the forbearance of a single man, in such a situation, and to relinquish those means of defence which have hitherto carried us safe through all the storms of the Revolution, if we were to ask what are the principles and character of this stranger, to whom fortune has suddenly committed the concerns of a great and powerful nation?

But is this the actual state of the present question? Are we talking of a stranger of whom we have heard nothing? No, sir, we have heard of him; we, and Europe, and the world, have heard both of him and of the satellites by whom he is surrounded, and it is impossible to discuss fairly the propriety of any answer which could be returned to his overtures of negotiation without taking into consideration the inferences to be drawn from his personal character and conduct. I know it is the fashion with some gentlemen to represent any reference to topics of this nature as invidious and irritating; but the truth is, that they rise unavoidably out of the very nature of the question. Would it have been possible for ministers to discharge their duty, in offering their advice to their sovereign, either for accepting or declining negotiation, without taking into their account the reliance to be placed on the disposition and the principles of the person on whose disposition and principles the security to be obtained by treaty must, in the present circumstances, principally depend? Or would they act honestly or candidly towards Parliament and towards the country if, having been guided by these considerations, they forbore to state, publicly and distinctly, the real grounds which have influenced their decision; and if, from a false delicacy and groundless timidity, they purposely declined an examination of a point, the most essential towards enabling Parliament to form a just determination on so important a subject?

What opinion, then, are we led to form of the pretensions of the Consul to those particular qualities for which, in the official note, his personal character is represented to us as the surest pledge of peace? We are told this is his second attempt at general pacification. Let us see, for a moment, how his attempt has been conducted. There is, indeed, as the learned gentleman has said, a word in the first declaration which refers to general peace, and which states this to be the second time in which the Consul has endeavored to accomplish that object. We thought fit, for the reasons which have been assigned, to decline altogether the proposal of treating, under the present circumstances, but we, at the same time, expressly stated that, whenever the moment for treaty should arrive, we would in no case treat but in conjunction with our allies. Our general refusal to negotiate at the present moment does not prevent the Consul from renewing his overtures; but are they renewed for the purpose of general pacification? Though he had hinted at general peace in the terms of his first note; though we had shown by our answer that we deemed negotiation, even for general peace, at this moment inadmissible; though we added that, even at any future period, we would treat only in conjunction with our allies, what was the proposal contained in his last note? To treat for a separate peace between Great Britain and France.

Such was the second attempt to effect general pacification—a proposal for a separate treaty with Great Britain. What had been the first? The conclusion of a separate treaty with Austria; and there are two anecdotes connected with the conclusion of this treaty, which are sufficient to illustrate the disposition of this pacificator of Europe. This very treaty of Campo Formio was ostentatiously professed to be concluded with the Emperor for the purpose of enabling Bonaparte to take the command of the army of England, and to dictate a separate peace with this country on the banks of the Thames. But there is this additional circumstance, singular beyond all conception, considering that we are now referred to the treaty of Campo Formio as a proof of the personal disposition of the Consul to general peace. He sent his two confidential and chosen friends, Berthier and Monge, charged to communicate to the Directory this treaty of Campo Formio; to announce to them that one enemy was humbled, that the war with Austria was terminated, and, therefore, that now was the moment to prosecute their operations against this country; they used on this occasion the memorable words: "The kingdom of Great Britain and the French Republic cannot exist together." This,

I say, was the solemn declaration of the deputies and ambassadors of Bonaparte himself, offering to the Directory the first-fruits of this first attempt at general pacification.

So much for his disposition towards general pacification. Let us look next at the part he has taken in the different stages of the French Revolution, and let us then judge whether we are to look to him as the security against revolutionary principles. Let us determine what reliance we can place on his engagements with other countries, when we see how he has observed his engagements to his own. When the constitution of the third year was established under Barras, that constitution was imposed by the arms of Bonaparte, then commanding the army of the triumvirate in Paris. To that constitution he then swore fidelity. How often he has repeated the same oath, I know not, but twice, at least, we know that he has not only repeated it himself, but tendered it to others, under circumstances too striking not to be stated.

Sir, the House cannot have forgotten the Revolution of the fourth of September, which produced the dismissal of Lord Malmesbury from Lisle. How was that revolution procured? It was procured chiefly by the promise of Bonaparte, in the name of his army, decidedly to support the Directory in those measures which led to the infringement and violation of everything that the authors of the constitution of 1795, or its adherents, could consider as fundamental, and which established a system of despotism inferior only to that now realized in his own person. Immediately before this event, in the midst of the desolation and bloodshed of Italy he had received the sacred present of new banners from the Directory; he delivered them to his army with this exhortation: " Let us swear, fellow-soldiers, by the manes of the patriots who have died by our side, eternal hatred to the enemies of the constitution of the third year "—that very constitution which he soon after enabled the Directory to violate, and which at the head of his grenadiers he has now finally destroyed. Sir, that oath was again renewed, in the midst of that very scene to which I have last referred; the oath of fidelity to the constitution of the third year was administered to all the members of the Assembly then sitting, under the terror of the bayonet, as the solemn preparation for the business of the day; and the morning was ushered in with swearing attachment to the constitution, that the evening might close with its destruction.

If we carry our views out of France, and look at the dreadful catalogue of all the breaches of treaty, all the acts of perfidy at which I have only glanced, and which are precisely commensurate with the number of treaties which the Republic has made (for I have sought in vain for any one which it has made and which it has not broken); if we trace the history of them all from the beginning of the Revolution to the present time, or if we select those which have been accompanied by the most atrocious cruelty, and marked the most strongly with the characteristic features of the Revolution, the name of Bonaparte will be found allied to more of them than that of any other that can be handed down in the history of the crimes and miseries of the last ten years. His name will be recorded with the horrors committed in Italy, in the memorable campaign of 1796 and 1797, in the Milanese, in Genoa, in Modena, in Tuscany, in Rome, and in Venice.

His entrance into Lombardy was announced by a solemn proclamation, issued on April 27, 1796, which terminated with these words: " Nations of Italy! the French army is come to break your chains; the French are the friends of the people in every country; your religion, your property, your customs shall be respected." This was followed by a second proclamation, dated from Milan, twentieth of May, and signed " Bonaparte," in these terms: " Respect for property and personal security; respect for the religion of countries—these are the sentiments of the government of the French Republic and of the army of Italy. The French, victorious, consider the nations of Lombardy as their brothers." In testimony of this fraternity, and to fulfil the solemn pledge of respecting property, this very proclamation imposed on the Milanese a provisional contribution to the amount of twenty millions of livres, or near one million sterling, and successive exactions were afterwards levied on that single state to the amount, in the whole, of near six millions sterling. The regard to religion and to the customs of the country was manifested with the same scrupulous fidelity. The churches were given up to indiscriminate plunder. Every religious and charitable fund, every public treasure, was confiscated. The country was made the scene of every species of disorder and rapine. The priests, the established form of worship, all the objects of religious reverence, were openly insulted by the French troops; at Pavia, particularly, the tomb of St. Augustin, which the inhabitants were accustomed to view with peculiar veneration, was mutilated and defaced; this last provocation having roused the resentment of the people, they flew to arms, surrounded the French garrison and took them prisoners, but carefully abstained from offering any violence to a single soldier. In revenge for this conduct, Bonaparte, then on his march to the Mincio, suddenly returned, collected his troops, and carried the extremity of military execution over the country. He burned the town of Benasco, and massacred eight hundred of its inhabitants; he marched to Pavia, took it by storm, and delivered it over to general plunder, and published, at the same moment, a proclamation of the twenty-sixth of May, ordering his troops to shoot all those who had not laid down their arms and taken an oath of obedience, and to burn every village where the tocsin should be sounded, and to put its inhabitants to death.

The transactions with Modena were on a smaller scale, but in the same character. Bonaparte began by signing a treaty, by which the Duke of Modena was to pay twelve millions of livres, and neutrality was promised him in return; this was soon followed by the personal arrest of the duke, and by a fresh extortion of two hundred thousand sequins. After this he was permitted, on the payment of a farther sum, to sign another treaty, called a *convention de sureté*, which of course was only the prelude to the repetition of similar exactions.

Nearly at the same period, in violation of the rights of neutrality and of the treaty which had been concluded between the French Republic and the Grand Duke of Tuscany in the preceding year, and in breach of a positive promise given only a few days before, the French army forcibly took possession of Leghorn, for the purpose of seizing the British property which was deposited there and confiscating it as a prize; and shortly after, when Bonaparte agreed to evacuate Leghorn, in return for the evacuation of the island of Elba, which was in possession of the British troops, he insisted upon a separate article, by which, in addition to the plunder before obtained, by the infraction of the law of nations, it was stipulated that the Grand

Duke should pay the expense which the French had incurred by this invasion of his territory.

In the proceedings towards Genoa we shall find out only a continuance of the same system of extortion and plunder, in violation of the solemn pledge contained in the proclamations already referred to, but a striking instance of the revolutionary means employed for the destruction of independent governments. A French minister was at that time resident at Genoa, which was acknowledged by France to be in a state of neutrality and friendship; in breach of this neutrality Bonaparte began, in the year 1796, with the demand of a loan. He afterwards, from the month of September, required and enforced the payment of a monthly subsidy, to the amount which he thought proper to stipulate. These exactions were accompanied by repeated assurances and protestations of friendship; they were followed, in May, 1797, by a conspiracy against the government, fomented by the emissaries of the French embassy, and conducted by the partisans of France, encouraged and afterwards protected by the French minister. The conspirators failed in their first attempt. Overpowered by the courage and voluntary exertions of the inhabitants, their force was dispersed, and man of their number were arrested. Bonaparte instantly considered the defeat of the conspirators as an act of aggression against the French Republic; he despatched an aide-de-camp with an order to the Senate of this independent state; first, to release all the French who were detained; secondly, to punish those who had arrested them; thirdly, to declare that they had no share in the insurrection; and fourthly, to disarm the people. Several French prisoners were immediately released, and a proclamation was preparing to disarm the inhabitants, when, by a second note, Bonaparte required the arrest of the three inquisitors of state, and immediate alterations in the constitution. He accompanied this with an order to the French minister to quit Genoa, if his commands were not immediately carried into execution; at the same moment his troops entered the territory of the republic; and shortly after, the councils, intimidated and overpowered, abdicated their functions. Three deputies were then sent to Bonaparte to receive from him a new constitution. On the sixth of June, after the conferences at Montebello, he signed a convention, or rather issued a decree, by which he fixed the new form of their government; he himself named provisionally all the members who were to compose it, and he required the payment of seven millions of livres as the price of the subversion of their constitution and their independence. These transactions require but one short comment. It is to be found in the official account given of them at Paris; which is in these memorable words: "General Bonaparte has pursued the only line of conduct which could be allowed in the representative of a nation which has supported the war only to procure the solemn acknowledgment of the right of nations to change the form of their government. He contributed nothing towards the revolution of Genoa, but he seized the first moment to acknowledge the new government, as soon as he saw that it was the result of the wishes of the people."

It is unnecessary to dwell on the wanton attacks against Rome, under the direction of Bonaparte himself, in the year 1796, and in the beginning of 1797, which terminated first by the treaty of Tolentino concluded by Bonaparte, in which, by enormous sacrifices, the Pope was allowed to purchase the acknowledgment of his authority as a sovereign prince; and secondly, by the violation of that very treaty, and the subversion of the papal authority by Joseph Bonaparte, the brother and the agent of the general, and the minister of the French Republic to the Holy See. A transaction accompanied by outrages and insults towards the pious and venerable pontiff, in spite of the sanctity of his age and the unsullied purity of his character, which even to a Protestant seem hardly short of the guilt of sacrilege.

But of all the disgusting and tragical scenes which took place in Italy in the course of the period I am describing, those which passed at Venice are perhaps the most striking and the most characteristic. In May 1796, the French army, under Bonaparte, in the full tide of its success against the Austrians, first approached the territories of this republic, which from the commencement of the war had observed a rigid neutrality. Their entrance on these territories was, as usual, accompanied by a solemn proclamation in the name of their general:

"BONAPARTE TO THE REPUBLIC OF VENICE

"It is to deliver the finest country in Europe from the iron yoke of the proud House of Austria, that the French army has braved obstacles' the most difficult to surmount. Victory in union with justice has crowned its efforts. The wreck of the enemy's army has retired behind the Mincio. The French army, in order to follow them, passes over the territory of the Republic of Venice; but it will never forget that ancient friendship unites the two republics. Religion, government, customs, and property shall be respected. That the people may be without apprehension, the most severe discipline shall be maintained. All that may be provided for the army shall be faithfully paid for in money. The general-in-chief engages the officers of the Republic of Venice, the magistrates, and the priests, to make known these sentiments to the people, in order that confidence may cement that friendship which has so long united the two nations. Faithful in the path of honor as in that of victory, the French soldier is terrible only to the enemies of his liberty and his government.

" BONAPARTE."

This proclamation was followed by exactions similar to those which were practised against Genoa, by the renewal of similar professions of friendship, and the use of similar means to excite insurrection. At length, in the spring of 1797, occasion was taken, from disturbances thus excited, to forge in the name of the Venetian government a proclamation hostile to France, and this proceeding was made the ground for military execution against the country, and for effecting by force the subversion of its ancient government and the establishment of the democratic forms of the French Revolution. This revolution was sealed by a treaty, signed in May 1797, between Bonaparte and commissioners appointed on the part of the new and revolutionary government of Venice. By the second and third secret articles of this treaty, Venice agreed to give as a ransom to secure itself against all further exactions or demands, the sum of three millions of livres in money, the value of three millions more in articles of naval supply, and three ships of the line; and it received in return the assurances of the friendship and support of the French Republic. Immediately after the signature of this treaty, the arsenal, the library, and the palace of St. Mark were ransacked and plundered, and heavy additional contributions were imposed upon its inhabitants. And, in not more than four months afterwards, this very Republic of Venice, united by alliance to France, the creature of Bonaparte himself, from whom it had received the present of French liberty, was by the same Bonaparte transferred, under the treaty of Campo Formio, to "that iron yoke of the proud House of Austria," to deliver it from which he had represented in his first proclamation to be the great object of all his operations.

Sir, all this is followed by the memorable expedition into Egypt, which I mention, not merely because it forms a principal article in the catalogue of those acts of violence and perfidy in which Bonaparte has been engaged; not merely because it was an enterprise peculiarly his own, of which he was himself the planner, the executor, and the betrayer; but chiefly because when from thence he retires to a different scene, to take possession of a new throne, from which he is to speak upon an equality with the kings and governors of Europe, he leaves behind him, at the moment of his departure, a specimen, which cannot be mistaken, of his principles of negotiation. The intercepted correspondence which has been alluded to in this debate seems to afford the strongest ground to believe that his offers to the Turkish government to evacuate Egypt were made solely with a view to gain time; that the ratification of any treaty on this subject was to be delayed with the view of finally eluding its performance, if any change of circumstances favorable to the French should occur in the interval. But whatever gentlemen may think of the intention with which these offers were made, there will at least be no question with respect to the credit due to those professions by which he endeavored to prove in Egypt his pacific dispositions. He expressly enjoins his successor strongly and steadily to insist, in all his intercourse with the Turks, that he came to Egypt with no hostile design, and that he never meant to keep possession of the country; while, on the opposite page of the same instructions, he states in the most unequivocal manner his regret at the discomfiture of his favorite project of colonizing Egypt and of maintaining it as a territorial acquisition. Now, sir, if in any note addressed to the Grand Vizier or the Sultan Bonaparte had claimed credit for the sincerity of his professions, that he came to Egypt with no view hostile to Turkey, and solely for the purpose of molesting the British interests, is there any one argument now used to induce us to believe his present professions to us, which might not have been equally urged on that occasion? Would not those professions have been equally supported by solemn asseveration, by the same reference which is now made to personal character, with this single difference, that they would have then had one instance less of hypocrisy and falsehood, which we have since had occasion to trace in this very transaction?

It is unnecessary to say more with respect to the credit due to his professions, or the reliance to be placed on his general character. But it will, perhaps, be argued that whatever may be his character, or whatever has been his past conduct, he has now an interest in making and observing peace. That he has an interest in making peace is at best but a doubtful proposition, and that he has an interest in preserving it is still more uncertain. That it is his interest to negotiate, I do not indeed deny. It is his interest, above all, to engage this country in separate negotiation, in order to loosen and dissolve the whole system of the confederacy on the Continent, to palsy at once the arms of Russia, or of Austria, or of any other country that might look to you for support; and then either to break off his separate treaty, or, if he should have concluded it, to apply the lesson which is taught in his school of policy in Egypt, and to revive at his pleasure those claims of indemnification which may have been reserved to some happier period.

This is precisely the interest which he has in negotiation. But on what grounds are we to be convinced that he has an interest in concluding and observing a solid and permanent pacification? Under all the circumstances of his personal character, and his newly acquired power, what other security has he for retaining that power but the sword? His hold upon France is the sword, and he has no other. Is he connected with the soil, or with the habits, the affections, or the prejudices of the country? He is a stranger, a foreigner, and a usurper. He unites in his own person everything that a pure republican must detest; everything that an enraged Jacobin has abjured; everything that a sincere and faithful royalist must feel as an insult. If he is opposed at any time in his career, what is his appeal? He appeals to his fortune; in other words, to his army and his sword. Placing, then, his whole reliance upon military support, can he afford to let his military renown pass away, to let his laurels wither, to let the memory of his trophies sink in obscurity? Is it certain that with his army confined within France, and restrained from inroads upon her neighbors, that he can maintain, at his devotion, a force sufficiently numerous to support his power? Having no object but the possession of absolute dominion, no passion but military glory, is it to be reckoned as certain that he can feel such an interest in permanent peace as would justify us in laying down our arms, reducing our expense, and relinquishing our means of security, on the faith of his engagements? Do we believe that, after the conclusion of peace, he would not still sigh over the lost trophies of Egypt, wrested from him by the celebrated victory of Aboukir, and the brilliant exertions of that heroic band of British seamen, whose influence and example rendered the Turkish troops invincible at Acre? Can he forget that the effect of these exploits enabled Austria and Prussia, in one campaign, to recover from France all which she had acquired by his victories, to dissolve the charm which for a time fascinated Europe, and to show that their generals, contending in a just cause, could efface, even by their success and their military glory, the most dazzling triumphs of his victorious and desolating ambition?

Can we believe, with these impressions on his mind, that if, after a year, eighteen months, or two years of peace had elapsed, he should be tempted by the appearance of fresh insurrection in Ireland, encouraged by renewed and unrestrained communication with France, and fomented by the fresh infusion of Jacobin principles; if we were at such a moment without a fleet to watch the ports of France, or to guard the coasts of Ireland, without a disposable army, or an embodied militia capable of supplying a speedy and adequate reënforcement, and that he had suddenly the means of transporting thither a body of twenty or thirty thousand French troops; can we believe that, at such a moment, his ambition and vindictive spirit would be restrained by the recollection of engagements or the obligation of treaty? Or if, in some new crisis of difficulty and danger to the Ottoman Empire, with no British navy in the Mediterranean, no confederacy formed, no force collected to support it, an opportunity should present itself

for resuming the abandoned expedition to Egypt, for renewing the avowed and favorite project of conquering and colonizing that rich and fertile country, and of opening the way
to wound some of the vital interests of England, and to plunder the treasures of the East, in order to fill the bankrupt
coffers of France—would it be the interest of Bonaparte, under
such circumstances, or his principles, his moderation, his love
of peace, his aversion to conquest, and his regard for the independence of other nations—would it be all or any of these
that would secure us against an attempt which would leave us
only the option of submitting without a struggle to certain loss
and disgrace, or of renewing the contest which we had prematurely terminated, without allies, without preparation, with
diminished means, and with increased difficulty and hazard?

Hitherto I have spoken only of the reliance which we can
place on the professions, the character, and the conduct of the
present First Consul; but it remains to consider the stability
of his power. The Revolution has been marked throughout by
a rapid succession of new depositaries of public authority, each
supplanting its predecessor. What grounds have we to believe that this new usurpation, more odious and more undisguised than all that preceded it, will be more durable? Is it that
we rely on the particular provisions contained in the code of
the pretended constitution, which was proclaimed as accepted
by the French people as soon as the garrison of Paris declared
their determination to exterminate all its enemies, and before
any of its articles could even be known to half the country,
whose consent was required for its establishment?

I will not pretend to inquire deeply into the nature and effects
of a constitution which can hardly be regarded but as a farce
and a mockery. If, however, it could be supposed that its
provisions were to have any effect, it seems equally adapted to
two purposes: that of giving to its founder, for a time, an
absolute and uncontrolled authority; and that of laying the certain foundation of disunion and discord, which, if they once
prevail, must render the exercise of all the authority under
the constitution impossible, and leave no appeal but to the
sword.

Is, then, military despotism that which we are accustomed
to consider as a stable form of government? In all ages of

the world it has been attended with the least stability to the persons who exercised it, and with the most rapid succession of changes and revolution.   In the outset of the French Revolution its advocates boasted that it furnished a security forever, not to France only, but to all countries in the world, against military despotism; that the force of standing armies was vain and delusive; that no artificial power could resist public opinion; and that it was upon the foundation of public opinion alone that any government could stand.   I believe that in this instance, as in every other, the progress of the French Revolution has belied its professions; but, so far from its being a proof of the prevalence of public opinion against military force, it is instead of the proof, the strongest exception from that doctrine which appears in the history of the world.   Through all the stages of the Revolution military force has governed, and public opinion has scarcely been heard.   But still I consider this as only an exception from a general truth.   I still believe that in every civilized country, not enslaved by a Jacobin faction, public opinion is the only sure support of any government.   I believe this with the more satisfaction, from a conviction that, if this contest is happily terminated, the established governments of Europe will stand upon that rock firmer than ever; and, whatever may be the defects of any particular constitution, those who live under it will prefer its continuance to the experiment of changes which may plunge them in the unfathomable abyss of revolution, or extricate them from it only to expose them to the terrors of military despotism.   And to apply this to France, I see no reason to believe that the present usurpation will be more permanent than any other military despotism which has been established by the same means, and with the same defiance of public opinion.

What, then, is the inference I draw from all that I have now stated?   Is it that we will in no case treat with Bonaparte?   I say no such thing.   But I say, as has been said in the answer returned to the French note, that we ought to wait for " experience and the evidence of facts " before we are convinced that such a treaty is admissible.   The circumstances I have stated would well justify us if we should be slow in being convinced; but on a question of peace and war, everything depends upon degree and upon comparison. If, on the one hand, there should be an appearance that the policy of France is at length guided by different maxims from those which have hitherto prevailed; if we should hereafter see signs of stability in the government which are not now to be traced; if the progress of the allied army should not call forth such a spirit in France as to make it probable that the act of the country itself will destroy the system now prevailing; if the danger, the difficulty, the risk of continuing the contest should increase, while the hope of complete ultimate success should be diminished; all these, in their due place, are considerations which, with myself and, I can answer for it, with every one of my colleagues, will have their just weight. But at present these considerations all operate one way; at present there is nothing from which we can presage a favorable disposition to change in the French councils. There is the greatest reason to rely on powerful co-operation from our allies; there are the strongest marks of a disposition in the interior of France to active resistance against this new tyranny; and there is every ground to believe, on reviewing our situation and that of the enemy, that, if we are ultimately disappointed of that complete success which we are at present entitled to hope, the continuance of the contest, instead of making our situation comparatively worse, will have made it comparatively better.

If, then, I am asked how long are we to persevere in the war, I can only say that no period can be accurately assigned. Considering the importance of obtaining complete security for the objects for which we contend, we ought not to be discouraged too soon; but, on the contrary, considering the importance of not impairing and exhausting the radical strength of the country, there are limits beyond which we ought not to persist, and which we can determine only by estimating and comparing fairly, from time to time, the degree of security to be obtained by treaty, and the risk and disadvantage of continuing the contest.

But, sir, there are some gentlemen in the House who seem to consider it already certain that the ultimate success to which I am looking is unattainable. They suppose us contending only for the restoration of the French monarchy, which they believe to be impracticable, and deny to be desirable for this country.

We havé been asked in the course of this debate: Do you think you can impose monarchy upon France, against the will of the nation? I never thought it, I never hoped it, I never wished it. I have thought, I have hoped, I have wished, that the time might come when the effect of the arms of the allies might so far overpower the military force which keeps France in bondage, as to give vent and scope to the thoughts and actions of its inhabitants. We have, indeed, already seen abundant proof of what is the disposition of a large part of the country; we have seen almost through the whole of the Revolution the western provinces of France deluged with the blood of their inhabitants obstinately contending for their ancient laws and religion. We have recently seen, in the revival of that war, fresh proof of the zeal which still animates those countries in the same cause. These efforts (I state it distinctly, and there are those near me who can bear witness to the truth of the assertion) were not produced by any instigation from hence; they were the effects of a rooted sentiment prevailing through all those provinces forced into action by the "law of the hostages" and the other tyrannical measures of the Directory, at the moment when we were endeavoring to discourage so hazardous an enterprise. If, under such circumstances, we find them giving proofs of their unalterable perseverance in their principles; if there is every reason to believe that the same disposition prevails in many other extensive provinces of France; if every party appears at length equally wearied and disappointed with all the successive changes which the Revolution has produced; if the question is no longer between monarchy, and even the pretence and name of liberty, but between the ancient line of hereditary princes on the one hand, and a military tyrant, a foreign usurper, on the other; if the armies of that usurper are likely to find sufficient occupation on the frontiers, and to be forced at length to leave the interior of the country at liberty to manifest its real feeling and disposition; what reason have we to anticipate, that the restoration of monarchy under such circumstances is impracticable?

The learned gentleman has, indeed, told us that almost every man now possessed of property in France must necessarily be interested in resisting such a change, and that therefore it never can be effected. If that single consideration were con-

clusive against the possibility of a change, for the same reason
the Revolution itself, by which the whole property of the country was taken from its ancient possessors, could never have
taken place. But though I deny it tó be an insuperable obstacle, I admit it to be a point of considerable delicacy and
difficulty. It is not, indeed, for us to discuss minutely what arrangement might be formed on this point to conciliate and unite
opposite interests. But whoever considers the precarious tenure
and depreciated value of lands held under the revolutionary
title, and the low price for which they have generally been obtained, will think it, perhaps, not impossible that an ample
compensation might be made to the bulk of the present possessors, both for the purchase-money they have paid and for the
actual value of what they now enjoy; and that the ancient
proprietors might be reinstated in the possession of their former
rights, with only such a temporary sacrifice as reasonable men
would willingly make to obtain so essential an object.

The honorable and learned gentleman, however, has supported his reasoning on this part of the subject, by an argument which he undoubtedly considers as unanswerable—a reference to what would be his own conduct in similar circumstances; and he tells us that every landed proprietor in France
must support the present order of things in that country from
the same motive that he and every proprietor of three per cent.
stock would join in the defence of the constitution of Great
Britain. I must do the learned gentleman the justice to believe that the habits of his profession must supply him with
better and nobler motives for defending a constitution which
he has had so much occasion to study and examine, than any he
can derive from the value of his proportion, however large, of
three per cents, even supposing them to continue to increase in
price as rapidly as they have done during the last three years,
in which the security and prosperity of the country has been
established by following a system directly opposite to the counsels of the learned gentleman and his friends.

The learned gentleman's illustration, however, though it fails
with respect to himself, is happily and aptly applied to the state
of France; and let us see what inference it furnishes with respect to the probable attachment of moneyed men to the continuance of the revolutionary system, as well as with respect to

the general state of public credit in that country. I do not, indeed, know that there exists precisely any fund of three per cents in France, to furnish a test for the patriotism and public spirit of the lovers of French liberty. But there is another fund which may equally answer our purpose. The capital of three per cent. stock which formerly existed in France has undergone a whimsical operation, similar to many other expedients of finance which we have seen in the course of the Revolution This was performed by a decree which, as they termed it, republicanized their debt; that is, in other words, struck off at once two-thirds of the capital, and left the proprietors to take their chance for the payment of interest on the remainder. This remnant was afterward converted into the present five per cent. stock. I had the curiosity very lately to inquire what price it bore in the market, and I was told that the price had somewhat risen from confidence in the new government, and was actually as high as seventeen. I really at first supposed that my informer meant seventeen years' purchase for every pound of interest, and I began to be almost jealous of revolutionary credit; but I soon found that he literally meant seventeen pounds for every hundred pounds capital stock of five per cent., that is a little more than three and a half years' purchase. So much for the value of revolutionary property, and for the attachment with which it must inspire its possessors towards the system of government to which that value is to be ascribed!

On the question, sir, how far the restoration of the French monarchy, if practicable, is desirable, I shall not think it necessary to say much. Can it be supposed to be indifferent to us or to the world, whether the throne of France is to be filled by a prince of the House of Bourbon, or by him whose principles and conduct I have endeavored to develop? Is it nothing, with a view to influence and example, whether the fortune of this last adventurer in the lottery of revolutions shall appear to be permanent? Is it nothing whether a system shall be sanctioned which confirms, by one of its fundamental articles, that general transfer of property from its ancient and lawful possessors, which holds out one of the most terrible examples of national injustice, and which has furnished the great source of revolutionary finance and revolutionary strength against all the powers of Europe?

In the exhausted and impoverished state of France, it seems for a time impossible that any system but that of robbery and confiscation, anything but the continued torture, which can be applied only by the engines of the Revolution, can extort from its ruined inhabitants more than the means of supporting in peace the yearly expenditure of its government. Suppose, then, the heir of the House of Bourbon reinstated on the throne, he will have sufficient occupation in endeavoring, if possible, to heal the wounds, and gradually to repair the losses of ten years of civil convulsion; to reanimate the drooping commerce, to rekindle the industry, to replace the capital, and to revive the manufactures of the country. Under such circumstances, there must probably be a considerable interval before such a monarch, whatever may be his views, can possess the power which can make him formidable to Europe; but while the system of the Revolution continues, the case is quite different. It is true, indeed, that even the gigantic and unnatural means by which that revolution has been supported are so far impaired; the influence of its principles and the terror of its arms so far weakened; and its power of action so much contracted and circumscribed, that against the embodied force of Europe, prosecuting a vigorous war, we may justly hope that the remnant and wreck of this system cannot long oppose an effectual resistance.

But, supposing the confederacy of Europe prematurely dissolved; supposing our armies disbanded, our fleets laid up in our harbors, our exertions relaxed, and our means of precaution and defence relinquished; do we believe that the revolutionary power, with this rest and breathing-time given it to recover from the pressure under which it is now sinking, possessing still the means of calling suddenly and violently into action whatever is the remaining physical force of France, under the guidance of military despotism; do we believe that this revolutionary power, the terror of which is now beginning to vanish, will not again prove formidable to Europe. Can we forget that in the ten years in which that power has subsisted, it has brought more misery on surrounding nations, and produced more acts of aggression, cruelty, perfidy, and enormous ambition than can be traced in the history of France for the centuries which have elapsed since the foundation of its monarchy, including all the wars which, in the course of that period, have been waged by any of those sovereigns, whose projects of aggrandizement and violations of treaty afford a constant theme of general reproach against the ancient government of France? And if not, can we hesitate whether we have the best prospect of permanent peace, the best security for the independence and safety of Europe, from the restoration of the lawful government, or from the continuance of revolutionary power in the hands of Bonaparte?

In compromise and treaty with such a power placed in such hands as now exercise it, and retaining the same means of annoyance which it now possesses, I see little hope of permanent security. I see no possibility at this moment of such a peace as would justify that liberal intercourse which is the essence of real amity; no chance of terminating the expenses or the anxieties of war, or of restoring to us any of the advantages of established tranquillity, and, as a sincere lover of peace, I cannot be content with its nominal attainment. I must be desirous of pursuing that system which promises to attain, in the end, the permanent enjoyment of its solid and substantial blessings for this country and for Europe. As a sincere lover of peace, I will not sacrifice it by grasping at the shadow when the reality is not substantially within my reach.

Cur igitur pacem nolo? Quia infida est, quia periculosa, quia esse non potest.

If, sir, in all that I have now offered to the House, I have succeeded in establishing the proposition that the system of the French Revolution has been such as to afford to foreign powers no adequate ground for security in negotiation, and that the change which has recently taken place has not yet afforded that security; if I have laid before you a just statement of the nature and extent of the danger with which we have been threatened, it would remain only shortly to consider whether there is anything in the circumstances of the present moment to induce us to accept a security confessedly inadequate against a danger of such a description.

It will be necessary here to say a few words on the subject on which gentlemen have been so fond of dwelling, I mean our former negotiations, and particularly that at Lisle, in 1797. I am desirous of stating frankly and openly the true motives which induced me to concur in then recommending negotiation; and I will leave it to the House and to the country to judge whether our conduct at that time was inconsistent with the principles by which we are guided at present. That revolutionary policy which I have endeavored to describe, that gigantic system of prodigality and bloodshed by which the efforts of France were supported, and which counts for nothing the lives and the property of a nation, had at that period driven us to exertions which had, in a great measure, exhausted the ordinary means of defraying our immense expenditure, and had led many of those who were the most convinced of the original justice and necessity of the war, and of the danger of Jacobin principles, to doubt the possibility of persisting in it, till complete and adequate security could be obtained. There seemed, too, much reason to believe that, without some new measure to check the rapid accumulation of debt, we could no longer trust to the stability of that funding system by which the nation had been enabled to support the expense of all the different wars in which we have engaged in the course of the present century. In order to continue our exertions with vigor, it became necessary that a new and solid system of finance should be established, such as could not be rendered effectual but by the general and decided concurrence of public opinion. Such a concurrence in the strong and vigorous measures necessary for the purpose could not then be expected, but from satisfying the country, by the strongest and most decided proofs, that peace, on terms in any degree admissible, was unattainable.

Under this impression, we thought it our duty to attempt negotiation, not from the sanguine hope, even at that time, that its result could afford us complete security, but from the persuasion that the danger arising from peace, under such circumstances, was less than that of continuing the war with precarious and inadequate means. The result of those negotiations proved that the enemy would be satisfied with nothing less than the sacrifice of the honor and independence of the country. From this conviction, a spirit and enthusiasm was excited in the nation which produced the efforts to which we are indebted for the subsequent change in our situation. Having witnessed that happy change, having observed the increasing prosperity and security of the country from that period, seeing how much more satisfactory our prospects now are than any which we could then have derived from the successful result of negotiation, I have not scrupled to declare that I consider the rupture of the negotiation, on the part of the enemy, as a fortunate circumstance for the country. But because these are my sentiments at this time, after reviewing what has since passed, does it follow that we were at that time insincere in endeavoring to obtain peace? The learned gentleman, indeed, assumes that we were, and he even makes a concession, of which I desire not to claim the benefit. He is willing to admit that, on our principles and our view of the subject, insincerity would have been justifiable. I know, sir, no plea that would justify those who are entrusted with the conduct of public affairs in holding out to Parliament and to the nation one object, while they were, in fact, pursuing another. I did, in fact, believe, at the moment, the conclusion of peace, if it could have been obtained, to be preferable to the continuance of the war under its increasing risks and difficulties. I therefore wished for peace; I sincerely labored for peace. Our endeavors were frustrated by the act of the enemy. If, then, the circumstances are since changed; if what passed at that period has afforded a proof that the object we aimed at was unattainable; and if all that has passed since has proved that, provided peace had been then made, it could not have been durable, are we bound to repeat the same experiment, when every reason against it is strengthened by subsequent experience, and when the inducements which led to it at that time have ceased to exist?

When we consider the resources and the spirit of the country, can any man doubt that if adequate security is not now to be obtained by treaty, we have the means of prosecuting the contest without material difficulty or danger, and with a reasonable prospect of completely attaining our object? I will not dwell on the improved state of public credit; on the continually increasing amount, in spite of extraordinary temporary burdens, of our permanent revenue; on the yearly accession of wealth to an extent unprecedented even in the most flourishing times of peace, which we are deriving in the midst of war, from our extended and flourishing commerce; on the progressive improvement and growth of our manufactures; on the proofs which we see on all sides of the uninterrupted accumulation

of productive capital; and on the active exertion of every
branch of national industry which can tend to support and
augment the population, the riches, and the power of the country.

As little need I recall the attention of the House to the
additional means of action which we have derived from the
great augmentation of our disposable military force, the continued triumphs of our powerful and victorious navy, and the
events which, in the course of the last two years, have raised
the military ardor and military glory of the country to a height
unexampled in any period of our history.

In addition to these grounds of reliance on our own strength
and exertions, we have seen the consummate skill and valor
of the arms of our allies proved by that series of unexampled
successes in the course of the last campaign, and we have every
reason to expect a co-operation on the Continent, even to a
greater extent, in the course of the present year. If we compare
this view of our own situation with everything we can observe of the state and condition of our enemy—if we can trace
him laboring under equal difficulty in finding men to recruit his
army, or money to pay it—if we know that in the course of the
last year the most rigorous efforts of military conscription were
scarcely sufficient to replace to the French armies, at the end
of the campaign, the numbers which they had lost in the course
of it—if we have seen that that force, then in possession of
advantages which it has since lost, was unable to contend with
the efforts of the combined armies—if we know that, even while
supported by the plunder of all the countries which they had
overrun, those armies were reduced, by the confession of
their commanders, to the extremity of distress, and destitute
not only of the principal articles of military supply, but almost
of the necessaries of life—if we see them now driven back
within their own frontiers, and confined within a country whose
own resources have long since been proclaimed by their successive governments to be unequal either to paying or maintaining them—if we observe that since the last revolution no
one substantial or effectual measure has been adopted to remedy
the intolerable disorder of their finances, and to supply the
deficiency of their credit and resources—if we see through large
and populous districts of France, either open war levied against

the present usurpation, or evident marks of disunion and dis-
traction, which the first occasion may call forth into a flame—
if, I say sir, this comparison be just, I feel myself authorized to
conclude from it, not that we are entitled to consider ourselves
certain of ultimate success, not that we are to suppose ourselves
exempted from the unforeseen vicissitudes of war, but that,
considering the value of the object for which we are contending, the means for supporting the contest, and the probable
course of human events, we should be inexcusable, if at this
moment we were to relinquish the struggle on any grounds
short of entire and complete security; that from perseverance
in our efforts under such circumstances, we have the fairest
reason to expect the full attainment of our object; but that
at all events, even if we are disappointed in our more sanguine hopes, we are more likely to gain than to lose by the
continuation of the contest; that every month to which it is
continued, even if it should not in its effects lead to the final
destruction of the Jacobin system, must tend so far to weaken
and exhaust it, as to give us at least a greater comparative
security in any termination of the war; that, on all these
grounds, this is not the moment at which it is consistent with
our interest or our duty to listen to any proposals of negotiation with the present ruler of France; but that we are not,
therefore, pledged to any unalterable determination as to our
future conduct; that in this we must be regulated by the course
of events; and that it will be the duty of His Majesty's ministers from time to time to adapt their measures to any variation of circumstances, to consider how far the effects of the
military operations of the allies or of the internal disposition
of France correspond with our present expectations; and, on
a view of the whole, to compare the difficulties or risks which
may arise in the prosecution of the contest with the prospect
of ultimate success, or of the degree of advantage to be derived
from its farther continuance, and to be governed by the results
of all these considerations in the opinion and advice which
they may offer to their sovereign.

ON GRANTING AID TO PORTUGAL

—

BY

GEORGE CANNING

GEORGE CANNING

1770—1827

George Canning was the offspring of a love-match, his father having married a beautiful girl with a good education but with no fortune. His father died in 1781, and his mother attempted to make a living on the stage; but her beauty had more success than her dramatic talent; she was twice remarried, first to an actor, the last time to a worthy linen draper of Exeter. Canning attended school at Eton, showing himself an able scholar A literary tendency, derived from his father, prompted him to start and edit a periodical called " The Microcosm," the commendable prototype of many schoolboy magazines since then.

In 1787, at the age of seventeen, he went to Oxford, and enjoyed the advantage of passing his vacations with Sheridan, by whom he was made known to Burke, Fox, and other eminent Whig statesmen. Sheridan formed a high opinion of the youth's abilities, and regarded him as a coming light in the party; and by the influence of William Pitt, he was seated in the House of Commons in 1793. In 1796 he was made Secretary of State, and took up his permanent residence in London. About this time he and some others in sympathy with his ideas founded the " Anti-Jacobin," Canning becoming one of the leading contributors He joined Wilberforce in the motion to abolish the slave-trade, in 1798; and two years later he confirmed his claim to material as well as political good fortune by marrying Joanna Scott, with a fortune of one hundred thousand pounds sterling. While holding the office of Secretary of State for Foreign Affairs under the Portland administration, Canning quarrelled with Castlereagh, and they fought a duel, in which Canning was wounded. In 1810 he opposed the reference to the whole House of the Catholic claims, on the ground that the Catholics had offered no security; and on this theme some of his most brilliant speeches were delivered. He advocated Catholic admission not as a right, but as a matter of pure expediency; and this view led him, in 1813, to support the same measure which he had formerly opposed. It was Canning who aimed the first blow at Napoleon, and directed and animated the British policy in Spain; he declared that the English ought never to relinquish their hold on the Peninsula After two years abroad as minister to Portugal he returned to oppose Lord John Russell's Reform Bill During the ensuing years he constantly took a leading and influential part in foreign affairs, and in the debate over the proposition to intervene in the dispute between Spain and Portugal, he spoke the well-known words, " I resolved that if France had Spain, it should not be Spain with the Indies: I called the New World into existence, to redress the balance of the Old! " In 1827 he was chosen Prime Minister; and on the eighth of August of the same year he died, at the height of his renown. Few statesmen of any country have enjoyed a career of such uninterrupted success In spite of his fortune, enormous for those days, he is said to have died a poor man.

His foreign policy embraced the recognition of the South American states, the maintenance of Portugal's independence, and the treaty in behalf of Greece His attitude on the question of the British alliance with Portugal is well expressed in his oration, " On Granting Aid to Portugal." As an orator he took high rank; his eloquence was persuasive and impassioned, he was lucid and logical in his reasoning, and graceful in expression. His personal appearance was attractive; he had a brilliant wit, and in satire he was caustic and able. At his death it was voted that he be interred in that Valhalla of English statesmen of eminence, Westminster Abbey; and it is there that his remains repose.

ON GRANTING AID TO PORTUGAL

Delivered in the House of Commons, December 12, 1826 [1]

MR. SPEAKER: In proposing to the House of Commons to acknowledge, by an humble and dutiful address, His Majesty's most gracious message, and to reply to it in terms which will be, in effect, an echo of the sentiments and a fufilment of the anticipations of that message, I feel that, however confident I may be in the justice, and however clear as to the policy of the measures therein announced, it becomes me, as a British minister, recommending to Parliament any step which may approximate this country even to the hazard of a war, while I explain the grounds of that proposal, to accompany my explanation with expressions of regret.

I can assure the House that there is not within its walls any set of men more deeply convinced than His Majesty's ministers —nor any individual more intimately persuaded than he who has now the honor of addressing you—of the vital importance of the continuance of peace to this country and to the world. So strongly am I impressed with this opinion—and for reasons of which I will put the House more fully in possession before I sit down—that I declare there is no question of doubtful or controverted policy—no opportunity of present national advantage —no precaution against remote difficulty—which I would not gladly compromise, pass over, or adjourn, rather than call on Parliament to sanction, at this moment, any measure which had a tendency to involve the country in war. But, at the same time, sir, I feel that which has been felt, in the best times

[1] [In 1826, while Mr Canning was the English Minister of Foreign Affairs, a body of revolutionary Absolutists attempted to destroy the existing liberal government of Portugal, which had been recognized by all the great powers of Europe. In the course of the insurrection the Absolutists raised a body of troops on Spanish soil, and the Portuguese Government asked for the protection of England Five thousand troops were immediately sent to Portugal, this being in accordance with Canning's policy of allowing each nation to manage its internal affairs and of permitting no interference with the smaller nations by the larger.—Editor.]

of English history, by the best statesmen of this country, and by the Parliaments by whom those statesmen were supported— I feel that there are two causes, and but two causes, which cannot be either compromised, passed over, or adjourned. These causes are: adherence to the national faith, and regard for the national honor.

Sir, if I did not consider both these causes as involved in the proposition which I have this day to make to you, I should not address the House, as I now do, in the full and entire confidence that the gracious communication of His Majesty will be met by the House with the concurrence of which His Majesty has declared his expectation.

In order to bring the matter which I have to submit to you, under the cognizance of the House, in the shortest and clearest manner, I beg leave to state it, in the first instance, divested of any collateral considerations.   It is a case of law and of fact; of national law on the one hand, and of notorious fact on the other; such as it must be, in my opinion as impossible for Parliament, as it was for the government, to regard in any but one light, or to come to any but one conclusion upon it.

Among the alliances by which, at different periods of our history, this country has been connected with the other nations of Europe, none is so ancient in origin, and so precise in obligation—none has continued so long, and been observed so faithfully—of none is the memory so intimately interwoven with the most brilliant records of our triumphs, as that by which Great Britain is connected with Portugal.   It dates back to distant centuries; it has survived an endless variety of fortunes.   Anterior in existence to the accession of the House of Braganza to the throne of Portugal—it derived, however, fresh vigor from that event; and never from that epoch to the present hour, has the independent monarchy of Portugal ceased to be nurtured by the friendship of Great Britain.   This alliance has never been seriously interrupted; but it has been renewed by repeated sanctions.   It has been maintained under difficulties by which the fidelity of other alliances was shaken, and has been vindicated in fields of blood and of glory.

That the alliance with Portugal has been always unqualifiedly advantageous to this country—that it has not been sometimes inconvenient and sometimes burdensome—I am not bound nor prepared to maintain. But no British statesman, so far as I know, has ever suggested the expediency of shaking it off; and it is assuredly not at a moment of need that honor and what I may be allowed to call national sympathy would permit us to weigh, with an over-scrupulous exactness, the amount of difficulties and dangers attendant upon its faithful and steadfast observance. What feelings of national honor would forbid is forbidden alike by the plain dictates of national faith.

It is not at distant periods of history, and in bygone ages only, that the traces of the union between Great Britain and Portugal are to be found. In the last compact of modern Europe, the compact which forms the basis of its present international law—I mean the treaty of Vienna of 1815—this country, with its eyes open to the possible inconveniences of the connection, but with a memory awake to its past benefits, solemnly renewed the previously existing obligations of alliance and amity with Portugal. I will take leave to read to the House the third article of the treaty concluded at Vienna, in 1815, between Great Britain on the one hand and Portugal on the other. It is couched in the following terms: " The treaty of alliance, concluded at Rio de Janeiro, on February 19, 1810, being founded on circumstances of a temporary nature, which have happily ceased to exist, the said treaty is hereby declared to be void in all its parts, and of no effect; without prejudice, however, to the ancient treaties of alliance, friendship, and guarantee, which have so long and so happily subsisted between the two Crowns, and which are hereby renewed by the high contracting parties, and acknowledged to be of full force and effect."

In order to appreciate the force of this stipulation—recent in point of time, recent, also, in the sanction of Parliament—the House will, perhaps, allow me to explain shortly the circumstances in reference to which it was contracted. In the year 1807, when, upon the declaration of Bonaparte, that the House of Braganza had ceased to reign, the King of Portugal, by the advice of Great Britain, was induced to set sail for the Brazils; almost at the very moment of his most faithful Majesty's embarkation a secret convention was signed between His Majesty and the King of Portugal, stipulating that, in the event of his most faithful Majesty's establishing the seat of his government in Brazil, Great Britain would never acknowledge any other dynasty than that of the House of Braganza on the throne of Portugal. That convention, I say, was contemporaneous with the migration to the Brazils; a step of great importance at the time, as removing from the grasp of Bonaparte the sovereign family of Braganza. Afterwards, in the year 1810, when the seat of the King of Portugal's government was established at Rio de Janeiro, and when it seemed probable, in the then apparently hopeless condition of the affairs of Europe, that it was likely long to continue there, the secret convention of 1807, of which the main object was accomplished by the fact of the emigration to Brazil, was abrogated, and a new and public treaty was concluded, into which was transferred the stipulation of 1807, binding Great Britain, so long as his faithful Majesty should be compelled to reside in Brazil, not to acknowledge any other sovereign of Portugal than a member of the House of Braganza. That stipulation, which had hitherto been secret, thus became patent, and part of the known law of nations.

In the year 1814, in consequence of the happy conclusion of the war, the option was afforded to the King of Portugal of returning to his European dominions. It was then felt that, as the necessity of his most faithful Majesty's absence from Portugal had ceased, the ground for the obligation originally contracted in the secret convention of 1807, and afterwards transferred to the patent treaty of 1810, was removed. The treaty of 1810 was, therefore, annulled at the Congress of Vienna; and in lieu of the stipulation not to acknowledge any other sovereign of Portugal than a member of the House of Braganza, was substituted that which I have just read to the House.

Annulling the treaty of 1810, the treaty of Vienna renews and confirms (as the House will have seen) all former treaties between Great Britain and Portugal, describing them as " ancient treaties of alliance, friendship, and guarantee "; as having " long and happily subsisted between the two Crowns "; and as being allowed by the two high contracting parties, to remain " in full force and effect."

What, then, is the force—what is the effect of those ancient treaties? I am prepared to show to the House what it is. But before I do so, I must say, that if all the treaties to which this article of the treaty of Vienna refers had perished by some convulsion of nature, or had by some extraordinary accident been consigned to total oblivion, still it would be impossible not to admit, as an incontestable inference from this article of the treaty of Vienna alone, that, in a moral point of view, there is incumbent on Great Britain a decided obligation to act as the effectual defender of Portugal.   If I could not show the letter of a single antecedent stipulation, I should still contend that a solemn admission, only ten years old, of the existence at that time of " treaties of alliance, friendship, and guarantee," held Great Britain to the discharge of the obligations which that very inscription implies.   But fortunately there is no such difficulty in specifying the nature of those obligations.   All of the preceding treaties exist—all of them are of easy reference—all of them are known to this country, to Spain, to every nation of the civilized world.   They are so numerous, and their general result is so uniform, that it may be sufficient to select only two of them to show the nature of all.

The first to which I shall advert is the treaty of 1661, which was concluded at the time of the marriage of Charles II with the Infanta of Portugal.   After reciting the marriage, and making over to Great Britain, in consequence of that marriage, first, a considerable sum of money, and, secondly, several important places, some of which, as Tangier, we no longer possess, but others of which, as Bombay, still belong to this country, the treaty runs thus : " In consideration of all which grants, so much to the benefit of the King of Great Britain and his subjects in general, and of the delivery of those important places to his said Majesty and his heirs forever, etc., the King of Great Britain does profess and declare, with the consent and advice of his council, that he will take the interest of Portugal and all its dominions to heart, defending the same with his utmost power by sea and land, even as England itself "; and it then proceeds to specify the succors to be sent, and the manner of sending them.

I come next to the treaty of 1703, a treaty of alliance contemporaneous with the Methuen treaty, which has regulated, for upwards of a century, the commercial relations of the two countries.   The treaty of 1703 was a tripartite engagement between the States-General of Holland, England, and Portugal.   The second article of that treaty sets forth that " if ever it shall happen that the Kings of Spain and France, either the present or

the future, that both of them together, or either of them separately, shall make war, or give occasion to suspect that they
intend to make war, upon the kingdom of Portugal, either on
the Continent of Europe, or on its dominions beyond the seas,
Her Majesty the Queen of Great Britain, and the Lords the
States-General, shall use their friendly offices with the said
kings, or either of them, in order to persuade them to observe
the terms of peace towards Portugal, and not to make war
upon it." The third article declares that " in the event of these
good offices not proving successful, but altogether ineffectual,
so that war should be made by the aforesaid kings, or by
either of them, upon Portugal, the above-mentioned powers
of Great Britain and Holland shall make war with all their
force upon the aforesaid kings or king who shall carry hostile arms into Portugal; and towards that war, which shall
be carried on in Europe, they shall supply twelve thousand
men, whom they shall arm and pay, as well when in quarters
as in action; and the said high allies shall be obliged to keep
that number of men complete, by recruiting it from time to
time at their own expense."

I am aware, indeed, that with respect to either of the treaties
which I have quoted it is possible to raise a question—whether
variation of circumstances or change of times may not have
somewhat relaxed its obligations. The treaty of 1661, it might
be said, was so loose and prodigal in the wording—it is so unreasonable, so wholly out of nature, that any one country should
be expected to defend another, " even as itself "; such stipulations are of so exaggerated a character as to resemble effusions
of feeling rather than enunciations of deliberate compact.
Again, with respect to the treaty of 1703, if the case rested on
that treaty alone, a question might be raised, whether or not,
when one of the contracting parties—Holland—had since so
changed her relations with Portugal, as to consider her obligations under the treaty of 1703 as obsolete—whether or not, I
say, under such circumstances, the obligation on the remaining
party be not likewise void. I should not hesitate to answer
both these objections in the negative. But without entering
into such a controversy, it is sufficient for me to say that the
time and place for taking such objections was at the Congress
at Vienna. Then and there it was that if you, indeed, consid-

ered these treaties as obsolete, you ought frankly and fearlessly to have declared them to be so. But then and there, with your eyes open, and in the face of all modern Europe, you proclaimed anew the ancient treaties of alliance, friendship, and guarantee, "so long subsisting between the Crowns of Great Britain and Portugal," as still "acknowledged by Great Britain," and still "of full force and effect." It is not, however, on specific articles alone—it is not so much, perhaps, on either of these ancient treaties, taken separately, as it is on the spirit and understanding of the whole body of treaties, of which the essence is concentrated and preserved in the treaty of Vienna, that we acknowledge in Portugal a right to look to Great Britain as her ally and defender.

This, sir, being the state, morally and politically, of our obligations towards Portugal, it is obvious that when Portugal, in apprehension of the coming storm, called on Great Britain for assistance, the only hesitation on our part could be—not whether that assistance was due, supposing the occasion for demanding it to arise, but simply whether that occasion—in other words, whether the *casus fœderis*—had arisen.

I understand, indeed, that in some quarters it has been imputed to His Majesty's ministers that an extraordinary delay intervened between the taking of the determination to give assistance to Portugal and the carrying of that determination into effect. But how stands the fact? On Sunday, the third of this month, we received from the Portuguese ambassador a direct and formal demand of assistance against a hostile aggression from Spain. Our answer was, that although rumors had reached us through France, His Majesty's Government had not that accurate information—that official and precise intelligence of facts—on which they could properly found an application to Parliament. It was only on last Friday night that this precise information arrived. On Saturday His Majesty's confidential servants came to a decision. On Sunday that decision received the sanction of His Majesty. On Monday it was communicated to both Houses of Parliament; and this day, sir, at the hour in which I have the honor of addressing you, the troops are on their march for embarkation.

I trust, then, sir, that no unseemly delay is imputable to government. But undoubtedly, on the other hand, when the claim of Portugal for assistance—a claim clear, indeed, in justice, but at the same time fearfully spreading in its possible consequences, came before us, it was the duty of His Majesty's Government to do nothing on hearsay. The eventual force of the claim was admitted; but a thorough knowledge of facts was necessary before the compliance with that claim could be granted. The government here labored under some disadvantage. The rumors which reached us through Madrid were obviously distorted, to answer partial political purposes; and the intelligence through the press of France, though substantially correct, was, in particulars, vague and contradictory. A measure of grave and serious moment could never be founded on such authority; nor could the ministers come down to Parliament until they had a confident assurance that the case which they had to lay before the legislature was true in all its parts.

But there was another reason which induced a necessary caution. In former instances, when Portugal applied to this country for assistance, the whole power of the state in Portugal was vested in the person of the monarch. The expression of his wish, the manifestation of his desire, the putting forth of his claim, was sufficient ground for immediate and decisive action on the part of Great Britain, supposing the *casus fœderis* to be made out. But, on this occasion, inquiry was in the first place to be made whether, according to the new constitution of Portugal, the call upon Great Britain was made with the consent of all the powers and authorities competent to make it, so as to carry with it an assurance of that reception in Portugal for our army, which the army of a friend and ally had a right to expect. Before a British soldier should put his foot on Portuguese ground, nay, before he should leave the shores of England, it was our duty to ascertain that the step taken by the regency of Portugal was taken with the cordial concurrence of the legislature of that country. It was but this morning that we received intelligence of the proceedings of the Chambers at Lisbon, which establishes the fact of such concurrence. This intelligence is contained in a dispatch from Sir W. A'Court, dated the twenty-ninth of November, of which I will read an extract to the House. " The day after the news arrived of the entry of the rebels into Portugal, the ministers demanded from the Chambers an extension of power for the executive government, and the permission to apply for foreign succors, in virtue of ancient treaties, in the event of their being deemed necessary. The deputies gave the requisite authority by acclamation; and an equally good spirit was manifested by the peers, who granted every power that the ministers could possibly require. They even went further, and, rising in a body from their seats, declared their devotion to their country, and their readiness to give their personal services, if necessary, to repel any hostile invasion. The Duke de Cadaval, president of the Chamber, was the first to make this declaration; and the minister who described this proceeding to me, said it was a movement worthy of the good days of Portugal!"

I have thus incidentally disposed of the supposed imputation of delay in complying with the requisition of the Portuguese Government. The main question, however, is this: Was it obligatory upon us to comply with that requisition? In other words, had the *casus fœderis* arisen? In our opinion it had. Bands of Portuguese rebels, armed, equipped, and trained in Spain, had crossed the Spanish frontier, carrying terror and devastation into their own country, and proclaiming sometimes the brother of the reigning sovereign of Portugal, sometimes a Spanish princess, and sometimes even Ferdinand of Spain, as the rightful occupant of the Portuguese throne. These rebels crossed the frontier, not at one point only, but at several points; for it is remarkable that the aggression, on which the original application to Great Britain for succor was founded, is not the aggression with reference to which that application has been complied with.

The attack announced by the French newspapers was on the north of Portugal, in the province of Tras-os-Montes; an official account of which has been received by His Majesty's Government only this day. But on Friday an account was received of an invasion in the south of Portugal, and of the capture of Villa Vicosa, a town lying on the road from the southern frontier to Lisbon. This new fact established even more satisfactorily than a mere confirmation of the attack first complained of would have done, the systematic nature of the aggression of Spain against Portugal. One hostile irruption might have been made by some single corps escaping from their quarters—by some body of stragglers, who might have evaded the vigilance

of Spanish authorities; and one such accidental and unconnect-
ed act of violence might not have been conclusive evidence of
cognizance and design on the part of those authorities; but
when a series of attacks are made along the whole line of a
frontier, it is difficult to deny that such multiplied instances of
hostility are evidence of concerted aggression.

If a single company of Spanish soldiers had crossed the
frontier in hostile array, there could not, it is presumed, be a
doubt as to the character of that invasion. Shall bodies of
men, armed, clothed, and regimented by Spain, carry fire and
sword into the bosom of her unoffending neighbor, and shall
it be pretended that no attack, no invasion has taken place, because, forsooth, these outrages are committed against Portugal
by men to whom Portugal had given birth and nurture? What
petty quibbling would it be to say that an invasion of Portugal
from Spain was not a Spanish invasion, because Spain did not
employ her own troops, but hired mercenaries to effect her
purpose? And what difference is it, except as an aggravation,
that the mercenaries in this instance were natives of Portugal.

I have already stated, and I now repeat, that it never has
been the wish or the pretension of the British government to interfere in the internal concerns of the Portuguese nation. Questions of that kind the Portuguese nation must settle among
themselves. But if we were to admit that hordes of traitorous
refugees from Portugal, with Spanish arms, or arms furnished
or restored to them by Spanish authorities, in their hands, might
put off their country for one purpose, and put it on again for
another—put it off for the purpose of attack, and put it on
again for the purpose of impunity—if, I say, we were to admit
this juggle, and either pretend to be deceived by it ourselves,
or attempt to deceive Portugal, into a belief that there was
nothing of external attack, nothing of foreign hostility, in such
a system of aggression—such pretence and attempt would, perhaps, be only ridiculous and contemptible; if they did not require a much more serious character from being employed as an
excuse for infidelity to ancient friendship, and as a pretext for
getting rid of the positive stipulations of treaties.

This, then, is the case which I lay before the House of Commons. Here is, on the one hand, an undoubted pledge of national faith—not taken in a corner—not kept secret between the

parties, but publicly recorded among the annals of history, in the face of the world. Here are, on the other hand, undeniable acts of foreign aggression, perpetrated, indeed, principally through the instrumentality of domestic traitors, but supported with foreign means, instigated by foreign councils, and directed to foreign ends. Putting these facts and this pledge together, it is impossible that His Majesty should refuse the call that has been made upon him; nor can Parliament, I am convinced, refuse to enable His Majesty to fulfil his undoubted obligations. I am willing to rest the whole question of to-night, and to call for the vote of the House of Commons upon this simple case, divested altogether of collateral circumstances; from which I especially wish to separate it, in the minds of those who hear me, and also in the minds of others, to whom what I now say will find its way. If I were to sit down this moment, without adding another word, I have no doubt but that I should have the concurrence of the House in the address which I mean to propose.

When I state this it will be obvious to the House that the vote for which I am about to call upon them is a vote for the defence of Portugal, not a vote for war against Spain. I beg the House to keep these two points entirely distinct in their consideration. For the former I think I have said enough. If, in what I have now further to say, I should bear hard upon the Spanish Government I beg that it may be observed that, unjustifiable as I shall show their conduct to have been—contrary to the law of nations, contrary to the law of good neighborhood, contrary, I might say, to the laws of God and man—with respect to Portugal!—still I do not mean to preclude a *locus pœnitentiæ*, a possibility of redress and reparation. It is our duty to fly to the defence of Portugal, be the assailant who he may. And, be it remembered, that, in thus fulfilling the stipulation of ancient treaties, of the existence and obligation of which all the world are aware, we, according to the universally admitted construction of the law of nations, neither make war upon that assailant, nor give to that assailant, much less to any other power, just cause of war against ourselves.

Sir, the present situation of Portugal is so anomalous, and the recent years of her history are crowded with events so unusual, that the House will, perhaps, not think that I am unprofitably wasting its time, if I take the liberty of calling its attention, shortly and succinctly, to those events, and to their influence on the political relations of Europe.   It is known that the consequence of the residence of the King of Portugal in Brazil was to raise the latter country from a colonial to a metropolitan condition ; and that, from the time when the King began to contemplate his return to Portugal, there grew up in Brazil a desire of independence that threatened dissension, if not something like civil contest, between the European and American dominions of the House of Braganza.   It is known, also, that Great Britain undertook a mediation between Portugal and Brazil, and induced the King to consent to a separation of the two crowns—confirming that of Brazil on the head of his eldest son.   The ink with which this agreement was written was scarcely dry when the unexpected death of the King of Portugal produced a new state of things, which reunited on the same head the two crowns which it had been the policy of England, as well as of Portugal and of Brazil, to separate.   On that occasion Great Britain and another European Court, closely connected with Brazil, tendered advice to the Emperor of Brazil, now become King of Portugal, which advice it cannot be accurately said that his Imperial Majesty followed, because he had decided for himself before it reached Rio de Janeiro; but in conformity with which advice, though not in consequence of it, his Imperial Majesty determined to abdicate the crown of Portugal in favor of his eldest daughter.   But the Emperor of Brazil had done more.   What had not been foreseen—what would have been beyond the province of any foreign power to advise—his Imperial Majesty had accompanied his abdication of the crown of Portugal with the grant of a free constitutional charter for that kingdom.

It has been surmised that this measure, as well as the abdication which it accompanied, was the offspring of our advice No such thing—Great Britain did not suggest this measure.   It is not her duty nor her practice to offer suggestions for the internal regulation of foreign states.   She neither approved nor disapproved of the grant of a constitutional charter to Portugal ; her opinion upon that grant was never required.   True it is, that the instrument of the constitutional charter was brought to Europe by a gentleman of high trust in the service of the Brit-

ish government. Sir C. Stuart had gone to Brazil to negotiate the separation between that country and Portugal. In addition to his character of plenipotentiary of Great Britain, as the
mediating power, he had also been invested by the King of
Portugal with the character of his most faithful Majesty's plenipotentiary for the negotiation with Brazil. That negotiation
had been brought to a happy conclusion; and therewith the
British part of Sir C. Stuart's commission had terminated. But
Sir C. Stuart was still resident at Rio de Janeiro, as the plenipotentiary of the King of Portugal, for negotiating commercial
arrangements between Portugal and Brazil. In this latter character it was that Sir C. Stuart, on his return to Europe, was requested by the Emperor of Brazil to be the bearer to Portugal
of the new constitutional charter. His Majesty's government
found no fault with Sir C. Stuart for executing this commission;
but it was immediately felt that if Sir C. Stuart were allowed to
remain at Lisbon it might appear, in the eyes of Europe, that
England was the contriver and imposer of the Portuguese constitution. Sir C. Stuart was, therefore, directed to return home
forthwith, in order that the constitution, if carried into effect
there might plainly appear to be adopted by the Portuguese
nation itself, not forced upon them by English interference.

As to the merits, sir, of the new constitution of Portugal I
have neither the intention nor the right to offer any opinion.
Personally, I may have formed one; but as an English minister,
all I have to say is: May God prosper this attempt at the establishment of constitutional liberty in Portugal! and may that
nation be found as fit to enjoy and to cherish its new-born privileges as it has often proved itself capable of discharging its duties among the nations of the world!

I, sir, am neither the champion nor the critic of the Portuguese constitution. But it is admitted on all hands to have proceeded from a legitimate source—a consideration which has
mainly reconciled continental Europe to its establishment; and
to us, as Englishmen, it is recommended by the ready acceptance which it has met with from all orders of the Portuguese
people. To that constitution, therefore, thus unquestioned in
its origin, even by those who are most jealous of new institutions—to that constitution, thus sanctioned in its outset by the
glad and grateful acclamations of those who are destined to live

under it—to that constitution, founded on principles, in a great degree, similar to those of our own, though differently modified —it is impossible that Englishmen should not wish well. But it would not be for us to force that constitution on the people of Portugal, if they were unwilling to receive it, or if any schism should exist among the Portuguese themselves, as to its fitness and congeniality to the wants and wishes of the nation. It is no business of ours to fight its battles. We go to Portugal in the discharge of a sacred obligation, contracted under ancient and modern treaties. When there nothing shall be done by us to enforce the establishment of the constitution; but we must take care that nothing shall be done by others to prevent it from being fairly carried into effect. Internally, let the Portuguese settle their own affairs; but with respect to external force, while Great Britain has an arm to raise, it must be raised against the efforts of any power that should attempt forcibly to control the choice and fetter the independence of Portugal.

Has such been the intention of Spain? Whether the proceedings which have lately been practised or permitted in Spain were acts of a government exercising the usual power of prudence and foresight (without which a government is, for the good of the people which live under it, no government at all), or whether they were the acts of some secret illegitimate power —of some furious fanatical faction, overriding the counsels of the ostensible government, defying it in the capital, and disobeying it on the frontiers—I will not stop to inquire. It is indifferent to Portugal, smarting under her wrongs—it is indifferent to England, who is called upon to avenge them— whether the present state of things be the result of the intrigues of a faction, over which, if the Spanish government has no control, it ought to assume one as soon as possible; or of local authorities, over whom it has control, and for whose acts it must, therefore, be held responsible. It matters not, I say, from which of these sources the evil has arisen. In either case Portugal must be protected; and from England that protection is due.

It would be unjust, however, to the Spanish government to say that it is only among the members of that government that an unconquerable hatred of liberal institutions exists in Spain. However incredible the phenomena may appear in this country,

I am persuaded that a vast majority of the Spanish nation entertain a decided attachment to arbitrary power, and a predilection for absolute government. The more liberal institutions of countries in the neighborhood have not yet extended their influence into Spain, nor awakened any sympathy in the mass of the Spanish people. Whether the public authorities of Spain did or did not partake of the national sentiment, there would almost necessarily grow up between Portugal and Spain, under present circumstances, an opposition of feelings which it would not require the authority or the suggestions of the government to excite and stimulate into action. Without blame, therefore, to the government of Spain—out of the natural antipathy between the two neighboring nations—the one prizing its recent freedom, the other hugging its traditionary servitude—there might arise mutual provocations and reciprocal injuries, which, perhaps, even the most active and vigilant ministry could not altogether restrain. I am inclined to believe that such has been, in part at least, the origin of the differences between Spain and Portugal. That in their progress they have been adopted, matured, methodized, combined, and brought into more perfect action, by some authority more united and more efficient than the mere feeling disseminated through the mass of the community, is certain; but I do believe their origin to have been as much in the real sentiment of the Spanish population as in the opinion or contrivance of the government itself.

Whether this be or be not the case is precisely the question between us and Spain. If, though partaking in the general feelings of the Spanish nation, the Spanish government has, nevertheless, done nothing to embody those feelings, and to direct them hostilely against Portugal; if all that has occurred on the frontier has occurred only because the vigilance of the Spanish government has been surprised, its confidence betrayed, and its orders neglected; if its engagements have been repeatedly and shamefully violated, not by its own good-will, but against its recommendation and desire, let us see some symptoms of disapprobation, some signs of repentance, some measures indicative of sorrow for the past and of sincerity for the future. In that case His Majesty's message, to which I propose this night to return an answer of concurrence, will retain the character which I have ascribed to it—that of a measure of defence for Portugal, not a measure of resentment against Spain.

With these explanations and qualifications let us now proceed to the review of facts. Great desertions took place from the Portuguese army into Spain, and some desertions took place from the Spanish army into Portugal. In the first instance, the Portuguese authorities were taken by surprise; but in every subsequent instance, where they had an opportunity of exercising a discretion, it is but just to say that they uniformly discouraged the desertions of the Spanish soldiery. There exist between Spain and Portugal specific treaties, stipulating the mutual surrender of deserters. Portugal had, therefore, a right to claim of Spain that every Portuguese deserter should be forthwith sent back. I hardly know whether from its own impulse, or in consequence of our advice, the Portuguese government waived its right under those treaties; very wisely reflecting that it would be highly inconvenient to be placed by the return of their deserters in the difficult alternative of either granting a dangerous amnesty or ordering numerous executions. The Portuguese government, therefore, signified to Spain that it would be entirely satisfied if, instead of surrendering the deserters, Spain would restore their arms, horses, and equipments; and, separating the men from their officers, would remove both from the frontiers into the interior of Spain. Solemn engagements were entered into by the Spanish government to this effect—first with Portugal, next with France, and afterwards with England. Those engagements, concluded one day, were violated the next. The deserters, instead of being disarmed and dispersed, were allowed to remain congregated together near the frontiers of Portugal, where they were enrolled, trained, and disciplined for the expedition which they have since undertaken. It is plain that in these proceedings there was perfidy somewhere. It rests with the Spanish government to show that it was not with them. It rests with the Spanish government to prove that, if its engagements have not been fulfilled —if its intentions have been eluded and unexecuted—the fault has not been with the government, and that it is ready to make every reparation in its power.

I have said that these promises were made to France and to Great Britain as well as to Portugal. I should do a great injustice to France if I were not to add that the representations of that government upon this point to the Cabinet of Madrid have been as urgent, and, alas! as fruitless, as those of Great Britain. Upon the first irruption into the Portuguese territory the French government testified its displeasure by instantly recalling its ambassador; and it further directed its *chargé d'affaires* to signify to his Catholic Majesty that Spain was not to look for any support from France against the consequences of this aggression upon Portugal. I am bound, I repeat, in justice to the French government, to state that it has exerted itself to the utmost in urging Spain to retrace the steps which she has so unfortunately taken. It is not for me to say whether any more efficient course might have been adopted to give effect to their exhortations; but as to the sincerity and good faith of the exertions made by the government of France to press Spain to the execution of her engagements I have not the shadow of a doubt, and I confidently reckon upon their continuance.

It will be for Spain, upon knowledge of the step now taken by His Majesty, to consider in what way she will meet it. The earnest hope and wish of His Majesty's Government is that she may meet it in such a manner as to avert any ill consequences to herself from the measure into which we have been driven by the unjust attack upon Portugal.

Sir, I set out with saying that there were reasons which entirely satisfied my judgment that nothing short of a point of national faith or national honor would justify, at the present moment, any voluntary approximation to the possibility of war. Let me be understood, however, distinctly as not meaning to say that I dread war in a good cause (and in no other way may it be the lot of this country ever to engage!) from a distrust of the strength of the country to commence it, or of her resources to maintain it. I dread it, indeed—but upon far other grounds: I dread it from an apprehension of the tremendous consequences which might arise from any hostilities in which we might now be engaged. Some years ago, in the discussion of the negotiations respecting the French war against Spain, I took the liberty of adverting to this topic. I then stated that the position of this country in the present state of the world was one of neutrality, not only between contending nations, but

between conflicting principles; and that it was by neutrality
alone that we could maintain that balance, the preservation of
which I believed to be essential to the welfare of mankind. I
then said that I feared that the next war which should be
kindled in Europe would be a war not so much of armies as
of opinions. Not four years have elapsed, and behold my apprehension realized! It is, to be sure, within narrow limits that
this war of opinion is at present confined; but it is a war of opinion that Spain (whether as government or as nation) is now
waging against Portugal; it is a war which has commenced in
hatred of the new institutions of Portugal. How long is it
reasonable to expect that Portugal will abstain from retaliation?
If into that war this country shall be compelled to enter we
shall enter into it with a sincere and anxious desire to mitigate
rather than exasperate—and to mingle only in the conflict of
arms, not in the more fatal conflict of opinions. But I much
fear that this country (however earnestly she may endeavor to
avoid it) could not, in such case, avoid seeing ranked under
her banners all the restless and dissatisfied of any nation with
which she might come in conflict. It is the contemplation of
this new power in any future war which excites my most anxious apprehension. It is one thing to have a giant's strength,
but it would be another to use it like a giant. The consciousness of such strength is, undoubtedly, a source of confidence
and security; but in the situation in which this country stands,
our business is not to seek opportunities of displaying it, but to
content ourselves with letting the professors of violent and exaggerated doctrines on both sides feel that it is not their interest
to convert an umpire into an adversary. The situation of England, amid the struggle of political opinions which agitates more
or less sensibly different countries of the world, may be compared to that of the Ruler of the Winds, as described by the
poet:

> " Celsâ sedet Æolus arce,
> Sceptra tenens; mollitque animos et temperat iras
> Ni faciat, maria ac terras cœlumque profundum
> Quippe ferant rapidi secum, verrantque per auras."

The consequence of letting loose the passions at present
chained and confined would be to produce a scene of desolation

which no man can contemplate without horror; and I should not sleep easy on my couch if I were conscious that I had contributed to precipitate it by a single moment.

This, then, is the reason—a reason very different from fear—the reverse of a consciousness of disability—why I dread the recurrence of hostilities in any part of Europe; why I would bear much, and would forbear long; why I would (as I have said) put up with almost anything that did not touch national faith and national honor, rather than let slip the furies of war, the leash of which we hold in our hands—not knowing whom they may reach, or how far their ravages may be carried. Such is the love of peace which the British government acknowledges; and such the necessity for peace which the circumstances of the world inculcate. I will push these topics no further.

I return, in conclusion, to the object of the address. Let us fly to the aid of Portugal, by whomsoever attacked, because it is our duty to do so; and let us cease our interference where that duty ends. We go to Portugal not to rule, not to dictate, not to prescribe constitutions, but to defend and to preserve the independence of an ally. We go to plant the standard of England on the well-known heights of Lisbon. Where that standard is planted foreign dominion shall not come.

ON THE RIGHTS OF CATHOLICS

—

BY

DANIEL O'CONNELL

DANIEL O'CONNELL

1775—1847

The great Irish agitator was born in Cahirciveen, County Kerry, Ireland, on August 6, 1775; his death took place when he had reached his seventy-third year, at Genoa, on the coast of Italy. His parents destined him for the priesthood, and sent him to the Jesuits' college at St Omer for instruction, but after he had finished his course, he announced that he preferred the law of man to the priesthood as a profession. To the Middle Temple therefore he went, and after duly completing his terms there, was admitted to the Irish bar in 1798, at which date it had been just opened to the Catholics. He had great powers as an advocate, and his skill and versatility in conducting defences before the Crown courts caused him sometimes to be charged with inconsistencies. But his extraordinary merits could not be obscured; and in 1831 he received his silk gown.

Long before this, however, he had become famous elsewhere than in forensic matters. He was not satisfied to be the foremost advocate of the Irish bar; it was not long before he had won the reputation of being also the leader of the Irish Catholics in the political field. He was resolved to obtain for his countrymen admission to all the rights of other British subjects; and he was chiefly instrumental in forwarding the results obtained by the Catholic Board and the Catholic Association. All this was not accomplished without animated personal collisions; and he was challenged for having applied the epithet of "beggarly corporation" to the corporation of Dublin, which opposed the Catholic claims. He met his antagonist, and killed him. He was subsequently challenged by Mr. Peel, at the time when the latter was Secretary for Ireland; but two attempts to fight a duel were frustrated by the authorities.

The repeal of the union and the removal of Catholic disabilities were the two measures to the securing of which he devoted his main energies Before the relief bill was passed he had expressed the opinion that it was possible for him to sit in Parliament; and he had accordingly been elected to the seat for County Clare; but he made no attempt to take his seat until after the bill had been passed. He was then required to take the usual oaths of allegiance, supremacy, and abjuration, and when he claimed the benefit of the bill, it was decided that he was not entitled to the advantage of its provisions; and he was not permitted to sit. But upon being re-elected, the prohibition was removed. In 1831 he was elected to sit for Kerry; in the same year he was arrested for sedition, or the suspicion of it, together with several others, but the prosecution came to nothing, and all were released. In 1841 he headed the repeal agitation, and during the two following years he promoted vast mass-meetings; in 1843 he was again arrested; but in 1844 the sentence which had been passed upon him was reversed.

O'Connell's natural manner of speaking, in accordance with his nature and temperament, was bold and aggressive; but he could at will adopt the most suave and cautious methods In short, he was a master of the oratorical and rhetorical arts; and his indomitable courage and persistence rendered him a most formidable parliamentary debater. The speech "On the Rights of Catholics" is a good example of his oratory in the cause to which he devoted the greatest efforts of his life.

ON THE RIGHTS OF CATHOLICS

Delivered at a meeting in Dublin, February 23, 1814

I WISH to submit to the meeting a resolution, calling on the different counties and cities in Ireland to petition for unqualified emancipation. It is a resolution which has been already and frequently adopted; when we have persevered in our petitions, even at periods when we despaired of success; and it becomes a pleasing duty to present it, now that the symptoms of the times seem so powerfully to promise an approaching relief.

Indeed, as long as truth or justice can be supposed to influence man; as long as man is admitted to be under the control of reason; so long must it be prudent and wise to procure discussions on the sufferings and the rights of the people of Ireland. Truth proclaims the treacherous iniquity which has deprived us of our chartered liberty; truth destroys the flimsy pretext under which this iniquity is continued; truth exposes our merits and our sufferings; whilst reason and justice combine to demonstrate our right—the right of every human being to freedom of conscience—a right without which every honest man must feel that to him, individually, the protection of government is a mockery, and the restriction of penal law a sacrilege.

Truth, reason, and justice are our advocates; and even in England let me tell you that those powerful advocates have some authority. They are, it is true, more frequently resisted there than in most other countries; but yet they have some sway among the English at all times. Passion may confound and prejudice darken the English understanding; and interested passion and hired prejudice have been successfully employed against us at former periods; but the present season appears singularly well calculated to aid the progress of our cause, and to advance the attainment of our important objects.

79

I do not make the assertion lightly. I speak after deliberate investigation, and from solemn conviction, my clear opinion that we shall, during the present session of Parliament, obtain a portion, at least, if not the entire, of our emancipation. We cannot fail, unless we are disturbed in our course by those who graciously style themselves our friends, or are betrayed by the treacherous machinations of part of our own body.

Yes, everything, except false friendship and domestic treachery, forebodes success. The cause of man is in its great advance. Humanity has been rescued from much of its thraldom. In the states of Europe, where the iron despotism of the feudal system so long classed men into two species— the hereditary masters and the perpetual slaves; when rank supplied the place of merit, and to be humbly born operated as a perpetual exclusion—in many parts of Europe man is reassuming his natural station, and artificial distinctions have vanished before the force of truth and the necessities of governors.

France has a representative government; and as the unjust privileges of the clergy and nobility are abolished; as she is blessed with a most wise, clear, and simple code of laws; as she is almost free from debt, and emancipated from odious prejudices, she is likely to prove an example and a light to the world.

In Germany the sovereigns who formerly ruled at their free will and caprice are actually bribing the people to the support of their thrones, by giving them the blessings of liberty. It is a wise and glorious policy. The prince regent has emancipated his Catholic subjects of Hanover, and traced for them the grand outlines of a free constitution. The other states of Germany are rapidly following the example. The people, no longer destined to bear the burdens only of society, are called up to take their share in the management of their own concerns, and in the sustentation of the public dignity and happiness. In short, representative government, the only rational or just government, is proclaimed by princes as a boon to their people, and Germany is about to afford many an example of the advantages of rational liberty. Anxious as some kings appear to be in the great work of plunder and robbery, others of them are now the first heralds of freedom.

It is a moment of glorious triumph to humanity; and even one instance of liberty, freely conceded, makes compensation for a thousand repetitions of the ordinary crimes of military monarchs. The crime is followed by its own punishment; but the great principle of the rights of man establishes itself now on the broadest basis, and France and Germany now set forth an example for England to imitate.

Italy, too, is in the paroxysms of the fever of independence. Oh, may she have strength to go through the disease, and may she rise like a giant refreshed with wine! One thing is certain, that the human mind is set afloat in Italy. The flame of freedom burns; it may be smothered for a season; but all the whiskered Croats and the fierce Pandours of Austria will not be able to extinguish the sacred fire. Spain, to be sure, chills the heart and disgusts the understanding. The combined Inquisition and the Court press upon the mind, whilst they bind the body in fetters of adamant. But this despotism is, thank God, as unrelentingly absurd as it is cruel, and there arises a darling hope out of the very excess of the evil. The Spaniards must be walking corpses—they must be living ghosts, and not human beings, unless a sublime reaction be in rapid preparation. But let us turn to our own prospects.

The cause of liberty has made, and is making, great progress in states heretofore despotic. In all the countries in Europe, in which any portion of freedom prevails, the liberty of conscience is complete. England alone, of all the states pretending to be free, leaves shackles upon the human mind; England alone, amongst free states, exhibits the absurd claim of regulating belief by law, and forcing opinion by statute. Is it possible to conceive that this gross, this glaring, this iniquitous absurdity can continue? Is it possible, too, to conceive that it can continue to operate, not against a small and powerless sect, but against the millions, comprising the best strength, the most affluent energy of the empire?—a strength and an energy daily increasing, and hourly appreciating their own importance. The present system, disavowed by liberalized Europe, disclaimed by sound reason, abhorred by genuine religion, must soon and forever be abolished.

Let it not be said that the princes of the Continent were forced by necessity to give privileges to their subjects, and that

England has escaped from a similar fate. I admit that the
necessity of procuring the support of the people was the main-
spring of royal patriotism on the Continent; but I totally deny
that the ministers of England can dispense with a similar
support. The burdens of the war are permanent; the dis-
tresses occasioned by the peace are pressing; the financial
system tottering, and to be supported in profound peace
only by a war taxation. In the mean time, the resources of
corruption are mightily diminished. Ministerial influence is
necessarily diminished by one-half of the effective force of
indirect bribery; full two-thirds must be disbanded. Peculation
and corruption must be put upon half-pay, and no allowances.
The ministry lose not only all those active partisans; those
outrageous loyalists, who fattened on the public plunder during
the seasons of immense expenditure; but those very men will
themselves swell the ranks of the malcontents, and probably
be the most violent in their opposition. They have no sweet
consciousness to reward them in their present privations; and
therefore they are likely to exhaust the bitterness of their souls
on their late employers. Every cause conspires to render this
the period in which the ministry should have least inclination,
least interest, least power, to oppose the restoration of our
rights and liberties.

I speak not from mere theory. There exist at this moment
practical illustrations of the truth of my assertions. Instances
have occurred which demonstrate, as well the inability of the
ministry to resist the popular voice, as the utility of re-echoing
that voice, until it is heard and understood in all its strength
and force. The ministers had determined to continue the
property tax; they announced that determination to their
partisans at Liverpool and in Bristol. Well, the people of
England met; they petitioned; they repeated—they reiterated
their petitions, until the ministry felt they could no longer
resist; and they ungraciously, but totally, abandoned their
determination; and the property tax now expires.

Another instance is also now before us. It relates to the
Corn Laws. The success of the repetition of petitions in that
instance is the more remarkable, because such success has
been obtained in defiance of the first principles of political
economy, and in violation of the plainest rules of political
justice.

This is not the place to discuss the merits of the Corn Laws; but I cannot avoid, as the subject lies in my way, to put upon public record my conviction of the inutility as well as the impropriety of the proposed measure respecting those laws. I expect that it will be believed in Ireland that I would not volunteer thus an opposition of sentiment to any measure, if I was not most disinterestedly, and in my conscience, convinced that such measure would not be of any substantial or permanent utility to Ireland.

As far as I am personally concerned, my interest plainly is to keep up the price of lands; but I am quite convinced that the measure in question will have an effect permanently and fatally injurious to Ireland. The clamor respecting the Corn Laws has been fomented by parsons who were afraid that they would not get money enough for their tithes, and absentee landlords, who apprehended a diminution of their rack rents; and if you observed the names of those who have taken an active part in favor of the measure, you will find amongst them many, if not all, the persons who have most distinguished themselves against the liberty and religion of the people. There have been, I know, many good men misled, and many clever men deceived, on this subject; but the great majority are of the class of oppressors.

There was formed, some time ago, an association of a singular nature in Dublin and the adjacent counties. Mr. Luke White was, as I remember, at the head of it. It contained some of our stoutest and most stubborn seceders; it published the causes of its institution; it recited that, whereas butcher's meat was dearer in Cork, and in Limerick, and in Belfast than in Dublin, it was therefore expedient to associate, in order that the people of Dublin should not eat meat too cheap. Large sums were subscribed to carry the patriotic design into effect, but public indignation broke up the ostensible confederacy; it was too plain and too glaring to bear public inspection. The indignant sense of the people of Dublin forced them to dissolve their open association; and if the present enormous increase of the price of meat in Dublin beyond the rest of Ireland be the result of secret combination of any individuals, there is at least this comfort, that they do not presume to beard the public with the open avowal of their design to increase the difficulties of the poor in procuring food.

Such a scheme as that, with respect to meat in Dublin—such a scheme, precisely, is the sought-for Corn Law. The only difference consists in the extent of the operation of both plans. The corn plan is only more extensive, not more unjust in principle, but it is more unreasonable in its operation, because its necessary tendency must be to destroy that very market of which it seeks the exclusive possession. The Corn Law men want, they say, to have the exclusive feeding of the manufacturers; but at present our manufacturers, loaded as they are with taxation, are scarcely able to meet the goods of foreigners in the markets of the world. The English are already undersold in foreign markets; but if to this dearness produced by taxation there shall be added the dearness produced by dear food, is it not plain that it will be impossible to enter into a competition with foreign manufacturers, who have no taxes and cheap bread? Thus the Corn Laws will destroy our manufactures, and compel our manufacturers to emigrate, in spite of penalties; and the Corn Law supporters will have injured themselves and destroyed others.

I beg pardon for dwelling on this subject. If I were at liberty to pursue it here, I would not leave it until I had satisfied every dispassionate man that the proposed measure is both useless and unjust; but this is not the place for doing so, and I only beg to record at least the honest dictates of my judgment on this interesting topic. My argument, of the efficacy of petitioning, is strengthened by the impolicy of the measure in question; because, if petitions, by their number and perseverance, succeed in establishing a proposition impolitic in principle, and oppressive to thousands in operation, what encouragement does it not afford to us to repeat our petitions for that which has justice for its basis, and policy as its support!

The great advantages of discussion being thus apparent, the efficacy of repeating, and repeating, and repeating again our petitions being thus demonstrated by notorious facts, the Catholics of Ireland must be sunk in criminal apathy if they neglect the use of an instrument so efficacious for their emancipation.

There is further encouragement at this particular crisis. Dissension has ceased in the Catholic body. Those who paralyzed our efforts, and gave our conduct the appearance and reality of weakness, and wavering, and inconsistency, have all retired. Those who were ready to place the entire of the Catholic feelings and dignity, and some of the Catholic religion too, under the feet of every man who pleased to call himself our friend, and to prove himself our friend, by praising on every occasion, and upon no occasion, the oppressors of the Catholics, and by abusing the Catholics themselves; the men who would link the Catholic cause to this patron and to that, and sacrifice it at one time to the minister, and at another time to the opposition, and make it this day the tool of one party, and the next the instrument of another party; the men, in fine, who hoped to traffic upon our country and our religion—who would buy honors, and titles, and places, and pensions, at the price of the purity, and dignity, and safety of the Catholic Church in Ireland; all those men have, thank God, quitted us, I hope forever. They have returned into silence and secession, or have frankly or covertly gone over to our enemies. I regret deeply and bitterly that they have carried with them some few who, like my Lord Fingal, entertain no other motives than those of purity and integrity, and who, like that noble lord, are merely mistaken.

But I rejoice at this separation—I rejoice that they have left the single-hearted, and the disinterested, and the indefatigable, and the independent, and the numerous, and the sincere Catholics to work out their emancipation unclogged, unshackled, and undismayed. They have bestowed on us another bounty also —they have proclaimed the causes of their secession—they have placed out of doubt the cause of the divisions. It is not intemperance, for that we abandoned; it is not the introduction of extraneous topics, for those we disclaimed; it is simply and purely, veto or no veto—restriction or no restriction—no other words; it is religion and principle that have divided us; thanks, many thanks to the tardy and remote candor of the seceders, that has at length written in large letters the cause of their secession—it is the Catholic Church of Ireland—it is whether the Church shall continue independent of a Protestant ministry or not. We are for its independence—the seceders are for its dependence.

Whatever shall be the fate of our emancipation question, thank God we are divided forever from those who would wish

that our Church should crouch to the partisans of the Orange
system. Thank God, secession has displayed its cloven foot,
and avowed itself to be synonymous with vetoism.

Those are our present prospects of success. First, man is
elevated from slavery almost everywhere, and human nature
has become more dignified, and, I may say, more valuable.
Secondly, England wants our cordial support, and knows that
she has only to secede to us justice in order to obtain our
affectionate assistance. Thirdly, this is the season of successful
petition, and the very fashion of the times entitles our petition
to succeed. Fourthly, the Catholic cause is disencumbered of
hollow friends and interested speculators. Add to all these the
native and inherent strength of the principle of religious freedom and the inert and accumulating weight of our wealth, our
religion, and our numbers, and where is the sluggard that shall
dare to doubt our approaching success?

Besides, even our enemies must concede to us that we act
from principle, and from principle only. We prove our sincerity
when we refuse to make our emancipation a subject of traffic
and barter, and ask for relief only upon those grounds which, if
once established, would give to every other sect the right to the
same political immunity. All we ask is " a clear stage and no
favor." We think the Catholic religion the most rationally
consistent with the divine scheme of Christianity, and, therefore, all we ask is that everybody should be left to his unbiassed
reason and judgment. If Protestants are equally sincere, why
do they call the law, and the bribe, and the place, and the
pension, in support of their doctrines? Why do they fortify
themselves behind pains, and penalties, and exclusions, and
forfeitures? Ought not our opponents to feel that they de-
grade the sanctity of their religion when they call in the profane aid of temporal rewards and punishments, and that they
proclaim the superiority of our creed when they thus admit
themselves unable to contend against it upon terms of equality,
and by the weapons of reason and argument, and persevere in
refusing us all we ask—" a clear stage and no favor "?

Yes, Mr. Chairman, our enemies, in words and by actions,
admit and proclaim our superiority. It remains to our friends
alone, and to that misguided and ill-advised portion of the
Catholics who have shrunk into secession—it remains for

those friends and seceders alone to undervalue our exertions, and underrate our conscientious opinions.

Great and good God, in what a cruel situation are the Catholics of Ireland placed! If they have the manliness to talk of their oppressors as the paltry bigots deserve—if they have the honesty to express, even in measured language, a small portion of the sentiments of abhorrence which peculating bigotry ought naturally to inspire—if they condemn the principle which established the Inquisition in Spain and Orange lodges in Ireland, they are assailed by the combined clamor of those parliamentary friends and title-seeking, place-hunting seceders. The war-whoop of "intemperance" is sounded, and a persecution is instituted by our advocates and our seceders, against the Catholic who dares to be honest, and fearless, and independent!

But I tell you what they easily forgive—nay, what our friends, sweet souls, would vindicate to-morrow in Parliament, if the subject arose there. Here it is—here is the "Dublin Journal" of the twenty-first of February, printed just two days ago. In the administration of Lord Whitworth, and the secretaryship of Mr. Peel, there is a government newspaper—a paper supported solely by the money of the people; for its circulation is little, and its private advertisements less. Here is a paper continued in existence like a wounded reptile—only whilst in the rays of the sun, by the heat and warmth communicated to it by the Irish administration. Let me read two passages for you The first calls "Popery the deadly enemy of pure religion and rational liberty." Such is the temperate description the writer gives of the Catholic faith. With respect to purity of religion I shall not quarrel with him. I only differ with him in point of taste; but I should be glad to know what this creature calls rational liberty. I suppose such as existed at Lacedæmon—the dominion of Spartans over Helots—the despotism of masters over slaves, that is his rational liberty. We will readily pass so much by. But attend to this:

"I will," says this moderate and temperate gentleman, "lay before the readers such specimens of the popish superstition as will convince him that the treasonable combinations cemented by oaths, and the nocturnal robbery and assassination which have prevailed for many years past in Ireland, and still exist in many parts of it, are produced as a necessary consequence by its intolerant and sanguinary principles."

Let our seceders—let our gentle friends who are shocked at our intemperance, and are alive to the mild and conciliating virtues of Mr. Peel—read this passage, sanctioned I may almost say, certainly countenanced by those who do the work of governing Ireland. Would to God we had but one genuine, unsophisticated friend, one real advocate in the House of Commons! How such a man would pour down indignation on the clerks of the Castle, who pay for this base and vile defamation of our religion—of the religion of nine-tenths of the population of Ireland !

But perhaps I accuse falsely; perhaps the administration of Ireland are guiltless of patronizing these calumnies. Look at the paper and determine; it contains nearly five columns of advertisements—only one from a private person—and even that is a notice of an anti-popery pamphlet, by a Mr. Cousins, a curate of the Established Church. Dean Swift has somewhere observed that the poorest of all possible rats was a curate; and if this rat be so, if he have as usual a large family, a great appetite, and little to eat, I sincerely hope that he may get what he wants—a fat living. Indeed, for the sake of consistency, and to keep up the succession of bad pamphlets, he ought to get a living.

Well, what think you are the rest of the advertisements?

First, there are three from the worthy Commissioners of Wide Streets; one dated August 6, 1813, announcing that they would, the ensuing Wednesday, receive certain proposals. Secondly, the barony of Middlethird is proclaimed, as of the sixth of December last, for fear the inhabitants of that barony should not as yet know they were proclaimed. Thirdly, the proclamation against the Catholic Board, dated only the third day of June last, is printed lest any person should forget the history of last year. Fourthly, there is a proclamation stating that gunpowder was not to be carried coastwise for six months, and this is dated the fifth of October last. But why should I detain you with the details of state proclamations, printed for no other purpose than as an excuse for putting so much of the public money into the pocket of a calumniator of the Catholics. The abstract of the rest is that there is one other proclamation, stating that Liverpool is a port fit for importation from the East Indies; another forbidding British subjects from serving in the American forces during the present, that is, the past war; and another stating that although we had made peace with France, we are still at war with America, and that, therefore, no marine is to desert; and to finish the climax, there is a column and a half of extracts from several statutes; all this printed at the expense of Government—that is, at the expense of the people.

Look now at the species of services for which so enormous a sum of our money is thus wantonly lavished! It consists simply of calumnies against the Catholic religion—calumnies so virulently atrocious as, in despite of the intention of the authors, to render themselves ridiculous. This hireling accuses our religion of being an enemy to liberty, of being an encourager of treason, of instigating to robbery, and producing a system of assassination. Here are libels for which no prosecution is instituted. Here are libels which are considered worthy of encouragement, and which are rewarded by the Irish treasury. And is it for this—is it to supply this waste, this abuse of public money—is it to pay for those false and foul calumnies, that we are, in a season of universal peace, to be borne down with a war taxation? Are we to have two or three additional millions of taxes imposed upon us in peace, in order that this intestine war of atrocious calumny may be carried on against the religion of the people of Ireland with all the vigor of full pay and great plunder. Let us, agitators, be now taunted by jobbers in Parliament with our violence, our intemperance. Why, if we were not rendered patient by the aid of a dignified contempt, is there not matter enough to disgust and to irritate almost beyond endurance!

Thus are we treated by our friends, and our enemies, and our seceders; the first to abandon, the second oppress, the third betray us, and they all join in calumniating us; in the last they are all combined. See how naturally they associate—this libeller in the " Dublin Journal," who calls the Catholic religion a system of assassination, actually praises in the same paper some individual Catholics; he praises, by name, Quarantotti, and my Lord Fingal, and the respectable party (those are his words) who join with that noble lord.

Of Lord Fingal I shall always speak with respect, because I

entertain the opinion that his motives are pure and honorable;
but can anything, or at least ought anything, place his secession
in so strong a point of view to the noble lord himself as to find
that he and his party are praised by the very man who, in the
next breath, treats his religion as a system of assassination?
Let that party have all the enjoyment which such praises can
confer; but if a spark of love for their religion or their country
remains with them, let them recollect that they could have
earned those praises only by having, in the opinion of this
writer, betrayed the one and degraded the other.

This writer, too, attempts to traduce Lord Donoughmore.
He attacks his lordship in bad English, and worse Latin, for
having, as he says, cried *peccavi* to popish thraldom.   But the
ignorant trader in virulence knew not how to spell that single
Latin word, because they do not teach Latin at the charter
schools.

I close with conjuring the Catholics to persevere in their
present course.

Let us never tolerate the slightest inroad on the discipline of
our ancient, our holy Church. Let us never consent that she
should be made the hireling of the ministry. Our forefathers
would have died, nay, they perished in hopeless slavery rather
than consent to such degradation.

Let us rest upon the barrier where they expired, or go back
into slavery rather than forward into irreligion and disgrace!
Let us also advocate our cause on the two great principles—
first, that of an eternal separation in spirituals between our
Church and the State; secondly, that of the eternal right to
freedom of conscience—a right which, I repeat it with pride and
pleasure, would exterminate the Inquisition in Spain and bury
in oblivion the bloody Orange flag of dissension in Ireland!

PROTEST AGAINST SENTENCE AS A TRAITOR

—

BY

ROBERT EMMET

ROBERT EMMET

1778—1803

The romantic and tragic career of this young Irish patriot, and the one memorable speech which he made at his trial, after he had been condemned to death on the gibbet, entitle him to be recorded among the great company of orators. Robert Emmet was born in Dublin in 1778, and was hanged in the same city twenty-five years afterwards. From the purest and most generous motives, he embraced the cause of the Irish revolutionists. The English dealt with these men with the most strenuous severity; and every leader knew that in espousing the cause he not only took his life in his hand, but faced the imminent peril of death by the rope. Robert Emmet was betrothed to a beautiful girl, whom he loved with all the ardor of his nature, and who returned his affection with equal intensity. In July, 1803, a rising of the revolutionists was planned in Dublin; and Emmet put himself at its head. The rising was unsuccessful; the forces were scattered, and Emmet succeeded in making good his escape to the mountains of Wicklow. It would have been easy for him to make his way thence to France or America, and be in safety; but the woman he loved was in Dublin, and he could not leave his country without an interview with her. Accordingly, he returned secretly to Dublin; but he was detected and seized, and, after a brief form of trial, sentenced to be hanged. The judge who passed the sentence was Lord Norbury, and the place was the Session-house. Emmet had been charged with acting as the emissary of France, with a view to that country's assuming rights of sovereignty over Ireland, should the revolution by their aid prove successful. When asked, according to the form, whether he had anything to say why sentence should not be pronounced upon him, he made the immortal address which must always remain a model of eloquence in the shadow of the scaffold. Never did a noble and high-minded gentleman repel in more burning and fearless words an aspersion upon his honor. Continually interrupted by the court, he fought his way through his speech to the end; and told such stern truths to his judges as perhaps were never heard before in a court of justice. In Robert Emmet Ireland lost one of the most precious of her patriot sons; a man to be compared only with the highest names on the roll of martyrs for their country, to be placed on equal terms with the most honored among the world's patriots.

PROTEST AGAINST SENTENCE AS A TRAITOR

Delivered at his trial before Lord Norbury, Dublin, September 19, 1803

MY LORDS: I am asked what have I to say why sentence of death should not be pronounced on me, according to law. I have nothing to say that can alter your predetermination, nor that it will become me to say, with any view to the mitigation of that sentence which you are to pronounce, and I must abide by. But I have that to say which interests me more than life, and which you have labored to destroy. I have much to say why my reputation should be rescued from the load of false accusation and calumny which has been cast upon it. I do not imagine that, seated where you are, your mind can be so free from prejudice as to receive the least impression from what I am going to utter. I have no hopes that I can anchor my character in the breast of a court constituted and trammelled as this is. I only wish, and that is the utmost that I expect, that your lordships may suffer it to float down your memories untainted by the foul breath of prejudice, until it finds some more hospitable harbor to shelter it from the storms by which it is buffeted. Were I only to suffer death, after being adjudged guilty by your tribunal, I should bow in silence and meet the fate that awaits me without a murmur; but the sentence of the law which delivers my body to the executioner, will, through the ministry of the law, labor in its own vindication to consign my character to obloquy; for there must be guilt somewhere; whether in the sentence of the court, or in the catastrophe, time must determine. A man in my situation has not only to encounter the difficulties of fortune, and the force of power over minds which it has corrupted or subjugated, but the difficulties of established prejudice. The man dies, but his memory lives. That mine may not perish, that it may live in the respect of my countrymen, I seize upon this opportunity to vindicate myself from some of the charges alleged against me. When my spirit shall be wafted to a more friendly port—when my shade shall have joined the bands of those martyred heroes who have shed their blood on the scaffold and in the field, in the defence of their country and of virtue, this is my hope; I wish that my memory and my name may animate those who survive me, while I look down with complacency on the destruction of that perfidious government which upholds its domination by blasphemy of the Most High; which displays its power over man, as over the beasts of the forest; which sets man upon his brother, and lifts his hand, in the name of God, against the throat of his fellow who believes or doubts a little more or a little less than the government standard—a government which is steeled to barbarity by the cries of the orphans and the tears of the widows it has made.

[Here Lord Norbury interrupted, saying that "the mean and wicked enthusiasts who felt as Emmet did were not equal to the accomplishment of their wild designs."]

I appeal to the immaculate God—I swear by the throne of Heaven, before which I must shortly appear—by the blood of the murdered patriots who have gone before me—that my conduct has been, through all this peril, and through all my purposes, governed only by the conviction which I have uttered, and by no other view than that of the emancipation of my country from the superinhuman oppression under which she has so long and too patiently travailed; and I confidently hope that, wild and chimerical as it may appear, there is still union and strength in Ireland to accomplish this noblest of enterprises. Of this I speak with the confidence of intimate knowledge, and with the consolation that appertains to that confidence. Think not, my lord, I say this for the petty gratification of giving you a transitory uneasiness. A man who never yet raised his voice to assert a lie will not hazard his character with posterity by asserting a falsehood on a subject so important to his country, and on an occasion like this. Yes, my lords, a man who does not wish to have his epitaph written until his country is liberated will not leave a weapon in the power of envy, or a pretence to impeach the probity which he means to preserve even in the grave to which tyranny consigns him.

[Here he was again interrupted by the court.]

Again I say that what I have spoken was not intended for your lordship, whose situation I commiserate rather than envy —my expressions were for my countrymen. If there is a true Irishman present, let my last words cheer him in the hour of his affliction.

[Here he was again interrupted. Lord Norbury said he did not sit there to hear treason.]

I have always understood it to be the duty of a judge, when a prisoner has been convicted, to pronounce the sentence of the law. I have also understood that judges sometimes think it their duty to hear with patience and to speak with humanity; to exhort the victim of the laws, and to offer, with tender benignity, their opinions of the motives by which he was actuated in the crime of which he was adjudged guilty. That a judge has thought it his duty so to have done, I have no doubt; but where is the boasted freedom of your institutions—where is the vaunted impartiality, clemency, and mildness of your courts of justice, if an unfortunate prisoner, whom your policy, and not justice, is about to deliver into the hands of the executioner, is not suffered to explain his motives clearly and truly, and to vindicate the principles by which he was actuated? My lords, it may be a part of the system of angry justice to bow a man's mind by humiliation to the purposed ignominy of the scaffold; but worse to me than the purposed shame or the scaffold's terrors would be the shame of such foul and unfounded imputations as have been made against me in this court. You, my lord, are a judge; I am the supposed culprit. I am a man; you are a man also. By a revolution of power we might change places, though we never could change characters. If I stand at the bar of this court and dare not vindicate my character, what a farce is your justice! If I stand at this bar and dare not vindicate my character, how dare you calumniate it? Does the sentence of death, which your unhallowed policy inflicts on my body, condemn my tongue to silence and my reputation to reproach? Your executioner may abridge the period of my existence; but while I exist, I shall not forbear to vindicate my character and motives from your aspersions; and, as a man, to whom fame is dearer than life, I will make the last use of that life in doing justice to that reputation which is to live after me, and which is the only legacy I can leave to those I honor and love, and for whom I am proud to perish. As men, my lords, we must appear on the great day at one common tribunal; and it will then remain for the Searcher of all Hearts to show a collective universe who was engaged in the most virtuous actions, or swayed by the purest motive—my country's oppressors, or—

[Here he was interrupted and told to listen to the sentence of the law.]

My lords, will a dying man be denied the legal privilege of exculpating himself in the eyes of the community from an undeserved reproach, thrown upon him during his trial, by charging him with ambition, and attempting to cast away for a paltry consideration the liberties of his country? Why did your lordships insult me? Or rather, why insult justice, in demanding of me why sentence of death should not be pronounced against me? I know, my lords, that form prescribes that you should ask the question. The form also presents the right of answering. This, no doubt, will be dispensed with, and so might the whole ceremony of the trial, since sentence was already pronounced at the Castle before the jury were empanelled. Your lordships are but the priests of the oracle, and I insist on the whole of the forms.

I am charged with being an emissary of France. An emissary of France! and for what end? It is alleged that I wish to sell the independence of my country; and for what end? Was this the object of my ambition? And is this the mode by which a tribunal of justice reconciles contradiction? No; I am no emissary; and my ambition was to hold a place among the deliverers of my country, not in power nor in profit, but in the glory of the achievement. Sell my country's independence to France! and for what? Was it a change of masters? No, but for ambition. O! my country! was it personal ambition that could influence me? Had it been the soul of my actions, could I not, by my education and fortune, by the rank and consideration of my family, have placed myself amongst the proudest of your oppressors? My country was my idol! To it I sacrificed every selfish, every endearing sentiment; and for it I now offer up myself, O God! No, my lord; I acted as an Irishman; determined on delivering my country from the yoke of a foreign and unrelenting tyranny, and the more galling yoke of a domestic faction, which is its joint partner and perpetrator in the patricide, from the ignominy existing with an exterior of splendor and a conscious depravity. It was the wish of my heart to extricate my country from this doubly riveted despotism —I wished to place her independence beyond the reach of any power on earth. I wished to exalt her to that proud station of the world. Connection with France was, indeed, intended, but only as far as mutual interest would sanction or require. Were the French to assume any authority inconsistent with the purest independence it would be the signal for their destruction. We sought their aid—and we sought it as we had assurance we should obtain it—as auxiliaries in war, and allies in peace. Were the French to come as invaders or enemies, uninvited by the wishes of the people, I should oppose them to the utmost of my strength. Yes! my countrymen, I should advise you to meet them upon the beach with a sword in one hand and a torch in the other. I would meet them with all the destructive fury of war. I would animate my countrymen to immolate them in their boats, before they had contaminated the soil of my country. If they succeed in landing, and if forced to retire before superior discipline, I would dispute every inch of ground, burn every blade of grass, and the last entrenchment of liberty should be my grave. What I could not do myself, I should leave as a last charge to my countrymen to accomplish; because I should feel conscious that life, any more than death, is unprofitable when a foreign nation holds my country in subjection. But it was not as a enemy that the succors of France were to land. I looked, indeed, for the assistance of France; but I wished to prove to France and to the world that Irishmen deserved to be assisted; that they were indignant at slavery, and ready to assert the independence and liberty of their country. I wished to procure for my country the guarantee which Washington procured for America; to procure an aid which, by its example, would be as important as its valor; discipline, gallant, pregnant with science and experience; that of a people who would perceive the good, and polish the rough points of our character. They would come to us as strangers, and leave us as friends, after sharing in our perils and elevating our destiny. These were my objects: not to receive new taskmasters, but to expel old tyrants. It was for these ends I sought aid from France; because France, even as an enemy, could not be more implacable than the enemy already in the bosom of my country.

[Here he was interrupted by the court.]

I have been charged with that importance in the emancipation of my country as to be considered the keystone of the combination of Irishmen; or as your lordship expressed it, "the life and blood of the conspiracy." You do me honor overmuch: you have given to the subaltern all the credit of a superior. There are men engaged in this conspiracy who are not only superior to me, but even to your own conceptions of yourself, my lord—men before the splendor of whose genius and virtues I should bow with respectful deference, and who would think themselves disgraced by shaking your blood-stained hand.

What, my lord, shall you tell me, on the passage to the scaffold, which that tyranny (of which you are only the intermediary executioner) has erected for my murder, that I am accountable for all the blood that has been and will be shed in this struggle of the oppressed against the oppressor—shall you tell me this, and must I be so very a slave as not to repel it? I do not fear to approach the Omnipotent Judge to answer for the conduct of my whole life; and am I to be appalled and falsified by a mere remnant of mortality here? By you, too, although, if it were possible to collect all the innocent blood that you have shed in your unhallowed ministry in one great reservoir, your lordship might swim in it.

[Here the judge interrupted.]

Let no man dare, when I am dead, to charge me with dishonor; let no man attaint my memory, by believing that I could have engaged in any cause but that of my country's liberty and independence; or that I could have become the pliant minion of power, in the oppression and misery of my country. The proclamation of the provisional government speaks for our views; no inference can be tortured from it to countenance barbarity or debasement at home, or subjection, humiliation, or treachery from abroad. I would not have submitted to a foreign oppressor, for the same reason that I would resist the foreign and domestic oppressor. In the dignity of freedom I would have fought upon the threshold of my country, and its enemy should enter only by passing over my lifeless corpse.

And am I, who lived but for my country, and who have subjected myself to the dangers of the jealous and watchful oppressor, and the bondage of the grave, only to give my countrymen their rights, and my country her independence—am I to be
loaded with calumny, and not suffered to resent it? No, God
forbid!

[Here Lord Norbury told Mr. Emmet that his sentiments and
language disgraced his family and his education, but more particularly his father, Doctor Emmet, who was a man, if alive, that
would not countenance such opinions. To which Emmet replied:]

If the spirits of the illustrious dead participate in the concerns
and cares of those who are dear to them in this transitory life,
O ever dear and venerated shade of my departed father! look
down with scrutiny upon the conduct of your suffering son, and
see if I have, even for a moment, deviated from those principles of morality and patriotism which it was your care to in-
still into my youthful mind, and for which I am now about to
offer up my life. My lords, you are impatient for the sacrifice.
The blood for which you seek is not congealed by the artificial
terrors which surround your victim—it circulates warmly and
unruffled through the channels which God created for noble
purposes, but which you are now bent to destroy for purposes
so grievous that they cry to heaven. Be ye patient! I have
but a few more words to say—I am going to my cold and silent
grave—my lamp of life is nearly extinguished—my race is run
—the grave opens to receive me, and I sink into its bosom. I
have but one request to ask at my departure from this world:
it is—the charity of its silence. That no man write my epitaph;
for, as no man who knows my motives dares now vindicate them,
let not prejudice or ignorance asperse them. Let them and me
rest in obscurity and peace, and my tomb remain uninscribed,
and my memory in oblivion, until other times and other men can
do justice to my character. When my country takes her place
among the nations of the earth, then, and not till then, let my
epitaph be written. I have done.

CHOICE EXAMPLES OF CLASSIC SCULPTURE.

FAUNUS.

Photo-engraving from the marble bust in the Glyptothek at Munich

This bust is called *Fauno colla macchia*—the faun with the blemish or excrescence—in allusion to the small wen on the right of the neck, intended, doubtless, to be an appendage corresponding with the side tassels of the goat Winckelmann considers this one of the most exquisite creations of the antique sculptor It belongs to the later period of Greek sculpture, probably the end of the fourth century before Christ The name of the artist is unknown The bust was placed in the sculpture gallery at Munich during the reign of Louis I, Elector of Bavaria, who founded the artistic pre-eminence of the city The satyrs of Greek mythology, and the fauns of Roman mythology, were wild creatures haunting the woodland, half human, half bestial They have their counterparts in such imaginary beings as Puck and Ariel The satyr had the goat's feet and horns, but in the refinement of later art the coarser elements of the conception were eliminated, and we are presented with a figure of human though animal beauty, emblematic of the vital forces of nature The intellectual part of man is eliminated, and wild and wanton impulse is the controlling power in the acts, gestures and expression of the faun, whose fitting attribute is the timid, capricious and swiftly moving hare, the denizen of the forest

GOD'S SYMPATHY FOR MAN

—

BY

THOMAS CHALMERS

THOMAS CHALMERS

1780—1847

Thomas Chalmers was born at East Anstruther, in Fifeshire, March 17, 1780. He received his education at St. Andrews and was licensed to preach when but nineteen years old, and, four years later, ordained a minister During the first years of his ministry his attention was chiefly absorbed by the study of mathematics and natural philosophy. He formed classes in those subjects in St. Andrews and became very popular as a teacher and lecturer. An " Inquiry into the Extent and Stability of National Resources," which he published in 1808, showed that he had some understanding of the principles of political economy and a capacity to deal with its problems

At about this time Chalmers experienced a great change in his inner life and became keenly susceptible to religious impressions and religious truths While engaged in preparing an article on Christianity for the Edinburgh Encyclopædia, after an extensive study and prolonged meditation, he was convinced that Christianity was a fact and the Bible " the veritable word of God." Under the quickening influence of this new inspiration he grew more devoted to his pastoral duties, more earnest in his life, and more eloquent in his discourses. When he was appointed minister to the Tron church in Glasgow, in July, 1815, the fervor and eloquence of his preaching soon made him very popular. His " Astronomical Discourses," which he published in 1817, gave convincing proof of his great intellectual powers and his lofty imagination We can speak but briefly here of the great and good work Chalmers accomplished during his ministry in Glasgow, especially after he was transferred to St. John's Parish in 1819 His views on political economy were put into practice in his parish with such marked results that when he was entrusted with the management of its poor he reduced the pauper expenditure to less than one-third of the usual charges in four years He founded some fifty Sabbath-schools, and in many other ways ameliorated the lot of the poor in his parish Chalmers accepted an appointment to the chair of moral philosophy in St Andrews in 1823, and after five years of faithful labor he was called to fill the chair of theology at Edinburgh. Chalmers's most remarkable work during this period, a book which gained for him many literary honors and the degree of Doctor of Laws from Oxford, was his treatise " On the Adaptation of External Nature to the Moral and Intellectual Constitution of Man " The later years of Chalmers's life became somewhat disturbed by the dissensions springing up within the Church itself When the secular courts were appealed to, the crisis came, and Chalmers, with four hundred and seventy clergymen, left the Church rather than sacrifice principles he held indispensable to its welfare The rest of his life was given in the cause of the Free Church, of which he was thus the virtual founder He died suddenly at Morningside, Edinburgh, May 31, 1847.

As an orator Chalmers's fame is undisputed. As a man he seems to have been universally esteemed, admired, and loved. One biographer has truly said of him: " There have been some loftier and more purely original minds in Scotland than Chalmers, but there has never been a truer one, nor a heart whose Christian faith and piety were more intense, sincere, and humane " His sermon entitled " God's Sympathy for Man," is a discourse typical of Chalmers, showing his eternal, unshaken confidence in Him who marks the sparrow's flight, and who will guard and protect his children on the awful day when the heavens shall be rolled away like a scroll.

GOD'S SYMPATHY FOR MAN

I HAVE already attempted at full length to establish the position that the infidel argument of astronomers goes to expunge a natural perfection from the character of God, even that wondrous property of His, by which He, at the same instant of time, can bend a close and a careful attention on a countless diversity of objects, and diffuse the intimacy of His power and of His presence, from the greatest to the minutest and most insignificant of them all. I also adverted shortly to this other circumstance, that it went to impair a moral attribute of the Deity. It goes to impair the benevolence of His nature. It is saying much for the benevolence of God to say that a single world, or a single system, is not enough for it —that it must have the spread of a mightier region, on which it may pour forth a tide of exuberancy throughout all its provinces—that as far as our vision can carry us, it has strewed immensity with the floating receptacles of life, and has stretched over each of them the garniture of such a sky as mantles our own habitation—and that even from distances which are far beyond the reach of human eye, the songs of gratitude and praise may now be arising to the one God, who sits surrounded by the regards of His one great and universal family.

Now it is saying much for the benevolence of God, to say that it sends forth these wide and distant emanations over the surface of a territory so ample, that the world we inhabit, lying imbedded as it does amidst so much surrounding greatness, shrinks into a point that to the universal eye might appear to be almost imperceptible. But does it not add to the power and to the perfection of this universal eye, that at the very moment it is taking a comprehensive survey of the vast, it can fasten a steady and undistracted attention on each minute and separate portion of it; that at the very moment it is looking at all worlds, it can look most pointedly and most intelligently to each of them; that at the very moment it sweeps the field of immensity, it can settle all the earnestness of its regards upon every distinct handbreadth of that field; that at the very moment at which it embraces the totality of existence, it can send a most thorough and penetrating inspection into each of its details, and into every one of its endless diversities? You cannot fail to perceive how much this adds to the power of the all-seeing eye. Tell me, then, if it do not add as much perfection to the benevolence of God, that while it is expatiating over the vast field of created things, there is not one portion of the field overlooked by it; that while it scatters blessings over the whole of an infinite range, it causes them to descend in a shower of plenty on every separate habitation; that while His arm is underneath and round about all worlds, He enters within the precincts of every one of them, and gives a care and a tenderness to each individual of their teeming population. Oh! does not the God, who is said to be love, shed over this attribute of His its finest illustration, when, while He sits in the highest heaven, and pours out His fulness on the whole subordinate domain of nature and of providence, He bows a pitying regard on the very humblest of His children, and sends His reviving spirit into every heart, and cheers by His presence every home, and provides for the wants of every family, and watches every sick-bed, and listens to the complaints of every sufferer; and while, by His wondrous mind the weight of universal government is borne, oh! is it not more wondrous and more excellent still that He feels for every sorrow, and has an ear open to every prayer?

" It does not yet appear what we shall be," says the apostle John, " but we know that when He shall appear, we shall be like Him, for we shall see Him as He is." It is the present lot of the angels, that they behold the face of our Father in heaven, and it would seem as if the effect of this was to form and to perpetuate in them the moral likeness of Himself, and that they reflect back upon Him His own image, and that thus a diffused resemblance to the Godhead is kept up amongst all those adoring worshippers who live in the near and rejoicing contemplation of the Godhead. Mark, then, how that peculiar and endearing feature in the goodness of the Deity, which we have just now adverted to—mark how beauteously it is reflected downwards upon us in the revealed attitude of angels. From the high eminences of heaven are they bending a wakeful regard over the men of this sinful world; and the repentance of every one of them spreads a joy and a high gratulation throughout all its dwelling-places. Put this trait of the angelic character into contrast with the dark and lowering spirit of an infidel. He is told of the multitude of other worlds, and he feels a kindling magnificence in the conception, and he is seduced by an elevation which he cannot carry, and from this airy summit does he look down on the insignificance of the world we occupy, and pronounces it to be unworthy of those visits and of those attentions which we read of in the New Testament. He is unable to wing his upward way along the scale, either of moral or of natural perfection; and when the wonderful extent of the field is made known to him, over which the wealth of the Divinity is lavished—there he stops, and wilders, and altogether misses this essential perception, that the power and perfection of the Divinity are not more displayed by the mere magnitude of the field than they are by that minute and exquisite filling up, which leaves not its smallest portions neglected; but which imprints the fulness of the Godhead upon every one of them; and proves, by every flower of the pathless desert, as well as by every orb of immensity, how this unsearchable Being can care for all, and provide for all, and, throned in mystery too high for us, can, throughout every instant of time, keep His attentive eye on every separate thing that He has formed, and by an act of His thoughtful and presiding intelligence, can constantly embrace all.

But God, compassed about as He is with light inaccessible, and full of glory, lies so hidden from the ken and conception of all our faculties, that the spirit of man sinks exhausted by its attempts to comprehend Him. Could the image of the Supreme be placed direct before the eye of the mind, that flood of splendor, which is ever issuing from Him on all who have the privilege of beholding, would not only dazzle, but overpower us. And therefore it is that I bid you look to the reflection of that image, and thus to take a view of its mitigated glories, and to gather the lineaments of the Godhead in the face of those righteous angels, who have never thrown away from them the resemblance in which they were created; and, unable as you are to support the grace and the majesty of that countenance, before which the sons and the prophets of other days fell, and became as dead men, let us, before we bring this argument to a close, borrow one lesson of Him who sitteth on the throne, from the aspect and the revealed doings of those who are surrounding it.

The infidel, then, as he widens the field of his contemplations, would suffer its every separate object to die away into forgetfulness: these angels, expatiating as they do over the range of a loftier universality, are represented as all awake to the history of each of its distinct and subordinate provinces. The infidel, with his mind afloat among suns and among systems, can find no place in his already occupied regards for that humble planet which lodges and accommodates our species: the angels, standing on a loftier summit, and with a mightier prospect of creation before them, are yet represented as looking down on this single world, and attentively marking the every feeling and the every demand of all its families. The infidel, by sinking us down to an unnoticeable minuteness, would lose sight of our dwelling-place altogether, and spread a darkening shroud of oblivion over all the concerns and all the interests of men; but the angels will not so abandon us; and undazzled by the whole surpassing grandeur of that scenery which is around them, are they revealed as directing all the fulness of their regard to this our habitation, and casting a longing and a benignant eye on ourselves and on our children. The infidel will tell us of those worlds which roll afar, and the number of which outstrips the arithmetic of the human understanding—and then, with the hardness of an unfeeling calculation, will he consign the one we occupy, with all its guilty generations, to despair. But He who counts the number of the stars is set forth to us as looking at every inhabitant among the millions of our species, and by the word of the gospel beckoning to him with the hand of invitation, and, on the very first step of his return, as moving towards him with all the eagerness of the prodigal's father, to receive him back again into that presence from which he had wandered. And as to this world, in favor of which the scowling infidel will not permit one solitary movement, all heaven is represented as in a stir about its restoration; and there cannot a single son or a single daughter be recalled from sin unto righteousness without an acclamation of joy amongst the hosts of paradise. Ay, and I can say it of the humblest and the unworthiest of you all, that the eye of angels is upon him, and that his repentance would at this moment send forth a wave of delighted sensibility throughout the mighty throng of their innumerable legions.

Now, the single question I have to ask is, On which of the two sides of this contrast do we see most of the impress of heaven? Which of the two would be most glorifying to God? Which of them carries upon it most of that evidence which lies in its having a celestial character? For if it be the side of the infidel, then must all our hopes expire with the ratifying of that fatal sentence, by which the world is doomed, through its insignificancy, to perpetual exclusion from the attentions of the Godhead. I have long been knocking at the door of your understanding, and have tried to find an admittance to it for many an argument. I now make my appeal to the sensibilities of your heart; and, tell me, to whom does the moral feeling within it yield its readiest testimony—to the infidel, who would make this world of ours vanish away into abandonment—or to those angels who ring throughout all their mansions the hosannas of joy, over every one individual of its repentant population?

And here I cannot omit to take advantage of that opening with which our Saviour has furnished us by the parables of this chapter, and admits us into a familiar view of that principle on which the inhabitants of heaven are so awake to the deliverance and the restoration of our species. To illustrate the difference in the reach of knowledge and of affection between a man and an angel, let us think of the difference of reach between one man and another. You may often witness a man who feels neither tenderness nor care beyond the precincts of his own family; but who, on the strength of those instinctive fondnesses which nature has implanted in his bosom, may earn the character of an amiable father or a kind husband, or a bright example of all that is soft and endearing in the relations of domestic society. Now, conceive him, in addition to all this, to carry his affections abroad without, at the same time, any abatement of their intensity towards the objects which are at home—that, stepping across the limits of the house he occupies, he takes an interest in the families which are near him—that he lends his services to the town or the district wherein he is placed, and gives up a portion of his time to the thoughtful labors of a humane and public-spirited citizen. By this enlargement in the sphere of his attention he has extended his reach; and, provided he has done so at the expense of that regard which is due to his family—a thing which, cramped and confined as we are, we are very apt, in the exercise of our humble faculties, to do—I put it to you, whether, by extending the reach of his views and his affections, he has not extended his worth and his moral respectability along with it?

But I can conceive a still further enlargement. I can figure to myself a man, whose wakeful sympathy overflows the field of his own immediate neighborhood—to whom the name of country comes with all the omnipotence of a charm upon his heart, and with all the urgency of a most righteous and resistless claim upon his services—who never hears the name of Britain sounded in his ears, but it stirs up all his enthusiasm in behalf of the worth and the welfare of its people—who gives himself up, with all the devotedness of a passion, to the best and purest objects of patriotism—and who, spurning away from him the vulgarities of party ambition, separates his life and his labors to the fine pursuit of augmenting the science, or the virtue, or the substantial prosperity of his nation. Oh! could such a man retain all the tenderness, and fulfil all the duties which home and which neighborhood require of him, and at the same time expatiate, in the might of his untired faculties, on so wide a field of benevolent contemplation—would not this extension of reach place him still higher than before, on the scale both of moral and intellectual gradation, and give him a still brighter and more enduring name in the records of human excellence?

And lastly, I can conceive a still loftier flight of humanity —a man, the aspiring of whose heart for the good of man knows no limitations—whose longings, and whose conceptions on this subject, overleap all the barriers of geography—who,

looking on himself as a brother of the species, links every
spare energy which belongs to him with the cause of its
melioration—who can embrace within the grasp of his ample
desires the whole family of mankind—and who, in obedience
to a heaven-born movement of principle within him, separates
himself to some big and busy enterprise, which is to tell on
the moral destinies of the world. Oh! could such a man mix
up the softenings of private virtue with the habit of so sublime a comprehension—if, amid those magnificent darings of
thought and of performance, the mildness of his benignant
eye could still continue to cheer the retreat of his family,
and to spread the charm and the sacredness of piety among
all its members—could he even mingle himself, in all the gentleness of a soothed and a smiling heart, with the playfulness
of his children—and also find strength to shed blessings of
his presence and his counsel over the vicinity around him;
oh! would not the combination of so much grace with so much
loftiness, only serve the more to aggrandize him? Would
not the one ingredient of a character so rare, go to illustrate
and to magnify the other? And would not you pronounce
him to be the fairest specimen of our nature, who could so
call out all your tenderness, while he challenged and compelled all your veneration?

Nor can I proceed, at this point of my argument, without
adverting to the way in which this last and this largest style
of benevolence is exemplified in our own country—where the
spirit of the gospel has given to many of its enlightened disciples the impulse of such a philanthropy as carries abroad
their wishes and their endeavor to the very outskirts of human
population—a philanthropy, of which, if you asked the extent
or the boundary of its field, we should answer, in the language
of inspiration, that the field is the world—a philanthropy which
overlooks all the distinctions of caste and of color, and spreads
its ample regards over the whole brotherhood of the species
—a philanthropy which attaches itself to man in the general;
to man throughout all his varieties; to man as the partaker
of one common nature, and who, in whatever clime or latitude
you may meet with him, is found to breathe the same sympathies, and to possess the same high capabilities both of bliss
and of improvement. It is true that, upon this subject, there

is often a loose and unsettled magnificence of thought, which
is fruitful of nothing but empty speculation. But the men to
whom I allude have not imaged the enterprise in the form of
a thing unknown. They have given it a local habitation. They
have bodied it forth in deed and in accomplishment. They
have turned the dream into a reality. In them, the power of
a lofty generalization meets with its happiest attemperment
in the principle and preservance, and all the chastening and
subduing virtues of the New Testament. And, were I in
search of that fine union of grace and of greatness which I
have now been insisting on, and in virtue of which the enlightened Christian can at once find room in his bosom for
the concerns of universal humanity, and for the play of kind-
liness towards every individual he meets with—I could nowhere more readily expect to find it, than with the worthies
of our own land—the Howard of a former generation, who
paced it over Europe in quest of the unseen wretchedness
which abounds in it—or in such men of our present generation as Wilberforce, who lifted his unwearied voice against the
biggest outrage ever practised on our nature, till he wrought
its extermination—and Clarkson, who plied his assiduous task
at rearing the materials of its impressive history, and at length
carried, for this righteous cause, the mind of Parliament—
and Carey, from whose hand the generations of the East are
now receiving the elements of their moral renovation—and,
in fine, those holy and devoted men, who count not their lives
dear unto them; but, going forth every year from the island
of our habitation, carry the message of Heaven over the face
of the world; and in the front of severest obloquy are now
laboring in remotest lands; and are reclaiming another and
another portion from the wastes of dark and fallen humanity;
and are widening the domains of gospel light and gospel principle amongst them; and are spreading a moral beauty around
the every spot on which they pitch their lowly tabernacle; and
are at length compelling even the eye and the testimony of
gainsayers, by the success of their noble enterprise; and are
forcing the exclamation of delighted surprise from the charmed
and the arrested traveller, as he looks at the softening tints
which they are now spreading over the wilderness, and as he
hears the sound of the chapel bell, and as in those haunts where,

at the distance of half a generation, savages would have scowled
upon his path, he regales himself with the hum of missionary schools, and the lovely spectacle of peaceful and Christian
villages.

Such, then, is the benevolence, at once so gentle and so
lofty, of those men, who, sanctified by the faith that is in
Jesus, have had their hearts visited from heaven by a beam
of warmth and of sacredness. What, then, I should like to
know, is the benevolence of the place from whence such an
influence cometh? How wide is the compass of this virtue
there, and how exquisite is the feeling of its tenderness, and
how pure and how fervent are its aspirings among those un-
fallen beings who have no darkness, and no encumbering
weight of corruption to strive against! Angels have a mightier
reach of contemplation. Angels can look upon this world,
and all which it inherits, as the part of a larger family. Angels
were in the full exercise of their powers even at the first infancy of our species, and shared in the gratulations of that
period, when at the birth of humanity all intelligent nature
felt a gladdening impulse, and the morning stars sang together
for joy. They loved us even with the love which a family on
earth bears to a younger sister; and the very childhood of our
tinier faculties did only serve the more to endear us to them;
and though born at a later hour in the history of creation, did
they regard us as heirs of the same destiny with themselves,
to rise along with them in the scale of moral elevation, to bow
at the same footstool, and to partake in those high dispensations of a parent's kindness and a parent's care, which are
ever emanating from the throne of the Eternal on all the members of a duteous and affectionate family. Take the reach of
an angel's mind, but, at the same time, take the seraphic fervor
of an angel's benevolence along with it; how, from the eminence on which he stands he may have an eye upon many
worlds, and a remembrance upon the origin and the successive concerns of every one of them; how he may feel the full
force of a most affecting relationship with the inhabitants of
each, as the offspring of one common Father; and though it
be both the effect and the evidence of our depravity, that we
cannot sympathize with these pure and generous ardors of a
celestial spirit; how it may consist with the lofty comprehen-

sion, and the ever-breathing love of an angel, that he can both shoot his benevolence abroad over a mighty expanse of planets and of systems, and lavish a flood of tenderness on each individual of their teeming population.

Keep all this in view, and you cannot fail to perceive how the principle, so finely and so copiously illustrated in this chapter, may be brought to meet the infidelity we have thus long been employed in combating. It was nature—and the experience of every bosom will affirm it—it was nature in the shepherd to leave the ninety-and-nine of his flock forgotten and alone in the wilderness, and, betaking himself to the mountains, to give all his labor and all his concern to the pursuit of one solitary wanderer. It was nature; and we are told in the passage before us, that it is such a portion of nature as belongs not merely to men, but to angels; when the woman, with her mind in a state of listlessness as to the nine pieces of silver that were in secure custody, turned the whole force of her anxiety to the one piece which she had lost, and for which she had to light a candle, and to sweep the house, and to search diligently until she found it. It was nature in her to rejoice more over that piece, than over all the rest of them, and to tell it abroad among friends and neighbors, that they might rejoice along with her—ay, and sadly effaced as humanity is, in all her original lineaments, this is a part of our nature, the very movements of which are experienced in heaven, " where there is more joy over one sinner that repenteth, than over ninety-and-nine just persons who need no repentance." For anything I know, the every planet that rolls in the immensity around me may be a land of righteousness; and be a member of the household of God; and have her secure dwelling-place within that ample limit which embraces His great and universal family. But I know at least of one wanderer; and how wofully she has strayed from peace and purity; and how in dreary alienation from Him who made her, she has bewildered herself amongst those many devious tracts, which have carried her afar from the path of immortality; and how sadly tarnished all those beauties and felicities are, which promised, on that morning of her existence when God looked on her, and saw that all was very good—which promised so richly to bless and to adorn her; and how, in the eye of the whole un-

fallen creation, she has renounced all this goodliness, and is
fast departing away from them into guilt, and wretchedness,
and shame.   Oh! if there be any truth in this chapter, and any
sweet or touching nature in the principle which runs throughout all its parables, let us cease to wonder, though they who
surround the 'throne of love should be looking so intently
towards us—or though, in the way by which they have singled
us out, all the other orbs of space should, for one short season,
on the scale of eternity, appear to be forgotten—or though,
for every step of her recovery, and for every individual who is
rendered back again to the fold from which he was separated,
another and another message of triumph should be made to
circulate amongst the hosts of paradise—or though, lost as
we are, and sunk in depravity as we are, all the sympathies of
heaven should now be awake on the enterprise of Him who
has travailed, in the greatness of His strength, to seek and to
save us.

And here I cannot but remark how fine a harmony there
is between the law of sympathetic nature in heaven and the
most touching exhibitions of it on the face of our world. When
one of a numerous household droops under the power of disease, is not that the one to whom all the tenderness is turned,
and who, in a manner, monopolizes the inquiries of his neighborhood, and the care of his family? When the sighing of
the midnight storm sends a dismal foreboding into the mother's
heart, to whom of all her offspring, I would ask, are her
thoughts and her anxieties then wandering? Is it not to her
sailor boy whom her fancy has placed amid the rude and angry
surges of the ocean? Does not this, the hour of his apprehended danger, concentrate upon him the whole force of her
wakeful meditations? And does not he engross, for a season,
her every sensibility, and her every prayer? We sometimes
hear of shipwrecked passengers thrown upon a barbarous
shore; and seized upon by its prowling inhabitants; and hurried away through the tracks of a dreary and unknown wilderness; and sold into captivity; and loaded with the fetters
of irrecoverable bondage; and who, stripped of every other
liberty but the liberty of thought, feel even this to be another
ingredient of wretchedness, for what can they think of but
home, and as all its kind and tender imagery comes upon their
remembrance, how can they think of it but in the bitterness of

despair?   Oh, tell me, when the fame of all this disaster reaches
his family, who is the member of it to whom is directed the
full tide of its griefs and of its sympathies? Who is it that,
for weeks and for months, usurps their every feeling, and calls
out their largest sacrifices, and sets them to the busiest expedients for getting him back again? Who is it that makes
them forgetful of themselves and of all around them; and tell
me if you can assign a limit to the pains, and the exertions,
and the surrenders which afflicted parents and weeping sisters
would make to seek and to save him?

Now conceive, as we are warranted to do by the parables
of this chapter, the principle of all these earthly exhibitions to
be in full operation around the throne of God. Conceive the
universe to be one secure and rejoicing family, and that this
alienated world is the only strayed, or only captive member
belonging to it; and we shall cease to wonder, that from the
first period of the captivity of our species, down to the consummation of their history in time, there should be such a
movement in heaven; or that angels should so often have sped
their commissioned way on the errand of our recovery; or
that the Son of God should have bowed Himself down to the
burden of our mysterious atonement; or that the spirit of
God should now, by the busy variety of His all-powerful influences, be carrying forward that dispensation of grace which
is to make us meet for readmittance into the mansions of the
celestial. Only think of love as the reigning principle there;
of love, as sending forth its energies and aspirations to the
quarter where its object is most in danger of being forever
lost to it; of love, as called forth by this single circumstance
to its uttermost exertion, and the most exquisite feeling of its
tenderness; and then shall we come to a distinct and familiar
explanation of this whole mystery. Nor shall we resist by
our incredulity the gospel message any longer, though it tells
us that throughout the whole of this world's history, long in
our eyes, but only a little month in the high periods of immortality, so much of the vigilance, and so much of the earnestness of heaven, should have been expended on the recovery
of its guilty population.

There is another touching trait of nature, which goes finely
to heighten this principle, and still more forcibly to demonstrate its application to our present argument. So long as

the dying child of David was alive, he was kept on the stretch of anxiety and of suffering with regard to it. When it expired, he arose and comforted himself. This narrative of King David is in harmony with all that we experience of our own movements, and our own sensibilities. It is the power of uncertainty which gives them so active and so interesting a play in our bosoms; and which heightens all our regards to a tenfold pitch of feeling and of exercise; and which fixes down our watchfulness upon our infant's dying bed; and which keeps us so painfully alive to every turn and to every symptom in the progress of its malady; and which draws out all our affections for it to a degree of intensity that is quite unutterable; and which urges us on to ply our every effort and our every expedient, till hope withdraw its lingering beam, or till death shut the eyes of our beloved in the slumber of its long and its last repose.

I know not who of you have your names written in the book of life—nor can I tell if this be known to the angels which are in heaven. While in the land of living men, you are under the power and application of a remedy, which, if taken as the gospel prescribes, will renovate the soul, and altogether prepare it for the bloom and the vigor of immortality. Wonder not then that with this principle of uncertainty in such full operation, ministers should feel for you; or angels should feel for you; or all the sensibilities of heaven should be awake upon the symptoms of your grace and reformation; or the eyes of those who stand upon the high eminences of the celestial world, should be so earnestly fixed on the every footstep and new evolution of your moral history. Such a consideration as this should do something more than silence the infidel objection. It should give a practical effect to the calls of repentance. How will it go to aggravate the whole guilt of our impenitency, should we stand out against the power and the tenderness of these manifold applications—the voice of a beseeching God upon us—the word of salvation at our very door —the free offer of strength and of acceptance sounded in our hearing—the spirit in readiness with His agency to meet our every desire and our every inquiry—angels beckoning us to their company—and the very first movements of our awakened conscience drawing upon us all their regards and all their earnestness!

ARBITRATION

—

BY

LORD PALMERSTON

(Henry John Temple)

HENRY JOHN TEMPLE, VISCOUNT PALMERSTON

1784—1865

There was an Irish strain in Henry John Temple, Viscount Palmerston, which colored his character, and without which he would very likely have failed to impress himself upon the imagination of the English people. His intellectual abilities were not extraordinary; but there was an easy jollity about him, an audacity, or faculty of "bluff," which, in combination with more commonplace qualities, and with remarkable good fortune, not always deserved, made him a leading figure in English politics for many years, and, during the last ten years of his long life, Prime Minister. He loved the bustle of affairs, and had the power of applying himself diligently to business; or at all events—what for practical purposes was almost as good, if not better—of seeming busy; so that men his superiors in intellect, but less active and omnipresent, delegated important functions to him, and placed a confidence in him which he was clever enough not to forfeit, even when he did not fairly merit it. Upon the whole, he was a man of prodigious native talent, and his position in life gave him an immense experience; he dominated or silenced men far his superiors in real ability by his humorous *savoir-faire* and cool imperturbability. The people made a pet of him; he was known to them as few public men have been, largely owing to the caricatures of John Tenniel in "Punch," which hit off his happy-go-lucky air and optimistic temperament, his shrewdness, his shallowness, and his knowingness, in a way which captivated the general fancy, and made him immensely popular.

Palmerston was born at the family estate of Broadlands in 1784, and died at Brocket Hall in Hertfordshire in 1865. The Temple family had an English and an Irish branch, and Palmerston belonged to the latter. He went to Harrow School; afterwards he went to the University of Edinburgh; and matriculated at St John's College, Cambridge.

His father died in 1802, and he inherited his title and the family estates. In 1807 he took his seat in Parliament as member for Newtown, Isle of Wight, and held office as Junior Lord of the Admiralty under the Duke of Portland. From 1809 to 1828 he was Secretary of War. Taking Pitt for his political ideal, he was a consistent Tory, and favored the emancipation of the Roman Catholics. But when Lord Grey came into power in 1830, he embraced Whiggism, and made a reputation in foreign affairs, being active in the policy which placed Leopold of Saxe-Coburg on the Belgian throne. After 1840 he went out of office for five years; but became prominent again under Lord John Russell, and expressed his sympathy with the revolutionary party which was so much in evidence on the Continent in those days. His dallying with Louis Napoleon caused him to be dismissed from the foreign office; but he came in once more with Aberdeen in 1853. In 1855 he became Prime Minister, thus shouldering the responsibility of the Crimean War. He retained the office of Prime Minister, with the interval of Lord Derby's administration in 1858, until his death.

His discourses were business-like, off-hand affairs, such as business men address to one another. His self-confidence bred confidence in his hearers, and prompted them to believe that he could do anything, and would never be at the end of his resources. It was not so much by speeches as by his management of debates, and by his work behind the scenes, that he produced his results and carried his purposes. His speech on "Arbitration" is an excellent example of his practical, common-sense manner of reasoning on public affairs.

ARBITRATION

Delivered in the House of Commons, June 12, 1849

S IR, I beg to assure my honorable friend, the member for the West Riding, that in rising to state my intention of opposing his motion, I am far from wishing to speak either of the sentiments he has himself expressed, or of the opinions of those whose organ he is, with anything but the greatest possible respect. I entirely agree with my honorable friend, and with those of whose opinion he has been on this occasion the organ, in attributing the utmost possible value to this motion, and in feeling the greatest dislike, and I may say horror, of war in any shape. I will not go into those commonplace remarks which must be familiar to the mind of every man who has contrasted the calamities of war with the various blessings and advantages which attend upon peace. I cannot conceive that there exists in this country the man who does not attach the utmost value to the blessings of peace, and who would not make the greatest sacrifices to save his country from the calamities attendant upon war. And although I differ from my honorable friend, and although I am not ready to accede to his motion, yet I cannot say but that I am glad he has made that proposition, because it will be useful for this country and for Europe at large that every man should know that in this assembly, and among the vast masses of men of whom we are the representatives, there is a sincere and honest disposition to maintain peace. But that which I wish to guard against —the impression that I wish should not be entertained anywhere, either in this country or out of it—is that while there is in England a fervent love of peace, an anxious and steady desire to maintain it, there should not exist the impression that the manly spirit of Englishmen is dead—that

England is not ready, as she is ever, to repel aggression and resent injury, and that she is ready to defend her rights, although she never will be found acting aggressively against any other power. Sir, it would be most dangerous indeed to the interests of peace that a contrary opinion should prevail. I can conceive nothing that would bring more into jeopardy the peaceful relations of this country, than that an idea should prevail among foreign nations, that we are so attached to peace that we dare not make war, and that, therefore, any aggression or any injury may be safely ventured against English subjects, because England has such a rooted aversion to war that she will not repel it. That is the principle on which I differ from the observations made by my honorable friend, when he condemned those provident supplies—so I may call them—for military defence, which he said, he had found by his examination in a committee above stairs had béen laid up in store by this and the last Government. I quite agree with those who think that it is a useless expenditure of the public money to keep in pay an excessive number of men, either by sea or by land, beyond what the existing service of the country may demand, on an imaginary expectation of future and contingent hostilities. I think that is a wasteful application of the public money, but I cannot go along with the honorable member in condemning that provident provision of things which cannot be created at a moment's notice—which would be necessary if we were called on to defend ourselves from foreign aggression—and the absence of which, if known to foreign countries, would form an incitement and temptation to commit wrong against this country. Therefore I think that a Government acts wisely and prudently when they gradually and without overstraining the burden on the country, lay up a store of those things which may be wanted on the first outbreak of war, if it should unfortunately occur, and which must be provided beforehand, while they abstain from useless augmentations of men, which can be raised when the emergency arises, and in a short period would be just as effective as if they had been longer in military training. Sir, I cannot agree with the proposal of my honorable friend because I think it is founded on an erroneous principle, and that it would be impracticable if attempted to be carried out. My honorable friend comes to his conclusion by an analogy which he draws between private life and the intercourse of nations. He says, in the ordinary transactions between man and man, what is so common as an agreement between individuals, that in the event of disputes occurring they shall be referred to arbitration? It is very true that is a common and very advantageous practice, but how stand these individuals? Why, if the sentence of arbitration is not conformable to the opinion of both parties there is a higher and superior authority—the authority of some legal tribunal, which enforces concurrence; to that tribunal the parties previously agree to submit, and it is this superior force that gives value and efficacy to the agreement for arbitration. But my honorable friend at once perceives, and fairly acknowledges, that that element is wanting in the machine by which he proposes to settle international differences; and unless we have recourse to the plan of my honorable friend who spoke last for a general tribunal of nations, with a military force to compel compliance with its decrees, it is plain that the arbitration of my honorable friend the member for the West Riding would, in truth, simply, and in most cases, resolve itself into mediation, that is, the proposal by a third party of an arrangement of differences between two other parties. Honorable members ought not to lose sight of the distinction, which is frequently forgotten, between arbitration and mediation—arbitration consisting in the pronouncing of a final decision by a third party which is to be binding on the other two; mediation consisting in the good offices of a third party to bring about, by the consent and acquiescence of the other two, an amicable termination of differences that may have arisen between them. Now, sir. my honorable friend is so internally aware of the difficulty attending the practical execution of his own idea, that he has been obliged to abandon that which most persons imagined to be his plan.

[Mr. Cobden here said: I beg pardon; I never altered or abandoned my motion in the slightest degree.]

Viscount Palmerston: I will not say my honorable friend has abandoned, but he has been obliged not to propose, what many persons, myself included, imagined to be his plan— namely, that the court of arbitration should consist of some foreign government or governments: in turning over the matter, and bringing it to a practical bearing, he has found it necessary to substitute commissions taken from private life. Now, sir, it is obvious that that which would be to any person thinking of this matter for the first time the natural arrangement—and whenever the principle of my honorable friend has been acted upon the plan that has been fully practised—is that of making the arbitrator the government of some foreign state. The plan of my honorable friend, so far as I am aware, has never been attempted. It is perfectly true that there are cases in which arbitration has been resorted to, but in those cases the arbitrator chosen has been a sovereign or a government; in no case has final arbitration been consented to resting on private individuals. What are the reasons why my honorable friend abstained from that proposal which was generally expected to come from him on the present occasion? My honorable friend who has just sat down said that it would be a very desirable thing if an European tribunal could be composed that would act invariably on the principle of justice and of right, which would always give equitable decisions, and which of course, should have force to compel acquiescence in its judgments; but unfortunately the world is not yet come to that happy state of things. If you could find the governments of Europe all perfectly just, perfectly impartial, perfectly disinterested, and, by the possession of these qualities competent to form the tribunal my honorable friend imagines, why, such a tribunal would supersede itself; because if all governments were perfectly just, impartial, and disinterested, they would settle any little disputes that might arise between their respective subjects without having recourse to the extreme of war, which this tribunal was intended to prevent. But, unfortunately, it so happens that in the present imperfect condition of human nature, governments, like individuals, are actuated by unfounded and suspicious jealousies of each other—by that which, in men, is called covetousness, which in nations is called ambition—by interested motives of various kinds, interests conflicting with each other; and it is a matter so difficult that it may almost be deemed impossible to find, in a quarrel between two nations, a third party whose judgment each of the two contending parties would place confidence in. If you were to propose to the governments of Europe to enter now, to-day or to-morrow, into a prospective agreement that in cases of difference they would submit their disputes to any third party to be named now or to be named afterwards—if the engagement were that the third party should be named now, you never would get them to consent; and if the engagement were to name the third party when the dispute arose, you would have made very little progress towards the establishment of your arbitration. There is one case where a dispute arose between this country and the government of the United States, with respect to the Maine boundary, which was by the Treaty of Ghent submitted to arbitration. My honorable friend would have said, " You only want geographers for such a purpose; two members of the Geographical Society have only to draw the line, and there it is." But my honorable friend can hardly imagine how much time elapsed before we could come to any agreement as to the choice of the sovereign who was to be the arbitrator in that case, which certainly is not a happy illustration of the results of arbitration; because the King of the Netherlands, having been chosen by the two powers as arbitrator in that difference, did after a very long period of time, pronounce an award, which the United States, not finding suitable to their notions of the terms of reference, refused to submit to; the matter was left in a worse condition than before the arbitration began; and if that arbitration did not lead to war, I can assure my honorable friend it was no merit of the principle of arbitration, but only because the two governments were mutually inspired by a most intense desire to settle the question without having recourse to arms. Well, then, I say, if my honorable friend had proposed, as men generally thought he intended to propose, a court of arbitration, to consist of some third or foreign governments, the answer would have been that the mutual jealousies of governments, the rivalry of conflicting interests, the—I was going to say—intrigues, but the hostile policy of nations towards each other, would make it, I am satisfied, perfectly impossible to bring countries to acquiesce in the prospective arrangement, and I, for one, must say, it would be dangerous to the interests of this country to submit the vital rights and interests of England to the chances of a decision by the judgment of any foreign power. Well, but my honorable friend very wisely steers clear of that difficulty, and proposes the appointment of commissioners. I am not sure that I quite comprehend the proposal of my honorable friend, but he will correct me if I am wrong. I understand him to propose that a treaty should be made containing a stipulation that, in the event of differences, each government should name commissioners of its own to discuss the point at issue, and that they, either before they met, or after they met, should name some third person not in the employment of either government; but a man of science, or a man in private life, to be the arbitrator between the commissioners in case they should not be able to agree. That, so far as I understood, was the manner in which the proposal of my honorable friend was to be carried out. Now, sir, if it is objectionable, as I think it is, to commit the interests of a great country to the decision of what may be a rival power, upon matters of vital interest, or upon matters concerning most important and essential rights, I must say my objection to submit such matters to the arbitration and final decision of a third party would not be removed by substituting for a government, which at least is a public and responsible body, persons irresponsible and taken from private life. At all events, a government acts in the face of the world; it is accustomed to deal with matters of the kind submitted to it for decision; but if you take a man from private life he is perfectly irresponsible in any public way; his habits and pursuits may have been very different from those that would qualify for the decision of questions submitted to him; in my humble opinion almost all the same objections would apply, and other objections apply which would not apply to a government. There was one instance, to be sure, to show that these learned men are not always persons who are the readiest to come to a decision on a simple matter. There is one well known problem the difficulty of solving which is universally acknowledged. No one denies the difficulty of finding the longitude. But if a man be required to ascertain the latitude of any given place, or the position of any parallel of latitude, it it deemed to be a very simple process. Now, by the Treaty of Ghent, the commissioners appointed to settle the boundary dispute were to trace a line which should coincide with or come within a specified distance of a certain given parallel of latitude. Of course it will be said that nothing could be more easy than that; nothing was easier, it might be said, than to appoint two geographers as two commissioners, who would at once determine the matter, it being the simplest thing possible; they had only their boundary to mark along the line indicated by the treaty: that was precisely the sort of thing that suited the views of my honorable friend the member for the West Riding—nothing seemed easier than to find two learned men such as he would elect, and put them at once to find the parallel of latitude. But it so happened that there was not a chance of agreeing upon any such point, for one maintained that the parallel was to depend upon calculations commencing at the centre of the earth, and the other that the computations were to be made from the centre of the sun; they were, therefore, as far apart as the earth from the sun—they were further than the poles asunder—they were unable to agree about that which might be settled at once by anyone who was able to set a village sun-dial. Neither Baron von Humboldt nor Professor Tiarcks, who was associated with him in the undertaking, could arrive at any satisfactory result. [Mr. Cobden: The question is settled.] True, but not by geographers. However, I feel assured that the House will agree with me when I say that it would not be safe to trust such interests as those, or at all events such interests as usually give rise to differences between nations—it would not be safe to leave them to arbitration; and, though the matter was eventually settled in the usual way, I do think that the case is less of an example to be followed, than of a beacon to be avoided. Then m honorable friend says there is nothing new at bottom in the proposition which he has made to the House, for he says that the powers which we were accustomed to give to negotiators we might in future give to two commissioners, one to be appointed by either nation concerned, giving them power to call in a third as final arbitrator, and my honorable friend instanced the case of Lord Castlereagh, who, on behalf of this country, attended the Congress of Vienna, and took a part in the transactions which occurred on that memorable occasion. Lord Castlereagh was then enabled to say *adsum qui feci;* he might say he had done it; he was there upon his own responsibility, for least to a considerable extent upon his own responsibility, for Lord Castlereagh at that time held the office of Secretary of State for Foreign Affairs. But here it may be necessary for me to mention a matter well deserving to be borne in mind during the discussion which now occupies the attention of the House. It is this—that no person goes out from this country, or usually from any other, with full powers in the strict sense of those words. Some discretion may be left to him, but he does not go out with full and entire discretion—quite the contrary. Every minister plenipotentiary receives instructions. He is always told what he may agree to and what he may not, and he has opportunities, of which ministers often avail themselves, to send home for further instructions. As long as he confines himself to his instructions he may proceed with some degree of confidence; but the government by which he is accredited are still not finally bound by his acts, and everything that an ambassador does he does subject to the approbation of the government which he represents. It is perfectly competent to that government to disavow the acts of the minister whom they have sent out as an ambassador, and to disavow and reject all that he has done, if they think it expedient so to do; and a striking example has been furnished in the occurrences of the past week of the exercise of this power. It is, therefore, quite a mistake to suppose that, according to the present and prevailing practice, governments are at the mercy of their envoys; nothing is binding upon a government unless it be in strict accordance with communications made to other governments in the precise words of the instructions. A treaty may be signed and concluded but it is of no value without ratification, and this sort of provision is necessary in order that no government may be bound by the indiscreet or unauthorized act of any of its agents; and therefore if an envoy should go against his instructions, the arrangements he may make are of no value beyond the paper on which they are written. Therefore do I state that my honorable friend the member for the West Riding makes an admission that his plan is new in principle. The House will not have forgotten that my honorable friend quoted several cases of international transactions; but he did not succeed in making out the case which he appeared to think was necessary for his purpose. The cases which he mentioned were not cases of arbitration, but of mediation, or else they were cases of no mediation at all, settled neither by arbitration nor by intervention—such as those which he mentioned between Russia and England, and the case also of the Vixen. In the boundary case it seemed as if there had been some show of arbitration; but it was notorious that in that case arbitration failed; and when arbitration had totally failed, the parties concerned settled the matter for themselves in the usual manner; and let the fact not be overlooked, that the Oregon question was settled in pretty nearly the same way; at all events it was not settled by geographers, in the manner that my honorable friend would propose. If it were to have been so settled by geographers, I confess, I should not very much envy the gentlemen who might be employed upon such an undertaking; for I believe there can be no doubt that the district through which they would have had to penetrate is one of extraordinary wildness and difficulty, where the means of subsistence are hardly to be obtained. Now, the case of the Caroline was a remarkable one in reference to the question of arbitration, and it was one of those few cases in which it was manifest that it would be unavailing to arbitrate. It was not a case of dispute between this country and the United States, for the federal authority of that government was not sufficient to meet the exigency of the case. The government of the United States said they were sorry for what had occurred, but they had no power to interfere—the supreme government of the United States possessed no power over the local authority or government with which the dispute arose. Now, if we in that case possessed a treaty of arbitration, of what use would it be to us? For the Government of the United States would repeat its declaration that it could not interfere with the local government. They would say, " We are very sorry, but we can obtain you no redress from the State of New York." Your principle then of arbitration would be of not the least avail in such a case. It leaves you precisely where you were before the introduction of such a plan. The cases then which my honorable friend has quoted, are cases in which the principle of arbitration proved useless, or they are cases which have been settled by the ordinary authorities, or they are cases of mediation in which a friendly power has exercised its good offices, as in the sulphur question with France, or they are cases settled in the usual way after arbitration has wholly failed. I do think, however, and I have always thought, that when two nations have had any difference capable of being settled by arbitration, it is most desirable that they should allow a third party to come in to assist them in the good work of making a satisfactory arrangement—

it is at all times most desirable that a third party not actuated by the same passions which heat those immediately concerned, should step in, and bring the disputants to something like a compromise—there must be a giving and taking on both sides, for neither party in such cases can expect to get all that he may reasonably or fairly demand, and all such negotiations should therefore be entered upon in a spirit of accommodation and mutual concession, with a view to prevent an appeal to arms, and with a view to open the door to that kind of negotiation which may lead to peace, in the course of which the ministers engaged on both sides may receive from their respective governments fresh instructions, in which answers may be received, in which remonstrances may be made, further replies given, and thus a long time elapses before any actual rupture occurs, and before recourse is had to that appeal which arms alone afford. In the course of those proceedings opportunities occur for one or other of the parties to obtain the opinion of a third nation friendly to both, and having no private or separate interest to promote. A nation so circumstanced may, I think, well offer its mediation, and I have incurred no small amount of obloquy, and perhaps ridicule also, on the ground that I have been too forward to offer mediation in such cases as those which I have just been describing. But I confess that I feel perfectly easy under the influence of such attacks, for I feel quite persuaded that the good-will, at least manifested in such attempts, cannot fail eventually to be appreciated, and that in cases where England has nothing either to gain or to lose, a sincere desire to prevent war must, sooner or later, be attended with beneficial results; and I cannot help thinking that it must be most satisfactory to my honorable friend the member for the West Riding, and to those who support his motion, to know that mediation has been of much more frequent occurrence of late years than in times past; but those honorable gentlemen must, at the same time, bear in mind that the principle of arbitration is not applicable to the present state of Europe. Wars are now proceeding in various parts of the Continent, blood is being shed, lives being sacrificed; but these occurrences do not arise from international wars. It is to civil wars that they must be imputed, and, except in rare instances indeed, the intervention of foreigners, or third parties, or arbitrators, would be either impracticable, or, if possible, might be mischievous; and it must be obvious to everyone that the kind of war now prevailing on the Continent of Europe is not the species of hostility to which the principle of arbitration can be applied In those wars, however, I am happy to be able to perceive striking evidence of the improved civilization of the people of Europe—evidence not only of improvement in the governments of Europe, but of advancing civilization amongst the masses of the people. If such events as have recently taken place in Europe had occurred half a century ago we should have had not only civil wars, but conflicts between nations of the most fatal character—fatal alike to prosperity and civilization. It is consoling, then, to see that great masses of men, instead of standing forth as the aggressors of their neighbors, confine their disputes to their own territories, to the communities to which they properly belong, and to their own internal affairs It is gratifying to think that they have not been led into warfare with other nations, either by feelings of ambition or by any different description of impulse. I hope, then, that now sufficient proof has been given that we should not advance the interest of nations by recognizing the principle for which my honorable friend contends, at the same time that I cannot find fault with him for introducing this question, or for affording an opportunity for the expression of that general feeling which animates members of this House upon the present occasion The cultivation of that feeling forms a great example to the rest of Europe—it tends to inspire not only governments but nations with the sentiments which my honorable friend feels and has made known to the House this evening; and I conceive that it will take away nothing from the force of those sentiments, but rather add to their influence, when I say that ever since the year 1825 down to the present period, the practice of mediation has been preferred by many governments, and several cases have arisen in which it has been advantageously adopted. I believe that the present government, and any other which may succeed to the task of conducting the affairs of this country, would feel it not only their duty, but their pride, to avail themselves of every occasion when they think they can do good by softening the asperities between conflicting powers, and by effecting between governments and countries that may differ, an amicable

settlement of their disputes, either without war, or by shorten-
ing war if war should unfortunately arise. The proposition of
my honorable friend, however, is not one to which I can advise
the House to accede. I do not quarrel with the principle upon
which it is founded; but I think its practical effect would be
dangerous to this country, and that its practical adoption by
other countries would be impossible. Indeed, I believe that no
country would agree to such a proposal. No country would
consent blindfold to submit its interests and its rights on all
future occasions to the decision of any third party, whether
public or private, whether governments or men of science; and
I think, therefore, the proposition is one which would be attended with no possible results as regards foreign countries.
I confess also that I consider it would be a very dangerous
course for this country itself to take, because there is no country
which from its political and commercial circumstances, from its
maritime interests, and from its colonial possessions, excites
more envious and jealous feelings in different quarters than
England does; and there is no country that would find it more
difficult to discover really disinterested and impartial arbiters.
There is also no country that would be more likely than England to suffer in its important commercial interests from submitting its case to arbiters not disinterested, not impartial, and
not acting with a due sense of their responsibility. For these
reasons it is not in my power to assent to the motion. I should,
however, be sorry to meet it in a way that might, even by mis-
construction, be considered as negativing the principle upon
which it is founded. I shall not, therefore, propose a direct negative, although that is the mode which, according to the usual
practice of the House, ought to be adopted by those who differ
from my honorable friend. The " previous question " is not
technically applicable to this case, but the previous question
being the most courteous mode of disposing of such a motion
as that before the House, and one less liable than any other to
the imputation—however unfounded it may be—of negativing
the principle of peace, which is the foundation of my honorable
friend's proposal, I beg leave to move the previous question.

THE CHURCH OF IRELAND

—

BY

LORD JOHN RUSSELL

LORD JOHN RUSSELL

1792—1878

John Russell, the record of whose life is so intimately interwoven with the fortunes of the Whig party for nearly half a century, was born in London, August 18, 1792. He was the third son of the sixth duke of Bedford He received his early education at Westminster school and with a private tutor in Woodnesborough, in Kent He studied at Edinburgh from the autumn of 1809 till the summer of 1812. Lord Russell visited the Peninsula in 1812, and during this visit he met Wellington at Burgos, and in 1814 Napoleon at Elba While still under age, in July, 1813, he was elected member of Parliament for the borough of Tavistock in the interest of the Whig party. And with his return to Parliament began his long and useful career as a statesman At the general election in 1820 he was returned for Huntingdonshire Henceforth, for twelve years, he devoted himself to the pressing of Parliamentary reforms After the accession to power ,of Earl Grey, Lord Russell, though then not a member of Parliament, was intrusted with the task of explaining the Government Reform Bill to the House of Commons. His speech on this occasion marks an epoch in his career. In March, 1835, Russell brought in a motion to consider the temporalities of the Irish Church, which was carried by a considerable majority after a three nights' debate, and when Lord Melbourne's ministry again came into power during the same year he was made Home Secretary with a seat in the Cabinet

As Colonial Secretary in 1839 Russell pacified the Canadians, whose claims to self-government he allowed. His proposal of a fixed duty on foreign grain led to the defeat of Melbourne's administration and made way for Peel, who in 1845 made public announcement of his conversion to the immediate repeal of the Corn Laws After Peel's resignation in consequence, his recall to power, and another resignation, all within a twelvemonth, Russell became what he in reality had been under the Melbourne administration—Prime Minister. In 1846, 1847, and 1848 we find him engaged in adjusting the affairs of Ireland In the Cabinet of the Earl of Aberdeen, Russell became Foreign Secretary with the leadership of the House of Commons, but was forced to resign on account of the unpopularity incurred by his attitude at the Congress of Vienna. In 1859 Russell became Foreign Secretary a second time under the second administration of Palmerston, which office he held till 1865. He threw his whole influence on the side of Italian unity and preserved a strict neutrality in the Civil War in America He was created Earl Russell in 1861, and entered the House of Lords On the death of Lord Palmerston in 1865 he became Prime Minister a second time The reform bill which he introduced with Gladstone in 1866 was rejected and his ministry shortly after resigned. From now on, up to the time of his death, May 28, 1878, he remained an active member of the Liberal party in the House of Lords In private life, says a competent authority, Russell was a genial companion, never happier than when surrounded by his children and his books.

As a statesman he was a sincere, but not a demonstrative, patriot. He championed every measure that he believed would increase the happiness of his people. Though his voice was weak and his delivery somewhat affected, Earl Russell was an admirable and successful debater, his speeches rising to a high order of eloquence. The speech on " The Church of Ireland " is characteristic of Russell's style of oratory.

THE CHURCH OF IRELAND

Delivered in the House of Commons, March 30, 1835

I RISE fully sensible of the arduous task I have undertaken;
but although I am well aware both of the difficulty of that
task, and of the responsibility I incur, yet the confidence
I feel in the nature of the question I am to bring forward dimin-
ishes much of my anxiety, because I cannot but think that the
clearness of the proposition I shall submit will compensate for
any obscurity in the arguments I may use to enforce it. I am
confident that the truth and justice of the cause will prevail
though the weakness and incompetence of the advocate should
be manifest.

With no further preface, therefore, I shall enter upon the
consideration of the subject of the Church of Ireland; and
in doing so, let me advert, in the first instance, to a motion
made on April 22, in the last year. The honorable member for
the city of Dublin then introduced a motion for a committee to
inquire into the means by which the union with Ireland had
been effected, and as to the expediency of continuing it. The
honorable member was met by an amendment in the form of an
address to the Crown, which was carried by a large majority,
and in the minority appeared only one member for England,
and no member for Scotland. The answer to the motion of the
honorable and learned member, therefore, was given by the
Representatives of England and Scotland, supported by a great
part of those from Ireland. The address was in these terms:
" We, your Majesty's most dutiful and loyal subjects, the Commons, in Parliament assembled, feel it our duty humbly to approach your Majesty's throne, to record in the most solemn
manner our fixed determination to maintain unimpaired and
undisturbed the legislative union between Great Britain and
Ireland, which we consider to be essential to the strength and

stability of the empire, to the continuance of the connection between the two countries, and to the peace, and security, and happiness, of all classes of your Majesty's subjects. We feel this our determination, to be as much justified by our views of the general interests of the state, as by our conviction that to no other portion of your Majesty's subjects is the maintenance of the legislative union more important than to the inhabitants of Ireland themselves. We humbly represent to your Majesty that the imperial Parliament have taken the affairs of Ireland into their most serious consideration, and that various salutary laws have been enacted, since the union, for the advancement of the most important interests of Ireland, and of the empire at large. In expressing to your Majesty our resolution, to maintain the legislative union inviolate, we humbly beg leave to assure your Majesty that we shall persevere in applying our best attention to the removal of all just causes of complaint, and to the promotion of all well-considered measures of improvement."

This address was carried by the House to the foot of the throne, and His Majesty was pleased to return an answer in which he stated that he should be " at all times anxious to afford his best assistance in removing all just causes of complaint, and in sanctioning all well-considered measures of improvement." This was the answer of His Majesty to the claim in the petitions of a large portion of the people of Ireland, enforced by a member of this House, in whom they had the greatest confidence, and who undoubtedly possessed abilities to place his arguments in the best and strongest point of view. In pursuance of this answer which was adopted by the House of Lords, and thereby became, as it were, a solemn compact between the Parliament of the United Kingdom and the people, given by the King, received by the Commons, and approved by the Lords, I am come before you to-day to represent to you what I consider " a well-considered measure of improvement." My complaint is, that nothing of that sort has yet been done or attempted, and I have referred to this discussion, not only on account of its strict connection with my motion, but because I think it ought to refute any answer to it founded upon some supposed danger, some distant apprehension, that what we may do to remove a " just cause of complaint," and to adopt a " well-considered measure of improvement " with regard to Ireland, may have an injurious effect at some distant and indefinite time on one of the institutions of the country. I say you are not at liberty, after having agreed to this address, to put in that answer, and thus to bar a remedy.

One of two things must be admitted: Either you are prepared to do justice to Ireland—to consider her grievances, and redress her wrongs—or you are not. But if you tell us that your position is such that any measure of that kind would be injurious to England, and dangerous to her church establishment, which prevents the remedy of the abuses of the Church of Ireland, you surely, then, have no right to say that it is fit to enforce the legislative union. You are not to tell us that you cannot listen to the well-founded grievances of Ireland, and are not prepared to do her justice, and yet insist on an adherence to the legislative union. I hold that such an answer would be most impolitic as regards Ireland, and most dangerous as regards the whole empire. I am one of those who think that, with perfect safety to the Church of England, you may remedy what is defective in the Church of Ireland, and, remedying that, may persist in your demand for the preservation of the legislative union. I own I cannot understand how any members of this House can confess their inability to remove the grievances of Ireland; on account of a remote and contingent apprehension; and yet can maintain, as absolutely as I do, that the legislative union ought not to be disturbed. The state of Ireland has long been, and is now, a source of great embarrassment to every statesman of this country. There is no doubt that the moral, no less than the physical condition of that people, is one of great degradation. With respect to the physical condition—with respect to the poverty and distress prevalent in Ireland—if I were to bring forward a motion on that subject, I should be obliged to state grounds for thinking that some measures were necessary, by assessment or otherwise, to lessen that serious evil. But that is a question of another kind, and for another day. The question which I have to consider is, the moral condition of the people, and how far the church established in Ireland bears on that condition. Whether our acts of temporary coercion—our acts for enforcing the collection of tithes, and to compel the due administration of the law, have, or have not been effectual, there exists, as we unhappily know, a strong propensity to violence and outrage, not merely among a few lawless and ill-regulated persons, but among all, or nearly all, classes of the community. This defiance of the law arises from an opinion that the law is not fairly and equally administered. Dreadful acts of murder have been committed in various parts of Ireland. A murder has been perpetrated, at one time, on a clergyman of a most unoffending character, and at another time a Roman Catholic has fallen a victim to the animosity of those whom he had never intended to injure. It not infrequently has happened that an individual, wishing to preserve the safety of his own person, has had more reason to fear the combinations of those who set up against the law, than the ministers who execute the law. It has too often happened that when Justice has raised her head, a stronger power has resisted her efforts, her balance has been destroyed, and her sword turned aside from its purpose by the intervention of a multitude.

Every relation of life in Ireland, as Viscount Melbourne said in the House of Lords last year, has been, and still is, liable to be disturbed, by this lawless condition of affairs. The payment of rent, the hiring of land, the settlement of wages between employer and servant, in short, the conclusion of every bargain has been frequently impeded by threats on the part of those who appear to have no concern with making the engagements, and to complete them would be attended with personal danger. If we look to the causes, although no doubt many might be named, yet we cannot help being struck by the fact that there has been no time in the history of Ireland since this country obtained footing and dominion there, in which there was not some dreadful contest, something amounting to a civil war, and a state of law which induced the people to consider themselves rather as the victims of tyranny than the subjects of just government.

It has happened, by a kind of fatality, that those periods most remarkable and most glorious in English history have been marked by indications of some new calamity in Ireland. While we justly boast of the statutes passed in the reign of our first Edward, an epoch remarkable in our civil history, for Edward has been called the English Justinian, the inhabitants of Ireland vainly petitioned for a removal of those invidious distinctions which deprived them of the benefit of English laws. A similar remark applies to the reign of Edward IV. Throughout the reign of Elizabeth, when the Reformation was so prosperously completed, and when the glory of England was so resplendent, not only in arms, but in arts of literature, the Irish suffered the most grievous oppressions, and a new distinction was introduced, viz., that distinction of which I shall have so much to say to-day, brought about by changing the faith of the great body of the clergy, without the faith of the people undergoing the same change. Passing over the period óf the Commonwealth, the great event of the Revolution, to which we look back with such proud and just satisfaction, was attended with new calamities to Ireland. New distinctions were made, to the disadvantage of that unhappy people; and on the score of their religion they were suspected of an attachment to the monarch whom England had banished. They were accordingly visited by laws which Mr. Burke truly designated as a barbarous code—they were proscribed, humiliated, and degraded, and treated as enemies, both to the throne and to the altar. At the same time our ingenuity was tormented to discover modes of restricting the trade of Ireland with our colonies, and the progress of her internal improvement was industriously impeded; such were the circumstances which in Ireland corresponded with the most glorious events of English history.

Towards the end of the last and the beginning of the present century, a better era seemed promised to Ireland; many odious restrictions were removed, and she freed herself from bonds which had previously most unjustly confined her. The power of legislation was restored to her, and about this period some religious distinctions were removed, and she approached nearer to the enjoyment of equal laws and to the possession of civil rights. The conviction of a long course of injustice and suffering, which naturally impressed the minds of the people, induced them, even in this dawn of a happier day, to look a little into the cause of improvement in their prospects and condition. It was said by a statesman, of no democratic turn, no lover of popular innovation—the late Lord Grenville—that concession to Ireland was always the result, not of kindness, but of necessity.

Such was the case when, in the midst of the American war, with eighty thousand volunteers in arms, England was obliged to make an appeal to Ireland. Such was the case in 1792, when the elective franchise, first obstinately denied, was at length conceded, because a French war was impending. Such was the case, I am sorry to add, since the period when Lord Grenville spoke, when Catholic emancipation was reluctantly granted. That concession arose out of no admission of the justice of the claim on the part of those who proposed it, but proceeded avowedly from the fear of civil war. The point having been yielded in this manner, it cannot be expected that the minds of the people of Ireland should be so changed as to be reconciled to their remaining disadvantages; ancient hatred and former animosities still necessarily prevail, and it seems to have been too often thought by them that what force once extorted, force could again compel. I now come to you, and ask you to legislate in a different and a liberal spirit. I come to you, to ask you, although the Reformation and the Revolution were periods of calamity, and not of gratulation to Ireland, to make this era (when a Parliament has been assembled representing, I believe, fairly, the opinions of the united people) celebrated in her annals for its justice and impartiality, inspiring her inhabitants with better hopes, and laying the foundation of a lasting settlement.

In considering the state of the Church of Ireland I am obliged to look back and consider a question that has been of late a good deal mooted, viz.: the utility and object of a church establishment. I am one of those fully concurring in the defence set up last year by one of our prelates, that an establishment tends to promote religion, to maintain good order, and I further agree with him as to the fact that it is agreeable to the sentiments of the majority of the people of this part of the empire. But as a friend of the United Kingdom, I call upon you to consider whether with respect to the Church of Ireland you can set up the same defence? Does it tend to promote religion, or to maintain good order? On this part of the subject I will take the liberty of reading a passage from Archdeacon Paley, where he speaks of a church establishment. " The authority of a church establishment is founded in its utility, and whenever, upon this principle, we deliberate concerning the form, propriety, or comparative excellency of different establishments, the single view under which we ought to consider any of them is, that of 'a scheme of instruction,' the single end we ought to propose by them is, 'the preservation and communication of religious knowledge.' Every other idea, and every other end, that have been mixed with this, as the making of the Church an engine, or even an ally of the State, converting it into the means of strengthening or diffusing influence; or regarding it as a support of regal, in opposition to popular, forms of government; have served only to debase the institution, and to introduce into it numerous abuses and corruptions." I agree also with a right reverend prelate, who stated in one of his charges last year, that the " avowed object for which the Church is established is the spiritual instruction of all classes of the people." He adds, elsewhere, that the whole controversy is reduced to this—"whether the religious instruction of a nation is not more effectually carried on by means of an endowed and an established church? " That is precisely the question I propose to apply to the state of Ireland, and I ask whether this great object has been advanced by the mode in which the Church revenues are at present appropriated in Ireland— whether the religious instruction of the people has been promoted by the establishment of the Protestant Church? I will first consider what are now the revenues of the Irish Church as compared with its revenues in former times. Upon this point a passage which I shall beg to read from a letter of Archbishop King to Archbishop Wake, after the death of the Archbishop of Tuam, dated March 29, 1716, is instructive. He says, " We have but about six hundred beneficed clergymen in Ireland, and perhaps of these hardly two hundred have £100 per annum, and for you to send your supernumeraries to be provided out of the least of these, does look too like the rich man in Nathan's parable." At that period, then, it will be seen that there were not more than six hundred benefices in Ireland, and the total revenue of the Church at that time, even including lay impropriations, was not more than £110,000. Now, my honorable friend [Mr. Ward], in his speech of last year, made a statement of the present revenues of the Church of Ireland, which has not been disputed, and the exactness of which I believe there is no reason to doubt. It is as follows: " The

total number of benefices is 1,456, of which seventy-four range
from £800 to £1,000 a year; seventy-five from £1,000 to £1,500;
seventeen from £1,500 to £2,000, and ten from £2,000 to £2,800,
which is the maximum. There are four hundred and seven
livings, varying from £400 to £800 per annum; and three hundred and eighty-six livings exceeding £200." I have before
mentioned that the total revenue of the Church of Ireland in
1716 was £110,000, being made up of the sum of £60,000 for
benefices, and about £50,000 for lay impropriations. Now, let
us see what is its amount at present. I find it thus stated:

Tithe composition	£534,433
Episcopal revenues exclusive of tithes	141,896
Deans and chapters and economy estates	5,399
Minor canons and vicars choral	5,183
Dignitaries, prebendaries, and canons	6,560
Glebe lands	68,250 at 15s.
Perpetuity purchase fund	30,000
Total	£791,721

These are the present revenues of the Church of Ireland, so
that in the whole they amount to little less than £800,000. We
therefore at once come to the question whether this large sum
has really been applied to the religious instruction of the people,
or to whose benefit it has been applied?—whether, while during
the last century, there has been this enormous increase in the
revenues of the Church, there has been a corresponding increase in the number of conversions to the Protestant religion?
—whether the activity and zeal of the clergy have been such,
and whether such has been their success, that the greater portion of the inhabitants of Ireland have become attached to the
Protestant Church, and whether this beneficial change has been
owing to the instructions of its ministers? I am sorry to say,
that the result has been the reverse. I am afraid that in the last
century, although it is not so now, it was considered rather an
advantage, that there were but a few Protestant clergymen residing on their benefices; as they had no glebe-houses, and no
churches, they had a very fair plea for neglecting their spiritual
duties. It is mentioned by more than one traveller that such
was the ordinary case, and even at a late date, many of the
clergy considered themselves rather part of a large political

body than as persons appointed for the spiritual instruction of the people.

It has been stated to me by a reverend gentleman who has addressed me, and who once held a benefice in Ireland, that when first he went there he considered the character of the clergy of that Church very different from the character of the Church of England. They had many very small flocks; they had difficulty in collecting their tithes. Their attention was therefore too much absorbed by the means of collecting their tithes, and they did not partake of the character which does so much honor to the clergy of the Church of England. This statement was made to me by a highly respected gentleman, who held a benefice in Ireland for many years and afterwards gave it up and returned to this country; and he mentioned an instance of a clergyman who thought himself aggrieved in being deprived of his benefice because he would persist in holding a commission in a yeomanry corps. All the information that we have, and it is abundant, tends to show that such was formerly the actual condition of the Church. By Tighe's " History of Kilkenny," it appears that the number of Protestant families in 1731 was 1,055, but in 1800 they had been reduced to nine hundred and forty-one. The total number of Protestants at the former period was 5,238, while the population of the country, which in 1800 was 108,000, in 1731 was only 42,108 souls. From Stewart's " History of Armagh," we find that sixty years ago the Protestants in that county were as two to one; now they are as one to three. In 1733, the Roman Catholics in Kerry were in the proportion of twelve to one Protestant, and now the former are much more numerous than even that proportion. In Tullamore, in 1731, there were sixty-four Protestants to six hundred and thirteen Roman Catholics, but according to Mason's " Parochial Survey," in 1818, the Protestants had diminished to only five, while the Roman Catholics had augmented to 2,455. On the whole, from the best computation I have seen, and I believe it is not exaggerated one way or the other, the entire number of Protestants belonging to the Established Church in Ireland can hardly be stated higher than 750,000; and of those, 400,000 are resident in the ecclesiastical province of Armagh. Without going into particulars, for which indeed I do not pretend to be prepared, it may be said that in Armagh the numbers are seven or eight to one, and in other parts of Ireland the disproportion is larger. I have, however, an account relating to different dioceses, which I believe to be very accurate, and which I will state to the House.

The noble lord read several particulars, of which the following table is a summary:

Dioceses	Members of Established Church	Roman Catholics	Presbyterians	Other Protestant Dissenters	Total
Ardfert	7,529	297,131	....	27	304,687
Down.........	30,583	61,465	101,627	3,557	197,232
Dromore......	35,677	58,516	59,385	818	154,409
Kildare	13,986	122,577	9	334	136,956
Kilfenora......	235	34,606	4	.....	34,845
Killaloe... ...	19,149	359,585	6	326	379,076
Leighlin.......	20,404	170,083	198	281	190,966
Lismore.......	8,002	207,688	164	382	216,236
Meath	25,626	377,430	671	199	403,926
Waterford.....	5,301	43,371	110	433	49,225
Total	166,492	1,732,452	162,174	6,357	2,067,558

Thus, in the diocese of Ardfert, the Protestants only form one forty-first part of the population; in Down, one-eighth; in Lismore, one twenty-seventh; in Waterford, one-ninth; in Killaloe, one-nineteenth; and in Dromore, one-fourth of the population. Thus, too, it will be seen, that while in some parts of Ireland the members of the Established Church form a considerable proportion of the population, and it is therefore held that they require a considerable number of clergymen, in other parts they form but a small proportion—so small that it cannot be necessary or right that there should be so large an establishment as in other parts of the country. Having shown that these are the general results with respect to the proportions of the population—and everyone knows, that by no computation can the members of the Established Church be made to form more than one-ninth of the whole population—I may venture, with the less fear, to give some particular instances of the proportions which the members of the Church of England bear to the amount of money drawn from tithes, and applied to the spiritual instruction of a small portion of the people. The instances which I will state to the House are taken from a memorandum furnished by my right honorable friend, the member for Staffordshire [Mr. Littleton]. They are as follows:

Parishes	Value	Established Church	Roman Catholic
Taghmon....................	£446, Glebe £50	133	2,920
Ballycormick.................	95	10	501
Ballynilty....................	82	21	390
Dunleer	153, Glebe £6	159	1,460
Drumcar.....................	53	120	1,528
Monachebone................	107	9	737
Moyleary....................	173, Glebe £30	13	1,148
Cuppog......................	120	1	530
Rathdrummin................	82, Glebe £20	7	662
Carrickbogget...............	57	..	332
Port........................	142, Glebe £5	5	800
Ullard......................	280, Glebe £45	50	2,213
Graig.......................	440	63	4,779
Ossory	62	4	107
Balsoon	69	7	313

This, sir, will be sufficient for my present purpose. I believe that similar instances, without end, might be produced from the knowledge, and, I may say, the personal acquaintance, of gentlemen residing in Ireland. Their tendency is to show that there is a very large mass of the £800,000 raised for the spiritual instruction of a small class of the people, while all the rest of the people derive no benefit whatever from that expenditure. I believe that more care and more attention have been given of late years, particularly during the last seven years, to the spiritual cure of members of the Church of England, than have been afforded at a former period. I believe that, in this respect, the Church of Ireland now stands high, and that there are clergymen belonging to that church who exert themselves to the utmost to afford spiritual instruction to the people. But we must not fall into the error of supposing that it is only necessary to build churches and glebe-houses in order to convert men to the religion which we ourselves profess. There were times, perhaps—I know not whether it were so or not—when, by kindness and care, the English Church might have obtained a much more extensive footing in Ireland than it possesses

now; but it is evident that, as regards a people, so much attached to their own faith as the Roman Catholics are, you cannot hope, by merely placing a clergyman in a glebe-house, and
advising him to preach every Sunday—you cannot hope that,
by such means, any real advances will be made in their conversion. Everything contradicts such a supposition; and, if it
were not contradicted merely by the present state of the facts,
I am sorry to say, that what has occurred of late years would
tend to diminish very much any such hopes that might have
been entertained. It was thought fit some years ago to call together public meetings in Ireland, and to endeavor by controversy and dispute to bring over members of the Catholic
Church to the Protestant Church. Now, sir, I must say
that those who took this course acted in defiance of all
history and all experience. I can well conceive, that in
the case of a rich Church established in a country in which
it was enjoying large benefits without attending properly
to the cure of souls, individuals, even though themselves
were in error, might hope, by pointing out the corruptions
and defects of such a Church, to obtain many converts;
but that persons belonging to a Church like the Church of England—that they, belonging to a Church so large, and maintained by tithes paid by the people generally who dissent from
it—that they should attempt a sort of crusade against the voluntary leaders of men who support their own Church, and hope
to gain the supremacy in the controversy, does show, I think,
greater zeal and rashness than prudence or wisdom. What,
sir, was the consequence? It might have happened that things
might have gone on in their usual course; but this controversy
being commenced, the Catholic clergy considered themselves
attacked, and raised a spirit of resistance to the legal payment
of that clergy to whom they were religiously and theologically
opposed. I am far from thinking that that resistance was justified; still less do I think that encouragement ought to have
been given to it. But I feel it to be my duty to place before
you the facts—to acquaint you with the state of things which
naturally resulted from what was attempted, in order that you
may see that the effect was to throw an additional obstacle in
the way of the success of the Church of England in its endeavors to win over a large class of the Roman Catholics to its

spiritual doctrines. In the parish of Graig a system of violence was commenced, and it was said that the Roman Catholic priests advised the people not to pay tithes. If they did so all parties must blame them. A Protestant clergyman, on the other hand, seized a horse from a tithe-payer who was the Roman Catholic parish priest, and blame must be given to him for taking that course. I do think it is most lamentable, that instead of the clergy of the different persuasions recommending the mild precepts of the gospel which they teach in common, they should have been the originators of disputes and strife; it is surely most lamentable, I say, that such differences should have been commenced by those who ought to be the ministers of peace. Unfortunately there has prevailed throughout Ireland, for several years, a spirit of resistance to the payment of tithes, so inveterate that no exertions of the clergy, and no efforts of the government, have succeeded in enforcing the collection of them. The extent of the evil is admitted by all parties. The laws passed during the late administration having proved ineffectual, the right honorable gentleman opposite, the Chief Secretary for Ireland, the other night came down to the House, and, in his introduction of a measure relating to this subject, earnestly deprecated the use of military force for the collection of tithes. What, then, is the state of the Church of Ireland? You, in the first place, are unable to diffuse its spiritual and religious doctrines amongst the great mass of the people; and you have, in the second place, by your system of tithes, been constantly brought into collision with them. You have been constantly producing a state of things which, while it has led to the disturbance of the country, was irreconcilable with those spiritual objects for which the Bishop of London has said a church establishment alone ought to exist. Allow me, sir, to call the attention of the House to the principle which the great authority I have quoted lays down. That authority states that church establishments should be considered as the means of moral and spiritual instruction, and nothing else; the great object in establishing them was to be essentially useful.

Bearing in mind what has occurred at Graig and Rathcormac, I would ask whether the great permanent objects of a church establishment can ever be secured by your determining that funds shall be demanded for the purpose of enforcing the doctrines of the Church of England, and for no other purpose whatever? Well, then, what do I propose to do in this case? I propose that there should be instituted such a reform of the Church of Ireland as would enable us to adapt the establishment to the spiritual instruction of those who belong to the Church, and that there should be no unnecessary surplus. If you adopt this principle, you cannot do otherwise than greatly reduce the Church of Ireland. I propose, therefore, that you should undertake this object, and that you should apply what shall appear to be the surplus in some way by which the moral and religious improvement of the people of Ireland may be advanced, by which their interests may be considered, and by which they may hereafter believe that the funds which are raised nominally for their benefit, are used for their benefit in reality. It is with this view, then, that I mean to propose this resolution to the House, of which I have given notice. That resolution is as follows: " That this house resolve itself into a committee of the whole House to consider the temporalities of the Church of Ireland." The House having resolved itself into a committee, I shall move, " That it is the opinion of this committee that any surplus which may remain after fully providing for the spiritual instruction of the members of the established church in Ireland, ought to be applied locally to the general education of all classes of Christians." In proposing this course I feel that I am not doing more than the case requires. A similar course was taken in 1828 with respect to the Catholic claims, on the proposition of my honorable friend the member for Westminster. I beg leave to explain the view I take, because I shall thus answer the honorable gentleman opposite who asked me in what manner I intended to proceed. The motion to which I have alluded, that the House should resolve itself into a committee of the whole House to consider the state of the Roman Catholics, was carried by a majority of six. The committee then did resolve that it was expedient to consider the state of the laws affecting the Roman Catholics, with a view to their final adjustment. It was then moved that the resolution be sent to the Lords, in order that their concurrence might be asked. The Commons and the Lords held a conference on the subject, after which the latter fixed a day for the debate, the result being that the motion for their concurrence to the resolution that had been adopted by the House of Commons was lost. I now propose that this House shall resolve to go into committee, I shall propose a resolution which will embody the spirit and substance of my present motion. On that resolution being reported, I shall move an address to the Crown. I shall move that the resolution be presented to the Crown, with a humble entreaty to His Majesty that His Majesty would be most graciously pleased to enable the House to carry it into effect. I think that this is the course which we took on the question of the " Church Temporalities Act." After that bill had been read a first time, the question was raised whether we could dispose of the ecclesiastical patronage of the Crown without the special approval of His Majesty ; and it was decided, sir, by your predecessors, that the question having been brought under the consideration of the House by the King's speech, the bill might be read a second time, but that, afterwards, it would be proper that a special message should be received. I call the attention of the House to that question, because I think the manner of proceeding which I recommend is the best, not only in point of form, but because I do also think that the only manner in which a satisfactory measure can be proposed to the House, is by the concurrence of the Crown. In proposing this, I know not whether the right honorable gentleman opposite [the Chancellor of the Exchequer] will think it proper to follow the course he took in 1829. After a resolution had been carried by a majority of six the right honorable gentleman went down to the King, and informed His Majesty that the House of Commons had decided by a majority in favor of the Roman Catholic claims, and that the state of Ireland being such as to induce well-founded alarm, it was his duty to change his course, and to propose a measure of relief. Whether the right honorable gentleman opposite will follow that precedent or not, I know not ; but I do think that it is as competent to him to adopt such a course on the present occasion as it was for him to adopt the course he took on the Roman Catholic question. The right honorable gentleman has, I know, stated his opinion on the subject, and that is an opinion which is against this proposition ; but he has spoken in no more decided terms against it than he did with respect to the Roman Catholic question—a measure which he afterwards introduced. The right honorable baronet, in his address to his constituents, which he professed to be a declaration of the principles on which he intended to act, stated, with respect to church reform: " Then, as to the great question of church reform, on that head I have no new professions to make. I cannot give my consent to the alienation of church property, in any part of the United Kingdom, from strictly ecclesiastical purposes. But I repeat now the opinion that I have already expressed in Parliament, in regard to the church establishment in Ireland—that if by an improved distribution of the revenues of the Church, its just influence can be extended, and the true interest of the established religion promoted, all other considerations should be made subordinate to the advancement of objects of such paramount importance." The right honorable gentleman stated his opinion, in this very emphatic manner, very soon after he took office. When subsequently the right honorable gentleman was asked a question in this House, as to what he proposed to do in regard to measures resulting from the commission now making inquiries in Ireland, he answered that he was averse to any new distribution of the revenues of the Church, which would promote the interest and extend the influence of the Church; but any measure to which he consented must be confined in its object to the promotion of the doctrines of the Church. In some observations upon the Tithe Bill lately brought before the House, in which the question of the appropriation of Church revenues was involved, the right honorable baronet said that he would consent to their application to their present purposes, but the amount must be confined to those purposes, spiritual and ecclesiastical, viz., those purposes for which the Church of England at present exists. Now, I do say, sir, that the right honorable baronet having stated his opinion thus broadly on this question, it is quite clear, that whatever may be the result of the inquiries which the commission is yet to pursue, it is necessary that the House of Commons should come to some decision on that point, and either adopt or reject the principle adopted by the right honorable baronet.

If the House be determined to confine the revenues of the Church to purposes strictly ecclesiastical,ʻ it is better for that determination to be declared; but if the House is not

of that opinion, it is certainly of no use for us to be passing
through the different stages of the bills for the commutation
of tithes.' We ought, in my opinion, to proceed with that bill,
while this great question is unsettled—while it is yet unknown
whether the ministers and the House of Commons agree as to
the question, or are at variance upon it. I think, sir, that this
consideration is a full justification of the course I take in proposing this resolution to the House. It is quite clear that the
late ministry, or any similar ministry, on the report of the
Church commissioners becoming known, would have been disposed to act on the spirit of that report, and, if necessary, would
have proposed to reduce the church establishment in Ireland.
But the right honorable baronet tells us at once, immediately
on his assuming office, again on appearing in this House, and
also in proposing the Tithe Bill—three separate times he tells
us—that the commission may go on prosecuting its inquiries,
but he should care for its report no otherwise than as it would
enable him to effect a better distribution of Church property
among the members of the Church ; and whatever the nature of
the report, whatever the surplus, however extensive the reduction which the Protestant Church might bear consistently with
the preservation of its stability, and the extension of its really
beneficial influence, he has made up his mind already not to
consent to forego the principle of maintaining the property of
the Church to its present purposes. That being the case, it is
quite necessary, as it appears to me, to come to some distinct
resolution on the question. It is for the advantage of everyone
—for the advantage of this country—for the advantage of Ireland—and, indeed, for the general advantage of the empire—
that there should be, on this great and vital question, an administration in harmony with the House of Commons, acting
according to its sense   And if the right honorable gentleman
has the confidence of the House, or if his opinions and the opinions of those acting with him being adverse, he is prepared to
take the course he took on a former occasion—in either case
it is far better that at once we should come to some decision,
and not be voting supplies and not going on night after night,
and week after week, without knowing whether the ministers
of the Crown do enjoy the confidence of the House on this
great question, or do not. Well, then, sir, I think that what I

have said will be considered a sufficient answer to any argument that may be drawn from the fact of the report of the commission not being yet on the table of the House. The honorable gentleman opposite may say that it is inconsistent thus to bring forward a motion on this subject, without the report being before us, and they are quite welcome, if they please, to throw those taunts upon us; but I think it sufficient to state in reply that the state of the question has been entertained, that it is a question no longer open—on the contrary, it is one on which a decided opinion has been formed by the honorable gentleman on the other side of the House; and that decided opinion having been pronounced, it is quite necessary that we should ask whether or no the principle which we propose—whether the appropriation of the revenue of the Church of Ireland, or any part of it, to uses by which the people of Ireland generally can be benefited—will secure the sanction of the House. I come now to the question with respect to the purposes to which I would apply the surplus.

The other night an honorable gentleman asked me whether I proposed that any part of the money should go for the purpose of affording religious education to the Roman Catholics, on the principles of the Roman Catholic religion. My answer is, that I propose to adopt the principle acted on by the National Board of Education for Ireland. The measure, constituting that board, was proposed by my noble friend, the member for Lancashire; and, according to that measure, members of all creeds, children of all persuasions, can receive religious and moral instruction, and are brought up in harmony and at peace with each other. I have considered that, in the present state of Ireland, no measure would tend so much to its future peace as the expending of large funds for the purpose of promoting education. From the earliest times it will be found that the Protestants have been desirous of improving the condition of the people of Ireland by means of education. It was the object of the 12th of Elizabeth, chapter first. The preamble of that act actually states that much good is expected to result from the establishment of a good system of education in Ireland. But, in after times, and in times much later, there have been those who considered that it was of the utmost importance that instruction should be given to the people of

Ireland in such a manner as would not interfere with their religious faith.   In support of this statement, I beg the attention of the House, while I read to them the copy of a letter from the Lord Bishop of Clonfert to the Rev. Mr. Moore, of Boughton-Blean, near Canterbury: "Though I had not the pleasure of receiving your very informing discourse on Sunday-schools at the time you intended, I have since got it, and read it with the greatest satisfaction. It is an admirable defence and recommendation of this new institution, which I hope will daily become more general, and produce the best moral effects, by impressing the children of the poor with a sense of duty and religion, at the only time and age when they are capable of impressions. A poor man's creed need not be long, but it should be struck in early, and a true and right one. If he believes, as the common proverb says, that he is to die like a dog, he will undoubtedly live like one. The communication of education is certainly a very great blessing to the poor; and had Mandeville, and they who, to serve political purposes, are for denying all instruction to the lower classes, only pushed their argument far enough, they might have proved that they had a right to maim, or put out the eyes of, the common people, in order to make them more manageable, and more in the power of their superiors.

Having never seen the paragraph in the English papers concerning me, to which you allude in your appendix, I can say nothing to it; but what I have endeavored to do in my diocese, ever since my appointment, is this—there are twenty Catholics to one Protestant in it. To attempt their conversion, or to think of making them read Protestant books, would be in vain. I have, therefore, circulated amongst them some of the best of their own authors, particularly one Gother, whose writings contain much pure Christianity, useful knowledge, and benevolent sentiments. He wrote eighteen volumes of religious extracts, and died about the year 1696. Unable to make the peasants about me good Protestants, I wish to make them good Catholics, good citizens, and good anything. I have established, too, a Sunday-school, open to both Protestants and Catholics, at my residence in the country, have recommended the scheme to my clergy, and hope to have several on foot in the summer. Pastoral works, however, of this nature, go on very heavily in a kingdom so unsettled and so intoxicated with politics as this is. I return you my best thanks for your obliging present."

I cannot conceive, sir, that funds intended for the religious instruction of the people can be misapplied when devoted to objects likely to make them good subjects of the State, and religious and moral. Objects of a similar kind were kept in view, when, in 1806 a commission was appointed, which consisted of the Archbishop of Armagh, Mr. Grattan, and Mr. Edgeworth. After several years spent in inquiry, they agreed to a report, in which they carefully laid down the principle that any new system of education ought to be such as would not interfere with the religious tenets of any particular party.   In an appendix to the report there is a letter from Mr. Grattan, who, in speaking of the sort of schools that should be formed, says that they ought to be founded on more extensive and comprehensive principles. The board for promoting Irish education is composed of the Archbishop of Dublin, the Duke of Leinster, and others. I am sure that all must have heard that the schools of the kind established by the recommendation of that board, have been conducted with the utmost harmony, and attended with the most beneficial effects—moral and religious instruction has been conveyed generally to the people without reference to one particular and exclusive creed.   I come now to meet one or two objections which have been urged, but which I do not think well founded.

The first is the assertion of that principle that the property of the Church ought not to be diverted from the use of the Church to which it belongs. With respect to that principle, I am not disposed to go at large into the general question as to Church property being considered private or not.   I am disposed to consider that question as Burke was disposed to consider the right of taxation over a colony, as he expressed his opinion in his speech made on the motion for the conciliation of America.   And I believe that if I were to attempt entering on that question, I should run great risk of overwhelming myself in that

" —— great Serbonian bog
Betwixt Damiata and Mount Casius old,
Where armies whole have sunk."

Burke has also said, "From the earliest considerations of religion and constitutional policy, from their opinion of a duty to make a sure provision for the consolation of the feeble and the instruction of the ignorant, they have incorporated and identified the estate of the church with the mass of private property, of which the State is not the proprietor, either for use or dominion, but the guardian only and the regulator. They have ordained that the provision of the Establishment might be as stale as the earth on which it stands, and should not fluctuate with the Euripus of funds and actions." Now, I do not hold the opinion that this is private property, and that we can no more interfere with the revenues of a bishop than with the estate of an earl. Mine, however, is not the doctrine of right honorable gentlemen opposite. If they made their stand on the question of private right—if they said that ecclesiastical property shall not be disposed of otherwise than as it was originally devised or distributed—I could easily understand them; but this is not their argument. They hold that the State may distribute Church property otherwise than as at present; that the State, for example, can take from a bishop, and give to a rector or curate. Does that doctrine, then I ask, bear any resemblance whatever to the law which recognizes private property? Does Parliament ever proceed on that principle in the latter case, and say, "There are one hundred or two hundred great proprietors in this country, and it is expedient that wealth should be more equally distributed?" If Church property be private property, we cannot, for a moment, stop to inquire whether the Bishop of Durham has too much. We are satisfied it is private, and we cannot touch it. On what principle, then, do we proceed, and to what conclusion does our proceeding necessarily lead? My noble friend, the member for Lancashire, Lord Stanley, proposed a bill, which was passed into a law, and which diminished the number of bishops in Ireland. The number was too great, and the funds were to be distributed—in what manner? To those next in order—to deans and chapters. But supposing there was enough for them, and still a surplus, what then? Why, then it was to be applied to rectors, to churches, and glebe-houses. But it might also happen, that the bishops had too great a revenue still, so that there would be a surplus after all these objects had been accomplished. How is it possible to say that we can redistribute this property, and yet not carry out the principle to its legitimate length, and distribute the surplus in a manner in which it may be most useful? On what principle do we go? Upon no other than this—that it is useful for the purpose of religious instruction that there should be a redistribution. And what do we come to? To a principle totally distinct from, and at variance with, every law by which private property is affected. I maintain, we can only do that on the grounds of public expediency, of public right, and of public advantage.

If then, I show that public right, public expediency, and public advantage, require the application of some portion of those revenues to works of religious education and charity, where, I would ask, is the distinction between them? and how can the right honorable gentleman pretend that he left that property more sacred than I do? I confess, that to my mind the right honorable gentleman and his colleagues have no ground to stand upon, and I cannot see how they keep themselves out of the Serbonian bog to which Mr. Burke alluded. 'On the one hand, they may stand on the notion of private property, and maintain the ecclesiastical revenues intact and inviolate to their original destination; or, on the other hand, admitting the right of Parliament to interfere, they must hold that, for the benefits of the subjects of the realm, for their religious instruction, for the well-being and harmony of the State, it may so interfere. But there is resting between the two propositions; to say that it should be partly distributed, and partly kept sacred, partly interfered with for public objects, and partly considered private property, does seem to me to couple, in one proposition, the utmost absurdity with the utmost inefficiency. Sir, I do hope that honorable gentlemen opposite will grapple with this great question on clear and intelligible grounds. I must protest against any proposition not founded on distinct and known principles, and which does not tend directly to the good of the State. But we are told, in defence of the present mode of applying Church property in Ireland—that the greatest number—fifteen to one, it is said—of the owners of the land in fee—are members of that Church. Sir, if I could fancy that anyone would hold such a doctrine as this—that a church establishment was intended originally for the exclusive benefit of the rich—that spiritual instruction should be given only to men who had an estate of inheritance—that none but a man who possessed a freehold estate should be entitled to the comforts and consolations of religion—I could then understand the argument to which I have alluded; but when I refer to any of the great authorities I have quoted, who cannot be questioned or repudiated, and when I find it laid down that a church establishment is intended for the benefit of all classes, and more especially for the benefit, the instruction, and consolation of the poor, it is not enough to tell me that those who originally contribute the sums which constitute the revenues of the Church are Protestants and members of that Church; for I am bound to look at the effect of the payment of tithe, on the whole, as a system. Besides, on whomsoever the charge of maintaining the Establishment may fall ultimately, it is perfectly notorious that those, on whom, for the most part, the tithe is levied, and on whom it first falls, are members of the Roman Catholic faith.

The right honorable gentleman [Sir Henry Hardinge] stated to the House the other evening that sums were collected every day, and will continue to be collected as long as leases are in force, of sixpence, fourpence, and one penny from those who do not belong to the Establishment—from which, indeed, they derive no benefit whatever. The alleged circumstance, then, that the original proprietors of land happen to be members of the Church ought not to be an objection to the proposition for which I contend. On these grounds, and unaffected by those objections I have noticed, I am prepared to move the resolution which I call on the House to sanction and affirm. I do think, that if—without adopting some such course as that which I venture to recommend—we pass the Tithe Bill in the shape in which it has been proposed, appropriating solely to the benefit of the Irish Church all its existing revenues, we shall neither obtain peace, nor act ultimately for the harmony and advantage of Ireland. I believe that the Irish people have warm affections, and are strongly attached to those who confer any benefit on them. Notwithstanding those outrages and acts of violence to which I referred in the commencement of my speech, it is a singular fact that no traveller ever goes into Ireland who does not declare that he has been received everywhere by the poorest peasant, not only in the most hospitable manner, but with the utmost friendly and open-hearted kindness. Those who do not belong to Ireland, but

have lived in that country, have assured me, over and over again,
that the gratitude, and the overflowing of the affection of the
peasantry towards those who manifest kindness towards them is
very great.   Such being the feeling, and such the conduct of that
nation to individuals, the House has now an opportunity of earn-
ing that gratitude and making that affection its own, by asserting
the principle for which I contend, and by thus doing justice to
the people of Ireland.   We have now the power of acting free
from fear—free from any compulsion; there is no fear of foreign
war before us, nor of civil war in Ireland.   It is in our power at
length to settle and gain the affections of that country, to silence
the question of a repeal of the union, to gain the tribute of grateful homage from a people so warm-hearted, so eminently brave
and loyal; while we shall, at the same time, have the satisfaction
of reflecting, that in doing justice to Ireland we shall have contributed more, than by any other measure we can adopt, to the
future prosperity of the empire, making her unconquerable by
her enemies, and an example of religious liberality to the rest of
the world.   I shall now conclude by moving, " That the House
do resolve itself into a committee of the whole House to consider the temporalities of the Church of Ireland."

LIFE AND CULTURE

—

BY

THE EARL OF DERBY

(Edward Henry Smith Stanley)

EDWARD HENRY SMITH STANLEY, EARL OF DERBY

1826—1893

Edward Henry Smith Stanley was born at the family seat of Knowsley, Lancashire, on July 21, 1826. He was at Rugby under Arnold and later went to Cambridge, where he graduated with highest honors. During his absence on a tour to America he was elected to Parliament for King's Lynn to succeed Lord George Bentinck, lately deceased. While absent on a tour in India he was appointed Under Secretary for Foreign Affairs under his father's first administration. During the succeeding year he joined Cobden and Bright in resisting "the policy of drifting into war," and, no doubt, influenced by these men, he became, and always remained, a strong supporter of movements for the benefit and improvement of the working classes and of all reforms of a moderate and liberal character. In the second administration of his father he became, in February, 1858, Colonial Secretary and, later, First Secretary of State for India. After the great mutiny he had a large share in the reconstruction of the government for India, performing his work with consummate skill and judgment.

In July, 1866, during his father's third administration, he was appointed Foreign Secretary. He kept Great Britain neutral during the war of Prussia and Italy with Austria, and acted as mediator between France and Prussia in the Luxembourg affair. He resigned on the accession of the Gladstone ministry in 1868.

Early in the following year he was made Lord Rector of the University of Glasgow, and in October of the same year, on the death of his father, he took his seat in the House of Lords. Derby again became Foreign Secretary under Disraeli in 1874, but owing to a disagreement with his chief on the Eastern question he resigned in March, 1878.

He severed his connection with the Conservatives in 1880, and was soon accepted as the leader of the Liberals. From December, 1882, to 1885 he was Colonial Secretary in Gladstone's second administration. Gladstone's Home Rule plans induced him to join the newly formed party of Liberal-Unionists early in 1886. He was their leader in the House of Lords till 1891, when he retired from public life to give his attention to the study of social questions. His last public speech was at the unveiling of the Bright monument at Manchester in October, 1892. He died April 21, 1893. In Parliament, though not a prominent debater, and though his enunciation was imperfect, he spoke impressively and had a great gift "of making speeches with which everyone must agree, and which at the same time were never commonplace." His oration on "Life and Culture," delivered on assuming the Lord Rectorship of Glasgow University, is one of the most perfect orations ever delivered within the walls of that historic institution.

LIFE AND CULTURE

*Delivered on assuming the Lord Rectorship of Glasgow
University, April 1, 1869*

IT is with no common satisfaction, but at the same time with
a sense of diffidence which I cannot shake off, and do not
care either to deny or to conceal, that I take my place for
the first time in this hall among those by whom I have been
raised to a post of honor on my part unsought and unsolicited,
but on that very account doubly gratifying, not the less so because just thirty-five years ago it fell to my father's lot to stand
in this room, and with powers very different from mine, but certainly not with more anxiety to exert them to the utmost in
your service, to discharge the honorable function which de-
volves on me to-day.

Gentlemen, the Lord Rector of this university, be he who he
may, looks back on a series of more than ordinarily illustrious
predecessors, and cannot but feel honored by the association,
although but casual and temporary, of his name with theirs.   It
is something to be the successor, however unworthily, of Burke
and Adam Smith, of Jeffrey, Mackintosh, and Brougham, of
literary men such as Campbell and Lytton; of politicians like
Palmerston and Peel.   Rightly and wisely, you have not confined the highest honor at your disposal within either local or
professional limits.   Rightly and wisely, you have sought in
your Lord Rectors for representative men, not literary men
alone, nor men of science, nor politicians, nor lawyers, but each
and all of these in their turn; sympathizing with honest and
strenuous effort in whatever branch of human exertion, and
recognizing that not literature exclusively, nor exclusively
science, but action directed to useful public objects, is the true
end and purpose of that large and comprehensive training
which it is your glory and your privilege to bestow.

Gentlemen, if I came here merely to indulge in the language of compliment I might justly congratulate you on the patriotic munificence which has given to your ancient university a new and suitable home—on your four centuries of energetic and successful existence, dating from a time when Glasgow itself was little more than what we should now call a village—on your 1,200 students, your twenty-five professorial chairs—on the encouragement you afford to struggling and otherwise unaided talent—on the practical and varied character of the instruction given within these walls—on the long list of justly distinguished names, which, from the days of Buchanan to our own, has testified to the reality of the work you do, and illustrated the long series of your annals.   But, gentlemen, it is not merely in the language of compliment that I wish to speak here.   Words that lead to nothing are words wasted, and I should very ill repay your kindness if, on the only occasion when it will probably ever be my lot to meet you face to face, I should confine myself to expressions of gratitude, however sincerely felt, or to the language of vague and general panegyric, however much I might feel it to be deserved.

But there is one circumstance connected with the studies of this place that seems to me worthy of notice, because it may very well serve as a model to other and even greater communities than Glasgow—I mean the facilities supplied here to comparatively poor men to obtain the knowledge they seek for, and to compete on equal terms with the rich.   Comparisons are notoriously invidious, but I believe it is not to be denied that in that respect you set us, the English, a good example, and one which we should do well to follow.   No doubt, it is difficult to check undue expenditure in the case of young men whose means allow it; but if I were to say that both in our English schools and colleges more might be done in that respect than is now done I believe I should express an opinion which is very generally entertained among those whom it most directly concerns.

The combination of high attainments, persevering study, and limited means, is perhaps rarer in these islands, taking them as a whole, than in some other European countries.   Yet, though learning needs some degree of leisure, there is no natural connection between learning and opulence.   Scholarship has few greater names than that of Heine—yet Heine's existence, up to the age of thirty, was a constant struggle against poverty and privation, extending even to privation of the very means of subsistence. Simpson, the mathematician, a weaver's boy, was taken away from the humble school which he frequented, from want of means to keep him there. The early struggles of our great painter, Turner, are well known to all who have followed the history of modern art in the pages of perhaps the most eloquent of living English writers. I do not multiply such examples—they are recorded in a hundred familiar works; but Scotland, and Glasgow especially, owes much to Buchanan; and never more strikingly than in Buchanan's case were the hardships and trials of a poor scholar's life displayed.

I might, indeed, carry the argument one step further, and say that, as on the one hand mental energy is stunted and chilled by absolute penury, and the necessity of daily labor for daily bread, so on the other it is at least as likely to be repressed and destroyed by too abundant leisure, by the sense of security which belongs to an assured position, and by the thousand opportunities of easy enjoyment which wealth and leisure confer. I am not speaking here from theory. It is a matter of which illustrations occur in every-day existence. A middle station, equally removed from poverty and luxury, is that temperate zone of life (if I may so speak) in which mental development appears most to flourish. And the reason is simple. Work, as work, is not pleasant to anyone at first. The taste for it is an acquired taste. It becomes, I believe, with some men one of the strongest tendencies of their nature; the active brain requires its accustomed exercise as much as the active limbs need theirs. But the apprenticeship in ninety-nine cases out of one hundred is not pleasant, and perhaps there is no one respect in which the importance of early training is more deeply felt. Men may supply, well or ill, in later life, the want of acquired knowledge. They may accommodate their habits and thoughts to the necessities of a changed position; they may develop their natures in ways wholly unexpected; but one defect, I believe, can hardly ever be made good when the time of youth and early manhood is past—or, if made good, it can be so only as a result of painful and singular effort: the want, I mean, of habits of steady application and industry. They are

mostly hard at any age to acquire, but there is this counter-
vailing advantage about them, that once acquired they are not
easily lost.

To the man who has made intellectual work the habit of his
life it is actual pain to be long unemployed. And, be sure of
this, that, apart from all merely material and practical results
(though I do not undervalue these), apart from these chances
of rising in the world, of professional, or literary, or artistic
distinction, of which we are perhaps all apt to think too much
because, after all, they are prizes which can fall to the lot of
very few, and which those who have got them generally find
worth less than they supposed—apart, I say, from accidental
and adventitious results, there is no greater blessing for a man
than to have acquired that healthy and happy instinct which
leads him to take delight in his work for the work's sake; not
slurring it over, not thinking how soon it will be done and got
rid of, nor troubling himself greatly about what men will say
of it when it is done (I suspect the best kind of workers think
as little of that as Newton did when he hesitated whether to
publish his discoveries or not), but putting his whole heart
and mind into it, feeling that he is master of it, feeling that
the thing which he has turned out—be it a legal argument, or
a book, or a picture, or anything else—is conscientiously and
honestly perfected to the best of his power.

Look at the matter only from a point of view of a man's
personal happiness and welfare. What is the secret of the low
amusements, the pleasure that is not pleasure, with which so
many unhappy men contrive at once to waste and to shorten
their lives? Why these things are, in ninety-nine cases out of
one hundred, merely the resources which they adopt to fill up
vacant hours—to get rid of the intolerable weariness of unemployed existence—to kill the sense of apathy and *ennui* which is
killing them. I am not trying or desiring to lay down for all
men a single and uniform rule. There are some of us who
seem born for action rather than for study, to whom abstract
thought is repugnant, and who want always to be doing something, and to see the result of their labor before them. There
are others whose natural turn is rather for thinking—for the
exercise of the intellectual powers purely and simply—than for
what are called, by a somewhat unmeaning distinction, the

practical pursuits of life. Each temperament is probably better for having some admixture of the other, and the most
complete and perfect organization is that which combines both
in the most equal proportions. But there is room in the world
for both; and no greater folly can be committed by men than
that of seeking to assimilate all individual character to one and
the same type.

What I do say is that, whether the bent of a man's mind be
study or business, whatever it is, let him throw himself heartily
into it. I do not believe that an unemployed man; however
amiable and otherwise irreproachable, ever was, or ever can be,
really happy. Our work is our life; show me what you can do
and I will show you what you are. I have spoken of love of
one's work as being the best preventive of merely low and
vicious tastes. I will go further and say I believe it is the best
preservative against petty anxieties and the annoyances which
arise out of indulged self-love. Men have thought before now
that they could take a refuge from trouble and vexation by shel·
tering themselves, as it were, in a world of their own. The
experiment has often been tried, and always with one result.
You cannot escape from anxiety and labor—it is the destiny
of humanity. You may avoid, indeed some at least may to a
great extent, taking part in the struggle of life in the sharp and
eager competition of an open profession, or the not less intense
pursuit of some worthy object of study. But, by what seems
to me a just and wholesome retribution, those who shrink from
facing trouble find that trouble comes to them. The indolent
man may contrive that he shall have less than his share of the
world's work to do; but Nature, proportioning the instrument
to the work, contrives that that little shall to him be much and
hard. The man who has only himself to please finds, sooner or
later, and probably sooner rather than later, that he has got a
very hard master, and the more excusable weakness which
shrinks from responsibility has its own punishment, too; for
where great interests are excluded little matters become great,
and the same wear and tear of mind that might have been at
least usefully and healthfully expended on the real business of
life is often wasted on petty and imaginary vexations such as
breed and multiply in the unoccupied brain.

There is yet another point from which I may press upon you

the duty of industry. We sometimes hear it said, " So-and-so
is a man of fortune, who can afford to do nothing." There are,
of course, in a country like this many thousands who do not
need to earn their bread, or to increase their income, and who,
perhaps, would be doing more harm than good if they embarked
in any one of our already overcrowded professions. But there
is a moral as well as a material aspect of these questions. No
one can pass through his allotted term of years—no matter how
plainly and simply—much less can he do so living as the wealth-
ier classes live, without profiting by and consuming the fruits of
other men's toil. All capital is accumulated labor. Of course,
as far as human law and the regulations of society go, he may
legitimately do that, rendering himself no labor in return, so
long as he pays honestly for what he uses. But if the matter
is to be dealt with *in foro conscientiæ*, I think a scrupulous and
high-minded man will always feel that to pass out of the world
in the world's debt—to have consumed much and produced
nothing, to have sat down, as it were, at the feast and gone away
without paying his reckoning—is not, to put it in the mildest
way, a satisfactory transaction, however unimpeachable, and
rightly so, it may be in the eye of economical and social law.
You cannot very well lay down a formula for these things ; it
is often easier to ask for suitable occupation than to find it ; but
I think it is only a natural feeling for anyone living at his ease
to wish and strive that at least his country shall be no loser by
him, that in some form, by some means, whether by speech or
writing, or useful action, no matter how obscure, he shall replace to the public the expenditure of human labor that has been
made upon him.

I know very well that with the best will in the world that feeling is not always easy to act upon. It is one thing to wish for
a suitable sphere of duty and another to be able to obtain one.
There are many persons who, if not wholly idle, are yet unable
to employ their faculties as they best might from the mere
want of opportunity. I own that for such persons, assuming
the fault not to rest with them, I have more compassion than for
those who may be inclined to complain of the chances and
struggles of professional life. Overwork, or what we may be
inclined to consider as such, is bad enough ; but it is probably a
cause of less suffering in the aggregate than the consciousness
of faculties unused and of energies which can find no vent.

But, gentlemen, I do not forget that in addressing you I am speaking to young men who, for the most part, have every external, as well as internal, inducement to lead an energetic and industrious life. To warn you, therefore, against mere indolence and neglect of opportunities is, I hope, superfluous. It is perhaps more to the purpose to ask you—at least to ask some of you—to recollect that overwork and overhaste (they are mostly the same thing) are as fatal as carelessness. We live in days of perhaps overstrained competition; and even those who, so far as their personal feelings are concerned, would probably be satisfied with moderate success and a tranquil career, have, in most professions, hardly the choice. A rising lawyer cannot refuse briefs, a young surgeon or physician cannot decline practice. It is rarely, I fancy, in the power of any professional man to say, " Up to such a limit I will work, and no farther." It may be, for my own part I think it is, a misfortune that such should be the case—that, from the tendency of mankind to run after well-known names, one competitor in a profession should have more labor cast upon him than it is physically possible that he should attend to properly; while others, hardly, if at all, less capable, are standing by unemployed. But that is a result—I suppose an inevitable result—of open competition in a fair field, and we can only accept the laws of the game as we find them. Every man, therefore, who works with his brain must be prepared, in an open profession, to find, in the event of obtaining the success which he hopes for, that his bodily as well as mental powers will be taxed to the utmost. And if that possibility is realized, the question, all-important for him, whether he will be able to hold his own or whether he will break down, will depend very much on the nature of his early training.

This is a subject on which there exists, I think, a good deal of prejudice and want of information. We have often heard of men crushed in youth by excessive mental strain. That such cases do occur I cannot in the face of evidence deny. But I believe that nine times out of ten they are the result of simple mismanagement. I doubt whether—speaking of young men, not of very young boys or children—honest work, steadily and regularly carried on, ever yet hurt anybody. The men who fail, and whose failure is pointed to as an illustration of the evils of over-study, are generally those who, rashly and foolishly, try to make up for past neglect by excessive temporary efforts; or else those who, absorbed in a single idea, and possibly ignorant of their own physical constitution, overlook the most ordinary requirements of bodily health. We used to say at Cambridge that any man who had it in him to become a senior wrangler—that is, to take the highest honor known to the university in the driest and most laborious branch of study—could do so by means of six or seven hours' reading in the twenty-four. Never to hurry, never except for some brief interval wholly to relax—to remember that neglected bodily health involves a weakened brain, and that it is possible to wear out in preparation the strength that should be reserved for the final effort—above all, to content one's self with the idea that one is doing one's best, and to await the event with as little of worry or anxiety as is compatible with the infirmity of nature—these are, I know, very simple and homely rules, but for being simple they are not less true; and though assuredly I do not say to anyone that their observance is a guarantee for well-doing, I believe it will, to say the least, strike off from the list certain causes of otherwise inevitable failure. There is nothing new to be said in these matters. The *mens sana in corpore sano* is, as much now as it was two thousand years ago, the most rational object of human wishes, and the most necessary condition of human success.

One word, and only one word, more on this subject. I am convinced that as a rule we overrate—I think our tendency is enormously to overrate—the difference between men's powers for purposes of practical action. Of course, these differences, after all deductions made, remain very great. But it is a matter of common observation in every profession, even the most intellectual—I think I have noticed it myself again and again—how often the very acutest intellects, for some reason or another, do not seem able to procure for their possessors the first place; while that place is often secured and kept by powers which seem, and which, intellectually considered, are very greatly inferior. I believe that with no extraordinary quickness or brilliancy, but with perseverance, memory, accuracy, and that soundness of judgment which habits of patient inquiry confer—all qualities with which cultivation has more to do than nature—a man may rise very high in almost any department of human labor, and may pass by in the race many whom at school or at college, or possibly even in later life, he regarded as hopelessly superior to himself. But of all these qualities, for every purpose, whether for action or speculation, I hold that one to be most valuable which it is almost entirely within our own power to acquire, and which nature unassisted never yet gave to any man. I mean a perfectly accurate habit of thought and expression. This is, as far as I can see, one of the very rarest acquirements. For it implies a good deal—carefulness, close attention to details, a certain power of memory, and the habit of distinguishing between things which are alike but not identical. I lay stress on this because it seems to me the characteristically distinguishing mark of good and faulty teaching, of real and unreal learning. The best thing is to know your subject thoroughly—the next best to know nothing about it, and to be aware that you do know nothing—the worst is to know a little, and to know that little vaguely and confusedly.

Much is said in the present day for and against the system of competitive examinations. Like most other things, they may have their defects, but this advantage they undoubtedly possess, that if well managed they are an effective check—a check, I think, more effective than any other—on the imposture of half-knowledge. What man can write out clearly, correctly, and briefly, without book or reference of any kind, that he undoubtedly knows, whatever else he may be ignorant of. For knowledge that falls short of that—knowledge that is vague, hazy, indistinct, uncertain—I, for one, profess no respect at all. And I believe that there never was a time nor a country where the influences of careful training were in that respect more needed. Men live in haste, write in haste—I was going to say think in haste, only that perhaps the word thinking is hardly applicable to that large number who, for the most part, purchase their daily allowance of thought ready made. You find ten times more people now than ever before who can string together words with facility and with a general idea of their meaning, and who are ready with a theory of some kind about most matters. All that is very well as far as it goes; but it is one thing to be able to do this and quite another to know how to use words as they should be used, or really to have thought out the subject which you discuss.

For one of these purposes there is, I believe, no training better than the old classical training whose merits are now so much
disputed.   I do not deny that in English schools it has been carried to folly and pedantry.   I doubt if any human being was
ever the better or the wiser for being set to spin verses in a
foreign and dead language.   But, speaking of the rational use
and not the abuse of classical literature, I think it has one great
merit which is not easily to be found elsewhere.   Even those
who feel most strongly the incomparably wider range of modern thought will seldom deny that in precision, in conciseness,
in dignity of style, and in verbal felicity, the great writers of
ancient times have scarcely been equalled.   It is suggestive to
think how, under the influence of the mercantile principle, making books to be paid for in proportion, not to their merits, but to
their length, and of the lifelong hurry which prevents us from
studying condensation, such narratives as those of Cæsar and
Tacitus would in modern hands have swelled into the dimen-
sions of a modern historical composition, with the certain result
that they would have occupied in men's memories no more enduring place than this last.   Posterity preserves only what will
pack into small compass.   Jewels are handed down from age to
age; less portable valuables tend to disappear.   And do not
fancy that this is a question of words alone.   You cannot separate manner from matter.   It is very seldom, I fancy, that clear
thought and confused expression go together.   A man can
hardly give pains and time to the manner of saying a thing
without the idea at least crossing his mind—what do I really
mean?   What story have I got to tell?   What is the upshot of
all this?   I say, then, to those whose leisure will allow it, do
not be led into the folly of treating classical study as a thing antiquated and useless.   It is not what people used to think it, the
only training; but it is a training, and not the worst.   Only
let it be taken up in earnest, or not at all   If a young man has
time and taste for Latin literature, so much, I think, the better.
But a mere beginning of that—and, still more, a mere beginning both of Latin and Greek, which does not last long enough
to give familiar acquaintance with either language—is sheer
folly and waste of time.   In this, as in everything else, a man
should proportion his means to his ends, and not begin by laying the foundations of a house three times bigger than he can

ever hope to finish. It is, I think, the neglect of this very obvious rule, it is the aiming at more than can possibly be accomplished in the time allowed that more than anything else has tended to bring classical training into disrepute.

And what I say to you in regard to classics I would extend also to those other studies whose importance is being increasingly recognized in every modern system of education. I will not undertake to lay down a rule (I tell you frankly I do not see my way to do it) as to the proportion which the cultivation of science in its various forms should bear to that of literature and language. We are in a transition state as regards these matters, and it may last, for aught I can see, a long while yet. Much must depend, I conceive, on individual taste and temperament—something on the future destination of the student—something on the opportunities afforded, and the custom of the time and place. But this I think I do see clearly—and it adds to rather than lessens the intricacy of the whole question—that, looking on the one hand to the immense range of scientific knowledge, and on the other to the inevitable shortness of time allotted for learning, in the case of that great majority whose study here is a mere introduction to active life, it is idle to suppose that the actual amount of instruction acquired can bear any appreciable proportion to that which must remain untouched. To learn a little of everything under the sun is barely possible, and questionably useful, if it were possible. *Compendia, dispendia.* The value of all teaching, as I take it, consists far less in the facts acquired than in the action on the mind of the individual produced by the process of acquiring them.

The question which life asks of us all is not, " What do you know? " but, " What can you do? " I believe that any one study, steady and earnestly followed, is useful in that respect; and perhaps the difference in their respective values is less than we are apt to suppose. If a man wants only to train himself to be a good walker it matters very little what road he chooses to walk upon. But more than that—if you will allow me to express an opinion which I know may provoke dissent, but which I entertain very strongly—I believe that no course of reading or lecture-hearing is of much avail unless something is to follow, either in the way of public examination—which I hold to be best—or, failing that, of close and careful self-examination by the student himself, to test and measure how much of what has been read is retained. What is merely listened to or run over by the eye is mostly forgotten; what has to be assimilated and reproduced in another shape becomes, as it were, worked into the very substance of the brain.

One word more on these points and I shall have done. Every age has its fashions, some of them sensible, some very much the reverse; and one of the literary fashions of our time is to sneer at and depreciate what is termed " culture," as though it tended at best to make men skilful in doing things, which, being done, are worthless, and as though there were some natural connection between strength of mind and that kind of simplicity which arises from ignorance. It is noticeable, I think, that that tendency often appears strongest in those whose own culture has been carried to the highest point; and the explanation I would suggest of it is that the discontent with what has been accomplished, which is characteristic of a stirring and progressive time, and that painful sense of the shortness of individual life, compared with what has to be learned and done in it, takes in such minds the form of an undue disparagement of those acquirements which they are conscious of possessing, and a proportionably excessive appreciation of those which they have been compelled to neglect. As a general rule, I think that the aim of a liberal education ought to be not to fit men for this or that special profession exclusively, but to supply such acquirements and to sharpen such faculties as shall be useful in any walk of life. It is not good, I am sure, for anybody to be too early and exclusively buried in his own special pursuit. If from circumstances it is necessary that he should be, let him accept the necessity for that as for any other privation, without complaining But do not let him assert or think that it is in itself a good. Law, medicine, architecture, engineering, practical art—all these are pursuits of the highest usefulness, and even necessity; but no man can even dabble in them all; nor has the architect any particular use for law; nor the lawyer for architecture. What they both want, what they both have a use for, is accuracy of thought, clearness of expression, and that indefinable something—excluding pedantry on the one hand and vulgar coarseness on the other—which marks the man to whom literature has been more than the amusement of a casual hour.

You will sometimes hear it said—it is one of the crotchets of the day—that what is called culture is unfavorable to moral earnestness. Do not believe that. No doubt, like most untrue opinions, it has a shadow of plausibility. A man whose acquirements are few, whose range of knowledge is scanty and limited, is probably more apt than his educated neighbor to throw himself into some cause or controversy with an intense and unreasoning conviction that he is right, and that everybody else is wrong; and he is more likely also to underrate the complexity of human affairs, and to overvalue enormously the importance to mankind of that particular subject which has monopolized his attention. I do not say that that tendency is always and under all circumstances injurious. We are but weak at the best; and, perhaps, if the best and wisest of us all could see in how infinitesimal a degree the destinies of society can be affected by his utmost exertions, such clear-sightedness would serve rather to damp than to stimulate his energy. Happily, one may say in passing, there does not seem the slightest reason to apprehend, in the case of most of us, any process of that kind taking place.

But, admitting all this—admitting that knowledge is often a check on action, and that great questions are often most earnestly taken up by those who can only see one side of them— I think there can be no doubt on which side the balance of advantage lies. If cultivated apathy has done its share of mischief (and recollect that you are just as likely to have the apathy without the cultivation), unreasoning activity, enthusiasm without knowledge or judgment, has done a hundred times more. If increased intellectual light, or what seemed such, has weakened some men's convictions, shaken their faith in the principles which govern mankind, and left them simply perplexed and helpless in face of the great problems of existence, let us point on the other hand to the horrible calamities which men, from the earliest ages of the world to our own, have brought on one another—not, we may hope, in wilful wickedness, but in the confused struggle to defend errors ignorantly and honestly mistaken for truth. No, gentlemen, whatever may come of it, let us not ignore or shrink from our responsibility. Every one of us is bound, not merely to do the thing which seems to him right, but to do also what lies in his power, that the thing which seems to him right may be that which really is right. Good intentions will not help or save you if you take poison instead of medicine, and in social matters we well know that ignorant philanthropy has often caused, perhaps often causes even now, as much mischief as could be done by deliberate ill-will. We want zeal. We want earnestness for truth and justice. But the zeal of ignorance is a poor affair; and the earnestness must be very shallow and unreal which will not bear the strictest scrutiny of the objects to which it is directed. Action is the end of all thought, but to act justly and effectively you must think wisely. The time is not wasted which is spent in laying solid foundations for the future; nor that which soldiers pass in preparatory drill before they are trusted to take the field.

Recollect, too, that the stock of intellectual furniture which a man takes with him into business or professional life is not likely to be much increased afterwards. With most of us, I fear, the faculty of receiving new ideas is the very earliest part of our organization that decays. Special acquirements, professional experience, the caution and prudence and tact that come of protracted intercourse with the world, are the growth of middle age; but I suspect that most busy men if they took stock of their intellectual gains and losses, would find that after a certain time—say five-and-thirty, or forty—the former had not been considerable. Make the most, then, of your opportunity, for it will not last long. Waste no regret on the past if it has done less for you than it ought. There is leisure to redeem all that. Dream no dreams of the future, the future will take care of itself; and whatever may be the difficulties you foresee, whatever the successes you expect, it is a hundred to one that neither the former nor the latter will come upon you in the way you now anticipate. But make your footing good at every step you take; do manfully the task that is allotted to you, know thoroughly the thing you have to learn, discipline your energies without exhausting them, and have faith enough in yourselves and in the good sense of your own fellow-men to believe that whatever temporary success may be won by puffing and quackery (and, thank Heaven, such success is seldom more than temporary), the capable workman mostly gets the tools into his hands; opportunity sooner or later comes to nearly all who work and wait; and though I do not contend that there is no such thing as unmerited failure or unrewarded effort, yet even in that rare and painful case it is something to be able to think that you have tried your best, that though worsted in fair fight you have done justice to yourself and to yours, and that, if advancement and fortune have not been obtained you will have at least preserved that inward content, that sense of honest self-approval, with which neither obscurity nor poverty is an unendurable affliction—without which, neither by world-wide fame nor untold wealth, can any real and lasting happiness be secured.

Gentlemen, I have nothing more to add. It is, perhaps, presumption on my part to offer you advice as I have done. I only ask you to believe that it is sincerely given, and that it comes from one whose strongest sympathies are with intellectual labor. I know very well that spoken or written counsel cannot avail much—that to each man his own experience, his own mistakes, are the best, perhaps the only real, instruction. May your experience be as painless, your mistakes as few, as is compatible with the conditions under which we all live and work; and whatever you become, or wherever you go, I think you will always keep a warm corner in your hearts for that noble old university in which you have had your early training.

THE IMMORTALITY OF THE SOUL

—

BY

JOHN HENRY, CARDINAL NEWMAN

JOHN HENRY, CARDINAL NEWMAN

1801—1890

John Henry Newman was the son of a London banker, and his early days were therefore passed in the comfort and ease which, in men of his spiritual temperament, promote religious meditation and intellectual studies. English refinement and high-breeding were in him united with freedom from materiality and physical grossness. Newman was of a delicate make, yet so well were the elements of his organization balanced, that he lived for ninety years, devoting his whole existence to thought and action upon the highest subjects that can engage the human mind. He was born within a few weeks of the birthday of the nineteenth century—on February 25, 1801.

He went to Oxford, where he took his degree in 1820, from Trinity College, and two years later he was elected a fellow of Oriel. Here he began his friendship with Edward Bouverie Pusey, whose influence upon church thought and procedure was later to become historical. Pusey was less than a year older than Newman, was also a fellow of Oriel, and his mind tended to the same lines of development as did that of the future cardinal.

In 1832, Newman made a voyage up the Mediterranean, which in its effects might be called a religious sentimental pilgrimage. It was during this journey that the poem or hymn, "Lead, Kindly Light," was composed On returning to Oxford, he began to take an active part in the religious discussions of that epoch. There had been a strong drift towards liberalism in the Church of England, and the so-called Oxford Movement was designed to conteract this, and to bring the Church back to the primitive simplicity and faith of the Christian Fathers. Tracts were written and published with this end in view, and what is known as Tractarianism soon became important. Both Newman and Pusey contributed to the propaganda, and the tone of their writings gradually brought them nearer to a belief which was hardly to be distinguished from Roman Catholicism. Pusey was disbarred from preaching for three years for publishing his sermon on "The Holy Eucharist a Comfort to the Penitent", and it was from his initiative that the practice of confession was established among extreme ritualists of the Established Church. Pusey, however, never took the final step which would have separated him from the English communion; but Newman, though for some years he hoped that a middle ground between the Roman and the English dispensations might be found, finally gave up that hope, and in 1843 he formally withdrew from the Anglican Church; and two years afterwards the Roman Catholic Church accepted him as a convert. In 1849 he established an English branch of the Oratory of St Philip Neri, a Roman Catholic religious order founded in 1575, which is composed of simple priests, under no vows. The latter part of his pure and tranquil life was spent in writing and preaching, and under his influence, the Church of Rome received many recruits from England. Newman's literary style is exquisite; and his eloquence as a preacher had a sacred sweetness and fire, and a lofty gentleness of persuasion, unsurpassed in his day.

THE IMMORTALITY OF THE SOUL

What shall a man give in exchange for his soul?—Matt. xvi. 26

I SUPPOSE there is no tolerably informed Christian but considers he has a correct notion of the difference between our religion and the paganism which it supplanted. Everyone, if asked what it is we have gained by the gospel, will promptly answer, that we have gained the knowledge of our immortality, of our having souls which will live forever; that the heathen did not know this, but that Christ taught it and that His disciples know it. Everyone will say, and say truly, that this was the great and solemn doctrine which gave the gospel a claim to be heard when first preached, which arrested the thoughtless multitudes who were busied in the pleasures and pursuits of this life, awed them with the vision of the life to come, and sobered them till they turned to God with a true heart. It will be said, and said truly, that this doctrine of a future life was the doctrine which broke the power and the fascination of paganism. The poor benighted heathen were engaged in all the frivolities and absurdities of a false ritual, which had obscured the light of nature. They knew God, but they forsook Him for the inventions of men; they made protectors and guardians for themselves; and had " gods many and lords many." [1] They had their profane worship, their gaudy processions, their indulgent creed, their easy observances, their sensual festivities, their childish extravagance such as might suitably be the religion of beings who were to live for seventy or eighty years, and then die once for all, never to live again. " Let us eat and drink, for to-morrow we die," was their doctrine and their rule of life. " To-morrow we die; " this the Holy Apostles admitted. They taught so far as the heathen; " To-morrow we die; " but then they added, " And after death the judg-

[1] 1 Cor. viii. 5.

ment "; judgment upon the eternal soul, which lives in spite
of the death of the body. And this was the truth, which awakened men to the necessity of having a better and deeper religion
than that which had spread over the earth, when Christ came
—which so wrought upon them that they left that old false
worship of theirs, and it fell. Yes! though throned in all the
power of the world, a sight such as eye had never before seen,
though supported by the great and the many, the magnificence
of kings and the stubbornness of people, it fell. Its ruins
remain scattered over the face of the earth; the shattered works
of its great upholders, that fierce enemy of God, the pagan
Roman Empire. Those ruins are found even among ourselves,
and show how marvellously great was its power, and therefore
how much more powerful was that which broke its power;
and this was the doctrine of the immortality of the soul. So
entire is the revolution which is produced among men wherever
this high truth is really received.

I have said that every one of us is able fluently to speak of this
doctrine, and is aware that the knowledge of it forms the fundamental difference between our state and that of the heathen.
And yet, in spite of our being able to speak about it and our
" form of knowledge " [2] (as St. Paul terms it), there seems
scarcely room to doubt that the greater number of those who
are called Christians in no true sense realize it in their own
minds at all. Indeed, it is a very difficult thing to bring home
to us, and to feel that we have souls; and there cannot be a
more fatal mistake than to suppose we see what the doctrine
means as soon as we can use the words which signify it. So
great a thing is it to understand that we have souls, that the
knowing it, taken in connection with its results, is all one with
being serious, *i.e.*, truly religious. To discern our immortality
is necessarily connected with fear and trembling and repentance in the case of every Christian. Who is there but would
be sobered by an actual sight of the flames of hell-fire and the
souls therein hopelessly enclosed? Would not all his thoughts
be drawn to that awful sight, so that he would stand still, gazing
fixedly upon it, and forgetting everything else; seeing nothing
else, hearing nothing, engrossed with the contemplation of it;
and when the sight was withdrawn, still having it fixed in his

[2] Rom. ii. 20.

memory, so that he would be henceforth dead to the pleasures and employments of this world, considered in themselves, thinking of them only in their reference to that fearful vision? This would be the overpowering effect of such a disclosure, whether it actually led a man to repentance or not. And thus absorbed in the thought of the life to come are they who really and heartily receive the words of Christ and His Apostles. Yet to this state of mind, and therefore to this true state of knowledge, the multitude of men called Christians are certainly strangers; a thick veil is drawn over their eyes; and in spite of their being being able to talk of the doctrine, they are as if they never had heard of it. They go on just as the heathen did of old; they eat, they drink; or they amuse themselves in vanities, and live in the world, with fear and without sorrow, just as if God had not declared that their conduct in this life would decide their destiny in the next; just as if they either had no souls, or had nothing or little to do with the saving of them, which was the creed of the heathen.

Now let us consider what it is to bring home to ourselves that we have souls, and in what the special difficulty of it lies; for this may be of use to us in our attempt to realize that awful truth.

We are from our birth apparently dependent on things about us. We see and feel that we could not live or go forward without the aid of man. To a child this world is everything; he seems to himself a part of this world—a part of this world in the same sense in which a branch is part of a tree; he has little notion of his own separate and independent existence, that is, he has no just idea he has a soul. He views himself merely in his connection with this world, which is his all; he looks to this world for his good as to an idol; and when he tries to look beyond this life he is able to discern nothing in prospect, because he has no idea of anything, nor can fancy anything, but this life. And if he is obliged to fancy anything, he fancies this life over again; just as the heathen, when they reflected on those traditions of another life, which were floating among them, could but fancy the happiness of the blessed to consist in the enjoyment of the sun, and the sky, and the earth, as before, only as if these were to be more splendid than they are now.

To understand that we have souls is to feel our separation

from things visible, our independence of them, our distinct existence in ourselves, our individuality, our power of acting for ourselves this way or that way, our accountableness for what we do. These are the great truths which lie wrapped up indeed even in a child's mind, and which God's grace can unfold there in spite of the influence of the external world; but at first this outward world prevails. We look off from self to the things around us, and forget ourselves in them. Such is our state—a depending for support on the reeds which are no stay, and overlooking our real strength—at the time when God begins His process of reclaiming us to a truer view of our place in His great system of providence. And when He visits us, then in a little while there is a stirring within us. The unprofitableness and feebleness of the things of this world are forced upon our minds; they promise but cannot perform, they disappoint us. Or, if they do perform what they promise, still (so it is) they do not satisfy us. We still crave for something, we do not well know what; but we are sure it is something which the world has not given us. And then its changes are so many, so sudden, so silent, so continual. It never leaves changing; it goes on to change, till we are quite sick at heart; then it is that our reliance on it is broken. It is plain we cannot continue to depend upon it unless we keep pace with it and go on changing too; but this we cannot do. We feel that, while it changes, we are one and the same; and thus under God's blessing we come to have some glimpse of the meaning of our independence of things temporal, and our immortality. And should it so happen that misfortunes come upon us (as they often do), then still more are we led to understand the nothingness of this world; then still more are we led to distrust it, and are weaned from the love of it, till at length it floats before our eyes merely as some idle veil, which, notwithstanding its many tints, cannot hide the view of what is beyond it—and we begin by degrees to perceive that there are but two things in the whole universe—our own soul, and the God who made it.

Sublime, unlooked-for doctrine, yet most true! To every one of us there are but two beings in the whole world, himself and God; for, as to this outward scene, its pleasures and pursuits, its honors and cares, its contrivances, its personages, its kingdoms, its multitude of busy slaves, what are they to us?

Nothing—no more than a show. "The world passeth away and the lust thereof." And as to those others nearer to us, who are not to be classed with the vain world, I mean our friends and relations, whom we are right in loving, these, too, after all, are nothing to us here. They cannot really help or profit us; we see them, and they act upon us only (as it were) at a distance, through the medium of sense; they cannot get at our souls; they cannot enter into our thoughts, or really be companions to us. In the next world it will, through God's mercy, be otherwise; but here we enjoy, not their presence, but the anticipation of what one day shall be; so that, after all, they vanish before the clear vision we have, first, of our own existence, next of the presence of the great God in us and over us, as our governor and judge, who dwells in us and by our conscience, which is His representative.

And now consider what a revolution will take place in the mind that is not utterly reprobate, in proportion as it realizes this relation between itself and the Most High God. We never in this life can fully understand what is meant by our living forever, but we can understand what is meant by this world's *not* living forever, by its dying never to rise again. And, learning this, we learn that we owe it no service, no allegiance, it has no claim over us, and can do us no material good nor harm. On the other hand, the law of God written on our hearts bids us serve Him, and partly tells us how to serve Him, and Scripture completes the precepts which nature began. And both Scripture and conscience tell us we are answerable for what we do, and that God is a righteous judge; and, above all, our Saviour, as our visible Lord God, takes the place of the world as the only begotten of the Father, having shown himself openly, that we may not say that God is hidden. And thus a man is drawn forward by all manner of powerful influences to turn from things temporal to things eternal, to deny himself, to take up his cross and follow Christ. For there are Christ's awful threats and warnings to make him serious, His precepts to attract and elevate him, His promises to cheer him, His gracious deeds and sufferings to humble him to the dust, and to bind his heart once and forever in gratitude to Him who is so surpassing in mercy. All these things act upon him; and, as truly as St. Matthew rose from the receipt of custom when Christ called, heedless what bystanders would say of him, so they who, through grace, obey the secret voice of God, move onward contrary to the world's way, and careless what mankind may say of them, as understanding that they have souls, which is the one thing they have to care about.

I am well aware that there are indiscreet teachers gone forth into the world, who use language such as I have used, but mean something very different. Such are they who deny the grace of baptism, and think that a man is converted to God all at once. But I have no need now to mention the difference between their teaching and that of Scripture. Whatever their peculiar errors are, so far as they say that we are by nature blind and sinful, and must, through God's grace and our own endeavors, learn that we have souls and rise to a new life, severing ourselves from the world that is, and walking in what is unseen and future, so far they say true, for they speak the words of Scripture; which says, "Awake thou that sleepest, and arise from the dead, and Christ shall give thee light. See, then, that ye walk circumspectly, not as fools, but as wise, redeeming the time, because the days are evil. Wherefore be ye not unwise, but understanding what the will of the Lord is." [3]

Let us, then, seriously question ourselves, and beg of God grace to do so honestly, whether we are loosened from the world; or whether, living as dependent on it, and not on the eternal author of our being, we are in fact taking our portion with this perishing outward scene, and ignorant of our having souls. I know very well that such thoughts are distasteful to the minds of men in general. Doubtless, many a one there is, who, on hearing doctrines such as I have been insisting on, says in his heart that religion is thus made gloomy and repulsive; that he would attend to a teacher who spoke in a less severe way; and that in fact Christianity was not intended to be a dark, burdensome law, but a religion of cheerfulness and joy. This is what young people think, though they do not express it in this argumentative form. They view a strict life as something offensive and hateful; they turn from the notion of it. And then, as they get older and see more of the world, they learn to defend their opinion, and express it more or less in the way in which I have just put it. They hate and oppose the truth, as it were upon

[3] Eph. v. 14-17.

principle; and the more they are told that they have souls the more resolved they are to live as if they had not souls. But let us take it as a clear point from the first, and not to be disputed, that religion must ever be difficult to those who neglect it. All things that we have to learn are difficult at first; and our duties to God, and to man for His sake, are peculiarly difficult, because they call upon us to take up a new life, and quit the love of this world for the next. It cannot be avoided; we must fear and be in sorrow before we can rejoice. The gospel must be a burden before it comforts and brings us peace. No one can have his heart cut away from the natural objects of its love without pain during the process, and throbbings afterwards. This is plain from the nature of the case; and, however true it be that this or that teacher may be harsh and repulsive, yet he cannot materially alter things. Religion is in itself at first a weariness to the worldly mind, and it requires an effort and a self-denial in everyone who honestly determines to be religious.

But there are other persons who are far more hopeful than those I have been speaking of, who, when they hear repentance and newness of life urged on them, are frightened at the thought of the greatness of the work; they are disheartened at being told to do so much. Now let it be well understood that to realize our own individual accountableness and immortality, of which I have been speaking, is not required of them all at once. I never said a person was not in a hopeful way who did not thus fully discern the world's vanity and the worth of his soul. But a man is truly in a very desperate way who does not wish, who does not try, to discern and feel all this. I want a man on the one hand to confess his immortality with his lips, and on the other to live as if he tried to understand his own words, and then he is in the way of salvation; he is in the way towards heaven, even though he has not yet fully emancipated himself from the fetters of this world. Indeed none of us (of course) are entirely loosened from the world. We all use words, in speaking of our duties, higher and fuller than we really understand. No one entirely realizes what is meant by his having a soul; even the best of men is but in a state of progress towards the simple truth; and the most weak and ignorant of those who seek after it cannot but be in progress. And therefore no one need be alarmed at hearing that he has much to do before he arrives at a right view of his own condition in God's sight, *i.e.*, at faith; for we all have much to do, and the great point is, are we willing to do it?

Oh, that there were such a heart in us to put aside this visible world, to desire to look at it as a mere screen between us and God, and to think of Him who has entered in beyond the veil, and who is watching us, trying us, yes, and blessing, and influencing, and encouraging us towards good day by day! Yet, alas, how do we suffer the mere varying circumstances of every day to sway us! How difficult it is to remain firm and in one mind under the seductions or terrors of the world! We feel variously according to the place, time, and people we are with. We are serious on Sunday, and we sin deliberately on Monday. We rise in the morning with remorse at our offences and resolutions of amendment, yet before night we have transgressed again. The mere change of society puts us into a new frame of mind; nor do we sufficiently understand this great weakness of ours, or seek for strength where alone it can be found, in the unchangeable God. What will be our thoughts in that day, when at length this outward world drops away altogether, and we find ourselves where we ever have been, in His presence, with Christ standing at His right hand?

On the contrary, what a blessed discovery it is to those who make it, that this world is but vanity and without substance; and that really they are ever in their Saviour's presence. This is a thought which it is scarcely right to enlarge upon in a mixed congregation, where there may be some who have not given their hearts to God; for why should the privileges of the true Christian be disclosed to mankind at large, and sacred subjects, which are his peculiar treasure, be made common to the careless liver? He knows his blessedness, and needs not another to tell it him. He knows in whom he has believed; and in the hour of danger or trouble he knows what is meant by that peace which Christ did not explain when He gave it to His Apostles, but merely said it was not as the world could give.

" Thou wilt keep him in perfect peace whose mind is stayed on Thee; because he trusteth in Thee. Trust ye in the Lord forever: for in the Lord Jehovah is everlasting strength." [4]

<hr>

[4] Isaiah, xxvi. 3, 4.

CHOICE EXAMPLES OF EARLY PRINTING AND ENGRAVING.

Fac-similes from Rare and Curious Books.

EARLY VENETIAN PRINTING.

Roman missal printed at Venice in 1520 by Lucantonio de Giunta

A combination of red-lettering and black and white border which produces an effect pre-eminently rich and majestic   At the summit of the border St Peter is represented presiding at a conference of the apostles   Beneath this picture is a second, narrower border decorated with two sphinxes, whose tails, in true Roman fashion, are developed into double spirals of floriated ornaments.   This narrower border is continued down the two inner edges of the side panels, in which are seen a long series of ecclesiastical vestments and utensils   On the right is the papal tiara, below it the episcopal mitre, pastoral staffs, chalices, candlesticks, rosaries, a chasuble, a cross, the two keys, a cope, a stole and two cruets on a tray   The whole of these figures are symmetrically arranged on a central line and the general effect is that of a harmonious distribution of white and black—somewhat bizarre and lace-like, but rich and genuinely decorative   The other side of the page re peats the motive

Missale Romanū nouiter ipressuz
cū annotationibus in margine
ad facillime oia que i ipso ad
alias paginas remittútur
inueniéda: Et qñ alicu'
sancti missa iperfecta é:
notatus é locus vbi
inquiru debeat. In
super cū figuris
festiuitatum ac
euangelioꝝ initia exoꝛnanti
bus iuxta materiá cōtentá di
ligentissime accommodatis.

Lucantoniū de giunta floretinum. M.D.XX.

ON THE EFFECTS OF PROTECTION

—

BY

RICHARD COBDEN

RICHARD COBDEN

1804—1865

Richard Cobden was a man whom the English people loved, and who is held in affectionate remembrance by Americans, both on account of his labors for the welfare of humanity, and because, during the Civil War, he supported the cause of the North. He was born in Sussex in 1804, and died in London in 1865; and it was said by the man who knew him best that his was "the manliest and gentlest spirit that ever tenanted or quitted a human breast"

When a man of pure character and single ability devotes his entire life to advocating a measure of enlightened reform and philanthropy, the odds are in his favor, and Cobden, in his support of free trade, and of the repeal of the Corn Laws, seems not only to have reaped the natural reward of his persistent exertions, but to have been favored by Providence. His youth made him acquainted with the evils of poverty brought about by errors of political economy; and his young manhood was passed in a situation where he could personally examine the state of English industries, and the condition and needs of the working people. By the time his investigation had enabled him to formulate a policy by which the pressure of hard times could be relieved, he had accumulated, by the calico-printing industry, a fortune sufficient to support him while engaged in the work of impressing his views upon Parliament and the people; and for seven years he applied himself to this duty with such surprising energy, faith, and ability, that the end was victory. He instituted a vast propaganda, involving a house-to-house visitation throughout England, distributing pamphlets which presented the cause of free trade in such simple terms that anyone could understand them, and supplemented by open-air speeches, in which the multitude was instructed how they might act in order to obtain the repeal of the existing injurious laws Not less than one hundred and forty thousand pounds was expended in this work in the course of only two years, but the results warranted the outlay; and when all was ready, a bad agricultural season created such distress in the country and so powerful a feeling in favor of Cobden's measures, that Parliament was unable to withstand the pressure, and on June 26, 1846, the Reform Bill was passed Since then free trade has been the policy of England

Cobden entered Parliament in 1841, and at once made his mark there by a speech on his chosen theme In 1854 he visited the United States, and in 1859 he again entered Parliament His style of address was plain, simple, and direct, backed by an obvious honesty of purpose, and great keenness and persuasiveness of argument. He was able to move the great mass of the people, and to stimulate them to action, in a way that no contemporary could rival His speech, "On the Effects of Protection," delivered in the House on March 13, 1845, is one of the ablest and most characteristic speeches of his career.

ON THE EFFECTS OF PROTECTION

Delivered in the House of Commons, March 13, 1845

SIR: ,I am relieved upon the present occasion from any necessity for apologizing to the other side of the House for the motion which I am about to submit. It will be in the recollection of honorable members that a fortnight before putting this notice upon the book I expressed a hope that the matter would be taken up by some honorable member opposite. I do not think, therefore, that in reply to any observations I may have to make upon the question, I shall hear, as I did last year, an observation that the quarter from which this motion came was suspicious. I may also add, sir, that I have so framed my motion as to include in it the objects embraced in both the amendments which are made to it. I therefore conclude, that having included the honorable gentlemen's amendments [Mr. Stafford O'Brien and Mr. Wodehouse], they will not now feel it necessary to press them.

Sir, the object of this motion is to appoint a select committee to inquire into the present condition of the agricultural interests; and, at the same time, to ascertain how the laws regulating the importation of agricultural produce have affected the agriculturists of this country. As regards the distress among farmers, I presume we cannot go to a higher authority than those honorable gentlemen who profess to be the farmers' friends and protectors. I find it stated by those honorable gentlemen who recently paid their respects to the Prime Minister that the agriculturists are in a state of great embarrassment and distress. I find that one gentleman from Norfolk [Mr. Hudson] stated that the farmers in the county are paying their rents, but paying them out of capital, and not profits. I find Mr. Turner of Upton, in Devonshire, stating that one-half of the smaller farmers in that county are insolvent, and that the others

are rapidly falling into the same condition; that the farmers
with larger holdings are quitting their farms with a view of
saving the rest of their property; and that, unless some remedial
measures be adopted by this House, they will be utterly ruined.
The accounts which I have given you of those districts are
such as I have had from many other sources. I put it to honorable gentlemen opposite whether the condition of the farmers
in Suffolk, Wiltshire, and Hampshire, is better than that which
I have described in Norfolk and Devonshire? I put it to county
members, whether—taking the whole of the south of England,
from the confines of Nottinghamshire to the Land's End—
whether, as a rule, the farmers are not now in a state of the
greatest embarrassment? There may be exceptions; but I put
it to them whether, as a rule, that is not their condition in all
parts?

Then, sir, according to every precedent in this House, this
is a fit and proper time to bring forward the motion of which I
have given notice. I venture to state that had his grace of
Buckingham possessed a seat in this House, he would have done
now what he did when he was Lord Chandos—have moved
this resolution which I am now about to move. The distress of
the farmers being admitted, the next question which arises is,
What is its cause? I feel a greater necessity to bring forward
this motion for a committee of inquiry, because I find great
discrepancies of opinion among honorable gentlemen opposite
as to what is the cause of the distress among the farmers. In
the first place there is a discrepancy as to the generality or
locality of the existing distress. I find the right honorable
baronet at the head of the Government [Sir Robert Peel] saying
that the distress is local; and he moreover says it does not arise
from the legislation of this House. The honorable member for
Dorsetshire declares, on the other hand, that the distress is
general, and that it does not arise from legislation. I am at a
loss to understand what this protection to agriculture means,
because I find such contradictory accounts given in this House
by the promoters of that system. For instance, nine months
ago, when my honorable friend, the member for Wolverhamp-
ton [Mr. Villiers], brought forward his motion for the abolition
of the Corn Laws, the right honorable gentleman, then the
President of the Board of Trade, in replying to him, said that

the present Corn Law had been most successful in its operations. He took great credit to the government for the steadiness of price that was obtained under that law. I will read you
the quotation, because we find these statements so often controverted. He said:

" Was there any man who had supported the law in the year
1842 who could honestly say that he had been disappointed in
its workings? Could anyone point out a promise or a prediction hazarded in the course of the protracted debates upon the
measure, which promise or prediction had been subsequently
falsified? "

Now, recollect that the right honorable gentleman was speaking when wheat was fifty-six shillings per quarter, and that
wheat is now forty-five shillings. The right honorable baronet
at the head of the Government now says: " My legislation has
had nothing to do with wheat at forty-five shillings a quarter ";
but how are we to get over the difficulty that the responsible
member of Government at the head of the Board of Trade, only
nine months ago, claimed merit for the Government having kept
up the price of wheat at fifty-six shillings? These discrepancies
themselves between the Government and its supporters, render
it more and more necessary that this question of protection
should be inquired into. I ask, 'What does it mean? The price
of wheat is forty-five shillings this day. I have been speaking
to the highest authority in England upon this point—one who is
often quoted by this House—within the last week, and he tells
me, that with another favorable harvest, he thinks it very likely
that wheat will be thirty-five shillings a quarter. What does
this legislation mean, or what does it purport to be, if you are
to have prices fluctuating from fifty-six shillings down to thirty-
five shillings a quarter, and probably lower? Can you prevent
it by the legislation of this House? That is the question. There
is a great delusion spread abroad amongst the farmers; and
it is the duty of this House to have that delusion dissipated by
inquiring into the matter.

Now, there are these very different opinions on the other
side of the House; but there are members upon this side representing very important interests, who think that farmers are
suffering because they have this legislative protection. There
is all this difference of opinion. Now, is not that a fit and proper

subject for your inquiry? I am prepared to go into a select committee, and to bring forward evidence to show that the farmers are laboring under great evils—evils that I would connect with the legislation of this House, though they are evils which appear to be altogether dissociated from it. The first great evil under which the farmer labors is the want of capital. No one can deny that. I do not mean at all to disparage the farmers. The farmers of this country are just the same race as the rest of us; and, if they were placed in a similar position, theirs would be as good a trade—I mean that they would be as successful men of business—as others; but it is notorious, as a rule, that the farmers of this country are deficient in capital; and I ask, How can any business be carried on successfully where there is a deficiency of capital? I take it that honorable gentlemen opposite, acquainted with farming, would admit that ten pounds an acre, on an arable farm, would be a sufficient amount of capital for carrying on the business of farming successfully. I will take it, then, that ten pounds an acre would be a fair capital for an arable farm. I have made many inquiries upon this subject in all parts of the kingdom, and I give it you as my decided conviction, that at this present moment farmers do not average five pounds an acre capital on their farms. I speak of England, and I take England south of the Trent, though, of course, there are exceptions in every county; there are men of large capital in all parts—men farming their own land; but, taking it as a rule, I hesitate not to give my opinion —and I am prepared to back that opinion by witnesses before your committee—that, as a rule, farmers have not, upon an average, more than five pounds an acre capital for their arable land. I have given you a tract of country to which I may add all Wales; probably 20,000,000 of acres of cultivable land. I have no doubt whatever that there are £100,000,000 of capital wanting upon that land. What is the meaning of farming capital? There are strange notions about the word "capital." It means more manure, a greater amount of labor, a greater number of cattle, and larger crops. Picture a country in which you can say there is a deficiency of one-half of all those blessings which ought to, and might, exist there, and then judge what the condition of laborers wanting employment and food is.

But you will say, capital would be invested if it could be done

with profit. I admit it; that is the question I want you to inquire into. How is it that in a country where there is a plethora
of capital, where every other business and pursuit is overflowing with money, where you have men going to France for
railways and to Pennsylvania for bonds, embarking in schemes
for connecting the Atlantic with the Pacific by canals, railways
in the valley of the Mississippi, and sending their money to the
bottom of the Mexican mines; while you have a country rich
and overflowing, ready to take investments in every corner of
the globe; how is it, I say, that this capital does not find its
employment in the most attractive of all forms—upon the soil
of this country? The cause is notorious—it is admitted by your
highest authorities; the reason is, there is not security for
capital in land. Capital shrinks instinctively from insecurity
of tenure; and you have not in England that security which
would warrant men of capital investing their money in the soil.

Now, is it not a matter worthy of consideration, how far
this insecurity of tenure is bound up with that protective system of which you are so enamored? Suppose it can be shown
that there is a vicious circle; that you have made politics of
Corn Laws, and that you want voters to maintain them; that
you very erroneously think that the Corn Laws are your great
mine of wealth, and, therefore, you must have a dependent tenantry, that you may have their votes at elections to maintain
this law in Parliament. Well, if you will have dependent voters,
you cannot have men of spirit and capital. Then your policy
reacts upon you If you have not men of skill and capital, you
cannot have improvements and employment for your laborers.
Then comes round that vicious termination of the circle—you
have pauperism, poor-rates, county-rates, and all the other evils
of which you are now speaking and complaining.

But here I have to quote authorities, and I shall quote some
of the highest consideration with the opposite side of the
House. I will just state the opinion of the honorable member for Berkshire [Mr. Pusey], delivered at the meeting of the
Suffolk Agricultural Society. That honorable gentleman said:

" He knew this country well, and he knew there was not a
place from Plymouth to Berwick in which the landlords might
not make improvements; but when the tenant was short of
money, the landlord generally would be short of money too.

But he would tell them how to find funds. There were many districts where there was a great superfluity not only of useless, but of mischievous timber; and if they would cut that down which excluded the sun and air, and fed on the soil, and sell it, they would benefit the farmer by cutting it down, and they would benefit the farmer and laborer too by laying out the proceeds in underdraining the soil. There was another mode in which they might find money. He knew that on some properties a large sum was spent in the preservation of game. It was not at all unusual for the game to cost £500 or £600 a year; and if this were given up, the money would employ a hundred able-bodied laborers in improving the property. This was another fund for the landlords of England to benefit the laborers, and the farmers at the same time."

Again, at the Colchester agricultural meeting:

" Mr. Fisher Hobbes was aware that a spirit of improvement was abroad. Much was said about the tenant-farmers doing more. He agreed they might do more: the soil of the country was capable of greater production; if he said one-fourth more he should be within compass. But that could not be done by the tenant-farmer alone; they must have confidence; it must be done by leases—by draining—by extending the length of fields—by knocking down hedge-rows, and clearing away trees which now shielded the corn."

But there was still higher authority. At the late meeting at Liverpool, Lord Stanley declared:

" I say, and as one connected with the land I feel myself bound to say it, that a landlord has no right to expect any great and permanent improvement of his land by the tenant, unless that tenant be secured the repayment of his outlay, not by the personal character or honor of his landlord, but by a security which no casualties can interfere with—the security granted him by the terms of a lease for years."

Now, sir, not only does the want of security prevent capital flowing into the farming business, but it actually deters from the improvement of the land those who are already in the occupation of it. There are many men, tenants of your land, who could improve their farms if they had a sufficient security, and they have either capital themselves or their friends could supply it; but with the absence of leases, and the want of security, you are actually deterring them from laying out their money on your land. They keep everything the same from year to year. You know that it is impossible to farm your estates properly unless a tenant has an investment for more than one year. A man ought to be able to begin a farm with at least eight years before him, before he expects to see a return for the whole of the outlay of his money. You are, therefore, keeping your tenants-at-will at a yearly kind of cultivation, and you are preventing them carrying on their business in a proper way. Not only do you prevent the laying out of capital upon your land, and disable the farmers from cultivating it, but your policy tends to make them servile and dependent; so that they are actually disinclined to improvement, afraid to let you see that they can improve, because they are apprehensive that you will pounce upon them for an increase of rent. I see the honorable member for Lincolnshire opposite, and he rather smiled at the expression when I said that the state of dependence of the farmers was such that they were actually afraid to appear to be improving their land. Now that honorable gentleman, the member for Lincoln-shire [Mr. Christopher], upon the motion made last year for agricultural statistics, by my honorable friend, the member for Manchester [Mr. Milner Gibson], made the following state-ment:

" It is most desirable for the farmer to know the actual quan-tity of corn grown in this country, as such knowledge would in-sure steadiness of prices, which was infinitely more valuable to the agriculturist than fluctuating prices. But to ascertain this there was extreme difficulty. They could not leave it to the farmer to make a return of the quantity which he produced, for it was not for his interest to do so. If in any one or two years he produced four quarters per acre on land which had previously grown but three, he might fear that his landlord would say: ' Your land is more productive than I imagined, and I must therefore raise your rent.' The interest of the farmers, there-fore, would be to underrate, and to furnish low returns."

Now, I ask honorable gentlemen here, the landed gentry of England, what a state of things is that when, upon their own testimony respecting the farming capitalists in this country, they dare not appear to have a good horse—they dare not appear to be growing more than four quarters instead of three? [Mr.

Christopher: Hear!] The honorable member cheers, but I am quoting from his own authority. I say this condition of things, indicated by these two quotations, brings the tenant-farmers—if they are such as these gentlemen describe them to be—it brings them down to a very low point of servility. In Egypt Mehemet Ali takes the utmost grain of corn from his people, who bury it beneath their hearthstones in their cottages, and will suffer the bastinado rather than tell how much corn they grow. Our tenants are not afraid of the bastinado, but they are terrified at the rise of rent. This is the state of things amongst the tenant-farmers, farming without leases. In England leases are the exception, and not the rule. But even where you have leases in England—where you have leases or agreements—I doubt whether they are not in many cases worse tenures than where there is no lease at all; the clauses being of such an obsolete and preposterous character as to defy any man to carry on the business of farming under them profitably.

Now, I do not know why we should not in this country have leases for land upon similar terms to the leases of manufactories, or any " plant " or premises. I do not think that farming will ever be carried on as it ought to be until you have leases drawn up in the same way as a man takes a manufactory, and pays perhaps £1,000 a year for it. I know people who pay £4,000 a year for manufactories to carry on their business, and at fair rents. There is an honorable gentleman near me who pays more than £4,000 a year for the rent of his manufactory. What covenants do you think he has in his lease? What would he think if it stated how many revolutions there should be in a minute of the spindles, or if they prescribed the construction of the straps or the gearing of the machinery? Why, he takes his manufactory with a schedule of its present state—bricks, mortar, and machinery—and when the lease is over, he must leave it in the same state, or else pay a compensation for the dilapidation. [The Chancellor of the Exchequer: Hear! hear!] The right honorable gentleman, the Chancellor of the Exchequer, cheers that statement. I want to ask his opinion respecting a similar lease for a farm. I am rather disposed to think that the Anti-Corn-Law Leaguers will very likely form a joint-stock association, having none but free-traders in the body, that we may purchase an estate and have a model farm; taking care that it shall be in one of the rural counties, one of the most purely agricultural parts of the country, where we think there is the greatest need of improvement—perhaps in Buckinghamshire—and there shall be a model farm, homestead, and cottages; and I may tell the noble lord, the member for Newark, that we shall have a model garden, and we will not make any boast about it. But the great object will be to have a model lease. We will have as the farmer a man of intelligence and capital.

I am not so unreasonable as to tell you that you ought to let your land to men who have not a competent capital, or are not sufficiently intelligent; but I say, select such a man as that, let him know his business and have a sufficient capital, and you cannot give him too wide a scope. We will find such a man, and will let him our farm; there shall be a lease precisely such as that upon which my honorable friend takes his factory. There shall be no clause inserted in it to dictate to him how he shall cultivate his farm; he shall do what he likes with the old pasture. If he can make more by ploughing it up he shall do so; if he can grow white crops every year—which I know there are people doing at this moment in more places than one in this country—or if he can make any other improvement or discovery, he shall be free to do so. We will let him the land, with a schedule of the state of tillage and the condition of the homestead, and all we will bind him to will be this: " You shall leave the land as good as when you entered upon it. If it be in an inferior state it shall be valued again, and you shall compensate us; but if it be in an improved state it shall be valued, and we, the landlords, will compensate you." We will give possession of everything upon the land, whether it be wild or tame animals; he shall have the absolute control. Take as stringent precautions as you please to compel the punctual payment of the rent; take the right of reëntry as summarily as you like if the rent be not duly paid; but let the payment of rent duly be the sole test as to the well-doing of the tenant; and so long as he can pay the rent, and do it promptly, that is the only criterion you need have that the farmer is doing well; and if he is a man of capital, you have the strongest possible security that he will not waste your property while he has possession of it.

Now, sir, I have mentioned a deficiency of capital as being the primary want among farmers. I have stated the want of security in leases as the cause of the want of capital; but you may still say: "You have not connected this with the Corn Laws and the protective system." I will read the opinion of an honorable gentleman who sits upon this side of the House; it is in a published letter of Mr. Hayter, who, I know, is himself an ardent supporter of agriculture. He says:

" The more I see of and practise agriculture, the more firmly am I convinced that the whole unemployed labor of the country could, under a better system of husbandry, be advantageously put into operation; and, moreover, that the Corn Laws have been one of the principal causes of the present system of bad farming and consequent pauperism. Nothing short of their entire removal will ever induce the average farmer to rely upon anything else than the legislature for the payment of his rent; his belief being that all rent is paid by corn, and nothing else than corn, and that the legislature can, by enacting Corn Laws, create a price which will make his rent easy. The day of their [the Corn Laws'] entire abolition ought to be a day of jubilee and rejoicing to every man interested in land."

Now, sir, I do not stop to connect the cause and effect in this matter, and inquire whether your Corn Laws or your protective system has caused the want of leases and capital. I do not stop to make good my proof, and for this reason, that you have adopted a system of legislation in this House by which you profess to make the farming trade prosperous. I show you, after thirty years' trial, what is the depressed condition of the agriculturists; I prove to you what is the impoverished state of farmers, and also of laborers, and you will not contest any one of those propositions. I say it is enough, having had thirty days' trial of your specific with no better results than these, for me to ask you to go into committee to see if something better cannot be devised. I am going to contend that free trade in grain would be more advantageous to farmers—and with them I include laborers—than restriction; to oblige the honorable member for Norfolk, I will take with them also the landlords; and I contend that free trade in corn and grain of every kind would be more beneficial to them than to any other class of the community. I should have contended the same before the passing of the late tariff, but now I am prepared to do so with ten-fold more force. What has the right honorable baronet [Sir R. Peel] done? He has passed a law to admit fat cattle at a nominal duty. Some foreign fat cattle were selling in Smith-field the other day at about fifteen pounds or sixteen pounds per head, paying only about seven and one-half per cent. duty; but he has not admitted the raw material out of which these fat cattle are made. Mr. Huskisson did not act in this manner when he commenced his plan of free trade. He began by ad-mitting the raw material of manufactures before he admitted the manufactured article; but in your case you have commenced at precisely the opposite end, and have allowed free trade in cattle instead of that upon which they are fattened. I say give free trade in that grain which goes to make the cattle. I con-tend that by this protective system the farmers throughout the country are more injured than any other class in the community. I would take, for instance, the article of clover-seed. The hon-orable member for North Northamptonshire put a question the other night to the right honorable baronet at the head of the Government. He looked so exceedingly alarmed that I won-dered what the subject was which created the apprehension. He asked the right honorable baronet whether he was going to admit clover-seed into this country. I believe clover-seed is to be excluded from the schedule of free importation. Now, I ask for whose benefit is this exception made? I ask the honor-able gentleman, the member for North Northamptonshire, whether those whom he represents, the farmers of that district of the county, are, in a large majority of instances, sellers of clover-seed? I will undertake to say they are not. How many counties in England are there which are benefited by the pro-tection of clover-seed? I will take the whole of Scotland. If there be any Scotch members present, I ask them whether they do not in their country import the clover-seed from England? They do not grow it I undertake to say that there are not ten counties in the United Kingdom which are interested in the importation of clover-seed out of their own borders. Neither have they any of this article in Ireland. But yet we have clover-seed excluded from the farmers, although they are not interested as a body in its protection at all.

Again, take the article of beans. There are lands in Essex

where they can grow them alternate years with wheat. I find
that beans come from that district to Mark Lane; and I believe
also that in some parts of Lincolnshire and Cambridgeshire they
do the same; but how is it with the poor lands of Surrey or the
poor down-land of Wiltshire? Take the whole of the counties.
How many of them are there which are exporters of beans, or
send them to market? You are taxing the whole of the farmers
who do not sell their beans, for the pretended benefit of a few
counties or districts of counties where they do. Mark you,
where they can grow beans on the stronger and better soils, it
is not in one case out of ten that they grow them for the market.
They may grow them for their own use; but where they do
not cultivate beans, send them to market, and turn them into
money, those farmers can have no interest whatever in keeping
up the money price of that which they never sell.

Take the article of oats. How many farmers are there who
ever have oats down on the credit side of their books, as an
item upon which they rely for the payment of their rents?
The farmers may, and generally do, grow oats for feeding their
own horses; but it is an exception to the rule—and a rare exception, too—where the farmer depends upon the sale of his
oats to meet his expenses. Take the article of hops. You have a
protection upon them for the benefit of the growers in Kent,
Sussex, and Surrey; but yet the cultivators of hops are taxed
for the protection of others in articles which they do not themselves produce. Take the article of cheese. Not one farmer in
ten in the whole country makes his own cheese, and yet they
and their servants are large consumers of it. But what are the
counties which have the protection in this article? Cheshire,
Gloucestershire, Wiltshire, part of Derbyshire, and Leicester-
shire. Here are some four or five dairy counties having an interest in the protection of cheese; but recollect that those counties are peculiarly hardly taxed in beans and oats, because in
those counties where there are chiefly dairy farms, they are most
in want of artificial food for their cattle. There are the whole
of the hilly districts; and I hope my friend, the member for
Nottingham [Mr. Gisborne], is here, because he has a special
grievance in this matter. He lies in Derbyshire, and very com-
mendably employs himself in rearing good cattle upon the hills:
but he is taxed for your protection for his beans, peas, oats,

Indian corn, and everything which he wants for feeding them. He told me, only the other day, that he should like nothing better than to give up the little remnant of protection on cattle, if you would only let him buy a thousand quarters of black oats for the consumption of his stock. Take the whole of the hilly districts, and the down country of Wiltshire; the whole of that expanse of downs in the south of England; take the Cheviots, where the flock-masters reside; the Grampians in Scotland; and take the whole of Wales, they are not benefited in the slightest degree by the protection on these articles; but, on the contrary, you are taxing the very things they want. They require provender as abundantly and cheaply as they can get it. Allowing a free importation of food for cattle is the only way in which those counties can improve the breed of their lean stocks, and the only manner in which they can ever bring their land up to anything like a proper state of fertility.

I will go further and say, that farmers with thin soil—I mean the stock farmers, whom you will find in Hertfordshire and Surrey, farmers with large capitals, arable farmers—I say those men are deeply interested in having a free importation of food for their cattle, because they have thin, poor land. This land of its own self does not contain the means of its increased fertility; and the only way is the bringing in of an additional quantity of food from elsewhere, that they can bring up their farms to a proper state of cultivation. I have been favored with an estimate made by a very experiencéd, clever farmer in Wiltshire—probably honorable gentlemen will bear me out, when I say a man of great intelligence and skill, and entitled to every consideration in this House. I refer to Mr. Nathaniel Atherton, Kingston, Wilts. That gentleman estimates that upon four hundred acres of land he could increase his profits to the amount of £280, paying the same rent as at present, provided there was a free importation of foreign grain of all kinds. He would buy five hundred quarters of oats at fifteen shillings, or the same amount in beans or peas at fourteen shillings or fifteen shillings a sack, to be fed on the land or in the yard; by which he would grow additional one hundred and sixty quarters of wheat, and two hundred and thirty quarters of barley, and gain an increased profit of £300 upon his sheep and cattle. His plan embraces the employment of an additional capital of

£1,000; and he would pay £150 a year more for labor. I had an opportunity, the other day, of speaking to a very intelligent farmer in Hertfordshire. Mr. Lattimore, of Wheathampstead. Very likely there are honorable members here to whom he is known. I do not know whether the noble lord, the member for Hertfordshire is present; if so, he will, no doubt, know that Mr. Lattimore stands as high in Hertford market as a skilful farmer and a man of abundant capital as any in the county. He is a gentleman of most unquestionable intelligence; and what does he say? He told me that last year he paid £230 enhanced price on his beans and other provender which he bought for his cattle—£230 enhanced price in consequence of that restriction upon the trade in foreign grain, amounting to fourteen shillings a quarter on all the wheat he sold off his farm.

Now, I undertake to say, in the name of Mr. Atherton, of Wiltshire, and Mr. Lattimore, of Hertfordshire, that they are as decided advocates for free trade in grain of every kind as I am. I am not now quoting merely solitary cases. I told honorable gentlemen once before that I have probably as large an acquaintance among farmers as anyone in the House. I think I could give you from every county the names of some of the first-rate farmers who are as ardent free-traders as I am. I requested the secretary of this much dreaded Anti-Corn-Law League to make me out a list of the farmers who are subscribers to that association; and I find there are upwards of one hundred in England and Scotland who subscribe to the league fund, comprising, I hesitate not to say, the most intelligent men to be found in the kingdom. I went into the Lothians, at the invitation of twenty-two farmers there, several of whom were paying upwards of £1,000 a year rent. I spent two or three days among them, and I never found a body of more intelligent, liberal-minded men in my life. Those are men who do not want restrictions upon the importation of grain. They desire nothing but fair play. They say: " Let us have our Indian corn, Egyptian beans, and Polish oats as freely as we have our linseed cake, and we can bear competition with any corn-growers in the world." But by excluding the provender for cattle, and at the same time admitting the cattle almost duty free, I think you are giving an example of one of the greatest absurdities and perversions of nature and common-sense that ever was seen.

We have heard of great absurdities in legislation in commercial matters of late   We know that there has been such a case as sending coffee from Cuba to the Cape of Good Hope, in order to bring it back to England under the law; but I venture to say, that in less than ten years from this time, people will look back with more amazement in their minds, at the fact that, while you are sending ships to Ichaboe to bring back the guano, you are passing a law to exclude Indian corn, beans, oats, peas, and everything else that gives nourishment to your cattle, which would give you a thousand times more productive manure than all the guano of Ichaboe.

Upon the last occasion when I spoke upon this subject I was answered by the right honorable gentleman, the President of the Board of Trade. He talked about throwing poor lands out of cultivation, and converting arable lands into pasture. I hope that we men of the Anti-Corn-Law League may not be reproached again with seeking to cause any such disasters. My belief is—and the conviction is founded upon a most extensive inquiry among the most intelligent farmers, without stint of trouble and pains—that the course you are pursuing tends every hour to throw land out of cultivation, and make poor lands unproductive. Do not let us be told again that we desire to draw the laborers from the land in order that we may reduce the wages of the work-people employed in factories   I tell you that if you bestow capital on the soil and cultivate it with the same skill as manufacturers bestow upon their business, you have not population enough in the rural districts for the purpose. I yesterday received a letter from Lord Ducie, in which he gives precisely the same opinion. He says: " If we had the land properly cultivated there are not sufficient laborers to till it " You are chasing your laborers from village to village, passing laws to compel people to support paupers, devising every means to smuggle them abroad—to the antipodes—if you can get them there; why, you would have to run after them and bring them back again if you had your land properly cultivated. I tell you honestly my conviction, that it is by these means, and these only, that you can avert very great and serious troubles and disasters in your agricultural districts

Sir, I remember, on the last occasion when this subject was discussed, there was a great deal said about disturbing an inter-

est. · It was said this inquiry could not be gone into because
we were disturbing and unsettling a great interest. I have no
desire to undervalue the agricultural interest. I have heard
it said that they are the greatest consumers of manufactured
goods in this country; that they are such large consumers of
our goods that we had better look after the home trade, aand
not think of destroying it. But what sort of consumers of manufactures think you the laborers can be, with the wages they
are now getting in agricultural districts? Understand me; I
am arguing for a principle that I solemnly believe would raise
the wages of the laborers in the agricultural districts. I believe you would have no men starving upon seven shillings a
week if you had abundant capital and competent skill employed
upon the soil; but I ask what is this consumption of manufactured goods that we have heard so much about? I have taken
some pains, and made large inquiries as to the amount laid out
in the average of cases by agricultural laborers and their families. You have 960,000 agricultural laborers in England and
Wales, according to the last census; I undertake to say they do
not expend on an average thirty shillings a year on their families, supposing every one of them to be in employ. I speak
of manufactured goods, excluding shoes. I assert that the
whole of the agricultural peasantry and their families in England and Wales do not spend a million and a half per annum
for manufactured goods, in clothing and bedding. And, with
regard to your excisable and duty-paying articles, what can the
poor wretch lay out upon them, who out of eight shillings or
nine shillings a week has a wife and family to support? I undertake to prove to your satisfaction—and you may do it
yourselves if you will but dare to look the figures in the face—
I will undertake to prove to you that they do not pay, upon an
average, each family fifteen shillings per annum; that the whole
of their contributions to the revenue do not amount to £700,000.
Now, is not this a mighty interest to be disturbed? I would
keep that interest as justly as though it were one of the most
important; but I say, when you have by your present system
brought down your agricultural peasantry to that state, have
you anything to offer for bettering their condition, or at all
events to justify resisting an inquiry?

On the last occasion when I addressed the House on this

subject I recollect stating some facts to show that you had no reasonable ground to fear foreign competition; those facts I do not intend to reiterate, because they have never been contradicted. But there are still attempts made to frighten people by telling them: " If you open the ports to foreign corn you will have corn let in here for nothing." One of the favorite fallacies which are now put forth is this: " Look at the price of corn in England and see what it is abroad; you have prices low here, and yet you have corn coming in from abroad and paying the maximum duty. Now, if you had not twenty shillings duty to pay what a quantity of corn you would have brought in, and how low the price would be!" This statement arises from a fallacy—I hope not dishonestly put forth—in not understanding the difference between the real and the nominal price of corn. The price of corn at Dantzic now, when there is no regular sale, is nominal; the price of corn when it is coming in regularly is the real price. Now, go back to 1838. In January of that year the price of wheat at Dantzic was nominal; there was no demand for England; there were no purchasers except for speculation, with the chance, probably, of having to throw the wheat into the sea; but in the months of July and August of that year, when apprehensions arose of a failure of our harvest, then the price of corn in Dantzic rose instantly, sympathizing with the markets of England; and at the end of the year, in December, the price of wheat at Dantzic had doubled the amount at which it had been in January; and during the three following years, when you had a regular importation of corn—during all that time, by the averages laid upon the table of this House, wheat at Dantzic averaged forty shillings. Wheat at Dantzic was at that price during the three years 1839, 1840, and 1841. Now, I mention this just to show the fact to honorable gentlemen, and to entreat them that they will not go and alarm their tenantry by this outcry of the danger of foreign competition. You ought to be pursuing a directly opposite course—you ought to be trying to stimulate them in every possible way, by showing that they can compete with foreigners; that what others can do in Poland, they can do in England.

I have an illustration of this subject in the case of a society of which the honorable member for Suffolk is chairman. We have lately seen a new light spreading amongst agricultural

gentlemen.   We are told the salvation of this country is to arise
from the cultivation of flax.   There is a National Flax Society,
of which Lord Rendlesham is the president.   This Flax Society state in their prospectus, a copy of which I have here,
purporting to be the first annual report of the National Flax
Agricultural Improvement Association—after talking of the
ministers holding out no hope from legislation the report goes
on to state that upon these grounds the National Flax Society
call upon the nation for its support, on the ground that they
are going to remedy the distress of the country.   The founder
of this society is Mr. Warnes, of Norfolk.   I observe Mr.
Warnes paid a visit to Sussex, and he attended an agricultural
meeting at which the honorable baronet, the member for Shoreham [Sir Charles Burrell], presided.   After the usual loyal
toasts the honorable baronet proposed the toast of the evening:
" Mr. Warnes and the cultivation of flax."   The honorable baronet was not aware, I dare say, that he was then furnishing a
most deadly weapon to the lecturers of the Anti-Corn-Law
League.   We are told you cannot compete with foreigners unless you have a high protective duty.   You have a high protective duty on wheat, amounting at this moment to twenty
shillings a quarter.   A quarter of wheat at the present time is
just worth the same as one hundredweight of flax.   On a quarter of wheat you have a protective duty against the Pole and
Russian of twenty shillings ; upon the one hundredweight of flax
you have a protective duty of one penny   And I did not hear
a murmur from honorable gentlemen opposite when the Prime
Minister proposed to take off that protective duty of one penny,
totally and immediately.

But we are told that English agriculturists cannot compete
with foreigners, and especially with that serf labor that is to be
found somewhere up the Baltic   Well, but flax comes from the
Baltic, and there is no protective duty.   Honorable gentlemen
say we have no objection to raw materials where there is no labor connected with them ; but we cannot contend against foreigners in wheat because there is such an amount of labor in it.
Why, there is twice as much labor in flax as there is in wheat ;
but the member for Shoreham favors the growth of flax in order
to restore the country, which is sinking into this abject and
hopeless state for want of agricultural protection.   But the

honorable baronet will forgive me—I am sure he will, he looks as if he would—if I allude a little to the subject of leases.   The honorable gentleman on that occasion, I believe, complained that it was a great pity that farmers did not grow more flax.   I do not know whether it was true or not that the same honorable baronet's leases to his own tenants forbade them to grow that article.

Now, it is quite as possible that the right honorable baronet does not exactly know what covenants or clauses there are in his leases.   But I know that it is a very common case to preclude the growth of flax; and it just shows the kind of management by which the landed proprietors have carried on their affairs, that actually, I believe, the original source of the error that flax was very pernicious to the ground was derived from Vergil; I believe there is a passage in the Georgics to that effect.   From that classic authority, no doubt, some learned lawyer put this clause into the lease; and there it has remained ever since.

Now, I have alluded to the condition of the laborers at the present time; but I am bound to say that while the farmers at the present moment are in a worse condition than they have been for the last ten years, I believe the agricultural laborers have passed over the winter with less suffering and distress, although it has been a five-months' winter, and a severer one, too, than they endured in the previous year.   [Hear!]   I am glad to find that corroborated by honorable gentlemen opposite, because it bears out, in a remarkable degree, the opinion that we, who are in connection with the free-trade question, entertain. We maintain that a low price of food is beneficial to the laboring classes.   We assert, and we can prove it, at least in the manufacturing districts, that whenever provisions are dear wages are low, and whenever food is cheap wages invariably rise.   We have had a strike in almost every business in Lancashire since the price of wheat has been down to something like fifty shillings; and I am glad to be corroborated when I state that the agricultural laborers have been in a better condition during the last winter than they were in the previous one.   But does not that show that, even in your case, though your laborers have in a general way only just as much as will find them a subsistence, they are benefited by a great abundance of the first necessaries

of life? Although their wages may rise and fall with the price
of food—although they may go up with the advance in the
price of corn, and fall when it is lowered—still, I maintain that
it does not rise in the same proportion as the price of food rises,
nor fall to the extent to which food falls. Therefore in all cases
the agricultural laborers are in a better state when food is low
than when it is high. I have a very curious proof that high-
priced food leads to pauperism in the agricultural districts,
which I will read to you. It is a laborer's certificate seen at
Stowupland, in Suffolk, in July, 1844, which was placed upon
the mantelpiece of a peasant's cottage there:

"West Suffolk Agricultural Association, established in 1833
for the advancement of agriculture and the encouragement of
industry and skill and good conduct among laborers and servants in husbandry, President—the Duke of Grafton, Lord-
Lieutenant of the county: This is to certify that a prize of ten
pounds was awarded to William Burch, aged eighty-two, laborer of the parish of Stowupland, in West Suffolk, September
25, 1840, for having brought up nine children without relief,
except when flour was very dear; and for having worked on
the same farm twenty-eight years. (Signed) Rt. Rushbrooke,
Chairman."

Now I need not press that point. It is admitted by honorable
gentlemen opposite—and I am glad it is so—that after a very
severe winter, in the midst of great distress among farmers,
when there have been a great many able-bodied men wanting
employment, still there have been fewer in the streets and work-
houses than there had been in the previous year; and I hope
we shall not again be told by honorable gentlemen opposite that
cheap bread is injurious to the laborers.

But the condition of the agricultural laborer is a bad case
at the very best. You can look before you, and you have to
foresee the means of giving employment to those men. I need
not tell you that the late census shows that you cannot employ
your own increasing population in the agricultural districts.
But you say the farmer should employ them. Now, I am
bound to say that, whatever may be the condition of the agricultural laborer, I hold that the farmer is not responsible for
that condition while he is placed in the situation in which he is
now by the present system. I have seen during the last autumn

and winter a great many exhortations made to the farmers that they should employ more laborers. I think that is very unfair towards the farmer; I believe he is the man who is suffering most; he stands between you and your impoverished, suffering peasantry; and it is rather too bad to point to the farmer as the man who should relieve them. I have an extract from Lord Hardwick's address to the laborers of Haddenham. He says:

"Conciliate your employers, and if they do not perform their duty to you and themselves, address yourselves to the land-lords, and I assure you that you will find us ready to urge our own tenants to the proper cultivation of their farms, and, consequently, to the just employment of the laborer."

Now, I hold that this duty begins nearer home, and that the landed proprietors are the parties who are responsible if the laborers have not employment. You have absolute power; there is no doubt about that. You can, if you please, legislate for the laborers, or yourselves. Whatever you may have done besides, your legislation has been averse to the laborer, and you have no right to call upon the farmers to remedy the evils which you have caused. Will not this evil—if evil you call it—press on you more and more every year? What can you do to remedy the mischief? I only appear here now because you have proposed nothing. We all know your system of allotments, and we are all aware of its failure. What other remedy have you? for, mark you, that is worse than a plaything, if you were allowed to carry out your own views. [Hear!]   Aye, it is well enough for some of you that there are wiser heads than your own to lead you, or you would be conducting yourselves into precisely the same condition in which they are in Ireland, but with this difference—this increased difficulty—that there they do manage to maintain the rights of property by the aid of the English Exchequer and 20,000 bayonets; but divide your own country into small allotments, and where would be the rights of property? What do you propose to do now? That is the question. Nothing has been brought forward this year which I have heard, having for its object to benefit the great mass of the English population; nothing I have heard suggested which has at all tended to alleviate their condition.

You admit that the farmer's capital is sinking from under

him, and that he is in a worse state than ever. Have you distinctly provided some plan to give confidence to the farmer, to cause an influx of capital to be expended upon his land, and so bring increased employment to the laborer? How is this to be met? I cannot believe you are going to make this a political game. You must set up some specific object to benefit the agricultural interest. It is well said that the last election was an agricultural triumph. There are two hundred county members sitting behind the Prime Minister who prove that it was so. What, then, is your plan for this distressing state of things? That is what I want to ask you. Do not, as you have done before, quarrel with me because I have imperfectly stated my case; I have done my best; and I again ask you what you have to propose? I tell you that this "protection," as it has been called, is a failure. It was so when you had the prohibition up to eighty shillings. You know the state of your farming tenantry in 1821. It was a failure when you had a protection price of sixty shillings; for you know what was the condition of your farm tenantry in 1835 It is a failure now with your last amendment, for you have admitted and proclaimed it to us; and what is the condition of your agricultural population at this time? I ask, what is your plan? I hope it is not a pretence; a mere political game that has been played throughout the last election, and that you have not all come up here as mere politicians. There are politicians in the House; men who look with an ambition—probably a justifiable one—to the honors of office. There may be men who—with thirty years of continuous service, having been pressed into a groove from which they can neither escape nor retreat—may be holding office, high office, maintained there, probably at the expense of their present convictions which do not harmonize very well with their early opinions. I make allowances for them; but the great body of the honorable gentlemen opposite came up to this House, not as politicians, but as the farmers' friends, and protectors of the agricultural interests. Well, what do you propose to do? You have heard the Prime Minister declare that, if he could restore all the protection which you have had, that protection would not benefit agriculturists. Is that your belief? If so, why not proclaim it? and if it is not your conviction you will have falsified your mission in this House, by following the right honorable baronet out into the lobby, and opposing inquiry into the condition of the very men who sent you here.

With mere politicians I have no right to·expect to succeed in this motion. But I have no hesitation in telling you that, if you give me a committee of this House I will explode the delusion of agricultural protection! I will bring forward such a mass of evidence, and give you such a preponderance of talent and of authority that when the Blue-Book is published and sent forth to the world, as we can now send it, by our vehicles of information, your system of protection shall not live in public opinion for two years afterwards. Politicians do not want that. This cry of protection has been a very convenient handle for politicians. The cry of protection carried the counties at the last election, and politicians gained honors, emoluments, and place by it. But is that old tattered flag of protection, tarnished and torn as it is already, to be kept hoisted still in the counties for the benefit of politicians; or will you come forward honestly and fairly to inquire into this question? I cannot believe that the gentry of England will be made mere drumheads to be sounded upon by a Prime Minister to give forth unmeaning and empty sounds, and to have no articulate voice of their own. No! You are the gentry of England who represent the counties. You are the aristocracy of England. Your fathers led our fathers; you may lead us if you will go the right way. But, although you have retained your influence with this country longer than any other aristocracy, it has not been by opposing popular opinion, or by setting yourselves against the spirit of the age.

In other days, when the battle and the hunting-fields were the tests of manly vigor, your fathers were first and foremost there. The aristocracy of England were not like the *noblesse* of France, the mere minions of a court; nor were they like the hidalgos of Madrid, who dwindled into pygmies. You have been Englishmen. You have not shown a want of courage and firmness when any call has been made upon you. This is a new era. It is the age of improvement, it is the age of social advancement, not the age for war or for feudal sports. You live in a mercantile age, when the whole wealth of the world is poured into your lap. You cannot have the advantages of commercial rents and feudal privileges; but you may be what you always have been if you will identify yourselves with the spirit of the age. The English people look to the gentry and aristocracy of their country as their leaders. I, who am not one of you, have no hesitation in telling you that there is a deep-rooted, an hereditary prejudice, if I may so call it, in your favor in this country. But you never got it, and you will not keep it, by obstructing the spirit of the age. If you are indifferent to enlightened means of finding employment to your own peasantry; if you are found obstructing that advance which is calculated to knit nations more together in the bonds of peace by means of commercial intercourse; if you are found fighting against the discoveries which have almost given breath and life to material nature, and setting up yourselves as obstructives of that which destiny has decreed shall go on—why, then, you will be the gentry of England no longer, and others will be found to take your place.

And I have no hesitation in saying that you stand just now in a very critical position. There is a widespread suspicion that you have been tampering with the best feelings and with the honest confidence of your constituents in this cause. Everywhere you are doubted and suspected. Read your own organs, and you will see that this is the case. Well, then, this is the time to show that you are not the mere party politicians which you are said to be. I have said that we shall be opposed in this measure by politicians; they do not want inquiry. But I ask you to go into this committee with me. I will give you a majority of county members. You shall have a majority of the Central Society in that committee. I ask you only to go into a fair inquiry as to the causes of the distress of your own population. I only ask that this matter may be fairly examined. Whether you establish my principle or yours, good will come out of the inquiry; and I do, therefore, beg and entreat the honorable independent country gentlemen of this House that they will not refuse, on this occasion, to go into a fair, a full, and an impartial inquiry.

ON THE POLITICAL SITUATION

—

BY

BENJAMIN DISRAELI

(Lord Beaconsfield)

BENJAMIN DISRAELI, LORD BEACONSFIELD

1804—1881

For sheer original genius, which lifts a man from the ranks, and in the teeth of disheartening odds lands him at last in the highest place in a great kingdom, Benjamin Disraeli may perhaps be conceded to hold the first place in modern English political history. The problem, how to rise, is in England a far more difficult one than it is in America; and at the period of Disraeli's entrance into public life, it was vastly more difficult than it is to-day. But for him, in addition to the ordinary obstructions, there was the apparently insurmountable one of his Jewish parentage. There is nowhere any prouder, more self-satisfied body of people than the English aristocracy, none more exclusive, more difficult to subdue; and to none would they be less apt to bow than to a friendless and moneyless Jew. But Disraeli conquered the English aristocracy, and did it without allowing them to know or understand him. The situation is new in history, and of course can be explained only by the secret force of genius, working through all disguises, as a mighty magnet works beneath the wrappings which swathe it from sight. Not only did he become master of the House, not only did he hold the reins of government again and again; but according to his prophecy, he in due course took his seat in the House of Lords as a peer of England

Disraeli was born five years before his great rival, Gladstone, on December 21, 1804; and he died eighteen years before him, April 19, 1881. After a career in society, where he figured with success as a wit, and a season of travel on the Continent, he returned to London and obtained a seat in the Commons in 1837. Disraeli took his seat, and made his maiden speech, the reception of which was enough to quench the stoutest ambition, and destroy the most ingrained self-conceit. But it had only the effect of steeling him in his resolution; "the time shall come when you will hear me!" he said, and he made it his business thenceforward to keep that promise. By degrees he schooled himself to the style of speech which the House of Commons favors, that is, he cut off some of the Oriental adornments which he had at first affected. But in substance, the principle which guided him in rhetoric and argument was unaltered, it was the Commons that altered, and listened to him, at first respectfully, then with submissive admiration. In time he became one of the leaders of the Protectionist Tory party. He was Chancellor of the Exchequer three times, and in 1867 he carried his Reform Bill. He was Prime Minister in 1868, and again for six years, from 1874 to 1880. In 1876 he was created a peer of England with the title of Earl of Beaconsfield. In 1878 he was England's representative at the Congress of Berlin

Throughout their careers Gladstone and Disraeli were pitted against each other; and there can be no doubt that each of them benefitted greatly by their antagonism. Again and again, in their personal encounters in the House, did the Jew's wit and readiness give him at least the semblance of victory over his great antagonist; his sardonic tongue was a terrible weapon, and Gladstone often blenched under it. Disraeli's speeches well repay study. His speech "On the Political Situation" sums up, in a general way, his policy on many important political questions. They are clever, persuasive, cynical at times, but in general proposing measures, of foreign policy especially, that capture the imagination by their boldness or ingenuity. He aimed to make England the greatest nation in the world—an empire surpassing all empires of history; and his policy always held this end in view.

Disraeli also holds a prominent place in the list of English authors. He was a novelist of real genius. Among his most widely read works are "Vivian Grey," "Lothair," and "Endymion."

ON THE POLITICAL SITUATION

Delivered before the Glasgow Conservative Association November 22, 1873

GENTLEMEN: I believe I may describe the position of this country as one of very great prosperity. There is no doubt that during the last three years prosperity has been generally acknowledged. There are some who suppose that it may have received a check at the time when I paid my visit to Glasgow. If it has received a check it will increase, I hope, our circumspection, but I must express my own opinion that no substantial diminution in the sources of the prosperity so apparent during the last three years has occurred. I think we may fairly say the state of this country is one of great prosperity, and although I believe and know that it is a prosperity for which we are not indebted either to Whigs or Tories, although I know that it has been occasioned in a considerable degree, under Providence, by fortuitous though felicitous circumstances, I am perfectly ready, speaking to-day, as I hope to speak, in the fairest terms on public affairs, which I believe to be quite consistent with the position of the leader of a party—I am ready to give to Her Majesty's Government credit for the prosperity we feel and acknowledge. With regard to Her Majesty's ministers themselves, I will be equally candid, equally fair—I will take them at their own estimate. They have lost few opportunities of informing the country that they are men distinguished for commanding talent, admirable eloquence, and transcendent administrative abilities I dispute none of these propositions any more than I do the prosperity of the country. They also tell us that the country being so prosperous, and they having all these personal advantages, they have taken the opportunity during the last few years of passing measures of immense magnitude, only equalled by the benefit they have con-

ferred upon the people. Now, gentlemen, I will not question
their own estimate of their ability, or even for a moment their
own description of their achievements; but I ask this question,
What is the reason, when the country is so prosperous, when
its affairs are administered by so gifted a government, and when
they have succeeded during five years in passing measures
of such a vast character and beneficence—what is the reason
that her Majesty's ministers are going about regretting that
they are so unpopular? Now, gentlemen, I beg you to observe
that I did not say Her Majesty's ministers are unpopular. I
stated their own case and their own position; I say that under
the circumstances I have put fairly before you, it is a remarkable
circumstance, and the question must be inquired into—why
persons in the position of Her Majesty's Government should on
every occasion deplore the unpopularity they have incurred.
Now, my opinion, gentlemen, is that that is not a question of
mere curiosity—it is one that, as I think I shall show you, concerns the honor and the interests of the country. If the country is so prosperous—if Her Majesty's ministers are so gifted—
if they have had such an ample opportunity of showing the
talents which they possess—if they have done all this good—if
they have availed themselves of this signal opportunity to effect such great results, then the only inference we can draw
from the unpopularity which they themselves deplore is that
the people of this country is a fickle and ungrateful people.
Therefore, it is not a question of mere curiosity. It is a question that ought to be answered. If there be those who suppose that the people of this country, as I hold, are not a
fickle or ungrateful people—that they are a people who may
be mistaken—that they may be misled; but that they are a
people who on the whole are steadfast in their convictions and
especially in their political convictions, I cannot myself for
a moment doubt. I say, then, that this question, if left unan-
swered, would show that Her Majesty's ministers have placed
a slur on the character of the people of this kingdom, it ought
to be answered; and a short time since, some two months
ago, I answered it. It appeared to me, at that moment especially, when all those circumstances to which I have referred
were clearly before the country, and when Her Majesty's Government, by their ablest and most powerful representatives,

were deploring their unpopularity, and asking the reason why, or rather intimating by inference that it was the fault of the people, not of the Government, that someone should give an answer to that question. I gave it, and in a very brief form —in the most condensed and the most severely accurate form. There is not an expression in that description of the conduct of the Government which was not well weighed; there was not a word for which I had not warranty, for which I could not adduce testimony ample and abounding. There was only one characteristic of that description which was not noticed at the time, and which I will now confess—it was not original, for six months before in the House of Commons I had used the same expressions and made the same statement—not in a hole or corner, but on the most memorable night of the session, when there were six hundred members of the House of Commons present, when on the debate that took place avowedly the fate of the ministry depended. It was at midnight that I rose to speak, and made the statement almost similar in expression, though perhaps stronger and more lengthened than the one which has become the cause of recent controversy. The Prime Minister followed me in that debate. The House of Commons knew what was depending upon the verdict about to be taken, and with all that knowledge they came to a division, and by a majority terminated the existence of the Government. Gentlemen, it surprises me, then, that, having made that statement six months after, with the advantage of six months' more experience and observation, it should have so much offended Her Majesty's Government. The ministers sighed, and their newspapers screamed. The question I have to ask, and in this your interests are vitally concerned—the question is, was the statement I made a true and accurate one? You cannot answer statements of this kind by saying, " Oh, fie! how very rude." You must at least adduce arguments in order to prove that the statement which you do not sanction is one that ought not to have been made. And therefore I ask you to-day, in the first place, is it or is it not true that the Irish Church has been despoiled? Is it or is it not true that the gentlemen of Ireland have been severely amerced? Is it or is it not true that a royal commission has been issued which has dealt with the ancient endowments of this country in so ruthless a manner that Parlia-

ment has frequently been called upon to interfere, and has addressed the Crown to arrest their propositions? Are these facts
or are they not? Well, I did then venture to say that they had
" harassed trades and worried professions," as reasons why men
naturally become unpopular. Was that true or was it not?
Because, after all, everything depends on the facts of the statement. I won't enter into· a long catalogue of trades, commencing with the important trade of which we have heard so
much, and which has made itself felt at so many elections, down
to the humblest trade—the lucifer-match makers—who fell
upon their knees in Palace Yard. I suppose there are some
Scotch farmers present, or, at least, those who are intimately
connected with them. I want to know whether trade was harassed when a proposition was brought before the House of Commons to take their carts and horses, and all the machinery of
their cultivation? I know how the proposition was received in
England, and I doubt not the Scotch farmers, like the English,
felt extremely harassed by it. I want to know what is the reason why there is this crusade throughout the country against
schedule D of the Income Tax. The Income Tax has been
borne for thirty years with great self-sacrifice and with great
loyalty by the people of this country. It is at this moment at
the lowest pitch it has ever reached; how is it, then, that it is at
this moment more unpopular than it was at any time during the
long period we endured it at a much higher figure? It is on
account of the assessment of the trades of England under that
schedule. It is the vexatious and severe assessment that has
harassed tradesmen, who, like all those who come under that
act, are not particularly pleased, when they are paying five quarters of income tax in the year, to learn also that they are in ar-
rears. Then, have the professions been worried? Ask the
military profession. Is it not true that at this moment a
royal commission is examining in London into the grievances
of six thousand officers? Ask the naval profession whether
they have not been worried. During the course of the present
Government the whole administrative system of the Admiralty,
the council that had always great influence in the management
of the navy, and the peculiar office of the secretary, were all
swept away; and in spite I may say of the nightly warnings of
a right honorable friend who is now lost to us all and his coun-

try, the ablest minister of the Admiralty during the present reign—notwithstanding his nightly warnings that they were so conducting the administration of the navy that they would probably fall into some disaster, his remonstrances were in vain, till soon the most costly vessel of the State was lost, and the perilous voyage of the " Megæra " had been made, when the country would stand it no longer. They rescinded the whole of this worrying arrangement, and appointed a new First Lord to re-establish the old system. Is that worrying a profession, or is it not? Well, gentlemen, I can speak of another profession— a profession the most important in the State—the civil service profession. Has it been worried? Is it now in a process of worrying, or is it not? There are many even in this room well acquainted with the position of the civil service in all its departments. I might say the same of the legal profession, for I have heard lawyers on both sides of the House in the debates of last session agree in imploring the Government not to continue propositions which would infallibly weaken the administration of justice in this country. It is not only these professions and trades who are directly attacked, but it is every one that is harassed, because no one knows whose turn will come next. Well, I did say to the House of Commons—and I afterwards expressed it in another form—I said they had attacked every class and institution from the highest to the lowest in the country. Is that true or is it not? Is it not a fact that Her Majesty's Government on every occasion of which they could avail themselves during the last three years attacked the authority of the House of Lords, scoffed at the existence of its high functions, and even defied its decisions, until the result proved that the House of Lords was extremely popular in the country, and Her Majesty's Government were obliged to confess that they themselves were exceeding unpopular?' But you must remember this, that the same body who attacked the House of Lords also brought in a bill which would have attacked the poor inheritance of the widow and the orphan. Now, I think I have shown from the highest to the lowest the same system prevailed. What occurred in the interval? The Churches of England and Scotland have been threatened. It has been publicly said by the highest authority in the House of Commons that he did not believe that the House of Commons would sanction the views of those who wished to pull down the venerable establishments, but he recommended them to agitate out of doors and endeavor to excite public opinion against them. Then, again, I said jobs were perpetrated that outraged public opinion. Is that true or is it not? Is it not a fact that two years ago the whole country was outraged by persons being appointed to important offices in Church and State in direct violation of the language of Acts of Parliament?—that the ministry in that respect exercised that dispensing power which forfeited the crown of James II? Was not public indigation roused to the highest degree upon the Collier appointment and a similar one? Were these acts perpetrated, and did they outrage public opinion? Everyone knows from his own individual experience that public opinion was outraged. I have said, also, that they stumbled into errors which were always discreditable and sometimes ruinous. That was called violent language. Gentlemen, I never use violent language; violent language is generally weak language; but I hope my language is sometimes strong. Now, let us look at this statement. I said that they stumbled into errors which were always discreditable and sometimes ruinous. Was the Zanzibar contract not an " error," and was it not " discreditable " ? Was the conduct of the Treasury in allowing a subordinate officer to misappropriate nearly a million of the public money not an " error," and was it not " discreditable " ? When the Government had referred the Alabama claims to the arbitrament of a third State, was not the change of the law of nations by the three rules an " error " ? Was that not " discreditable," and in its consequences was it not " ruinous " ?

I have now given an answer to the question why the Government, with transcendent abilities, as they tell us, with magnificent exploits which they are always extolling, and with a country whose prosperity is so palpable—they ask us why they are unpopular, and I tell them why. They have harassed and worried the country, and there was no necessity for any of the acts they have committed. I have put it in condensed and, I am sure, accurate language. There was an illustrious writer, one of the greatest masters of our language, who wrote the history of the last four years of the reign of Queen Anne, which was the duration of an illustrious ministry. I have written the history of a ministry that has lasted five years, and I have immortalized the spirit of their policy in five lines. And now, gentlemen, I will tell you what is the unfortunate cause of this political embarrassment; why, with such favorable circumstances as the present Government have encountered; why, with the great ability which no man is more conscious than myself that they possess; why, with the most anxious and earnest desire, for which I give them entire credit, to do their duty to their sovereign and their fellow-countrymen, the result has been so mortifying. I told it two years ago to the assembled county of Lancaster, when I met not only the greatest proprietors of the soil, but deputations and delegations of the choicest citizens from every town and city of that great county. I told them, speaking with the sense of the deepest responsibility, which, I trust, also animates me now—I told them that the cause was that this Government, unfortunately, in its beginning, had been founded on a principle of violence, and that fatal principle had necessarily vitiated their whole course. And what have we gained by that principle of violence? Let us consider it, here even, with impartiality and perfect candor. I am now referring to the Irish policy of the ministry. I say it is quite possible for public men, with the view of obtaining some great object advantageous to the country, to devise and pass measures which may utterly fail in accomplishing their purpose, and yet, however mortifying to themselves, however disappointing to the country, there would be no stain upon their reputation. We cannot command, but we must endeavor in public life to deserve success. If, therefore, it is said that the Government proposed the large measures which they did with respect to Ireland in order to terminate the grievances of years and the embarrassment to England, which the state of Ireland certainly was, although they may have failed, their position was one which still might be a position of respect. That they have failed in this instance no one can doubt. A great portion of Ireland at this moment is in a state of veiled rebellion. But what I charge upon the Government is this, not that their measures fail—for all measures may fail—not that their measures fail to prevent or to suppress this veiled rebellion in Ireland, but that their measures, which they brought forward to appease and settle, to tranquillize and consolidate Ireland, are the very cause that this veiled rebellion is taking place. For, gentlemen, what was the

principle upon which the whole of their policy with respect to
Ireland was founded? What was the principle upon which
they induced Parliament to confiscate and to despoil Church
and private property in Ireland? It was that Ireland must be
governed on Irish principles—the administration of Ireland
must be carried on with reference to Irish feeling. If that is
a sound principle and a sound sentiment in politics, it is a perfect
vindication of what is occurring in the city of Dublin at this
moment—viz, an assembly of men whose great and avowed
object is to dissever the connection between the two countries.
If we are not to legislate for Ireland with reference to imperial
feelings and general and national interests—if we are only to
legislate with reference to Irish feelings, it is perfectly evident
that if there is a majority of the Irish people who may take any
idea in the world into their heads, however ruinous to themselves and however fatal to the empire, that policy must be recognized by this country. It is, therefore, to that principle,
avowedly and ostentatiously brought forward by the ministry as
the basis of their Irish policy, that I trace the dangerous condition in which Ireland is now placed. Well, then, I say this policy of violence for which such sacrifices were made, for which
institutions and interests which were, at least, faithful to Britain
were sacrificed—this policy of violence has led only to a state of
affairs, unfortunately, more unsatisfactory than that which prevailed before.

Now, gentlemen, I observe in the paper that the day is fixed
for the reassembling of Parliament. The time is not yet very
near, but when you find Her Majesty has appointed the day for
our reassembling, it is an intimation that we must begin to consider the public business a little, and, therefore, it is not altogether inconvenient that we should be talking upon these matters to-day. Now, when we meet Parliament, I apprehend the
first business that will be brought before us will be the Ashantee
war. Upon that subject my mouth is closed. I will not even
make an observation upon the railway which I believe has been
returned to England. Whenever this country is externally involved in a difficulty, whatever I may think of its cause or
origin, those with whom I act, and myself, have no other duty
to fulfil but to support the existing Government in extricating
the country from its difficulties and vindicating the honor and

interests of Great Britain. The time will come, gentlemen, no doubt, when we shall know something of the secret history of that mysterious mess of the Ashantee war, but we have now but one duty to fulfil, which is to give every assistance to the Government in order that they may take those steps which the interests of the country require. I should indeed, myself, from my own individual experience, be most careful not to follow the example which one of the most distinguished members of the present administration pursued with respect to us when we had to encounter the Abyssinian difficulty. Mr. Lowe thought proper to rise in Parliament when I introduced the necessity of interference in order to escape from difficulties which we had inherited and not created. Mr. Lowe rose in Parliament and violently attacked the Government of the day for the absurdity, the folly, the extreme imprudence of attempting any interference in the affairs of Abyssinia. He laughed at the honor of the country, he laughed at the interests of a few enslaved subjects of the Queen of England being compared, as he said, with the certain destruction and disaster which must attend any interference on our part. He described the horrors of the country and the terrors of the climate. He said there was no possibility by which any success could be obtained, and the people of England must prepare themselves for the most horrible catastrophe He described not only the fatal influences of the climate, but I remember he described one pink fly alone, which he said would eat up the whole British army He was as vituperative of the insects of Abyssinia as if they had been British workmen.

Now, gentlemen, there is a most interesting and important subject which concerns us all, and which it is not impossible may be submitted to the consideration of Parliament by Her Majesty's ministers, because I observe a letter published in a newspaper by the authority of the Prime Minister which is certainly calculated to arrest public attention. That is a letter respecting the subject of parliamentary reform. I think it is not undesirable that at a moment when letters of this kind are circulated, and when there is a good deal of loose talking prevalent in the country on the subject, I should take this opportunity of calling your attention to some considerations on this subject which may occupy you after my visit to Glasgow

has terminated, and may not be, I think, unprofitable. Her
Majesty's Government are not pledged, but after the letter of
the Prime Minister announcing his own opinion, and the indication of the probability of the Government considering the question of further parliamentary reform, there are two points which
the Government ought to consider when they come to that
question. The first is the expediency of having any further
parliamentary reform. They will have to remember that very
wise statesmen have been of opinion that there is no more dangerous and feeble characteristic of a state than perpetually to
be dwelling on what is called organic change. The habit, it
has been said in politics, of perpetually considering your political constitution can only be compared to that of the individual
who is always considering the state of his health and his physical constitution. You know what occurs in such circumstances—he becomes infirm and valetudinarian. In fact, there
is a school of politics which looks at the English constitution
as valetudinarian. They are always looking at its tongue and
feeling its pulse, and devising means by which they may give
it a tonic. The Government will have to consider that very
important point, first of all whether it is expedient. I am not
giving any opinion upon it—being only a private member of
Parliament, that is quite unnecessary—but I am indicating the
consideration that would occur to a responsible statesman.
They will also have to consider this important point, that whatever minister embarks in a campaign of parliamentary reform
must make up his mind that he will necessarily arrest the progress of all other public business in the country. I will show
you to what extent that consideration should prevail. Parliamentary reform, as a new question, was introduced in the
House of Commons in 1852 by Lord John Russell, and from
1852 to 1866, or the end of 1865, it was introduced annually;
four prime ministers had pledged themselves to the expediency
of parliamentary reform; the subject made no progress in Parliament, but took up a great deal of time; a great portion of
the parliamentary sessions for these twelve or thirteen years
was taken up by discussions on parliamentary reform; and the
country got very ill-tempered, finding that no reform was ever
advanced, and other and more important subjects were neglected. At last it was taken up by men determined to carry it

—first by Lord Russell, who did not carry it, and afterwards by others; but, observe, the whole of 1866, 1867, and 1868 was entirely absorbed by the subject of parliamentary reform. Therefore, you will observe that when important subjects in legislation are neglected you must be prepared to discourage any further demand for parliamentary reform unless you feel an insuperable necessity for it, because if you want parliamentary reform you cannot have any of those great measures with regard to local taxation or other subjects in which you are all so much interested. That is the first consideration for the Government of the present day to determine, whether they shall embark in the question of parliamentary reform. Is it necessary? Is the necessity of such a character that it outweighs the immense inconvenience of sacrificing all other public and progressive measures for the advancement of this particular measure? Then there comes another subject of consideration. I dwell upon these subjects because I apprehend that one of the reasons for our meeting this evening is that upon questions which are likely to engage the public attention so far as those whom you honor with your confidence can give you any guidance, it is as well that I should indicate to you briefly my general views of the situation. The next point, therefore, that Government will have to consider if they make up their minds to bring forward a measure of parliamentary reform, is the character of the measure, and that will be a most anxious question for them to decide. I think I may say without conceit that the subject of parliamentary reform is one that I am entitled to speak upon at least with some degree of authority. I have given to it the consideration of some forty years, and am responsible for the most important measure on the subject that has been carried. I would say this, that it is impossible to go further in the direction of parliamentary reform than the bill of 1867-68 without entirely subverting the whole of the borough representation of this country. I do not mean to say that if there was a place disfranchised to-morrow for corruption, it would not be possible to enfranchise a very good place in its stead; but, speaking generally, you cannot go beyond the Act of 1867 without making up your mind entirely to break up the borough representation of this country. The people of Great Britain ought to be aware that that is the necessary consequence. So far as I am concerned

I never could view the matter in a party light. If I were to accustom myself to view it in a party light I might look with unconcern on this difficulty, for the smaller boroughs of the country are not, on the whole, favorable to our views. I am proud to think our party is supported by the great counties, and now to a great extent by great towns and cities; but I do not consider the smaller boroughs favorable to Conservative views. It is the national sympathies and wide sentiments of those who live in our great cities that are much more calculated to rally round the cause in which we are deeply concerned— the greatness and glory of our country. This ought to be known, that if those who intend to have a further measure of parliamentary reform, and have digested that large meal which they had a few years ago, they should remember that there is no borough in England with under 40,000 inhabitants that would have any claim to be represented even by one member. Now that is a very important consideration if, as we are told, the small boroughs of between ten and fifteen thousand inhabitants are the backbone of the Liberal party. They may be, and I think they are, but I should be very sorry to see them disfranchised, for they are centres of public spirit and intelligence in the country, influencing very much the districts in which they are situated, and affording a various representation of the mind and life of the country. But it is inevitable that that would occur, and I think, therefore, it ought to be well understood by the country when you hear persons without the slightest consideration saying they are prepared to vote for this, or in favor of that, whereas they have not really mastered the question in any degree whatever. So far as I am concerned, any proposition to change the representation of the people brought forward by Her Majesty's Government will receive my respectful and candid consideration. But I say at once that I will vote for no measure of that kind, or of that class which is brought forward by some irresponsible individual, who, on the eve of a general election, wants to make a claptrap career. I think it is perfectly disgusting for individuals to jump up in the House of Commons without the slightest responsibility, official or moral, and make propositions which demand the gravest consideration of prolonged and protracted cabinets, with all the responsibility attaching to experienced statesmen. Now, gen-

tlemen, although I have rather exceeded the time I had intended, there are one or two more remarks I should like to make
on subjects which interest us all.   And first, as the only feature
in our domestic life that gives me uneasiness, are the relations
at present between capital and labor, and between the employers and employed.   I must say one word upon that subject.   If
there are any relations in the world which should be those of
sympathy and perfect confidence, they always appear to be the
relations which should subsist between employers and employed, and especially in manufacturing life.   They are, in fact,
much more intimate and more necessary relations than those
which subsist between landlords and tenants.   It is an extremely painful thing that of late years we so frequently hear of
misunderstandings between the employers and the employed—
that they look upon each other with suspicion—with mutual
suspicion—as if each were rapaciously inclined either to obtain or retain the greater share of the profits of their trade; and
those incidents with which you are all acquainted, of a very
painful nature, have been the consequence.   I am not talking
of demands for an increase of wages when men are carrying
on what is called a roaring trade—I believe that is the classical
epithet taken from the Manchester school.   When a roaring
trade is going on, I am not at all surprised that workingmen
should ask for an increase of wages.   But a trade sometimes ceases to roar, when wages naturally, on the same principle, assume a form more adapted to the circumstances.   No
doubt, during the last twenty years there appears to have been,
not a passing and temporary cause of disturbance like the
incidents of trade being very active or reduced, but some permanent cause disturbing prices, which alike confuses the employer in his calculations as to profits and embarrasses the
employer from the greater expenditure which they find it necessary to make.   Now, I cannot but feel myself—having given to
the subject as much consideration as I could—I cannot help
feeling that the large and continuous increase of the precious
metals, especially during the last twenty years, has certainly
produced no inconsiderable effect—not only in trade, but no inconsiderable effect in prices.   I will not, on an occasion like
this, enter into anything like an abstruse discussion.   I confine
myself to giving my opinion and the results which I draw from

it; and this moral, which I think is worthy of consideration. If it can be shown accurately and scientifically that there is a cause affecting a prominent class, reducing the average remuneration of the employed, and confusing and confounding the employer in his calculations as to profits—if that can be shown, and if it is proved to be the result of inexorable laws, far beyond the reach of legislation, and of circumstances over which human beings have no control—I think if that could be shown, and employers and employed had sufficient acuteness and knowledge—and I am sure that in Scotland both will have to acknowledge that result—it would very much change those mutual feelings of suspicion and sentiments of a not pleasant character which occasionally prevail when they find that they are both of them the victims, as it were, of some inexorable law of political economy which cannot be resisted. I think, instead of supposing that each wanted to take advantage of the other, they would feel inclined to put their shoulders to the wheel, accurately ascertain whether this be true, and come to some understanding which would very much mitigate the relations which subsist between them, and I have little doubt the effect would be to increase the average rate of wages, with my views as to the effect of the continuous increase of the precious metals. But, at the same time, I have not the slightest doubt the employer would, in the nature of things, find adequate compensation for the new position in which he would find himself. There is one point before I sit down to which I wish to call your attention, because if I am correct in saying that the question of the relations between the employer and employed is the only one that gives me anxiety at home, there is a subject abroad to which, I think, I ought, on an occasion like this, to draw your notice; and this is the contest that is commencing in Europe between the spiritual and temporal powers. Gentlemen, I look upon it as very grave, as pregnant with circumstances which may greatly embarrass Europe. The religious sentiment is often and generally taken advantage of by political classes, who use it as a pretext; and there is much going on in Europe at the present moment which, it appears to me, may occasion us soon much anxiety in this community. I should myself look upon it as the greatest danger to civilization if, in the struggle that is going on between faith and free thought, the respective sides should only be represented by the papacy and the red re-public; and here I must say that if we have before us the pros-pect of struggles—perhaps of wars and anarchy, ultimately—caused by the great question that is now rising in Europe, it will not easily be in the power of England entirely to withhold her-self from such circumstances. Our connection with Ireland will then be brought painfully to our consciousness, and I should not be at all surprised if the visor of Home Rule should fall off some day, and you beheld a very different countenance. Now, gentlemen, I think we ought to be prepared for those cir-cumstances. The position of England is one which is indica-tive of dangers arising from holding a middle course upon those matters. It may be open to England again to take a stand upon the Reformation which three hundred years ago was the source of her greatness and her glory, and it may be her proud destiny to guard civilization alike from the withering blast of atheism and from the simoom of sacerdotal usurpation. These things may be far off, but we live in a rapid age, and my appre-hension is that they are nearer than some suppose. If that struggle comes we must look to Scotland to aid us. It was once, and I hope is still, a land of liberty, of patriotism, and of religion. I think the time has come when it really should leave off mumbling the dry bones of political economy and munching the remainder biscuit of an effete Liberalism. We all know that a general election is at hand. I do not ask you to consider on such an occasion the fate of parties or of ministers. But I ask you to consider this, that it is very probable that the future of Europe depends greatly on the character of the next Parlia-ment of England. I ask you, when the occasion comes, to act as becomes an ancient and famous nation, and give all your en-ergies for the cause of faith and freedom.

ON PROGRESS

—

BY

HENRY EDWARD, CARDINAL MANNING

HENRY EDWARD, CARDINAL MANNING

1808—1892

Henry Edward Manning was born at Totteridge, Hertfordshire, in 1808   He began his education at Harrow, and in 1827 went to Oxford, where he was graduated, first in classics, in 1830, and two years after was elected Fellow of Merton College.   This was just at the beginning of the Tractarian movement, in which Manning took no active part at Oxford, for he left the university in 1833 for the rectorship of Woollavington and Graffham, Sussex   He was, however, a decided High Churchman   His abilities were early recognized by his appointment as archdeacon of Chichester in 1840, the year before the celebrated Tract " 90 " was published.   Manning must be called an ambitious man, if ambition means a consciousness of great powers coupled with a desire to exercise them in a wide field.   He had made himself famous as a striking preacher, and since his wife had died in 1837 there was nothing to prevent his ordination to the Roman Catholic priesthood when the " Gorham Judgment " moved him to join the Church of Rome in 185˙   Gorham was an Anglican clergyman, whose teachings on baptism, which Manning considered at variance with the English Prayer-book, were declared by the Privy Council to be the teachings of the Church of England

In 1865 Manning crowned a ministry of incessant activity and devotion by succeeding Cardinal Wiseman as Archbishop of Westminster, and five years later rose up in the Vatican Council of 1870 as one of the most ardent and uncompromising supporters of Papal infallibility.   He was made a Cardinal in 1875 and became a most powerful advocate of Roman Catholicism   He was, however, very much more than a mere ecclesiastic, and by his Christian charity and noble life he conciliated all religious parties and won their support in his humanitarian work   Manning belonged, as a great Englishman, rather to the whole nation, than to any denomination in England, being a broad-minded philanthropist and reformer, whose zeal and abilities the Government recognized by making him, in 1885, a member of the Royal Commission   During his later years he was to be found sitting side by side with laymen and ministers of all sorts of denominations on any platform where he could advocate the rights of labor and the cause of temperance   He died in 1892, leaving many writings, including sermons and addresses of commanding eloquence, as well as several polemical and controversial pamphlets   His address " On Progress " gives an excellent idea of his eloquence and erudition   He was an eloquent and impressive preacher, a dogmatic theologian, untainted by rationalism, indifferent to, and presumably not well acquainted with, the school of modern criticism.

ON PROGRESS

Delivered before a meeting of the Young Men's Catholic Association, October 10, 1871

WHEN a boy, I remember reading a book which had a great name nearly a century ago, in which one of the chapters was headed: " Our hero talks of what he does not understand." I have no doubt that I will hear that I am talking of what I do not understand; but in my defence I think I may say, I am about to talk of what I do not understand for this reason: I cannot get those who talk about it to tell me what they mean. I know what I mean by it, but I am not at all sure that I know what they mean by it; and those who use the same words in different senses are like men that run up and down the two sides of a hedge, and so can never meet. That perhaps will happen to me in talking about progress. I have tried all I can to find out some definition or description to give me an idea of what is meant by progress. The perpetual repetition of the word stuns and deafens us day by day. At the feet of newspaper editors and article-writers, the great teachers of the day—philosophers and sophists are gone—at the feet of these we sit, and hear constantly a great deal about progress, of which, if I could understand it to be something true and good, I should become one of the preachers; but these apostles of the nineteenth century will not tell us their meaning. They leave us in a state of blank amazement. I have tried to find some authorities to depend upon, and have found two—one the present Prime Minister of England, who, in a speech in Liverpool four years ago, says that progress is what the police say to the people on the pavement, " Move on! " My other authority is the leader of Her Majesty's Opposition who, in one of his books introduces his hero talking with a stranger from the other side of the Atlantic, who held very cheap our great commercial towns with their machinery and manufactures, saying that they were nothing at all compared with the States. At parting he presents his card to his companion, on which was written, " Mr. G. O. A. Head." These are the only two authoritative meanings I can gather from our two political parties as to what progress means. It is talked of by most people as if it were a Holy Grail of which people are in quest. Some of them spend their lives in great energy to promote progress; but unfortunately they appear to me to verify what St. Augustin said about men who make great speed after truth without finding the right way to it. He said: " You are making great strides, but are out of the road." And when I see people making for progress in different directions, we are quite sure they cannot all be right. Some people tell us progress means liberalism. It is difficult again to know what that is—and when you do get their definition of it, it seems to be the emancipation of the human will from every kind of law. I do not think that is progress, or that it leads to a good result. Then, again, plebiscites, or universal suffrage, are taken to be one of the tokens of progress, and the results of plebiscites do not seem to me to be the ultimate good of society— at least they are so frequently given in different directions, and one is so speedily necessary to correct another, and build up what another throws down, that neither does this seem to me progress, unless progress means perpetual motion, swaying to and fro. Again, we are told that material improvements, such as gas, railroads, and the abolition of intramural burials the other day, came among the evidences of progress; trades which are what we call roaring trades; steamboats, races between them, with the steam shut in, and excited passengers stamping upon the paddle-boxes—this is taken by some people as evidence of progress. One thing, however, I see. In every country of Europe there is what is called a " party of progress," but, unfortunately, this party of progress has a trail behind it like certain reptiles, and that trail is revolution. We have not, therefore, as yet arrived at a very clear notion of progress from the popular teachers of the day; I will therefore venture to give my own humble conception of what progress is.

I will say, then, that progress with us simple people means the growth and ripening of anything from its first principles to its perfection. We distinguish between progress which is growth, and progress which is decay; because decay is the reverse of growth, and it is a departure from first principles. It is the dissolution of perfection; and therefore we distinguish between growth and decay as between ripeness and rottenness —and growth we call progress, but decay we call ruin. Now I want to show what may be classified under progress of growth, and what under decay or ruin—that is my subject.

The growth of an oak is a very intelligible thing. The acorn planted in the clay strikes its tap-root, then rises into a stem, and spreads into branches; and in the whole tree completes its symmetry, stature, and perfection—this is an example of progress from a germ in nature. But when that oak has attained its maturity, and has run through its period of time, it begins to decay, which reverses this progress. The sap sinks to the root, the leaves begin to fall, the sprays wither, the branches decay and fall from the trunk, the rot in the substance of the tree gradually spreads, the trunk becomes hollow, and the tree disappears in dust: this is, then, the reverse of progress. The same is true of every fruit we hold in our hands; so Shakespeare tells us of man:

> " And so from hour to hour, we ripe and ripe;
> And then, from hour to hour, we rot and rot;
> And thereby hangs a tale."

Let us apply this to human things, and first to an individual man. The idea of physical progress in man is first of all the growth from childhood to manhood, the complete expansion and development of the whole man in stature, symmetry, strength, and countenance; the whole human being filling up as it were the outline and type which belongs not only to man in general, but to that particular individual—that is what we call progress. Then there is the moral progress in every man; that is, the progress of his character, which begins in the self-control of the will and in obedience; then in the rectitude of conduct; and then again in prudence and the whole range of duty, and, finally, in excellence—that is, in surpassing others according to the capacity of that which is in him by nature. For men are not all equal, they are variously endowed and some have capacities and qualities and energies far beyond others; and each individual has a progress of his own, which means, as I said before, the filling up of that which is not only due to the type of race to which he belongs, but also to his own individual gifts and capacities. In like manner of intellectual progress: there is a passive intellect in us all, which first receives the instruction of teachers, and then becomes an active intellect, whereby we educate and form ourselves; and then that active intellect becomes reflective, and has a power of research and discovery. The whole intellect of the man is thus matured and ripened according to his capacities and circumstances, and that from very small beginnings.

For instance, it is said in the life of St. Gregory VII, the greatest ruler the world ever saw, the loftiest of all legislators, the justest of all judges, and the most intrepid of all pontiffs, who ruled over the whole Christian world with a sway which for wisdom and fortitude has never been excelled—it is said that in his childhood he was kneeling at the feet of a carpenter who was hewing wood; and the chips, so traditions say, formed themselves into the words from the Book of Psalms, " He shall reign from sea to sea." This was taken as an indication of his future, which he fulfilled to the letter. The movement which connected this small beginning with his mighty end was a progress of the whole man, moral and intellectual. Take also the example of Fergusson, the astronomer, who, when a shepherd's boy, would lie on his back, and with a string of beads over his eye measure the distance or intervals of the stars, and then mark them down with his pencil—this was the beginning of his progress in astronomy. So again take another instance in the familiar anecdote of Nelson, who was perhaps one of the most intrepid and fearless of men. When a boy in Norfolk, he left his father's house, and was lost for the whole day, not coming home until after dark. His father said he wondered fear did not drive him home, upon which the boy asked: " Who is fear? I do not know him." I suppose that was the index of his genius, which progressed into the heroic fearless character which is written in history. That is my notion of progress in the individual man—a consistent growth of the same principles from first to last. The next example shall be the progress of a people.

I do not know whether any of you have read Carlyle's " Chartism " ; if so, you will find me a plagiarist, but I shall only take his outline, not his words. He says of the British Empire,

there was a time when we were Druids; and I recollect that
somebody in the House of Commons attacked Mr. Pitt for
speaking in favor of the abolition of slavery, on the ground that
it was useless to emancipate the negro, for he was of a lower and
baser race than the white man; in proof of which it was said
that they sold their children into slavery, sacrificed human beings to idols, covered themselves with paint, and I know not
what. Mr. Pitt answered that such was precisely the state of
our British ancestors—they painted themselves with woad, sold
their children into slavery, and offered human sacrifices under
their oaks. There is no doubt there was a time when we were in
that unprogressive state. After that came Hengist and Horsa,
in their leathern boats, upon the mud of Thanet, and springing
from them came the seven kingdoms of the Heptarchy, which
are described by Milton as " the flocking and the fighting of
crows and kites "—and that was pretty nearly the history of the
internecine wars of the seven Saxon kingdoms. After that
came an agency which was not of this world—St. Augustin
breathed Christianity into the Saxon race. Dioceses, churches,
and parishes were formed before the tithings, hundreds, and
shires had any existence. Christianity began to shape the community, which, under Alfred, gathered together in one the
whole Saxon people; and from Alfred to St. Edward the Con-
fessor England attained a state of high Christian civilization.
It is a history full of luminous beauty. In those days it is said
that along the high-roads there were drinking-fountains. We
of the nineteenth century imagine our drinking-fountains to be
the last perfection of humane and civilized invention, but our
ancestors had them along their roads; and it is said that so
strong was the reign of law in that time that a poor mother carrying her child might walk in safety from the Humber to the
southern sea. Well, then, progress had been made since the
Druids. After that came the Normans introducing the feudal
system of the continental kingdoms, consolidating and
strengthening the simpler, more primitive, and, I may say,
pastoral government of the Saxon kings. England became one
of the mightiest monarchies of Europe. The three kingdoms
were at least united together by the Norman conquest of Ireland and Scotland. This was the first outline of the British Empire. Thus unity has endured and confirmed itself from that day

to this. The civilization of the Normans was far higher than that of the Saxons. They introduced a refinement and literature and a higher grade of culture. This is to be traced in our language, in which, for the most part, the simple terms describing individual things are Saxon, but the more abstract terms which describe kind and species are from the Norman-French. At least this rule may be so extensively verified in English as to show that a wave of a higher civilization passed over a lower civilization and elevated it. After this, from age to age, came the introduction of manufactures. Then commercial towns began to grow: London, which once was surrounded by a single wall with its one tower, has never ceased to grow till it has reached its three millions of men; Liverpool has exceeded in its magnificence the docks of London, which were thought to be the wonder of the world; Glasgow sprang up suddenly into an enormous manufacturing world, with half a million of human beings; and Manchester, which in the memory of living men was a single parish with its parish church, has half a million likewise. I cannot omit to say, in passing, that only the other day a good old venerable Catholic went to her rest in Manchester, who remembered the time when she and her family came to Manchester and found there a humble priest and eight Catholics. The immigration of her family raised the Catholics of Manchester to seventeen. One poor church, one priest, and a flock of seventeen, was the slender beginning which she lived to see expanded to a diocese. It has now a bishop, twelve or fourteen magnificent churches, many priests, and one hundred thousand Catholics. Well this is an example of progress which I can understand.

In the seventeenth century Great Britain acquired its West Indian colonies, and in the eighteenth century it acquired the East Indies and Canada—it already possessed the plantations of America. It became therefore a colonial empire. The American plantations in the year 1775, by a happy law of progress, began to work out their own independence, and became a vast confederation. The North American Union, the greatest creation of civilized life, perhaps, in the world, sprang from Great Britain. The English tongue has gone with it throughout the whole breadth. The English tongue is more widely spread than any language, and the Anglo-Celtic race covers a wider surface of the earth than any other tongue or people. It may be very well said, then, that those leathern boats, which lay upon the mud of Thanet, brought over with them a very notable burden. When we look at the colonial empire of Great Britain, with England as its heart and centre, at the United States as its offspring and sister, it is true to say that here has been an example of true progress, and progress so grand, that perhaps in the history of the world it cannot be exceeded.

Well, now let me take another example, that is, the progress of Christianity. I will not dwell upon this, because it is so obvious; I need only give its outline. You remember the prophecy of Daniel, of a stone which became a great mountain and filled the earth; and the parable of our Lord, of the mustard-seed which took root and became a great tree. Christianity has fulfilled those two prophecies. If you consider for a moment what the faith was when it was received only by the Jews who believed, what it became when it was spread to the synagogue—the Jews who spoke the Greek language, and were dispersed abroad—when from them it passes to the pure heathen of the Roman Empire; how the very word " pagan " signifies " the peasantry " who lived out in the country, as distinguished from the cities which first became Christian; how Christianity spread itself over the whole mass, like the prophet Eliseus, who communicated his warmth to the body of the dead child, and so communicated the warmth of life to the populations of the world, that they lived with a new and vital spirit; then how over the whole population the universal episcopate began to extend its sway, and to organize it into the distinct divisions and flocks which constitute the dioceses and pastoral cure of the Catholic Church; then how the faith and morality of Christianity began to work in domestic life, and how from the homes and families of men spread into the public life of cities, and how gradually it took possession of Rome, until the world accepted it, and was penetrated through and through with the light of Christianity; how, after that, the literature and laws, customs, and even the very warfare of the Christian world, was guided and mitigated by the effects of Christianity; how thenceforward the universal church spread itself, the line of its Pontiffs continuing unbroken as its supreme rulers, the line of its councils legislating continuously, from age to age, for the necessities of the world; how, in its office of teacher of faith and judge of morals, the church has continually governed the Christian nations of the world, and is there still, standing imperishable, immutable, and ever progressive, always extending, always maturing and perfecting the work which it has in hand—there is the most perfect example of progress the world has ever seen, or ever will see.

Now let us take an example or two from the progress of science. There was a time when science hardly existed. It began by observation and reflection. A very learned and good man unhappily was lost to us some years ago by a fall from his horse, and a more lamented death among scholars these later days I have hardly known. I mean Whewell, the head of Trinity College, Cambridge. He was a man of powerful, original, mature, and just and scientific mind. He wrote two books which I dare say many who hear me know. The one on the " History of the Inductive Sciences," that is to say, the pure and applied sciences, in the true scientific sense of the term; not the chatter we hear about social and historical sciences, which can have no existence. That book, in three volumes, I believe, under correction, to be one of the most solid and precious books of these days. He wrote also two volumes on the " Philosophy of the Inductive Sciences," being an analysis of the intellectual processes of those sciences. Those two works trace out the progress of science from its beginning along the line of its advance. For example, he traces in astronomy the earliest observation of the Orientals; and then, how, by gradual discovery, the whole science has been developed; how its periods of observation were followed by periods of demonstration, and these again by periods of deduction, so that the science was always growing in conformity to its first principles, as the acorn into the oak-tree. The intellectual germ was always extending itself. There was a time when this earth was believed to be the fixed centre of all things, the sun revolving round it; and the solar system, as we know it, was supposed to be the whole universe. We know now that the sun, which is the centre of our system, together with all its planets, and they, with all their satellites and comets, are going at a speed which takes our breath away to hear, in the direction of the star λ in the constellation of Hercules. This is true and legitimate progress in science. Take another example. Whewell tells us of the tradition that the first idea of the octave in music sprang up in the mind of a Greek by hearing the constant ring and alternation of hammers beating on an anvil. From this the idea of number, rhythm, and sound, with the distinction of tones, grew in his mind, and the basis of scientific music was laid. In the history of music we read that in proportion as instruments have been perfected in compass, in that proportion has music been perfected. The organ on which Handel played had I know not how much less in compass than the organs of the present day. His music therefore was limited. And the sphere and range of music has been perpetually increasing as instruments have been perfected and their sphere enlarged. This again is an example of scientific and true progress. I might take another example in spectrum analysis, or in electricity, with its application to telegraphy, and many other uses, as an instance of true progress.

We will now take an example of progress in political government. The first law of political government in the beginning was club-law; and the way in which people made peace was by beating one another till one party had enough of it. Jurists tell us the first fiction of civil law was government by majority; that is to say, they no longer counted the number of clubs or bruises, but the number of votes; and the vote by majority and minority was taken as sufficient to settle any political controversy, which is at least a more comfortable way of settling a contest. When this mode of government sprang up, immediately there was found something which had the power of tying the hands of tyrants, of limiting the absolutism of despotic government. There was a time when the first principle of law was, " *Quod principi placuit legis habet vigorem;* " that is, what the prince wills has the force of law; so that the will of the prince was the law of the subject. Well, the introduction of this new theory of putting votes for clubs had a beneficial effect in England, and the dicta and axioms of our lawyers, going back to Bracton and Fleta, were recast. Our ancestors said, " *Lex facit regem*," not " *Rex facit legem.*" The law makes the king, not the king makes the law. There came in another idea of government, and that was monarchy limited by law; both by the unwritten customs of the people and the written law made legitimately by the king and his councillors. Well, from this has come gradually what we call self-government; but the government which is municipal and local depends ultimately upon the government of each individual man over himself; and no people are worthy to obtain, or can obtain, self-government, or if they had obtained could keep it, who do not train and discipline themselves, so that they begin by governing themselves before they govern their neighbors. There has been undoubtedly great progress in those things also. One more example I will give, and with that will end this dreary part of the subject; and that shall be progress in civilization.

I cannot deny that we are very much better off than when our ancestors smeared themselves with woad; that our manufactures, cheapening good articles of clothing, are a great blessing to everybody, rich and poor. I also think it is much better to live on good wheaten bread than on acorns; and if we cannot grow enough wheat at home, it is a good thing that we are able to import it. Also I think it is better to live in brick houses than in huts of mud and wicker-work; and it is better we should have machinery which will do ten thousand operations with great fineness and power rather than flint knives and burnt sticks. It seems, therefore, that progress in civilization as regards food, clothing, dwellings, and machinery, in the mechanical power of production, transit by railway, and the dynamic powers of machinery—that is, the mechanical powers applied to lift weights, build houses, and transport of goods which no human strength could lift—that all this is a vast progress in the material order. I may say also that the extension of the benefits of all these things, from the rich, or from the classes that might appropriate them to their own enjoyment, to the whole mass of the people, bringing them within the reach of the poor and those standing in greatest need of them—that this is a very just and legitimate idea of progress. Next I will say that what is called credit in commerce is a notable progress. Trading in kind would be very inconvenient nowadays, if, every time you had to buy a hat, you had to pay for it with a table, or if every time you had to purchase, it was necessary to put down the cash on the spot, you would have to carry a fortune with you; and if brass money were the chief currency, that would be still more difficult; so that the substitution of a gold and silver currency is a progress in civilization. But it seems to me that the introduction of the bank-note is much better; and bank-notes never could have existed, if there had not been confidence created between man and man, and recognized by public and social law, which gives value and reality to a piece of paper. Now that would appear to be the result of modern civilization, because I do not read of it either in Athens or Rome. This example, entirely the creation of a civilized state, I will not put high, but I think it an improvement, as it facilitates the transaction of business. Then, international law, that is, the law which runs from nation to nation, an extension of that domestic law which governs a people singly, by contract and mutual recognition, at last federates together and binds a number of nations in one family; and there arises what is called by lawyers a comity of nations, which means a certain mutually fair and benevolent dealing with one another. Just as charity binds individuals, so nations are bound by justice; and this is a distinction of civilization which grew and advanced so long as Christian civilization endured.

I hope that I have given a sufficient number of examples of progress in our own country, in Christianity, in science, in political government, and in civilization, to have cleared ourselves at least from the imputation of being opposed to progress.

Let me sum up what I have said in the first part of my subject in this way: It is a philosophical axiom, a certain truth of the reason, that everything is preserved by the same principles by which it is produced. The oak which springs from the acorn is preserved by the sap and fibre and wood and bark which belong to its kind; you cannot change that nature without destroying its perfection. This is true physically, it is true in science, it is true in moral character, as I will go on to show. Whenever anything grows from its root by the same principles of development to its perfection, it retains its own identity. The oak is always the oak, and Christian society is always Christian society. Another axiom is, that destruction is the change or perversion of the principles by which anything was produced; if you can change or pervert the principles from which anything springs, you destroy it. For instance, one single foreign element introduced into the blood produces death; one false assumption admitted into science destroys its certainty;

one false principle admitted into morals is fatal. As, for example, a portion of the Church separated from the unity of the
Church, therefore separated from the principles by which it
was first created and preserved, becomes a schism. A state
which rejects its own vital laws, which were founded upon
reason, justice, and Christianity, becomes an anomaly. A body
which has reached maturity, and loses the principle of its ani-
mation, becomes dust. The first of these axioms is what I may
call the law of progress, the second is the law of decay. We will
now consider the latter.

The last part of my subject is that which is opposed to progress. Let me take as an example the formation of character.
I dare say all of you have seen many a youth beginning life with
great promise, with piety, faith, conscientiousness, and so
growing to manhood; yet there has been about him something
which a keen observer has detected, yet feared even to think of,
lest he should do wrong. Just as some magnificent tree suddenly snaps in the night, its strength of stem overmastered by
a high wind, because at the heart there was a secret rottenness,
unseen without, yet it was there within, and when the pressure
came upon the branches the tree went asunder—so it is with
many a character. There is some false principle or passion,
something within, which, when it is tried, fails. The piety of
boyhood and of youth becomes careless, because there is a germ
of sloth, and ends in impiety. Faith has near its root, some secret germ of doubt, which begins to grow secretly, and at last
shows itself in the form of captious objection, and ends in un-
belief. Conscientiousness begins to manifest a certain laxity,
and ends in acts of dishonor. Here we see what may be called
a falling off from the first principles by which the character was
formed in the beginning. Apply this, then, to the case of nations.

Take the republic of Athens, which was cultivated, intellectually, morally, scientifically, and politically, to a very high degree, which established a colonial empire, and I may say a
dominion over the Greek race. It rose to a very high point of
civilization. It then became a luxurious and licentious democracy, and began at once to decay. Rome in like manner had
what its people called the *prisca virtus*, that old austerity of virtue, which carried the sway of its republic over the whole earth.

When it began to be luxurious and corrupt, an imperial tyranny was established over it. Thenceforward it went to pieces age after age, with the greatest havoc ever made on earth. Spain was a noble, Christian, and austere people, until by successful commerce, and the mines of the New World, it was inundated with gold. Among the causes of Spain's decline, the enormous influx of gold has a chief place. It brought on a relaxation of industry, a carelessness and luxuriousness of life, a disposition to live on acquired wealth, which paralyzed the energy of the people. Here, again, we find the principles of the nation's greatness discarded, and its greatness lost. Take the example of the Christian world as distinct from the Church. Always remember, when we speak of the Christian world, that the Christian world and the Christian Church are two different things. The Christian Church existed before the Christian world, and created it. The Christian world may go to pieces, and it seems at this moment to be on the breakers; but the Church will remain in all its vigor and plenitude of light and power until its Divine Head comes again. The Christian world is everywhere divided; and because divided, it is in perplexity and conflict everywhere. We hear Christian men complaining and contending about " the religious difficulty." They cannot act together or educate their children together, because of the religious difficulty. Do you know what the religious difficulty is? It is not the Catechism, it is not the Thirty-nine Articles—it is God, the truth of God, and the will of God. Because some men have determined to interpret the truth of God in their own fashion, and to reject everything else, and because others reject God altogether, therefore they can find no common basis upon which to educate or to legislate, without shutting out God, His truth and will, from the four corners of an act of Parliament. Here we have an example of the abandonment of those principles upon which the progress of the Christian civilization of the world was made.

Modern civilization, then, is civilization without Christianity. It is perfect when the religious difficulty is eliminated and excluded from the progress of man, intellectual, moral, and political. Take for example France, which has been for eighty years leading the way in modern civilization. A more refined people, a people more exquisite in the cultivation of the arts and sciences of the natural order, is not to be found; but a people more incoherent in political life, more wanting in the power of permanent combination, more stricken as it were with the impossibility of adhering together in any one constant form of civil government, can hardly be found in history. That noble people, full of intelligence and of genius, because it has abandoned the first principles which formed the great French monarchy of a thousand years, and has substituted in their place the shallow theories that are called the principles of '89, that majestic people has reduced itself for a time to an instability so great, that within the memory of living men it has had two empires, three republics, three kings dethroned, seventeen constitutions, and six or seven revolutions. The present state of that noble country is such, that we may justly take it as an example of the dissolution which follows upon the loss of those first principles from which Christian society springs, and by which alone Christian society can be preserved.

Let us now take England. England in the last three hundred years has been departing from those principles by which its progress was originally impelled, and by which that progress has been preserved. I will only touch upon three points. Three hundred years ago a legal Church was set up, which covered the whole country, and, excepting only the faithful Catholics who refused it, and a handful of dissenters, contained the whole population of England. At this moment the population of England has outgrown that legal religion by one-half its number. Next there was a political constitution of Church and State set up at that day which spread itself over the whole Anglican population. The population has outgrown the constitution; and, therefore, some twenty or thirty years ago we were perpetually hearing about Chartism, and now in these days we are hearing of trades-unions, political unions, strikes among trades —the masses of the people uniting together to accomplish, by combination against capital, that which the law of the land ought to do for them. Lastly, the effect of these and other causes is that one-half of the people of England have outgrown Christianity, they have passed beyond the moral restraints of Christianity, they have become materialized. They are not atheists, not infidels. It is not by the act of their own will; it is the pressure, and I may say the tyranny, of events or the logic of facts, of which we hear so much, that has robbed them of their inheritances of faith and culture. And this because the first principles of Christian civilization, which created the mature commonwealth of England, were violated three hundred years ago.

I was going to take next the example of the United States, but I will not venture upon any judgment of its state. In talking of England I am always willing to give hard knocks. Englishmen like it. They give us the privileges of sons and brothers; and we may say what we like about England, if we say it filially—I trust I never do otherwise. But of the New World I do not venture so freely to speak. I trust that in the United States good care will be taken of the faith, I mean of Christianity, of Christian education, of morals, of domestic life, and of strong-minded women—a race now rising among ourselves, and, with all good-will towards them, I hope they will be benignly kept in order. I hope that in the United States there will be great care taken to exclude political ambition and faction. About fifteen years ago I read what I believe to be an authentic statement—that a number of leading politicians and statesmen of America, of highest name and note, met together to consider the condition of the United States It was before the war, when there were already many causes of anxiety. It was said that there was a universal and growing license of the individual will, and that law and government were powerless to restrain it; that if the will of the multitude became licentious, it would seriously threaten the public welfare and liberty of the country. The conclusion they came to was, that unless there could be found some power which could restrain the individual will, this danger would at last seriously menace the United States. Now I think we are all ready to say what that power is It is the power which created the Christian society of the world. Whensoever it is weakened or lost, immediately all political society decays. I hope it may be restored and long retained in the American Union. I hope too that the prophecy of Bishop Berkeley may be abundantly fulfilled in America:

> " Westward the course of empire takes its way,
>   The first four acts already past;
> A fifth shall close the drama with the day:
>   Time's noblest offspring is the last."

I hope there is a future for America which will verify this prophecy; but I am confident it cannot be, unless those first principles of Christian civilization which have created and maintained the progress of the Christian world shall be restored and preserved.

Now I shall be asked what those principles are; and I will enunciate them as quickly as I can. First, they are the laws of God in nature and revelation. They are the laws of God in nature; that is, the reason rightly cultivated, the conscience rightly directed; the four cardinal virtues, prudence, justice, fortitude, and temperance; the law, that is, recognition of a rule and duty of obedience to the law. The idea of law is the foundation of all civil society, and the rule of the conscience and conduct of men. Second, the principles of God's law in Revelation, the Ten Commandments, a very old code, and very much forgotten; the twelve articles of the Creed, very much disliked by those who talk of the religious difficulty; the unity of the Christian Church, and its authority. Thirdly, the law of man made by rulers and legislatures when conformable to those of God. And so long as legislatures and governments conform themselves and their laws to the law of God, then there is progress. I utterly deny there is progress when they depart from it.

What, then, are the principles that convert progress to decay? The violation of God's laws, their perversion, and their privation or loss. I had put down a number of examples, but I have looked at my watch, and see I must not go on. Therefore I can only give one single example, which is the most fresh and vivid at this moment.

We have heard a great deal of the Munich Conference; well, now, this revolt is nothing new. Another, precisely the same, happened at the beginning of this century. In the year 1801, on the fifteenth of August, Pope Pius VII issued an apostolic letter, whereby, by the supreme authority of the Vicar of Jesus Christ, he extinguished the whole existing episcopate in France, subdivided anew all the dioceses, and thus created a new hierarchy over the whole of the country. At once, a certain number of men, in whom the Gallican spirit was strong—I have no doubt many were conscientious and good men, but they had admitted one false principle, which, as I said, like one little

globule of foreign matter in the blood is fatal—absolutely refused obedience, separated themselves from the Catholic
Church and set up what was called the Petite Église. This little
Church consisted of a considerable number of bishops, priests
and laity. The last bishop of the Petite Église submitted himself
to the Catholic Church in the year 1829, and died in peace. But
this separation is not extinct. In the year 1865, when I was at
Poictiers, the bishop told me that he had some five thousand of
the members of this little Church in his diocese, who had no
priests, no sacraments, no churches; nevertheless, that they
baptized their own children, and met, from time to time, to say
prayers and the rosary together. They are dying out. Yet they
began with a number of bishops; but they had no succession,
and they are now ceasing to exist.

What is now happening at Munich? The Holy Father, in the
Vatican Council, issued last year the constitution *Pastor
Æternus*, whereby the infallibility of the Head of the Church
was defined. The " Times " newspaper says all the bishops of
the Roman Catholic Church have accepted it, " having been
fairly caught and safely landed in the great Vatican net." Well,
this was too much for the professors of Germany. They are an
estate in the intellectual realm of Germany, and the consequence has been what you may read in the newspapers. Some
five hundred men from all countries have met together. The
names of the chief leaders from foreign countries have been
mentioned in the papers, except only the English deputies.
Who deputed them? Whom did they represent? I wish the
names had been published, as we should know more easily how
to deal with them. As it is, I can only say that every man who
has participated in that Munich Congress is either directly, explicitly, or implicitly excommunicated and incapable of sacraments. However, this Congress did a great many things.
It has resolved to begin a system of parishes and public
worship with priests, the greater part of whom have been
suspended, and are incapable of officiating in the Catholic
Church. It is a curious thing that the Petite Église of whom
I spoke at first commenced their schism upon the rejection of
the plenitude of the supreme authority of the Head of the
Church in matter of jurisdiction and discipline. These Munich
separatists are committing schism by rejecting the plenitude

of the doctrinal authority of the Head of the Church in matter
of faith. That is to say, these two schisms are made precisely
on the same ground: the plenitude of the primacy in jurisdiction and doctrinal authority; with what result, time is to show.
In the mean while we have the authority of the " Times " newspaper for saying that the great difficulty with them is, that,
though they have some laymen and some priests, they have no
bishop.

" Here," says the " Times," " are five hundred professors,
priests, and laymen, founding and constituting a Church—old,
say they; new, says Rome—and, as it were at the last moment,
they find they must have bishops to keep it going. They will
beg, borrow, or steal one. Are not bishops to be found somewhere? We, nevertheless, are sure that not even an English
' colonial,' not even a suffragan, not even a Scottish bishop,
without clergy, churches, or people, would hire himself out to
keep up the breed of old Catholics at Munich."

The broad English common-sense of the " Times " has saved
it. It goes on to say: " The last words in the description which
our correspondent, who was present, gives of the last public
meeting have, we suspect, a prophetic import. The assemblage
was vast for Catholic Munich; the city was much stirred up by
the strangeness of the event; but when all was over the impression left on the public was ' that much more remained to be
done.' All Englishmen must feel that. It is a common thing to
find men who retain the shell, as it were, of old conviction; who
live by old habits and use the words they did in their youth;
but whose inner nature, indeed, whose leading principles, are
bursting these bonds. The programme before us we venture to
pronounce utterly inconsistent in spirit with the conservative
part of its doctrinal propositions."

Here is good sense. Further on, the " Times," with the accuracy of a Catholic theologian, speaking of the Munich Congress, continues: " It retains the decrees of the Council of
Trent, including all former councils, but reopens—and, indeed, compels the reopening of—every controversy which that
council was summoned to close. ' A dogma,' it says, ' to be
valid, must be in accordance with Holy Writ and the old traditions of the Church, such as they have been conveyed to us in
the writings of the recognized fathers and the decrees of the

councils.' Then, having said this, it proceeds to point out that even were a council really ecumenical, it would be powerless against essential truth and history; nay, that no unanimity could confer validity on its decrees. The congress, some here will think, avows an intention to look still further ahead. It sets out boldly on the road of science and progressive Christian culture; it insists that the clergy shall be theologians, and also admitted freely to the culture of the century. This must all mean something, and most people will understand it better than the dogmatic portion of the programme. Which of the two con- flicting portions will survive the other on German soil is a question on which our English readers will not be long in making up their minds."

I must pass over much more that I had meant to say, and sum up in these words: We do not oppose any true material, scientific, social, or political progress. The reiterated and persistent way in which people say we are opposed to progress is cant. They who can believe it to be so are superstitious—they ought to believe in hobgoblins; and perhaps they do. Well, then, my general conclusion is. that the Church is progressing and always will progress, in strength, truth, unity of faith, in the self-evidence by which it proves itself to the world. Secondly, that nations are departing from the principles which created their civilization. Thirdly, that civilization is becoming every day more and more material. I shall keep you till midnight if I go on. Look for proof of what I say in any work on political economy; or in the production and use of wealth, its enjoyment; luxury, and the consequences of luxury, visible all around us. Fourthly, that this material civilization, while more and more material, is becoming less and less moral. Fifthly, that therefore this modern civilization is for this reason not progressive, because the nations are not growing happier, nor purer in their morals, nor more united in the charities of life. Sixthly, that society is not becoming more solid, more safe, more stable; that, on the contrary, the reverse of all these things is undubitably true and visible before our eyes. Seventhly, that individuals are becoming more anarchical, the intellect more licentious, the wills of man more stubborn; and this self-will expresses itself in their actions, so that it is true to say that the principles upon which the Christian world was founded, and by which it has hitherto been preserved, have been rejected and are being violated on every side. The Christian world therefore is not progressing, but is going back. Finally, civilization like everything else cannot stand still: *non progredi est regredi;* not to go onward is to go backward; and therefore it is that the Holy Father, when he condemned in the syllabus the proposition, "that the Roman Pontiff can and ought to reconcile and adjust himself to progress, liberalism, and modern civilization," condemned a great error, and proclaimed a great truth. There is no hope for either man or society, but to go back to the feet of the only true legislator, who said, " Come unto Me: take My yoke upon you; for My yoke is easy and My burden is light."

ON DOMESTIC AND FOREIGN
AFFAIRS

—

THE ESTABLISHED CHURCH IN
IRELAND

—

BY

WILLIAM EWART GLADSTONE

WILLIAM EWART GLADSTONE

1809—1898

William Ewart Gladstone happened to be born in Liverpool; but he was a Scot on both sides of his ancestry; and his father came of an ancient line of Gledstanes (Hawk-stones) who had figured with dignity and credit in Scottish history for generations. Born in 1809, he lived all but ninety years, retaining to the last the unimpaired use of his mind, and to the last interested in all that pertained to the welfare and honor of his country Though he had retired from active political life four or five years before his death, no one could act in the government without explicit or implied reference to him; and his opponents were never free from the apprehension that, if a crisis demanded it, the Grand Old Man would once more take the helm. Often invited to enter the peerage, he steadfastly and wisely declined, and remained to the end the Great Commoner—a title which he shared with the only other English statesman who could stand comparison with him—Lord Chatham previous to 1766. That he made many errors in the course of his long life was inevitable; though many of them were due less to his will than to the tyranny of circumstance; but the longer he lived the more firmly did the mass of the people pin their faith to him; and the worthier of their trust did he prove himself

It was in 1832, when twenty-three years of age, that he took his seat for the first time in Parliament; and with the exception of eighteen months, he sat there till his retirement from public life in 1894 Most of this time he represented the boroughs of Greenwich and Midlothian But his first constituency was Newark, a " pocket-borough " of the Duke of Newcastle, a Tory. When Sir Robert Peel came into power in 1834, Gladstone was appointed a Lord of the Treasury, and then Under Secretary of the Colonies. In 1841 he became Vice-President of the Board of Trade, and made a reputation by his handling of the scheme of tariff revision. Two years later he took his place in the Cabinet, but resigned in 1845 for reasons of political consistency Between this time and 1852 Gladstone's views underwent a progressive change, and as Chancellor of the Exchequer in the coalition ministry of Aberdeen, he appeared under Liberal colors Lord Palmerston and Lord Russell both continued him in the Exchequer, and when Palmerston died, in 1865, Gladstone became leader of the House of Commons. The Tories defeated his reform bill, and " dished the Whigs " by bringing in one of their own, but in 1868 he was chosen Prime Minister, and so remained till 1874. Nor was he content to fill this august office only; he combined with it those of First Lord of the Treasury, Chancellor of the Exchequer, and Lord Privy Seal The more he labored for the public weal, the more strength and ability to work did he seem to evince The disestablishment of the Irish Church was one of the earliest measures which, as Prime Minister, he introduced and advocated; and from that time the condition of Ireland was one of his leading preoccupations

Gladstone's oratory was always remarkable, even from the first; but it constantly improved as he advanced in age and experience, and his knowledge of men and affairs broadened and deepened. The almost savage earnestness with which he dealt with questions of moment never left him; but he gradually relieved it by a sunny and sympathetic treatment of the body of his subject, by touches or humor and wit, and by the extraordinary perspicacity and ease with which he handled matters which, till then, had been thought unsusceptible of any but formal and tedious treatment This was especially conspicuous in his speeches on finance. " Domestic and Foreign Affairs " and " The Established Church in Ireland " are typical examples of his Parliamentary speeches.

ON DOMESTIC AND FOREIGN AFFAIRS

Delivered at West Calder, November 27, 1879[1]

MR. CHAIRMAN AND GENTLEMEN: In addressing you to-day, as in addressing like audiences assembled for a like purpose in other places of the county, I am warmed by the enthusiastic welcome which you have been pleased in every quarter and in every form to accord to me. I am, on the other hand, daunted when I recollect, first of all, what large demands I have to make on your patience; and secondly, how inadequate are my powers, and how inadequate almost any amount of time you can grant me, to set forth worthily the whole of the case which ought to be laid before you in connection with the coming election.

To-day, gentlemen, as I know that many among you are interested in the land, and as I feel that what is termed " agricultural distress " is at the present moment a topic too serious to be omitted from our consideration, I shall say some words upon the subject of that agricultural distress, and particularly, because in connection with it there have arisen in some quarters of the country proposals, which have received a countenance far beyond their deserts, to reverse or to compromise the work which it took us one whole generation to achieve, and to revert to the mischievous, obstructive, and impoverishing system of protection. Gentlemen, I speak of agricultural distress as a matter now undoubtedly serious. Let none of us withold our sympathy from the farmer, the cultivator of the soil, in the struggle he has to undergo. His struggle is a struggle of competition with the United States. But I do not fully explain the case when I say the United States. It is not with the entire United States, it is with the western portion of these States—that portion remote from the sea-board; and I wish in the first place, gentlemen, to state to you all a fact of very great interest and importance, as it seems to me, relating to and defining the point at which the competition of the western States of America is most severely felt. I have in my hand a letter received recently from one well known, and honorably known, in Scotland—Mr. Lyon Playfair, who has recently been a traveller in the United States, and who, as you well know, is as well qualified as any man upon earth for accurate and careful investigation. The point, gentlemen, at which the competition of the western States of America is most severely felt is in the eastern States of America. Whatever be agricultural distress in Scotland, whatever it be, where undoubtedly it is more felt, in England, it is greater by much in the eastern States of America. In the States of New England the soil has been to some extent exhausted by careless methods of agriculture, and these, gentlemen, are the greatest of all the enemies with which the farmer has to contend.

But the foundation of the statement I make, that the eastern States of America are those that most feel the competition of the West, is to be found in facts—in this fact above all, that not only they are not in America, as we are here, talking about the shortness of the annual returns, and in some places having much said on the subject of rents, and of temporary remission or of permanent reduction. That is not the state of things; they have actually got to this point, that the capital values of land, as tested by sales in the market, have undergone an enormous diminution. Now I will tell you something that actually happened, on the authority of my friend Mr. Playfair. I will tell you something that has happened in one of the New England States—not, recollect, in a desert or a remote country—in an old cultivated country, and near one of the towns of these States, a town that has the honorable name of Wellesley.

Mr. Playfair tells me this: Three weeks ago—that is to say, about the first of this month, so you will see my information is tolerably recent—three weeks ago a friend of Mr. Playfair bought a farm near Wellesley for $33 an acre, for £6 12s. an acre—agricultural land, remember, in an old settled country. That is the present condition of agricultural property in the old States of New England. I think by the simple recital of that fact I have tolerably well established my case, for you have not come in England, and you have not come in Scotland, to the point at which agricultural land is to be had—not wild land, but improved and old cultivated land—is to be had for the price of £6 12s. an acre. He mentions that this is by no means a strange case, an isolated case, that it fairly represented the average transactions that have been going on; and he says that in that region the ordinary price of agricultural land at the present time is from $20 to $50 an acre, or from £4 to £10. In New York the soil is better, and the population is greater; but even in the State of New York land ranges for agricultural purposes from $50 to $100, that is to say, from £10 to £20 an acre.

I think those of you, gentlemen, who are farmers will perhaps derive some comfort from perceiving that if the pressure here is heavy the pressure elsewhere and the pressure nearer to the seat of this very abundant production is greater and far greater still.

It is most interesting to consider, however, what this pressure is. There has been developed in the astonishing progressive power of the United States—there has been developed a faculty of producing corn for the subsistence of man, with a rapidity and to an extent unknown in the experience of mankind. There is nothing like it in history. Do not let us conceal, gentlemen, from ourselves the fact; I shall not stand the worse with any of you who are farmers if I at once avow that this greater and comparatively immense abundance of the prime article of subsistence for mankind is a great blessing vouchsafed by Providence to mankind. In part I believe that the cheapness has been increased by special causes. The lands from which the great abundance of American wheat comes are very thinly peopled as yet. They will become more thickly peopled, and as they become more thickly peopled a larger proportion of their produce will be wanted for home consumption and less of it will come to you, and at a higher price. Again, if we are rightly informed, the price of American wheat has been unnaturally reduced by the extraordinary depression, in recent times, of trade in America, and especially of the mineral trades, upon which many railroads are dependent in America, and with which these railroads are connected in America in a degree and manner that in this country we know but little of. With a revival of trade in America it is to be expected that the freights of corn will increase, and all other freights, because the employment of the railroads will be a great deal more abundant, and they will not be content to carry corn at nominal rates. In some respects, therefore, you may expect a mitigation of the pressure, but in other respects it is likely to continue.

Nay, the Prime Minister is reported as having not long ago said—and he ought to have the best information on this subject, nor am I going to impeach in the main what he stated—he gave it to be understood that there was about to be a development of corn production in Canada which would entirely throw into the shade this corn production in the United States. Well, that certainly was very cold comfort, as far as the British agriculturist is concerned, because he did not say—he could not say—that the corn production of the United States was to fall off, but there was to be added an enormous corn production from Manitoba, the great province which forms now a part of the Canada Dominion. There is no doubt, I believe, that it is a correct expectation that vast or very large quantities of corn will proceed from that province, and therefore we have to look forward to a state of things in which, for a considerable time to come, large quantities of wheat will be forthcoming from America, probably larger quantities, and perhaps frequently at lower prices than those at which the corn-producing and corn-exporting districts of Europe have commonly been able to supply us. Now that I believe to be, gentlemen, upon the whole, not an unfair representation of the state of things.

How are you to meet that state of things? What are your fair claims? I will tell you. In my opinion your fair claims are, in the main, two. One is to be allowed to purchase every article that you require in the cheapest market, and have no needless burden laid upon anything that comes to you and can assist you in the cultivation of your land. But that claim has been conceded and fulfilled.

I do not know whether there is an object, an instrument, a tool of any kind, an auxiliary of any kind, that you want for the business of the farmer, which you do not buy at this moment in the cheapest market. But beyond that, you want to be relieved from every unjust and unnecessary legislative restraint. I say every unnecessary legislative restraint, because taxation, gentlemen, is unfortunately a restraint upon us all, but we cannot say that it is always unnecessary, and we cannot say that it is always unjust. Yesterday I ventured to state—and I will therefore not now return to the subject—a number of matters connected with the state of legislation in which it appears to me to be of vital importance, both to the agricultural interest and to the entire community, that the occupiers and cultivators of the land of this country should be relieved from restraints under the operation of which they now suffer considerably. Beyond those two great heads, gentlemen, what you have to look to, I believe, is your own energy, your own energy of thought and action, and your care not to undertake to pay rents greater than, in reasonable calculation, you think you can afford. I am by no means sure, though I speak subject to the correction of higher authority—I am by no means sure that in Scotland within the last fifteen or twenty years something of a speculative character has not entered into rents, and particularly, perhaps, into the rents of hill farms. I remember hearing of the augmentations which were taking place, I believe, all over Scotland—I verified the fact in a number of counties—about twelve or fourteen years ago, in the rents of hill farms, which I confess impressed me with the idea that the high prices that were then ruling, and ruling increasingly from year to year, for meat and wool, were perhaps for once leading the wary and shrewd Scottish agriculturist a little beyond the mark in the rents he undertook to pay. But it is not this only which may press. It is, more broadly, in a serious and manful struggle that you are engaged, in which you will have to exert yourselves to the uttermost, in which you will have a right to claim everything that the legislature can do for you; and I hope it may perhaps possibly be my privilege and honor to assist in procuring for you some of those provisions of necessary liberation from restraint; but beyond that, it is your own energies, of thought and action, to which you will have to trust.

Now, gentlemen, having said thus much, my next duty is to warn you against quack remedies, against delusive remedies, against the quack remedies that there are plenty of people found to propose, not so much in Scotland as in England; for, gentlemen, from Mid-Lothian at present we are speaking to England as well as to Scotland. Let me give a friendly warning from this northern quarter to the agriculturist of England not to be deluded by those who call themselves his friends in a degree of special and superior excellence, and who have been too much given to delude him in other times; not to be deluded into hoping relief from sources from which it can never come. Now, gentlemen, there are three of these remedies. The first of them, gentlemen, I will not call a quack remedy at all, but I will speak of it notwithstanding in the tone of rational and dispassionate discussion. I am not now so much upon the controversial portion of the land question—a field which, Heaven knows, is wide enough—as I am upon matters of deep and universal interest to us in our economic and social condition. There are some gentlemen, and there are persons for whom I for one have very great respect, who think that the difficulties of our agriculture may be got over by a fundamental change in the land-holding system of this country.

I do not mean, now pray observe, a change as to the law of entail and settlement, and all those restraints which, I hope, were tolerably well disposed of yesterday at Dalkeith; but I mean those who think that if you can cut up the land, or a large part of it, into a multitude of small properties, that of itself will solve the difficulty, and start everybody on a career of prosperity.

Now, gentlemen, to a proposal of that kind, I, for one, am not going to object upon the ground that it would be inconsistent with the privileges of landed proprietors. In my opinion, if it is known to be for the welfare of the community at large, the legislature is perfectly entitled to buy out the landed proprietors. It is not intended probably to confiscate the property of a landed proprietor more than the property of any other man; but the state is perfectly entitled, if it please, to buy out the landed proprietors as it may think fit, for the purpose of dividing the property into small lots. I don't wish to recommend it, because I will show you the doubts that to my mind hang about that proposal; but I admit that in principle no objection can be taken. Those persons who possess large portions of the spaces of the earth are not altogether in the same position as the possessors of mere personalty; that personalty does not impose the same limitations upon the action and industry of man, and upon the well-being of the community, as does the possession of land; and, therefore, I freely own that compulsory expropriation is a thing which for an adequate public object is in itself admissible and so far sound in principle.

Now, gentlemen, this idea about small proprietors, however, is one which very large bodies and parties in this country treat with the utmost contempt; and they are accustomed to point to France, and say: " Look at France." In France you have got 5,000,000—I am not quite sure whether it is 5,000,000 or even more; I do not wish to be beyond the mark in anything—you have 5,000,000 of small proprietors, and you do not produce in France as many bushels of wheat per acre as you do in England. Well, now I am going to point out to you a very remarkable fact with regard to the condition of France. I will not say that France produces—for I believe it does not produce —as many bushels of wheat per acre as England does, but I should like to know whether the wheat of France is produced mainly upon the small properties of France. I believe that the wheat of France is produced mainly upon the large properties of France, and I have not any doubt that the large properties of England are, upon the whole, better cultivated, and more capital is put into the land than in the large properties of France. But it is fair that justice should be done to what is called the peasant proprietary. Peasant proprietary is an excellent thing, if it can be had, in many points of view. It interests an enormous number of the people in the soil of the country, and in the stability of its institutions and its laws. But now look at the effect that it has upon the progressive value of the land—and I am going to give you a very few figures which I will endeavor to relieve from all complication, lest I should unnecessarily weary you. But what will you think when I tell you that the agricultural value of France—the taxable income derived from the land, and therefore the income of the proprietors of that land—has advanced during our lifetime far more rapidly than that of England? When I say England I believe the same thing is applicable to Scotland, certainly to Ireland; but I shall take England for my test, because the difference between England and Scotland, though great, does not touch the principle; and, because it so happens that we have some means of illustration from former times for England, which are not equally applicable for all the three kingdoms.

Here is the state of the case. I will not go back any further than 1851. I might go back much further: it would only strengthen my case. But for 1851 I have a statement made by

French official authority of the agricultural income of France, as well as the income of other real property, viz., houses. In 1851 the agricultural income of France was £76,000,000. It was greater in 1851 than the whole income from land and houses together had been in 1821. This is a tolerable evidence of progress; but I will not enter into the detail of it, because I have no means of dividing the two—the house income and the land income—for the earlier year, namely, 1821. In 1851 it was £76,-000,000—the agricultural income; and in 1864 it had risen from £76,000,000 to £106,000,000. That is to say, in the space of thirteen years the increase of agricultural values in France—annual values—was no less than forty per cent., or three per cent. per annum. Now, I go to England. Wishing to be quite accurate, I shall limit myself to that with respect to which we have positive figures. In England the agricultural income in 1813-14 was £37,000,000; in 1842 it was £42,000,000, and that year is the one I will take as my starting-point. I have given you the years 1851 to 1864 in France. I could only give you those thirteen years with a certainty that I was not misleading you, and I believe I have kept within the mark. I believe I might have put my case more strongly for France.

In 1842, then, the agricultural income of England was £42,-000,000; in 1876 it was £52,000,000—that is to say, while the agricultural income of France increased forty per cent. in thirteen years, the agricultural income of England increased twenty per cent. in thirty-four years. The increase in France was three per cent. per annum; the increase in England was about one-half or three-fifths per cent. per annum. Now, gentlemen, I wish this justice to be done to a system where peasant proprietary prevails. It is of great importance. And will you allow me, you who are Scotch agriculturists, to assure you that I speak to you not only with the respect which is due from a candidate to a constituency, but with the deference which is due from a man knowing very little of agricultural matters to those who know a great deal? And there is one point at which the considerations that I have been opening up, and this rapid increase of the value of the soil in France, bear upon our discussions. Let me try to to explain it. I believe myself that the operation of economic laws is what in the main dictates the distribution of landed property in this country I doubt if those economic laws will allow it to remain cut up into a multitude of small properties like the small properties of France. As to small holdings, I am one of those who attach the utmost value to them. I say that in the Lothians—I say that in the portion of the country where almost beyond any other large holdings prevail—in some parts of which large holdings exclusively are to be found—I attach the utmost value to them. But it is not on that point I am going to dwell, for we have no time for what is unnecessary. What I do wish very respectfully to submit to you, gentlemen, is this. When you see this vast increase of the agricultural value of France, you know at once it is perfectly certain that it has not been upon the large properties of France, which, if anything, are inferior in cultivation to the large properties of England. It has been upon those very peasant-properties which some people are so ready, to decry. What do the peasant-properties mean? They mean what, in France, is called the small cultivation—that is to say, cultivation of superior articles, pursued upon a small scale—cultivation of flowers, cultivation of trees and shrubs, cultivation of fruits of every kind, and all that, in fact, which rises above the ordinary character of farming produce, and rather approaches the produce of the gardener.

Gentlemen, I cannot help having this belief, that, among other means of meeting the difficulties in which we may be placed, our destiny is that a great deal more attention will have to be given than heretofore by the agriculturalists of England, and perhaps even by the agriculturalists of Scotland, to the production of fruits, of vegetables, of flowers, of all that variety of objects which are sure to find a market in a rich and wealthy country like this, but which have hitherto been consigned almost exclusively to garden production You know that in Scotland, in Aberdeenshire—and I am told also in Perthshire—a great example of this kind has been set in the cultivation of strawberries—the cultivation of strawberries is carried on over hundreds of acres at once. I am ashamed, gentlemen, to go further into this matter, as if I was attempting to instruct you. I am sure you will take my hint as a respectful hint—I am sure you will take it as a friendly hint. I do not believe that the large properties of this country, generally or universally, can or will be broken up into small ones. I do not believe that the land of this country will be owned, as a general rule, by those who cultivate it. I believe we shall continue to have, as we have had, a class of landlords and a class of cultivators, but I most earnestly desire to see—not only to see the relations of those classes to one another harmonious and sound, their interests never brought into conflict; but I desire to see both flourishing and prospering, and the soil of my country producing, as far as may be, under the influence of capital and skill, every variety of product which may give an abundant livelihood to those who live upon it. I say, therefore, gentlemen, and I say it with all respect, I hope for a good deal from the small culture, the culture in use among the small proprietors of France; but I do not look to a fundamental change in the distribution of landed property in this country as a remedy for agricultural distress.

But I go on to another remedy which is proposed, and I do it with a great deal less of respect; nay, I now come to the region of what I have presumed to call quack remedies. There is a quack remedy which is called reciprocity, and this quack remedy is under the special protection of quack doctors, and among the quack doctors, I am sorry to say, there appear to be some in very high station indeed; and if I am rightly informed, no less a person than Her Majesty's Secretary of State for Foreign Affairs has been moving about the country, and indicating a very considerable expectation that possibly by reciprocity agricultural distress will be relieved. Let me test, gentlemen, the efficacy of this quack remedy for your, in some places, agricultural pressure, and generally distress—the pressure that has been upon you, the struggle in which you are engaged. Pray watch its operation; pray note what is said by the advocates of reciprocity. They always say, We are the soundest and best free-traders. We recommend reciprocity because it is the truly effectual method of bringing about free trade. At present America imposes enormous duties upon our cotton goods and upon our iron goods. Put reciprocity into play and America will become a free-trading country. Very well, gentlemen, how would that operate upon you agriculturists in particular? Why, it would operate thus: If your condition is to be regretted in certain particulars, and capable of amendment, I beg you to cast an eye of sympathy upon the condition of the American agriculturist.   It has been very well said, and very truly said—though it is a smart antithesis—the American agriculturist has got to buy everything that he wants at prices which are fixed in Washington by the legislation of America, but he has got to sell everything that he produces at prices which are fixed in Liverpool—fixed by the free competition of the world.   How would you like that, gentlemen—to have protective prices to pay for everything that you use—for your manures, for your animals, for your implements, for all your farming stock, and at the same time to have to sell what you produce in the free and open market of the world?   But bring reciprocity into play, and then, if reciprocity doctors are right, the Americans will remove all their protective duties, and the American farmer, instead of producing, as he does now, under the disadvantage, and the heavy disadvantage, of having to pay protective prices for everything that constitutes his farming stock, will have all his tools, and implements, and manures, and everything else purchased in the free, open market of the world at free-trade prices.   So he will be able to produce his corn to compete with you even cheaper than he does now.   So much for reciprocity considered as a cure for distress. I am not going to consider it now in any other point of view.

But, gentlemen, there are another set of men who are bolder still, and who are not for reciprocity; who are not content with that milder form of quackery; but who recommend a reversion, pure and simple, to what I may fairly call, I think, the exploded doctrine of protection.   And upon this, gentlemen, I think it necessary, if you will allow me, to say to you a few words, because it is a very serious matter, and it is all the more serious because of Her Majesty's Government—I do not scruple to say —are coquetting with this subject in a way which is not right. They are tampering with it; they are playing with it.   A protective speech was made in the House of Commons in a debate last year by Mr. Chaplin, on the part of what is called " the agricultural interest."   Mr. Chaplin did not use the word protection, but what he did say was this: He said he demanded that the malt tax should be abolished, and the revenue supplied by a tax upon foreign barley or some other foreign commodity. Well, if he has a measure of that kind in his pocket I don't ask him to affix the word protection to it.   I can do that for myself.

Not a word of rebuke, gentlemen, was uttered to the doctrines of Mr. Chaplin. He was complimented upon the ability of his speech and the well-chosen terms of his motion. Some of the members of Her Majesty's Government—the minor members of Her Majesty's Government—the humbler luminaries of that great constellation—have been going about the country and telling their farming constituents that they think the time has come when a return to protection might very wisely be tried. But, gentlemen, what delusions have been practised upon the unfortunate British farmer! When we go back for twenty years, what is now called the Tory party was never heard of as the Tory party. It was always heard of as the party of protection. As long as the chiefs of the protective party were not in office, as long as they were irresponsible, they recommended themselves to the good-will of the farmer as protectionists, and said they would set him up and put his interests on a firm foundation through protection. We brought them into office in the year 1852. I gave with pleasure a vote that assisted to bring them into office. I thought bringing them into office was the only way of putting their professions to the test. They came into office, and before they had been six months in office they had thrown protection to the winds. And that is the way in which the British farmer's expectations are treated by those who claim for themselves in the special sense the designation of his friends.

It is exactly the same with the malt tax. Gentlemen, what is done with the malt tax? The malt tax is held by them to be a great grievance on the British farmer. Whenever a Liberal government is in office, from time to time they have a great muster from all parts of the country to vote for the abolition of the malt tax. But when a Tory government comes into office, the abolition of the malt tax is totally forgotten; and we have now had six years of a Tory government without a word said, as far as I can recollect—and my friend in the chair could correct me if I were wrong—without a motion made, or a vote taken, on the subject of the malt tax. The malt tax, great and important as it is, is small in reference to protection. Gentlemen, it is a very serious matter indeed if we ought to go back to protection, because how did we come out of protection to free trade? We came out of it by a struggle which in its crisis threatened to convulse the country, which occupied Parliaments, upon which elections turned, which took up twenty years of our legislative life, which broke up parties. In a word, it effected a change so serious that if, after the manner in which we effected that change, it be right that we should go back upon our steps, then all I can say is, that we must lose that which has ever been one of the most honorable distinctions of British legislation in the general estimation of the world—that British legislation, if it moves slowly, always moves in one direction—that we never go back upon our steps.

But are we such children that, after spending twenty years—as I may say from 1840 to 1860—in breaking down the huge fabric of protection, in 1879 we are seriously to set about building it up again? If that be right, gentlemen, let it be done, but it will involve on our part a most humiliating confession. In my opinion it is not right. Protection, however, let me point out, now is asked for in two forms, and I am next going to quote Lord Beaconsfield for the purpose of expressing my concurrence with him.

Mostly, I am bound to say, as far as my knowledge goes, protection has not been asked for by the agricultural interest, certainly not by the farmers of Scotland.

It has been asked for by certain injudicious cliques and classes of persons connected with other industries—connected with some manufacturing industries. They want to have duties laid upon manufactures.

But here Lord Beaconsfield said—and I cordially agree with him—that he would be no party to the institution of a system in which protection was to be given to manufactures, and to be refused to agriculture.

That one-sided protection I deem to be totally intolerable, and I reject it even at the threshold as unworthy of a word of examination or discussion.

But let us go on to two-sided protection, and see whether that is any better—that is to say, protection in the shape of duties on manufactures, and protection in the shape of duties upon corn, duties upon meat, duties upon butter and cheese and eggs, and everything that can be produced from the land. Now, gentlemen, in order to see whether we can here find a remedy for our difficulties, I prefer to speculation and mere abstract argument the method of reverting to experience. Experience will give us very distinct lessons upon this matter. We have the power, gentlemen, of going back to the time when protection was in full and unchecked force, and of examining the effect which it produced upon the wealth of the country. How, will you say, do I mean to test that wealth? I mean to test that wealth by the exports of the country, and I will tell you why, because your prosperity depends upon the wealth of your customers—that is to say, upon their capacity to buy what you produce. And who are your customers? Your customers are the industrial population of the country, who produce what we export and send all over the world. Consequently, when exports increase, your customers are doing a large business, are growing wealthy, are putting money in their pockets, and are able to take that money out of their pockets in order to fill their stomachs with what you produce. When, on the contrary, exports do not increase, your customers are poor, your prices go down, as you have felt within the last few years, in the price of meat, for example, and in other things, and your condition is proportionally depressed. Now, gentlemen, down to the year 1842 no profane hand had been laid upon the august fabric of protection. For recollect that the farmers' friends always told us that it was a very august fabric, and that if you pulled it down it would involve the ruin of the country. That, you remember, was the commonplace of every Tory speech delivered from a country hustings to a farming constituency. But before 1842 another agency had come into force, which gave new life in a very considerable degree to the industry of the country, and that was the agency of railways, of improved communication, which shortened distance and cheapened transit, and effected in that way an enormous economical gain and addition to the wealth of the country. Therefore, in order to see what we owe to our friend protection, I won't allow that friend to take credit for what was done by railways in improving the wealth of the country. I will go to the time when I may say there were virtually no railways—that is the time before 1830. Now, gentlemen, here are the official facts which I shall lay before you in the simplest form, and, remember, using round numbers. I do that because, although round numbers cannot be absolutely accurate, they are easy for the memory to take in, and they involve no material error, no falsification of the case.   In the year 1800, gentlemen, the exports of British produce were thirty-nine and a half millions sterling in value.   The population at that time—no, I won't speak of the exact figure of the population, because I have not got it for the three kingdoms.   In the years 1826 to 1830— that is, after a medium period of eight-and-twenty years—the average of our exports for those five years, which had been thirty-nine and a half millions in 1800, was thirty-seven millions. It is fair to admit that in 1800 the currency was somewhat less sound, and therefore I am quite willing to admit that the thirty-seven millions probably meant as much in value as the thirty-nine and a half millions; but substantially, gentlemen, the trade of the country was stationary, practically stationary, under protection.   The condition of the people grew, if possible, rather worse than better.   The wealth of the country was nearly stationary.   But now I show you what protection produced; that it made no addition, it gave no onward movement to the profits of those who are your customers.   But on these profits you depend; because, under all circumstances, gentlemen, this, I think, nobody will dispute—a considerable portion of what the Englishman or the Scotchman produces will, some way or other, find its way down his throat.

What has been the case, gentlemen, since we cast off the superstition of protection, since we discarded the imposture of protection?   I will tell you what happened between 1830, when there were no railways, and 1842, when no change, no important change, had been made as to protection, but when the railway system was in operation, hardly in Scotland, but in England to a very great extent, to a very considerable extent upon the main lines of communication.   The exports which in 1830 had been somewhere about £37,000,000, between 1840 and 1842 showed an average amount of £50,000,000.   That seems due, gentlemen, to the agency of railways; and I wish you to bear in mind the increasing benefit now derived from that agency, in order that I may not claim any undue credit for freedom of trade.   From 1842, gentlemen, onward, the successive stages of free trade began; in 1842, in 1845, in 1846, in 1853, and again in 1860, the large measures were carried which have completely reformed your customs tariff, and reduced it from a taxation of twelve hundred articles to a taxation of, I think, less than twelve.

Now, under the system of protection, the export trade of the country, the wealth and the power of the manufacturing and producing classes to purchase your agricultural products, did not increase at all. In the time when railways began to be in operation, but before free trade, the exports of the country increased, as I have shown you, by £13,000,000 in somewhere about thirteen years—that is to say, taking it roughly, at the rate of £1,000,000 a year.

But since 1842, and down to the present time, we have had, along with railways, always increasing their benefits—we have had the successive adoption of free-trade measures; and what has been the state of the export business of the country? It has risen in this degree, that that which from 1840 to 1842 averaged £50,000,000, from 1873 to 1878 averaged £218,000,000. Instead of increasing, as it had done between 1830 and 1842, when railways only were at work, at the rate of £1,000,000 a year—instead of remaining stagnant as it did when the country was under protection pure and simple, with no augmentation of the export trade to enlarge the means of those who buy your products, the total growth in a period of thirty-five years was no less than £168,000,000, or, taking it roughly, a growth in the export trade of the country to the extent of between £4,000,000 and £5,000,000 a year. But, gentlemen, you know the fact. You know very well, that while restriction was in force, you did not get the prices that you have been getting for the last twenty years. The price of wheat has been much the same as it had been before. The price of oats is a better price than was to be had on the average of protective times. But the price, with the exception of wheat, of almost every agricultural commodity, the price of wool, the price of meat, the price of cheese, the price of everything that the soil produces, has been largely increased in a market free and open to the world; because, while the artificial advantage which you got through protection, as it was supposed to be an advantage, was removed, you were brought into that free and open market, and the energy of free trade so enlarged the buying capacity of your customers that they were willing and able to give you, and did give you, a great deal more for your meat, your wool, and your products in general, than you would ever have got under the system of protection. Gentlemen, if that be true—and it cannot, I believe, be impeached or impugned—if that be true, I don't think I need further discuss the matter, especially when so many other matters have to be discussed.

I will therefore ask you again to cross the seas with me. I see that the time is flying onward, and, gentlemen, it is very hard upon you to be so much vexed upon the subject of policy abroad. You think generally, and I think, that your domestic affairs are quite enough to call for all your attention. There was a saying of an ancient Greek orator, who, unfortunately, very much undervalued what we generally call the better portion of the community—namely, women; he made a very disrespectful observation, which I am going to quote, not for the purpose of concurring with it, but for the purpose of an illustration.

Pericles, the great Athenian statesman, said with regard to women, their greatest merit was to be never heard of.

Now, what Pericles untruly said of women, I am very much disposed to say of foreign affairs—their great merit would be to be never heard of. Unfortunately, instead of being never heard of, they are always heard of, and you hear almost of nothing else; and I can't promise you, gentlemen, that you will be relieved from this everlasting din, because the consequences of an unwise meddling with foreign affairs are consequences that will for some time necessarily continue to trouble you, and that will find their way to your pockets in the shape of increased taxation.

Gentlemen, with that apology I ask you again to go with me beyond the seas. And as I wish to do full justice, I will tell you what I think to be the right principles of foreign policy; and then, as far as your patience and my strength will permit, I will, at any rate for a short time, illustrate those right principles by some of the departures from them that have taken place of late years. I first give you, gentlemen, what I think the right principles of foreign policy.

The first thing is to foster the strength of the empire by just legislation and economy at home, thereby producing two of the great elements of national power—namely, wealth, which is a physical element, and union and contentment, which are moral elements—and to reserve the strength of the empire, to reserve the expenditure of that strength for great and worthy occasions abroad. Here is my first principle of foreign policy: good government at home.

My second principle of foreign policy is this, that its aim ought to be to preserve to the nations of the world—and especially, were it but for shame, when we recollect the sacred name we bear as Christians, especially to the Christian nations of the world—the blessings of peace. That is my second principle.

My third principle is this: Even, gentlemen, when you do a good thing you may do it in so bad a way that you may entirely spoil the beneficial effect; and if we were to make ourselves the apostles of peace in the sense of conveying to the minds of other nations that we thought ourselves more entitled to an opinion on that subject than they are, or to deny their rights—well, very likely we should destroy the whole value of our doctrines. In my opinion the third sound principle is this: to strive to cultivate and maintain, aye, to the very uttermost, what is called the concert of Europe; to keep the powers of Europe in union together. And why? Because by keeping all in union together you neutralize, and fetter, and bind up the selfish aims of each. I am not here to flatter either England or any of them. They have selfish aims, as, unfortunately, we in late years have too sadly shown that we too have had selfish aims; but their common action is fatal to selfish aims. Common action means common objects; and the only objects for which you can unite together the powers of Europe are objects connected with the common good of them all. That, gentlemen, is my third principle of foreign policy.

My fourth principle is: That you should avoid needless and entangling engagements. You may boast about them, you may brag about them, you may say you are procuring consideration for the country. You may say that an Englishman can now hold up his head among the nations. You may say that he is now not in the hands of a Liberal ministry, who thought of nothing but pounds, shillings, and pence. But what does all this come to, gentlemen? It comes to this, that you are increasing your engagements without increasing your strength; and if you increase engagements without increasing strength, you diminish strength, you abolish strength; you really reduce the empire and do not increase it. You render

it less capable of performing its duties; you render it an inheritance less precious to hand on to future generations.

My fifth principle is this, gentlemen: To acknowledge the
equal rights of all nations. You may sympathize with one
nation more than another. Nay, you must sympathize in certain circumstances with one nation more than another. You
sympathize most with those nations, as a rule, with which you
have the closest connection in language, in blood, and in religion, or whose circumstances at the time seem to give the
strongest claim to sympathy. But in point of right all are
equal, and you have no right to set up a system under which one
of them is to be placed under moral suspicion or espionage, or
to be made the constant subject of invective. If you do that,
but especially if you claim for yourself a superiority, a pharisaical superiority over the whole of them, then I say you may
talk about your patriotism if you please, but you are a misjudg-
ing friend of your country, and in undermining the basis of the
esteem and respect of other people for your country you are
in reality inflicting the severest injury upon it. I have now
given you, gentlemen, five principles of foreign policy. Let me
give you a sixth, and then I have done.

And that sixth is: That in my opinion foreign policy, subject
to all the limitations that I have described, the foreign policy
of England should always be inspired by the love of freedom.
There should be a sympathy with freedom, a desire to give it
scope, founded not upon visionary ideas, but upon the long experience of many generations within the shores of this happy
isle, that in freedom you lay the firmest foundations both of loyalty and order; the firmest foundations for the development
of individual character, and the best provision for the happiness
of the nation at large. In the foreign policy of this country
the name of Canning ever will be honored. The name of Russell ever will be honored. The name of Palmerston ever will
be honored by those who recollect the erection of the kingdom
of Belgium, and the union of the disjoined provinces of Italy.
It is that sympathy, not a sympathy with disorder, but, on the
contrary, founded upon the deepest and most profound love of
order—it is that sympathy which in my opinion ought to be the
very atmosphere in which a foreign secretary of England ought
to live and to move.

Gentlemen, it is impossible for me to do more to-day than to attempt very slight illustrations of those principles. But in uttering those principles I have put myself in a position in which no one is entitled to tell me—you will hear me out in what I say—that I simply object to the acts of others, and lay down no rules of action myself. I am not only prepared to show what are the rules of action which in my judgment are the right rules, but I am prepared to apply them, nor will I shrink from their application. I will take, gentlemen, the name which, most of all others, is associated with suspicion, and with alarm, and with hatred in the minds of many Englishmen. I will take the name of Russia, and at once I will tell you what I think about Russia, and how I am prepared as a member of Parliament to proceed in anything that respects Russia. You have heard me, gentlemen, denounced sometimes, I believe, as a Russian spy, sometimes as a Russian agent, sometimes as perhaps a Russian fool, which is not so bad, but still not very desirable. But, gentlemen, when you come to evidence, the worst thing that I have ever seen quoted out of any speech or writing of mine about Russia is that I did one day say, or I believe I wrote these terrible words: I recommended Englishmen to imitate Russia in her good deeds. Was not that a terrible proposition? I cannot recede from it. I think we ought to imitate Russia in her good deeds, and if the good deeds be few I am sorry for it, but I am not the less disposed on that account to imitate them when they come. I will now tell you what I think just about Russia.

I make it one of my charges against the foreign policy of Her Majesty's Government that, while they have completely estranged from this country—let us not conceal the fact—the feelings of a nation of eighty millions, for that is the number of the subjects of the Russian Empire—while they have contrived completely to estrange the feelings of that nation, they have aggrandized the power of Russia. They have aggrandized the power of Russia in two ways, which I will state with perfect distinctness. They have augmented her territory. Before the European powers met at Berlin, Lord Salisbury met with Count Schouvaloff, and Lord Salisbury agreed that, unless he could convince Russia by his arguments in the open Congress of Berlin, he would support the restoration to the despotic power of

Russia of that country north of the Danube which at the moment constituted a portion of the free state of Roumania. Why, gentlemen, what had been done by the Liberal government, which, forsooth, attended to nothing but pounds, shillings, and pence? The Liberal government had driven Russia back from the Danube. Russia, which was a Danubian power before the Crimean War, lost this position on the Danube by the Crimean War; and the Tory government, which has been incensing and inflaming you against Russia, yet, nevertheless, by binding itself beforehand to support, when the judgment was taken, the restoration of that country to Russia, has aggrandized the power of Russia.

It further aggrandized the power of Russia in Armenia; but I would not dwell upon that matter if it were not for a very strange circumstance. You know that an Armenian province was given to Russia after the war, but about that I own to you I have very much less feeling of objection. I have objected from the first, vehemently, and in every form, to the granting of territory on the Danube to Russia, and carrying back the population of a certain country from a free state to a despotic state; but with regard to the transfer of a certain portion of the Armenian people from the government of Turkey to the government of Russia I must own that I contemplate that transfer with much greater equanimity. I have no fear myself of the territorial extensions of Russia, in Asia, no fear of them whatever. I think the fears are no better than old women's fears. And I don't wish to encourage her aggressive tendencies in Asia, or anywhere else. But I admit it may be, and probably is, the case that there is some benefit attending upon the transfer of a portion of Armenia from Turkey to Russia.

But here is a very strange fact. You know that that portion of Armenia includes the port of Batoum. Lord Salisbury has lately stated to the country that, by the Treaty of Berlin, the port of Batoum is to be only a commercial port. If the Treaty of Berlin stated that it was to be only a commercial port, which, of course, could not be made an arsenal, that fact would be very important. But, happily, gentlemen, although treaties are concealed from us nowadays as long and as often as is possible, the Treaty of Berlin is an open instrument   We can consult it for ourselves; and when we consult the Treaty of Berlin we find it states that Batoum shall be essentially a commercial port, but not that it shall be only a commercial port. Why, gentlemen, Leith is essentially a commercial port, but there is nothing to prevent the people of this country, if in their wisdom or their folly they should think fit, from constituting Leith as a great naval arsenal or fortification; and there is nothing to prevent the Emperor of Russia, while leaving to Batoum a character that shall be essentially commercial, from joining with that another character that is not in the slightest degree excluded by the treaty, and making it as much as he pleases a port of military defence. Therefore, I challenge the assertion of Lord Salisbury; and as Lord Salisbury is fond of writing letters to the " Times " to bring the Duke of Argyll to book, he perhaps will be kind enough to write another letter to the " Times " and tell in what clause of the Treaty of Berlin he finds it written that the port of Batoum shall be only a commercial port. For the present, I simply leave it on record that he has misrepresented the Treaty of Berlin.

With respect to Russia, I take two views of the position of Russia. The position of Russia in Central Asia I believe to be one that has, in the main, been forced upon her against her will. She has been compelled—and this is the impartial opinion of the world—she has been compelled to extend her frontier southward in Central Asia by causes in some degree analogous to, but certainly more stringent and imperative than, the causes which have commonly led us to extend, in a far more important manner, our frontier in India; and I think it, gentlemen, much to the credit of the late Government, much to the honor of Lord Clarendon and Lord Granville that, when we were in office, we made a covenant with Russia, in which Russia bound herself to exercise no influence or interference whatever in Afghanistan, we, on the other hand, making known our desire that Afghanistan should continue free and independent. Both the powers acted with uniform strictness and fidelity upon this engagement until the day when we were removed from office. But Russia, gentlemen, has another position—her position in respect to Turkey; and here it is that I have complained of the Government for aggrandizing the power of Russia; it is on this point that I most complain.

The policy of Her Majesty's Government was a policy of repelling and repudiating the Slavonic populations of Turkey in Europe, and of declining to make England the advocate for their interests. Nay, more, she became in their view the advocate of the interests opposed to theirs. Indeed, she was rather the decided advocate of Turkey; and now Turkey is full of loud complaints—and complaints, I must say, not unjust—that we allured her on to her ruin; that we gave the Turks a right to believe that we should support them; that our ambassadors, Sir Henry Elliot and Sir Austin Layard, both of them said we had most vital interests in maintaining Turkey as it was, and consequently the Turks thought if we had vital interests we should certainly defend them; and they were thereby lured on into that ruinous, cruel, and destructive war with Russia. But by our conduct to the Slavonic populations we alienated those populations from us. We made our name odious among them. They had every disposition to sympathize with us, every disposition to confide in us. They are, as a people, desirous of freedom, desirous of self-government, with no aggressive views, but hating the idea of being absorbed in a huge despotic empire like Russia. But when they found that we, and the other powers of Europe, under our unfortunate guidance, declined to become in any manner their champions in defence of the rights of life, of property, and of female honor—when they found that there was no call which could find its way to the heart of England through its government, or to the hearts of other powers, and that Russia alone was disposed to fight for them, why naturally they said, Russia is our friend. We have done everything, gentlemen, in our power to drive these populations into the arms of Russia. If Russia has aggressive dispositions in the direction of Turkey—and I think it probable that she may have them—it is we who have laid the ground upon which Russia may make her march to the south—we who have taught the Bulgarians, the Servians, the Roumanians, the Montenegrins, that there is one power in Europe, and only one, which is ready to support in act and by the sword her professions of sympathy with the oppressed populations of Turkey. That power is Russia, and how can you blame these people if, in such circumstances, they are disposed to say, Russia is our friend? But why did we make them say it? Simply because of the policy of the Government, not because of the wishes of the people of this country. Gentlemen, this is the most dangerous form of aggrandizing Russia. If Russia is aggressive anywhere, if Russia is formidable anywhere, it is by movements toward the south, it is by schemes for acquiring command of the straits or of Constantinople; and there is no way by which you can possibly so much assist her in giving reality to these designs as by inducing and disposing the populations of these provinces, who are now in virtual possession of them, to look upon Russia as their champion and their friend, to look upon England as their disguised, perhaps, but yet real and effective enemy.

Why, now, gentlemen, I have said that I think it not unreasonable either to believe, or at any rate to admit it to be possible, that Russia has aggressive designs in the east of Europe. I do not mean immediate aggressive designs. I do not believe that the Emperor of Russia is a man of aggressive schemes or policy. It is that, looking to that question in the long run, looking at what has happened, and what may happen in ten or twenty years, in one generation, in two generations, it is highly probable that in some circumstances Russia may develop aggressive tendencies towards the south.

Perhaps you will say I am here guilty of the same injustice to Russia that I have been deprecating, because I say that we ought not to adopt the method of condemning anybody without cause, and setting up exceptional principles in proscription of a particular nation. Gentlemen, I will explain to you in a moment the principle upon which I act, and the grounds upon which I form my judgment. They are simply these grounds: I look at the position of Russia, the geographical position of Russia relatively to Turkey. I look at the comparative strength of the two empires; I look at the importance of the Dardanelles and the Bosphorus as an exit and a channel for the military and commercial marine of Russia to the Mediterranean; and what I say to myself is this: If the United Kingdom were in the same position relatively to Turkey which Russia holds upon the map of the globe, I feel quite sure that we should be very apt indeed both to entertain and to execute aggressive designs upon Turkey. Gentlemen, I will go further, and will frankly own to you that I believe if we, instead of happily inhabiting this island, had been in the possession of the Russian territory, and in the circumstances of the Russian people, we should most likely have eaten up Turkey long ago. And consequently, in saying that Russia ought to be vigilantly watched in that quarter, I am only applying to her the rule which in parallel circumstances I feel convinced ought to be applied, and would be justly applied, to judgments upon our own country.

Gentlemen, there is only one other point on which I must still say a few words to you, although there are a great many upon which I have a great many words yet to say somewhere or other.

Of all the principles, gentlemen, of foreign policy which I have enumerated, that to which I attach the greatest value is the principle of the equality of nations; because, without recognizing that principle, there is no such thing as public right, and without public international right there is no instrument available for settling the transactions of mankind except material force.   Consequently the principle of equality among nations lies, in my opinion, at the very basis and root of a Christian civilization, and when that principle is compromised or abandoned, with it must depart our hopes of tranquillity and of progress for mankind.

I am sorry to say, gentlemen, that I feel it my absolute duty to make this charge against the foreign policy under which we have lived for the last two years, since the resignation of Lord Derby.   It has been a foreign policy, in my opinion, wholly, or to a perilous extent, unregardful of public right, and it has been founded upon the basis of a false, I think an arrogant and a dangerous, assumption, although I do not question its being made conscientiously and for what was believed the advantage of the country—an untrue, arrogant, and dangerous assumption that we are entitled to assume for ourselves some dignity, whic1 we should also be entitled to withhold from others, and to claim on our own part authority to do things which we would not permit to be done by others.   For example, when Russia was going to the Congress at Berlin, we said: " Your Treaty of San Stefano is of no value.   It is an act between you and Turkey; but the concerns of Turkey by the Treaty of Paris are the concerns of Europe at large.   We insist upon it that the whole of your treaty of San Stefano shall be submitted to the Congress at Berlin, that they may judge how far to open it in each and every one of its points, because the concerns of Turkey are the common concerns of the powers of Europe acting in concert."

Having asserted that principle to the world, what did we do? These two things, gentlemen: Secretly, without the knowledge of Parliament, without even the forms of official procedure, Lord Salisbury met Count Schouvaloff in London, and agreed with him upon the terms on which the two powers together should be bound in honor to one another to act upon all the most important points when they came before the Congress at Berlin. Having alleged against Russia that she should not be allowed to settle Turkish affairs with Turkey, because they were but two powers, and these affairs were the common affairs of Europe, and of European interest, we then got Count Schouvaloff into a private room, and on the part of England and Russia, they being but two powers, we settled a large number of the most important of these affairs in utter contempt and derogation of the very principle for which the Government had been contending for months before, for which they had asked Parliament to grant a sum of £6,000,000, for which they had spent that £6,000,000 in needless and mischievous armaments. That which we would not allow Russia to do with Turkey, because we pleaded the rights of Europe, we ourselves did with Russia, in contempt of the rights of Europe. Nor was that all, gentlemen. That act was done, I think, on one of the last days of May, in the year 1878, and the document was published, made known to the world, made known to the Congress at Berlin, to its infinite astonishment, unless I am very greatly misinformed.

But that was not all. Nearly at the same time we performed the same operation in another quarter. We objected to a treaty between Russia and Turkey as having no authority, though that treaty was made in the light of day—namely, to the Treaty of San Stefano; and what did we do? We went not in the light of day, but in the darkness of the night—not in the knowledge and cognizance of other powers, all of whom would have had the faculty and means of watching all along, and of preparing and taking their own objections and shaping their own policy—not in the light of day, but in the darkness of the night, we sent the ambassador of England in Constantinople to the minister of Turkey, and there he framed, even while the

Congress of Berlin was sitting to determine these matters of common interest, he framed that which is too famous, shall I say, or rather too notorious, as the Anglo-Turkish Convention.

Gentlemen, it is said, and said truly, that truth beats fiction; that what happens in fact from time to time is of a character so daring, so strange, that if the novelist were to imagine it and put it upon his pages, the whole world would reject it from its improbability. And that is the case of the Anglo-Turkish Convention. For who would have believed it possible that we should assert before the world the principle that Europe only could deal with the affairs of the Turkish empire, and should ask Parliament for six millions to support us in asserting that principle, should send ministers to Berlin who declared that unless that principle was acted upon they would go to war with the material that Parliament had placed in their hands, and should at the same time be concluding a separate agreement with Turkey, under which those matters of European jurisdiction were coolly transferred to English jurisdiction; and the whole matter was sealed with the worthless bribe of the possession and administration of the island of Cyprus! I said, gentlemen, the worthless bribe of the island of Cyprus, and that is the truth. It is worthless for our purposes—not worthless in itself; an island of resources, an island of natural capabilities, provided they are allowed to develop themselves in the course of circumstances, without violent and unprincipled methods of action. But Cyprus was not thought to be worthless by those who accepted it as a bribe. On the contrary, you were told that it was to secure the road to India; you were told that it was to be the site of an arsenal very cheaply made, and more valuable than Malta; you were told that it was to revive trade. And a multitude of companies were formed, and sent agents and capital to Cyprus, and some of them, I fear, grievously burned their fingers there. I am not going to dwell upon that now. What I have in view is not the particular merits of Cyprus, but the illustration that I have given you in the case of the agreement of Lord Salisbury with Count Schouvaloff, and in the case of the Anglo-Turkish Convention, of the manner in which we have asserted for ourselves a principle that we had denied to others—namely, the principle of overriding the European authority of the Treaty of Paris, and taking the matters which that treaty gave to Europe into our own separate jurisdiction.

Now, gentlemen, I am sorry to find that that which I call the pharisaical assertion of our own superiority has found its way alike into the practice, and seemingly into the theories of the government. I am not going to assert anything which is not known, but the Prime Minister has said that there is one day in the year—namely, the ninth of November, Lord Mayor's Day—on which the language of sense and truth is to be heard amidst the surrounding din of idle rumors generated and fledged in the brains of irresponsible scribes. I do not agree, gentlemen, in that panegyric upon the ninth of November. I am much more apt to compare the ninth of November—certainly a well-known day in the year—but as to some of the speeches that have lately been made upon it, I am very much disposed to compare it with another day in the year, well known to British tradition, and that other day in the year is the first of April. But, gentlemen, on that day the Prime Minister, speaking out —I do not question for a moment his own sincere opinion— made what I think one of the most unhappy and ominous allusions ever made by a minister of this country. He quoted certain words, easily rendered, as " empire " and " liberty "—words (he said) of a Roman statesman, words descriptive of the state of Rome—and he quoted them as words which were capable of legitimate application to the position and circumstances of England. I join issue with the Prime Minister upon that subject, and I affirm that nothing can be more fundamentally unsound, more practically ruinous, than the establishment of Roman analogies for the guidance of British policy. What, gentlemen, was Rome? Rome was indeed an imperial state, you may tell me—I know not, I cannot read the counsels of Providence—a State having a mission to subdue the world, but a State whose very basis it was to deny the equal rights, to proscribe the independent existence of other nations. That, gentlemen, was the Roman idea. It has been partially and not ill described in three lines of a translation from Vergil by our great poet Dryden, which run as follows:

> " O Rome! 'tis thine alone with awful sway
> To rule mankind, and make the world obey,
> Disposing peace and war thine own majestic way."

We are told to fall back upon this example.   No doubt the word " empire " was qualified with the word " liberty."   But what did the two words " liberty " and " empire " mean in a Roman mouth?   They meant simply this: " Liberty for ourselves, empire over the rest of mankind."

I do not think, gentlemen, that this ministry, or any other ministry, is going to place us in the position of Rome.   What I object to is the revival of the idea.   I care not how feebly, I care not even how, from a philosophic or historical point of view, how ridiculous the attempt at this revival may be. I say it indicates an intention—I say it indicates a frame of mind, and the frame of mind, unfortunately, I find, has been consistent with the policy of which I have given you some illustrations— the policy of denying to others the rights that we claim ourselves.   No doubt, gentlemen, Rome may have had its work to do, and Rome did its work.   But modern times have brought a different state of things.   Modern times have established a sisterhood of nations, equal, independent, each of them built up under that legitimate defence which public law affords to every nation, living within its own borders, and seeking to perform its own affairs; but if one thing more than another has been detestable to Europe, it has been the appearance upon the stage from time to time of men who, even in the times of the Christian civilization, have been thought to aim at universal dominion.   It was this aggressive disposition on the part of Louis XIV, King of France, that led your forefathers, gentlemen, freely to spend their blood and treasure in a cause not immediately their own, and to struggle against the method of policy which, having Paris for its centre, seemed to aim at an universal monarchy.

It was the very same thing, a century and a half later, which was the charge launched, and justly launched, against Napoleon, that under his dominion France was not content even with her extended limits, but Germany, and Italy, and Spain, apparently without any limit to this pestilent and pernicious process, were to be brought under the dominion or influence of France, and national equality was to be trampled under foot, and national rights denied. For that reason England in the struggle almost exhausted herself, greatly impoverished her people, brought upon herself, and Scotland, too, the consequences of a

debt that nearly crushed their energies, and poured forth their
best blood without limit, in order to resist and put down these
intolerable pretensions.

Gentlemen, it is but in a pale and weak and almost despicable
miniature that such ideas are now set up, but you will observe
that the poison lies—that the poison and the mischief lie—in
the principle and not the scale.

It is the opposite principle which, I say, has been compromised by the action of the ministry, and which I call upon
you, and upon any who choose to hear my views, to vindicate
when the day of our election comes; I mean the sound and
the sacred principle that Christendom is formed of a band of
nations who are united to one another in the bonds of right;
that they are without distinction of great and small; there is
an absolute equality between them—the same sacredness de-
fends the narrow limits of Belgium as attaches to the extended
frontiers of Russia, or Germany, or France. I hold that he who
by act or word brings that principle into peril or disparagement, however honest his intentions may be, places himself in
the position of one inflicting—I won't say intending to inflict—
I ascribe nothing of the sort—but inflicting injury upon his own
country, and endangering the peace and all the most fundamental interests of Christian society.

THE ESTABLISHED CHURCH IN IRELAND

Delivered in the House of Commons, March 1, 1869

T HE motion, sir, which, in concluding, I shall propose to
the committee is, that the chairman be directed to move
the House that leave be given to bring in a bill to put an
end to the Established Church in Ireland, and to make provision in respect of the temporalities thereof, and in respect
of the Royal College of Maynooth. I do not know, sir, whether
I should be accurate in describing the subject of this resolution as the most grave and arduous work of legislation that
ever has been laid before the House of Commons; but I am
quite sure I should speak the truth if I confined myself to
asserting that there has probably been no occasion when the
disproportion was so great between the demands of the subject that is to be brought before you, and the powers of the
person whose duty it is to submit it. I will not, however,
waste time in apologies that may be considered futile, and the
more so because I am conscious that the field I have to traverse
is a very wide one, and that nothing but the patient favor and
kindness of the committee can enable me in any degree to
attain the end I have in view—namely, that of submitting
with fulness and with clearness both the principles and the
details of a measure which, as far as regards its principles, is
singularly arduous, and, as far as regards its details, must
necessarily embrace matter of a character highly complex and
diverse.

Now, I cannot but be aware that, under ordinary circumstances, one who undertakes to introduce to the House of
Commons a subject of grave constitutional change ought to
commence by laying his ground strongly and broadly in historical and political reasons. On this occasion I shall feel
myself in the main dispensed from entering upon them. Un-

der ordinary circumstances, in discussing the subject of the Church of Ireland—I mean had nothing already occurred in this House or elsewhere in relation to it on which I might take my stand—I should endeavor to pass in review the numerous, I might say the numberless and powerful arguments which, in my opinion, may be adduced to prove that this Establishment cannot continue to exist with advantage to itself or without mischief to the country. I should be prepared to show how many benefices there are in Ireland where, although there is a church population, it can hardly be said to be more than an official church population, for the members of these benefices are too often restricted to those whom we may reasonably suppose to be supplied by the families of the clergyman, the clerk, and the sexton. I should show, sir, how buttresses have been devised for the maintenance of this extraordinary system in the shape of those grants from the consolidated fund in this country, on the one hand to the Presbyterians under the form of the *Regium Donum,* and on the other hand to the Roman Catholics under the form of the Maynooth grant, without which it was felt that the maintenance of such an Establishment in Ireland would be intolerable and impossible. I should endeavor to show how Parliament has been so conscious of the difficulties attending the position which it has held that it has actually been reduced upon more than one occasion to waste away, by positive provisions of legislation, the property of the Church, in order that its magnitude compared with the duties might not too much shock the public mind. I should endeavor to show how in past times, and through all the evil years of the penal legislation that has affected Ireland, the authorities of this Established Church have unfortunately stood in the foremost rank with respect to the enactment of those laws on which we cannot look back without shame and sorrow.

Sir, of the Established Church in Ireland I will only say that, although I believe its spirit to have undergone an immense change since those evil times, yet, unfortunately, it still remains, if not the home and the refuge, yet the token and the symbol of ascendancy, and, so long as that Establishment lives, painful and bitter memories of ascendancy can never die. But, sir, instead of lengthened discussion upon this and kindred topics, I hope I shall be sufficiently justified in passing at once to the measure of the Government by a reference to recent occurrences. In form, without doubt, this is the first, the very first stage of a great political measure, liable and open at every point to controversy; but in substance we cannot dismiss from our view that we are virtually taking up and are bound to prosecute the unfinished labors of last year.

I refer to those debates which formed the main, almost the only, subject of party difference in the discussions of this House during the session of 1868. I refer to the large majority which in a House of Commons undoubtedly Conservative in its general spirit affirmed, notwithstanding, the necessity of bringing the system of religious establishment in Ireland to a close. I refer to the autumn spent in incessant discussions of this subject before every constituency in the country. I refer to the elections in which the issue so clearly put was not less decisively answered. And lastly, but not least, I refer to that resignation of the late administration on which I have not to pronounce one word of censure, but about which I am sure I am justified in stating that it was an unusual course. I have not one word of censure to utter, but assuredly I am justified in saying that it forms the most emphatic testimony to the character of that judgment which has already been pronounced by the representatives and by the people of the three kingdoms. Nor shall I dwell in any detail upon the counter-arguments which have been ably, sincerely, and persistently used in defence of the Established Church. If I name them, it is to do little more than to say that we are responsible for this measure, and we who on this side are pledged to its general principles shall be ready upon every due occasion, with all respect to those who oppose us, to meet those counter-arguments.

It is said that the measure we are about to introduce will be adverse to religion. I believe it to be favorable, to be essential to the maintenance of those principles of right on which every religion must rest. We shall be told, more especially, that it is adverse to the interests of Protestantism; but we shall point to the condition of Ireland, and shall argue from the facts of that condition that the interests of Protestantism have not been promoted, but on the contrary have been injured by our perseverance in a system which reason does not justify.

We shall be told, perhaps, that we are invading the rights of property. No possible confidence can be greater than that with which we shall meet that argument. On former occasions, indeed, things have been done by Parliament, under the extreme pressure of the case, which it may be difficult to reconcile with the extreme assertion of the rights of property. There are clauses, and important clauses, of the Church Temporalities Act of 1833 which greatly strain the abstract theory of property, and which I for one am totally unable to reconcile with its general rules. But, so far as I know, there is no imputation that can fairly be made against the measure we propose with respect to the rights of property by any other persons than those who hold what appears to me the untenable —I may even say the extravagant—doctrine that although Parliament has a perfect right to direct the course of the descent of property in the case of natural descent, lineage by blood, yet it has no right, when once the artificial existence of what we call a corporation has been created, to control the existence of that corporation or to extinguish it even under the gravest public exigency. Well, we shall be told also of the Act of Union; and I cannot, nor shall I attempt to dissemble that on a point which has been described as essential we propose to alter that act. The Act of Union has been altered on other occasions, though never for so grave a cause as this; but we shall confidently contend that while we are altering this particular provision of the Act of Union, we are confirming its general purport and substance, and laboring to the best of our humble ability to give it those roots which unfortunately it has never yet adequately struck in the heart and affections of the people.

And lastly, sir, this claim I, for one, confidently, boldly, make on behalf of the measure that we are introducing—I say we are giving effect to the spirit of a former policy. The great minister who proposed the Act of Union neither said nor believed that it would be possible under a legislative union to maintain the system of religious inequality which he found subsisting in Ireland. On the contrary, he has left upon record his strong conviction that the countenance and support afforded from national sources to the Established Church must be extended to other religions of the country. I admit that we pursue religious equality by means different from those proposed by Mr. Pitt, but by means, as I believe, better suited to the purpose we have in view, and certainly more consonant to the spirit, to the opportunities, and to the possibilities of the times in which we live. Be that, however, as it may, and with all that allowance for difference of means, the end we have in view is the same, and for that end we are entitled to quote his great authority, and the authority of many of those who have followed him in their public career.

Sir, having referred to what I venture to call—although not in any technical or formal sense—the previous stages of this measure, I will briefly remind the committee of the character of the general declarations by which the late House of Commons was moved to action, and of those pledges—for I do not hesitate to recognize them in that capacity—which we are now called upon to do our best to redeem. I think, sir, it was well understood to be the view of those who supported the resolutions of last year that the system of Church Establishment in Ireland must be brought thoroughly and completely to a close —that although the word "disendowment" was never embodied in any resolution of this House, nor, so far as I recollect, was ever accepted without qualification in the speeches of those who most prominently supported it, yet, as a general rule and for every substantial purpose and effect, an end must likewise be put to the system of the public endowment of religion in Ireland. While the principles of the measure were laid thus broad and deep, it was likewise professed, and I think to a great degree accepted by the House, that in all the details, in all the modes of application, the rules not only of justice but of equity, and not only of equity, but, within every reasonable limit, even of indulgence, should be followed.

And while the measure was thus to be thorough and thus to be liberal, there were two other great characteristics which, in order fully to realize the desire we entertain, it ought to possess. The first of these, sir, is, in my judgment, that the measure ought to be prompt in its operation; for it is not for the interest of those with whom we deal any more than it is for the interest of the country that—I will not say the Irish Church, but—the Irish Establishment should be subjected to the pain of a lingering death. That promptitude of operation

cannot be absolute; it must necessarily be checked by considerations arising out of the vested interests with which we
have to deal. But yet, subject to those rules of right and of
prudence, it is an object which we ought to have in view in the
prosecution of our work. And lastly, sir, there is another characteristic which perhaps has hardly yet been mentioned in
debate, but which appears to me second to none in its importance as determining the value of the provisions of a measure such as this. It is that the legislation which we now
propose, so far as the Irish Church is concerned, so far as the
subjects of religious controversy growing out of legislative
establishment in the sister island are concerned, shall be final
legislation—that it shall put away, out of sight, out of hearing,
out of mind if it may be, this long-continued controversy—
a controversy almost of generations; and that even should it
necessarily happen, as commonly happens in the train of great
statutes, that in this or that point of detail it may require to
be either developed or amended, yet the bill which we propose
shall leave no question of principle unsolved, and shall permit
every man who takes part in its discussion to hope that when
it finally departs from within the walls of Parliament we shall
have heard the very last and latest of the controversy on the
Irish Church.

Subject, then, to those great principles, it is our duty—and
I am sure it will be recognized to be our duty—to seek every
means of softening the transition that is about to be effected.
We must not disguise from ourselves that we are calling upon
persons, upon large classes, upon individuals entitled to great
respect, to undergo a great change in their position under the
direct action of law. And every motive that can appeal to the
feelings of men of honor and of gentlemen must lead us, I
think, to feel it a duty so to proceed that this measure shall
carry with it no unnecessary penalty or pain. Sir, I am bound
to say that I think many of those who may be expected and
considered to take a special interest in this measure have given
us in this respect much encouragement. There are many eminent persons in Ireland connected with the Church who have
shown a great disposition to meet us in the fair field of discussion, to recognize the judgment which has been pronounced
at the tribunal of the nation, and to endeavor to arrive at a

just and equitable settlement.   Nay more, even upon that
Episcopal bench of England, from which oftentimes no sounds
but those of persistent resistance have proceeded, there have
been signs upon very recent occasions of a sense that it is
their duty to look to the future interests of the Church as well
as of the Establishment—of the religion as well as of the
property with which it is endowed.   And those counsels of
moderation, which impose on us corresponding obligations, are
likely to prevail, as we may hope, in those quarters during the
coming discussions.   In Ireland it has, indeed, been left only to
one single prelate—the Bishop of Down—among the Episcopal
order boldly to take his stand on behalf of the principle of
settlement and accommodation; but yet I cannot but hope and
believe that there are many, even among his Episcopal brethren, who are by no means disposed to prolong this hopeless
struggle or to make demands upon Parliament, as terms of
surrender, which it would be impossible for Parliament to
grant.

And now, sir, I think I may say that I will not trouble the
committee further upon general considerations connected with
this measure, but will at once proceed to use the best efforts
in my power to convey its character and all its leading provisions to the minds of the committee as nearly as I can in the
same light and in the same form as they present themselves
to the minds of the Government.   And I think, sir, searching
for a key by which I may suggest to the gentlemen who hear
me the best and most likely method of clearly apprehending
the nature of the provisions of the bill which I now hold in
my hand, I will venture to direct their attention to the points
of time—not, indeed, to all the points of time, because some
points of time have of necessity been chosen for secondary
and minor purposes—but to the three which I may call essential points of time, with reference to which I will endeavor to
state the provisions and operation of the bill so that the committee may have, as far as depends upon me, a clear understanding of the manner in which we shall endeavor to give
effect to the judgment of Parliament and of the country.

The first of these points of time, sir, is the passing of the
act, and I will first describe such of the effects of the act as
are to ensue either immediately upon its passing, or in the

provisional and preparatory period which will immediately follow its passing. The second of these points of time is a day named in the act. At present it stands January 1, 1871, affording an interval between the passing of the act—should it, as I trust it will, become law during the present session— of about eighteen months or something less for the prepara- tory arrangements; but with regard to that day I will presume to say that while we believe it is distinctly for the interest of the Church itself that this intermediate period should not be too long, and while it is the absolute limit of time which we have thought the best, yet it does not constitute a point of the measure to which, in case the limit is found to be too narrow, we should think ourselves irrevocably pledged. January 1, 1871, therefore, constitutes the second point of time.

The third point of time is one which we cannot define as a particular date, but I can describe it by stating the events which will bring it about. It is the point of time at which it shall be decided by the proper authorities that all the sub- sidiary arrangements connected with the winding up of the establishment of the Irish Church have been completed, and that thenceforth nothing remains to be done except to apply the property of the Irish Church, which will then have dis- charged every prior claim upon it, and will remain free for the purposes which Parliament may think fit to indicate.

Begging the committee to bear in mind these three points of time, I will now proceed to describe that portion of the effects of the measure which will follow immediately upon the passing of the bill. It is provided in almost the earliest clauses that the present Ecclesiastical Commission, which was ap- pointed for the purpose of administering the Church Estab- lishment, and not for the purpose of bringing it to an end, shall be wound up. In lieu of it new commissioners will be appointed, whose names we shall at a proper time propose and insert in the bill. We think very highly of the responsibility of their functions, and are very desirous that the men who may be proposed to discharge those functions should be men to whom Parliament shall have already, for the purposes of the measure, given its general approval. We shall propose that this commission shall endure for ten years, estimating, as far as present circumstances permit us to do, that this will be a term ample and sufficient for all the numerous and diversified purposes they will have to prosecute. In this commission, upon the passing of the bill, the entire property of the Church in Ireland will vest, subject to life interests. The committee will at once see the importance of that enactment. As far as legal and technical disendowment is concerned, it will have occurred on the day when the measure has received the royal assent, because there will no longer remain in the Church of Ireland any title whatever to its property other than that of the commissioners, and other than those temporary titles which we propose that Parliament should recognize. And all the subsequent arrangements which may be found necessary connected with fabrics or with any other points of the question, will be technically in the nature of a reëndowment, and will be brought by me separately under your consideration.

Then, sir, next to the vesting of the property, I have to mention the provision we propose to make for the government and management of the Church during this intermediate period. Last year we proposed and passed through this House a bill which suspended every appointment in Ireland from the day of its falling vacant, and we trusted entirely to collateral and subsidiary provisions of the law to make a supply for the time being of such assistance as might be necessary for the actual discharge of duties until Parliament should give its further judgment. Now, sir, it appears to be plain on the one hand that those provisions, which I think were very well adapted to the object we had in view last year of reserving the whole matter for the further judgment of Parliament, are not so well adapted to the purpose we now have in view—that is, to apply definite legislation to the determination of the whole question. On the other hand, it appears to us to be equally indisputable that there is one thing which we could not consistently or properly allow to be done during this intermediate period. We could not properly allow after the passing of the act the creation of new vested interests for life. We have therefore endeavored to steer as fairly as we can between these difficulties; on the one side proposing not to be parties to the creation of new vested interests, which I think everyone will see would from our point of view be highly inconsistent, and on the other side being equally anxious that the Irish Church, at a period when all its ministers and members will be called upon to exert themselves to the utmost in preparing for the future, should not be subjected to the disadvantage of a crippled ecclesiastical organization.

What we therefore propose is, that appointments may be made, generally speaking, to the spiritual offices without investing the person invested with a freehold; that he may receive during the interval the income as nearly as it can be calculated which he would have received if he had taken the freehold in the ordinary course, but that his title to it shall terminate when the provisional period is at an end, and when the links which connect the Establishment with the Church are finally broken. With respect, in particular, to Episcopal appointments, the provision we propose is as follows: We think it is very desirable after once the statute shall have passed for disestablishing the Church, to separate the Crown from the exercise of its old prerogative within the Church. We, therefore, propose that Episcopal appointments may be made by the Crown, but only on the prayer of the bishops themselves of the provinces of Ireland to consecrate a particular person to a vacancy. Such appointment, if made, will carry with it no vested interest, nor will it carry with it any right of peerage. The Irish Church being engaged in perfecting its organization for the future will probably not run the risk of having its sees and rectories vacant, but will have, so to speak, a staff fully adequate to deal with the coming contingency.

With respect to the exercise of Crown patronage as to livings, our view is this—while we take it for granted that at any rate as a general rule these livings would be filled up in the interval, they would be filled up on the same footing as bishoprics. In regard to the temporalities the disposition of the present advisers of the Crown, in making appointments wherever they have by law a right of patronage, would be to be guided within the limits of reason by the advice and recommendation of the ecclesiastical authorities. I think that is all I need say as regards the intermediate system that we shall now propose in lieu of the suspensory clauses of the bill of last year, except that in one point they would correspond more strictly with the provisions of the bill—namely, in this, that the commissioners would be inhibited from laying out money for permanent purposes, such as the building of new churches, during the interval, and would only be authorized to expend money for the purpose of substantial repairs, for the fulfilment of engagements actually entered into, and for the necessary charges for the performance of divine worship in the same manner as heretofore. So much for the scheme in relation to suspensory clauses.

The next important enactment which will take effect immediately on the passing of the bill is this. It is well known to the committee that certain disabilities affect the collective action of the clergy, and although the Convocations of England sit and have just been sitting, yet it is not in their power to proceed either to pass, or even to discuss with a view of passing, any canon, or regulation in the nature of a canon, without the assent of the Crown. In Ireland the case is different, and more adverse to the action of the Church, for there the Convocation has in point of fact never acted at all, excepting upon some very few occasions which may be specially pointed out, and the latest of those occasions, if I remember right, was a century and a half, if not fully two centuries ago. But besides the total disuse of that ecclesiastical machinery, and the difficulty in which the Crown is placed when it is called upon to revive or be a party to the revival of that which has never worked at all for two hundred years, and with respect to the working rules of which there are, even among lawyers, very grave doubts, there are in Ireland special provisions of the law called the Convention Act, which, though passed for purely political purposes, have the effect of preventing the clergy and laity of the Church from meeting in any general assembly. It is understood, I believe, that the clergy and laity of a parish may meet, but that the Church at large is incapacitated from meeting.

Now, it will, I presume, be deemed on both sides of the House to be obviously just and necessary that all disabilities whatsoever which in any manner fetter the action of the Church with reference to legislation for the future—and when I speak of legislation, I mean private legislation with respect to making voluntary contracts and regulations—ought, in passing a Disestablishment Act, to be at once and entirely swept away. When I say that, let it not be supposed I intend to insinuate any opinion to the effect that such a measure either is likely to cause or ought to be desired to cause a religious or spiritual separation between the Church of Ireland and the Church of England. The words of this measure have been carefully considered in reference to the Act of Union, so as to limit, as far as lies in our power, their repealing force to the establishment of those Churches, and we have been very desirous to do nothing which could possibly be held to interfere with their ecclesiastical relationship. At a later period I shall have to state to the committee what we have thought it our duty to propose, in order to prevent any kind of shock to their internal condition. But of this I am persuaded, that the best friends of religious union between the disestablished Church in Ireland and the Established Church in England will be those who most completely assert the liberty of the former to take its own course. Were we to attempt to apply to them constraint even in the faintest and feeblest form, for the purpose of seeking to secure their union, we should, I believe, engender reaction, even if such a proceeding were not open to the more palpable and obvious objection that, considering the general scope of our bill, it would be totally and radically unjust.

These, I think, are the positive and most important provisions which we propose as provisions which must take effect simultaneously with the passing of the bill. There is, however, another provision, for the operation of which we cannot precisely fix a time, because it does not depend altogether on us, but which this appears to me to be the proper place to mention. Inasmuch as there must necessarily grow out of the present position of the Church in Ireland, its property, and arrangements, a number of measures that in winding up this great system will have to be considered and discussed between some authority on the part of the State and some authority on the part of the Church, the course which we propose to Parliament to take is this: We presume that during the interval which the bill will create after the disabilities are removed, the bishops, clergy, and laity of the Church of Ireland will proceed to constitute for themselves, in the same manner as other religious communities have done, something in the nature of a governing body. We therefore take by this measure power to Her Majesty in Council—not to create such a body, but to recognize it when created, and we seek to avoid making Her Majesty the judge, either directly or by implication, whether this body is or is not for all purposes created wisely and well. But in the enacting words of the bill we should direct the attention of the Crown solely to one point —that it must be a representative body, representative alike of the bishops, clergy, and laity. In point of fact, Her Majesty's advisers would have to act simply as a jury, and to satisfy themselves that this body so constituted, according to the will and judgment of the Church, fulfilled in good faith the character of a representative body. Her Majesty would then recognize that body as such, and it would become incorporated under the provisions of the act for the purposes which I shall have presently to describe.

Now, the committee will see how far we have got. We have passed our provisions through the intermediate period, and we are coming to the day fixed in the act for the principal and final provisions of the bill to take effect. We have got in operation a commission which is to be the organ of the State in giving effect to the whole of our arrangements, and we have given time and every facility which properly belongs to us, not for bringing into operation, but for permitting to come into operation, that organ which we presume the members of the Church of Ireland will appoint in order to transact their share of the complicated business which will remain to be transacted. I now come to the second and most important period of time which stands at present fixed in the bill as January 1, 1871. On that day, according to the provisions of the bill, the union created by act of Parliament between the Churches of England and Ireland would be dissolved, and "the said Church of Ireland hereafter referred to as 'the said Church'"—I am now quoting the bill—would cease to be established by law. There would be at the same time a saving clause in the bill to prevent its having any effect on the Act of Union other than that which is thus strictly limited and defined. On that day the ecclesiastical courts in Ireland would be abolished, the ecclesiastical jurisdiction in Ireland would cease, the ecclesiastical laws in Ireland would no longer bind by any authority as law, the rights of peerage would lapse on the part of the bishops, and all ecclesiastical corporations in that country would be dissolved.

The committee is well aware that the Church itself is not a corporation, but an aggregate of corporations. I am, I believe, strictly accurate in saying that with these provisions in operation on January 1, 1871, the work of the disestablishment of the Irish Church would be legally completed. There is, at the same time, a point of great importance, which I think this is the place for me to mention. Though we feel it to be a necessary—and it will, I think, be admitted by the House generally to be necessary—part of such a plan as this that it should at once put an end to the force and authority of ecclesiastical laws, as such, in Ireland, yet we also feel that it is our duty not unnecessarily to subject that religious communion now called the Irish Established Church to shocks and inconveniences with respect to the management of its internal affairs not required by the scope of our measure. It is not our desire that this transition—this great political transition—should be attended with the maximum, but rather with the minimum, of ecclesiastical change. Whatever ecclesiastical change is made, ought, in our opinion, to be the result of the free deliberate will of the members of the Established Church, and not of the shock inconsiderately imparted by crude legislation to its machinery.

We, therefore, propose that although the ecclesiastical laws shall lose their force as laws, in which respect they have a certain relation to the whole community, yet they shall be understood to subsist as a form of voluntary contract, which shall continue to bind together the bishops, clergy, and laity now constituting the Established Church until and unless they shall be altered by the voluntary agency of the governing body which the members of that communion may appoint. In this way it appears to us that this great launch—and a great launch it undoubtedly is, so far as all the ecclesiastical arrangements, properly so called, are concerned—will be effected smoothly, and I am, indeed, very conscious that it is desirable, on every ground that it should be so, for there will be quite enough to tax the energy, the prudence, and the courage of the members of the Church of Ireland in making provision for the great change which we are going to bring about in its internal affairs. The committee, having followed me thus far, will have perceived that we have complete technical disendowment on the passing of the act, and complete and actual disestablishment on the day to be named in the act, and now standing for January 1, 1871.

Next comes a matter on which I fear it will be my duty to detain the committee for some time—the task of carrying out all those special arrangements, by means of which the interests of the parties affected by this great change will have to be settled and adjusted in detail. I am afraid I should, perhaps, alarm the committee were I to state how numerous those arrangements are, but they embrace the vested interests of incumbents—and by the word "incumbent" I wish to be understood as meaning a bishop or a dignitary of the Church, as well as a clergyman having parochial charge—the vested interests of curates, the case of lay and minor offices, the compensation for advowsons; the provisions to be adopted with respect to private endowments, the provisions with respect to churches, with respect to glebe houses, graveyards, all of those, of course, being subject to the life interests recognized by the bill. There are the arrangements connected with the winding-up of the *Regium Donum,* the arrangements connected with the winding-up of Maynooth, the arrangements for disposing of the tithe commutation rent-charge, the arrangements with respect to the large class of property affected by the property-purchase clauses, and the arrangements connected with the sale of the Church lands by the commissioners.

Let me say a word first with respect to that which is the largest of all these subjects—namely, the case of the vested interest of incumbents. Now, the vested interest of the incumbent is quite distinct, on the one hand, from his expectation of promotion. In all cases of the abolition of establishments, be they civil or ecclesiastical, I am afraid that expectation is a matter into which, however legitimate it may be, it is impossible for us to enter. The vested interest of the incumbent, then, is this—it is a title to receive a certain net income from the property of the Church, I say from the property of the Church, because I set apart receipts from pew-rents, receipts from fees, receipts from other casual sources with which it is no business of ours to deal. The vested interest with which we have to deal is the right of the incumbent to be secured in the receipt of a certain annual income from the property of the Church in consideration of the discharge of certain duties to which he is bound as the equivalent he gives for that income, and subject to the laws by which he is bound and the religious body to which he belongs. Therefore the committee will see in what sense it is true that, although the Church at large, and the congregations at large, have no vested interests, and it would be impossible to recognize anything of the kind, yet both the Church and the congregations are very largely concerned in the vested interest of the incumbent, because his title is not a simple, unconditional title to a certain payment of money, but it is a title to a payment of money in consideration of duty. In the performance of that duty the congregations and the Church are deeply concerned; and I think it will be the opinion of the committee that it would be unjust to them to expose them to unnecessary disparagement by worsening the conditions under which they now stand in reference to the clergy.

Such is the vested interest of the clergy; and I may here say that although, as a rule, it is for parents to set examples to children, yet, in the vicissitudes of human affairs, it sometimes happens that children may set a good example to parents. It has happened so in this instance, for the legislature of Canada, having to deal with a case undoubtedly far more simple, far less difficult and complicated than ours, yet, notwithstanding, in this one central and vital subject—the manner of dealing with the vested interests of the clergy upon whose incomes it was legislating, and the permanent source of whose incomes it was entirely cutting off—has undoubtedly proceeded upon principles which appear to balance, or rather to maintain very fairly the balance established between, the separate interests of the clergy and the general interests of the Church to which they belong, and the congregations to which they minister. Substantially, and after allowing for necessary differences of expression, we think the basis afforded by the Canadian measure supplies us with no unsuitable pattern after which to shape our own proceedings.

Such being the case, I will briefly describe to the committee how we propose to deal with the vested interest of the incumbent. The plan will be this: The amount of income to which each incumbent is entitled will be ascertained. It will be made subject to deduction for the curates he may have employed. That I will further explain when I come to the curate. It will be made payable, in the case of each, so long as he discharges the duty. And then there will be a provision that the annuity itself may be commuted upon the basis of capitalizing it as an annuity for life. Therefore, the commutation, taking the rate of interest at three and one-half per cent., will represent his whole interest in the income he receives, presuming it to last for life. This commutation can only be made upon the application of the incumbent. He must be the prime mover in bringing it about. Upon his application the sum of money will be paid to that which I shall call, for shortness, the Church body, but it will be paid to the Church body subject to the legal trust of discharging the obligation or covenant which we had ourselves to discharge to the incumbent—namely, to give him the annuity in full so long as he discharged the duties. The effect of that plan of commutation will be that, by means of the Church body, and of the inducements that will be given to arrangements between the Church body and the incumbents, we, the State, should escape, as we hope and believe, at a very early period from that which it is undoubtedly not desirable to maintain longer than is absolutely necessary—namely, a direct relation of administrator and recipient between the organs of the State and the individual clergy of the Church. That is the nature of the interest which the State possesses in commutation; and although, undoubtedly, commutation would be an arrangement so far favorable to the Church collectively— and the very same thing will apply *totidem verbis* to the Presbyterians of Ireland—as enabling the Church body and the individual to adjust their relations and to make a more economical application of their resources than would be possible by the maintenance of the original annuities, yet the interest of the State in bringing these transactions to a close will be felt amply to justify and strongly to recommend some arrangement of the kind.

Well, that is the mode in which we should propose to proceed with respect to the great subject of life interests. These life interests are in truth by far the greatest—and, indeed, much greater than all the rest put together—of the demands upon the fund of the Church before it becomes free and available for other purposes. I wish, however, to explain what I have not yet stated—that the recognition of life interests, which would be conditional as regards the performance of the duties that are now the equivalent for the income, would be unconditional in other respects. We should not attempt to interfere, in the main, with the position of the clergyman either as proprietor or occupier of land. In many cases, indeed, as we know, the clergy of Ireland do farm their own glebes. In many cases they let land from year to year. In many cases the land is let upon short leases; and although it would be desirable if we could to bring the clergy to give up the position of landlord as soon as possible, we do not propose to effect this result by any compulsory enactment. Commutation, we think, will offer inducements which will be sufficient for the purpose; but, speaking generally, we do not propose, by any compulsory provision in the bill to interfere with the position of the clergyman in relation to any part of his freehold.

There is, however, one exception which I must mention, because it is an exception which, perhaps, has a name and a bulk, though insignificant in every other respect. It is the tithe commutation rent-charge. We propose that the tithe commutation rent-charge shall at once and absolutely, and without any intervening life interest, vest in the commission under the act, and the reason is that the tithe commutation rent-charge, with the single exception of a certain amount of fluctuation, which, of course, is rather in the nature of an inconvenience than a convenience to the clergyman, is in every other respect a fixed interest; and inasmuch as it is very desirable immediately to put in action certain arrangements respecting it, we propose to take it at once into the hands of the commissioners, the faith of Parliament, of course, being pledged to the payment of the whole proceeds which the clergyman could derive from it. Besides that, there is ·nother very small exception which we have thought fit to make. I will speak by and by of the case of churches which are in use, but there are in Ireland cases of churches wholly ruinous, many in graveyards, but many apart from graveyards. In some cases the freehold may be in the incumbent of the parish. We propose at once to dispossess him of that freehold. It may be desirable that these sites should be disposed of either by throwing them into the burial-grounds or in some other manner, but there can be no advantage in keeping up that barren freehold, which is totally unproductive of practical results to the clergyman, and is purely incidental to his position as clergyman of a Church established by law.

There is another change which would be made immediately upon the disestablishment of the Church, and which it is my duty to bring specially to the notice of the committee, although probably the view of the committee will be not only in favor of the change, but is likely to be that under the circumstances of the case it is inevitable. The committee is aware of the peculiar nature of the title of an Irish bishop to sit in the House of Lords. He has a title to sit there for life, and yet it is an intermittent title. He is not a permanent member of that assembly, but he is placed in a certain legal rotation which brings him there for a session and then dismisses him, in the case of the archbishop for one, and in the case of the bishops for two or three sessions. We have had to ask ourselves whether it is desirable that a right of peerage so singular in its character and operation should continue after the disestablishment of the Church. I own that it is not without some regret and pain that I propose a provision which should seem in the slightest degree to convey a slight or disparagement in point of dignity to individuals who, as such, I believe to be fully and amply worthy of the honors they enjoy in the House of Lords. But the anomaly is so great, and then, again, it is so obvious that the Irish bishops are maintained in the House of Lords for the very purpose of representing a national and an Established Church, that—although not without regret as far as the individuals are concerned—I think we cannot hesitate to propose to the committee that these peerages should lapse with the disestablishment of the Church. It is because this proposal forms a qualification to the broad principle I have laid down as to respecting life interests in their integrity that I have been so particular in calling attention to it.

Well, now, sir, I come to the case of the curates, and I hope the committee will not be shocked at my endeavoring to state clearly the nature of the provisions we propose with regard to this most meritorious class of men, because, wearisome as it must necessarily be to you to pass through such a wilderness of details, yet there are many hundreds of persons for whom this question may be, or at least is believed by them to be, a matter of life or death, and who wait with the keenest anxiety to know the view that has been taken of their case. In speaking of the case of curates, I do not speak simply of those clergymen who have entered into transitory and fluctuating engagements for a week, month, or other short period. I speak of those who are regularly enlisted in the service of the Church as curates, and, in point of fact, are bound to that office by a long life-tenure, unless, as they hope may at some time happen, they should be presented to benefices. I speak of those who in a popular sense I may venture to call the permanent curates of the Irish Church. There is a great deal of difficulty in dealing with this class of persons, but the committee will observe that I am not now asking them to invade the public or the national fund for the purpose of compensation. In the main I am only studying to secure the due application to the benefit of the curate of those deductions which we have already made from the income of the incumbent, when proceeding to calculate his annuity for the purpose of ascertaining his vested interest. We propose to deal with the curates as follows: The commissioners are to determine who are curates permanently employed. In some cases the form of the instrument under which they are employed will adequately determine this point, but in others it would not. We propose to leave the matter to the commissioners, giving also to the incumbent the power of objecting that A. B., his curate, was not permanently employed. It is required, also, in order to enable the curate to take advantage of the provision on this point, that he should have been employed on January 1, 1869, and that he continue to be employed on January 1, 1871, or that, if he has ceased to be employed, the discontinuance of his employment shall be due to some cause other than his own free choice or misconduct. That will be the test. Being so eligible, he would, *primâ facie*, be entitled to have the interest in his curacy calculated for life, he would have a vested interest in it in the same way as the incumbent has in the income of his living or bishopric, and he would be entitled to have it commuted upon the same terms. He would also be subjected to the corresponding obligation to that which would be imposed on the incumbent—that is to say, he would be bound to continue the duties he now performs until he effects an arrangement for commutation; he would be bound to render the same services to the incumbent that he formerly did, or if he cease to render them, in order to maintain his qualification, that cessation must be due to some other cause than his own misconduct or free choice.

With regard to the curates of a more transitory class, we have a provision in the bill which appears to us a fair analogy to a similar provision in the Civil Service Superannuation Acts, according to which gratuities may be awarded in consequence of disadvantages they may have sustained. But that is a matter of minor importance and minute detail upon which I will not at present detain the committee.

I come now to the arrangements I shall have to make with regard to private endowments—and here it would be as well to refer to a misunderstanding that sprung up in the course of last session in consequence of an expression used by me. I said in the course of discussion on the Irish Church that not less than three-fifths, as far as I could reckon, of the whole money value of the property of the Church would be given back to the Church itself or to its members in any form of disestablishment that Parliament would probably agree to. It was not generally observed how important a part of that statement were the words " or its members," which I pronounced with some emphasis. What the Church will receive under the plan of the Government I will endeavor to separate from what its members will receive. No doubt its members will receive compensation, and the congregations of the Church have a very real interest, if not a vested interest, in those compensations. But with regard to the Church itself, the proposal of the Government would be to convey to it nothing in the shape of what I may call marketable property—I will by and by explain what I mean by that phrase—with the exception of private endowments which it may have received.

I beg the committee not to come prematurely to a conclusion as to the meaning of those words, but I think I shall be able to make them good, and to explain them in the course of what I am now going to say. With respect to these private endowments we do not propose that the enactments relating to them should embrace churches or glebe houses, because these are dealt with on grounds of their own, which take them out of this category. But there are private endowments in the Irish Church, and although they do not appear to be very large in amount they are various in form—such as endowments in glebe lands, in tithes, and in money. And the definition of private endowments we think it fair to take is this: In the first place, it must be money which has been contributed from private sources. It may have been given in a public character, as for example in the case of Primate Boulter and Primate Robinson; but though given by persons holding a public position, its having been given in a private capacity evidently constitutes it a private endowment. But we limit it by date, and the date we have chosen to propose to Parliament for limitation is the year 1660—the year of the Restoration.

The reason that has recommended the date to us is the fact that the Restoration was really the period at which the Church of Ireland—the Reformed or Protestant Church of Ireland—assumed its present legislative shape and character. Before the wars of Charles I, in all the three Churches of the three kingdoms there were more or less the different elements that finally developed themselves into different forms of Protestantism, and these were in conflict together within the bosom of the National Church. In England we had Puritanism and Anglicanism struggling for ascendancy within the pale of the Church, as we are told in Scripture that Jacob and Esau struggled together within the womb of their mother. In Scotland there was the same struggle, with the exception that there Presbyterian was really in the ascendancy. In Ireland Presbyterianism and Episcopacy were struggling powerfully together during the reigns of James I and Charles I. It may not be known to all who hear me—though it ought to be known, and it tends strongly to justify us in not going beyond the Restoration—that the very confession, the doctrinal confession of the Irish Church in the reigns of James I and Charles I was not the same as that in England. It was modelled by Archbishop Usher upon the highest Calvinistic frame, and it included nine articles which composed a document well known in England under the name of the Lambeth Articles, drawn up in the latter end of the sixteenth century. I hope I shall not wound the feelings of any man when I say that it was one of the most formidable collections of theology which ever proceeded from the pen of a divine in the whole history of Christendom. It was different in spirit to the Thirty-nine Articles of the Church of England, and the constitution of the Irish Church was practically different. Presbyterianism was not formally or legally recognized, but it had a real or practical recognition in Ulster, which was occupied by Scotch rather than English colonists, who were for the most part Presbyterians. I find no proof that when a Presbyterian minister went over from Scotland to Ireland he was obliged to submit to reordination, and if a bishop had to go into a place where ordination was going on, he was never allowed, as far as I can learn, in the case of a man of strong Presbyterian opinions, to assert his Episcopal character and his exclusive power of ordination, but had to beg for admission into the room where the ordination was going on. Even if we could trace the private endowments back to so remote a period, the first effect would be to raise a strong controversy between the friends of Presbytery and Episcopacy.

When we come to the time of Charles II, at which period the ecclesiastical condition both of England and Ireland became distinct, we ask you, then, to distinguish private and public endowments, because we know historically that a man, at any rate, knew what he was doing, and the fair presumption arises that if he gave his money to the Church, it was for the support of that form of religion to which it is now applied. That will be the definition we propose to take with respect to private endowments. They are not numerous in the Church of Ireland, but they are of extraordinary interest. Take the case of the parish of Laracor, the parish of which Swift was vicar before he was transferred to the deanery of St. Patrick's. When he went into it, Laracor had a glebe house and one acre. He left it with a glebe house and twenty acres. He improved and decorated it in many ways. It is sad and melancholy to learn, if only we look upon this place as one of the memorials of so extraordinary a man, that many of the embellishments, or what our Scotch friends would call " amenities " of the glebe which grew up under his fostering hand have since been effaced. He endowed the vicarage with certain tithes which he had purchased for the purpose; and I doubt whether it is generally very well known that a curious question arises on this bequest, because a portion of his property—by the by, consisting, I be-

lieve, of those very tithes—was left by him for what he calls—
I never knew the term to be used elsewhere—" the Episcopal
religion established in Ireland." But that extraordinary man,
even at the time when he wrote that the Irish Catholics were
so down-trodden and insignificant that no possible change could
ever bring them into a position of importance, appears to have
foreseen the day when the ecclesiastical arrangements of Ireland would be called to account; because, not satisfied with
leaving the property to maintain the Episcopal religion he proceeds to provide for the day when that Episcopal religion might
be disestablished, and be no longer the national religion of the
country. Apparently by some secret intimation he foresaw the
shortness of its existence as an Establishment, for he left the
property subject to a condition that in such case it should be
administered for the benefit of the poor.

The value of the private endowments, as far as we have been
able to ascertain, is not more than half-a-million, between land-
tithes and money. It is very uncertain. I may say here that I
think the committee will recognize the fairness of a step which
we propose to take. There may be a good deal of legal research
and legal expenditure requisite in order to obtain evidence upon
those titles. We propose, therefore, to authorize the commissioners to allow the parties reasonable expenses in cases where
they think those expenses have been fairly undertaken in ascertaining the title and establishing the fact of private endowments.
I now come to the churches. This is the way in which we propose to deal with churches. When I say churches, I mean
principally—indeed, I may say exclusively—churches which
are in use by the present Established Church. Now, it is quite
evident that churches cost a great deal of money to erect, but
that when erected they do not properly fall within the category
of " marketable property." Buyers will not easily be found,
and in Ireland, as far as I can understand, there is no great in-
sufficiency of churches—in the Establishment there is a pro-
fusion—among the Presbyterians or the Roman Catholics. Be
that as it may—whether founded on feeling or the inconverti-
bility of churches into marketable property—we have no doubt
whatever that, subject always to the general though not legal
obligation of applying them to religious purposes, we propose
that the churches of Ireland should be handed over to the gov-

erning body of the disestablished Church with as little difficulty, impediment, or embarrassment as possible.

What we propose, therefore, is, that within the trust those churches may be taken on the simple declaration of that body that it is their intention to take and maintain them for the purposes of worship, or else to take them down, which they wish to do in certain cases, where it is expedient for the purpose of substituting for them new churches, which the governing body may desire to build, and which may be more convenient, especially having reference to the altered temporal circumstances of their community. Under these circumstances, I have no doubt a great number of these churches will be taken over by the governing body of the disestablished Church; but, whether that be so or not, it is our duty to make provision for the accidental case of churches being refused. If churches be not taken over by the governing body, we are not led to think that it would be expedient for Parliament to contemplate their actual transfer, under operation of law, to any other religious community; nor are we led to believe that would be generally desired by any other party. We, therefore, take a general power to enable the commissioners to dispose of the site, or of the building itself, or, more properly, its materials.

Now, there is a case on which I should say a few words, because I think it is one in which equity requires or recommends that we should make a small allowance from the ecclesiastical fund to the disestablished Church. Unhappily, in Ireland there are not copiously scattered, as in England, churches which are beautiful and wonderful specimens of art, and which form one of the richest portions of our national treasury; but here and there in Ireland there are churches of that class. I need only mention one which has been before the public in a peculiar manner of late years—the Church of St. Patrick in Dublin. We cannot but admit these two propositions: In the first place, that it is desirable that such churches should be maintained, that it would not be desirable for the credit or character of the country that they should fall into decay; and the second proposition is that the maintenance of such fabrics is more than we have a right to expect by means of casual voluntary contributions. If such a congregation, founded on voluntary bases, should think to erect for itself such a church as St. Patrick's or Westminster

Abbey, it will be for them to be responsible for its maintenance; but, with respect to those fabrics which have been erected and have been held under the expectation of permanent maintenance, we propose—subject to very careful limitations, for we confine the number to twelve churches—that the commissioners should be authorized, where it is desirable that a church should be maintained as a national monument, and where it is found that the maintenance would be too heavy for a voluntary congregation, to allow a moderate sum for its maintenance to those to whom it is given up. This is not a very large provision, but it is one recommended by the distinct equity of the case.

I will say one word with regard to churches which are not in use in Ireland. Some of these national monuments are of a curious and interesting character; but, at the same time, as in the case of the churches at Glendalough, they are not suited or adapted to public worship. Therefore, we propose that such churches should be handed over to the Board of Works. with an allocation of funds sufficient for their due and becoming preservation. In other cases where there are remains of churches and sites of churches, they might form burial-grounds, or be taken up and restored by one of the religious communities of the country. Though their value may be insignificant, we ask Parliament to give power to the commissioners to dispose of them to those communities.

The next question, I am sorry to say, like that of the curates, is beset with complications. It is one which was before the public last year, and with respect to it my views are very much qualified, or, indeed, I may say almost overturned, by the state of facts that since then we have become more accurately acquainted with. It is the case of the glebe houses; and I wish when I speak of them to include the see houses, as I included the bishops when I spoke of the incumbents, because, in all essential respects, they stand on the same footing. With respect to the glebe houses, it is exceedingly difficult to analyze the sources from which the means of building them have proceeded. Parliamentary grants have had a share of it; and private endowments have had a share of it; but the greater part of those funds has hitherto been supplied by charges deducted from the incomes of the clergy under Acts of Parliament, enabling them to charge their successors as well as themselves. Now, a nice and knotty question arises, as to whether money so obtained is to be regarded as a public or a private endowment. I can imagine a whole night spent in the discussion of that point. The greatest difficulties have arisen upon this point, and I myself have inclined sometimes one way and sometimes another with reference to it. As, in the case of the churches, there are some men of a practical turn of mind, not perhaps open much on the side of their imagination, whose minds were materially influenced by the observation that churches were not a marketable property, so the same feeling obtains as a general rule with respect to glebe houses, the value of which, while immense to the body that may possess the churches, is very small indeed to any other persons.

How correct I am in making this statement the committee will be enabled to judge when I inform them that we can trace an expenditure upon the glebe houses, not including sites, amounting to £1,200,000, and yet the whole of the present value of them in Ireland, including the ground upon which they are built, is estimated at only £18,600 per annum. I hear a good deal of murmuring from some quarters of the House, and I am not surprised at it, because when these facts first came to my knowledge I was astonished myself.

[An honorable member inquired whether the sum mentioned included the value of the glebes]

No, if I wanted to confuse the matter thoroughly I should merely have to discuss the subjects of the glebe houses and the glebes together. I have alluded to this point because I desire to draw a distinction between the title of the Church to what may be looked upon as property, because it can be converted into a sensible amount of money, and its title to that which, however valuable to it as a body, has no marketable value.

However, I by no means wish to be understood as saying that the glebe houses of Ireland are worth nothing. On the contrary, I will prove to the House that they are not worth nothing, and I will do so by showing that we shall not get hold of them without paying for them, as, unfortunately, they are saddled with heavy building charges. It is a singular fact that upon these glebe houses, which are valued at the present moment at £18,600 per annum—perhaps you may be justified in adding twenty per cent. to that amount in order to bring the value to the rack rental—there should be in addition to the enormous sums already laid out upon them a building charge outstanding of about £250,000. That is the exact state of the case, and I cannot put it too pointedly to the committee. £1,200,000 has been already laid out upon this property, of which the annual value, according to the tenements valuation, amounts to £18,600, and a further sum of £250,000 is still payable upon it on account of a building charge—a sum which must be paid in order to enable us to come into legal possession of it. Now, that is not certainly a very inviting prospect. I confess I was greatly astonished when I found that property which last year I proposed to treat as convertible property of very considerable value turned out to have this large charge upon it and to be of such comparatively small marketable value. However, such as it is, we of course propose to take it.

If the statement I have made prove to be inaccurate, and should it turn out that the glebe houses are of more value than I am now stating them to be, what I am now about to say will be subject, of course, to reconsideration. Assuming, however, that my information is correct with reference to the value of this property, then it appears to me that the best course we can adopt under the circumstances is this: This building charge, which will have to be paid by us in the first instance, is not uniformly distributed over the whole of the glebe houses. It is probable that in some cases it will amount to almost their full marketable value, while in others no building charge at all will have to be paid. The necessity of paying the building charge where it exists is binding upon us, because in such a case the incumbent would have been entitled to recover it from his successor, and consequently when the incumbent dies or commutes under the provisions of this bill, either he or his family will be entitled to recover it from us as standing in the place of his successor. We are, therefore, bound by law and by justice to discharge this obligation, and we are not called upon to exercise any discretion in the matter. We shall come into possession of the glebe houses when the existing life interests are exhausted, because our interest will still be only in the nature of a reversionary interest in the property, and then we shall have to pay the amount of the building charge still outstanding at the time.

Having come into possession of the property upon those terms, we shall assume that the glebe house, where fully charged, is no property at all, but we shall still regard the land upon which it stands as valuable property. We shall say to the Church body: "You have taken the church, and you may now negotiate with us for the land upon which the glebe house is built, and also for a small glebe not exceeding ten acres in extent of adjacent land, which we will sell you at a fair valuation." But we shall add: "Where you take the land you may take the house; but you must reimburse us the whole of the building charge we have paid upon it, subject to the limitation that it shall not exceed ten years' valuation." After a great deal of consideration, and after finding that the treasure we believed we possessed in the glebe houses was merely visionary, we have come to the conclusion that this is the best plan we can adopt in dealing with this description of property. It has been said that facilities ought to be given, although not in the way of grants to the members of other communions, for the purpose of enabling them to erect glebe houses for themselves. Now, that is a principle which has been already adopted by Parliament in the case of the Act of William IV, under which public money was advanced—under somewhat onerous conditions, it is true— to the Roman Catholics and the Presbyterians of Ireland for the purpose of building glebe houses. Although we have not inserted any clause to carry out such a proposal in the present bill, we think it may be desirable that loans for this purpose may be granted upon easy terms contemporaneously with the winding-up arrangements to be conducted by the Ecclesiastical Commission. At the same time it will be necessary to limit the operation of that system within a certain period of time, because I think it is open to considerable doubt whether it would be desirable to keep a law of that kind permanently upon the statute-book, seeing that it might possibly lead to some controversy in Ireland.

The question relating to the burial-grounds may be disposed of very shortly. I propose that the burial-grounds belonging to a church shall pass along with it to the Church body holding the latter, provision however being made in all cases for the

preservation of existing interests in the burial-ground. It is
known to the committee that the law in Ireland, as recently adjusted with respect to burying-grounds, is very different from,
and is much more favorable to the public, than that in force in
England. We propose that all other burial-grounds shall be
given over to the guardians of the poor, and we propose to give
uniformity and simplicity to the provisions of the law which
is now in partial action.

I think I have now done with the winding-up arrangements
of the bill as far as the Established Church is concerned. There
still remains a portion of them which, although not very extensive in amount, is yet of very great importance, and one
which, I am bound to add, is by no means free in all its bearing from difficulty. It was at all times part of the views of
those who proposed the resolutions of last year that with the
disestablishment of the Church must come the final cessation
of all relations between the State and the Presbyterian clergy
in Ireland and between the State and the College of Maynooth.
I have now to consider in what manner effect is to be given to
that conviction, which was strongly entertained by the House,
and which was, in fact, embodied in a fourth resolution passed
by the House during the session of 1868, which was added to
the other three resolutions which had been previously agreed to.
The sum which we have now to deal with is an annual sum of
about £70,000. Of that amount £26,000 a year constitutes the
vote for Maynooth, and between £45,000 and £50,000 is the aggregate of the votes given for the various communities of Presbyterians. We are no longer dealing with a simple and single
body known to the law as the Established Church, but we are
dealing with classes which, in point of religious opinion, fall
under a threefold division.

The interest now before us is that of the Old or Scotch Presbyterians, as I may call them for distinction's sake; the next is
that of the minor bodies of Presbyterians, who are separated in
Ireland from the main body, not only by religious communion,
but by grave differences in those matters which lie at the foundations of the Christian faith. There are three or four of these
bodies, such as the Remonstrant Synod of Ulster, the Presbytery
of Antrim, and one or two more, who fall under a different
class of religionists; these, or some of them, entertaining Arian
or what are called Unitarian opinions.

Then there are the Roman Catholics, sufficiently known to us to dispense with the necessity for any description as regards their religious opinions. If I refer to these distinctions of religious belief it is only for the purpose of stating in the broadest manner that on the part of Her Majesty's Government I entirely decline on the present occasion to enter into such matters. I will not for one moment ask what are the political or the religious peculiarities of these bodies, professing the Christian name, with whom we are to deal; but I will endeavor to deal with them strictly, impartially, and equitably on the principles of civil justice, which apply to them all alike, and which render it iniquitous and wrong to raise controversial questions in regard to them or to matters of religious belief. The ground they stand on is that of citizenship—the claim they urge is that of general equity and good faith. We, the Government, have recognized that claim. I am confident that Parliament will recognize that claim in the case of the Established Church. Let us endeavor to proceed upon the same fair, and just, and liberal, though moderate, and prudent recognition of it in the case of these bodies exterior to the Established Church. Now, as respects the larger part of this sum of £70,000 a year, there is no difficulty—when you come to look at it in the light of a purely civil interest. Most of it is given in the shape of a direct vote of so much money passing immediately from the State to the individual through the synod, but in all cases the nature of the vested interest and expectancy—call it what you like—is the same. All we have to do is to take precisely the same course as with respect to the clergy of the Established Church. Take the question of income—which here being a mere matter of money can be at once ascertained—that is not given to him for nothing, but on the condition of the performance of duty. Hence, with a slight modification, which I need not here mention, a similar claim will arise in the case of the Presbyterian minister to that which I have already explained in the case of the incumbent; and the bill also will give to him a power of commutation in every substantial respect corresponding with that proposed to be made for the clergy of the Established Church.

So far with respect to the clergy and to life interests proper. Beside the ministers who perform spiritual offices in particular congregations, there is another class that appears to us to have a claim; they are what are called assistants and successors. Now these gentlemen are in a condition, not indeed as to the abundance of the interest at which they are ultimately to arrive, but otherwise I take it legally in a condition not very far removed from that of an heir of entail; they are already appointed to the assistant pastorship of a particular congregation; they derive no benefit from the *Regium Donum,* but the office of assistant which they hold entitles them to succeed after the death or resignation of the incumbent, and consequently it is urged that they have a just claim to the expectancy created by that right of succession. This is not a very large matter; it consists only of the difference in value between the life of the incumbent and the younger life of his successor; but to that extent we think it just that the claim should be provided for.

Then there is another class—the teachers of Presbyterian educational institutions under the general assembly of the Presbytery of Ulster. With regard to them, though they are not ministers, but professors only, we propose to deal with them precisely in the same manner as if they were pastors of churches, and to assure to them their salaries, together with a like power of commutation. But now comes a greater difficulty, with respect to those educational establishments to which I wish to call the attention of the committee for a few moments. When we disestablish a church, and when a particular congregation ceases to have a pastor found for it by public funds, it feels an immediate want, and a stimulus is applied to it to satisfy that want. But when you deal with an establishment for educational purposes, a rather different order of considerations comes into play. There are several points which ought to be taken into account, although I will not say precisely what amount of weight is to be given to them.

In dealing with these Presbyterian places of education we have information upon which to proceed, but in dealing with the professors of the College of Maynooth we know nothing as to the details of the arrangements made with them. We have chosen to constitute a trust by the authority of an act of Parliament, and to that trust we have committed the disposal of the grant which Parliament has thought fit to make. Well, now, what is the experience of England? The experience, in particular, of the training colleges proves that there should be some consideration in dealing with establishments for education. I ought not, perhaps, to bring into the present discussion the case of Trinity College, Dublin, for Her Majesty's Government make no proposal upon that subject at the present time. But it is perfectly plain that if the House and the legislature should adopt the measure that we now submit to it, Trinity College, Dublin, will have to be made the subject of legislation. It is also, I think, quite plain that it will be impossible to maintain the present exclusive application of the revenues of Trinity College to the purposes of a governing body and staff wholly connected with one religious persuasion. It is quite possible that Parliament may apply to Trinity College the same lenient method of dealing which it commonly adopts, and may think fit to leave some moderate provision applicable to the rearing, or to the teaching, at least, of the clergy, who will, as a clergy, become dependent entirely upon the resources of a voluntary communion. But undoubtedly when we come to deal with Trinity College we shall feel the force of this argument, that to put a sharp termination to the career of an educational establishment is a more trenchant operation than to do the same with the machinery for providing a parochial ministry, because one is a much stronger stimulus to persons to provide themselves with clergymen than the other is to induce them to maintain schools in which these clergymen can be trained. These general considerations, at the same time, are considerations which I know must not be pushed beyond their proper limits.

I hope the House will think, when I come to the end of this long and wearisome statement, that whatever the Government have done, they have endeavored to keep strict good faith. I believe that I have announced no proposal as yet to which that character will not be held to apply when it is compared with our former declarations; and I trust that my announcements will remain the same to the end of the chapter. I have now to consider in the light and spirit of our general arrangements, and, subject always to the full maintenance, in letter and in spirit, of that which we have heretofore declared, what appears to us the most equitable method of dealing with the *Regium Donum*, the grant to Maynooth, and all similar grants. The Presbyterians are interested in this matter in respect of the college which they have have in Belfast, and likewise in respect of a similar institution which exists for the benefit of minor Presbyterian bodies; the Roman Catholics are interested in it through the College of Maynooth; but there are also several other payments made by Parliament which, on the whole, fall under very much the same class of considerations. There is the payment made by Parliament to what is called the Presbyterian Widows' Fund. Now, that, of course, exists for the purpose of supplying wants that are coming into operation from year to year, and it would be very hard to withdraw that widows' fund without notice. In the same way it would be hard to withdraw without notice the grants now made to Presbyterian educational establishments and to the College of Maynooth. There is another class of payments made by the Presbyterians to their synodical officers. They hold an office regarding which it is very difficult to define the degree to which it should be considered a vested interest. But when we look at the whole of these matters, and read them in the light of the declarations and proceedings of last year, we have adopted—first, the principle that now permanent endowment can be given to them out of the public resources properly so called; and, secondly, the principle that no permanent endowment can be given to them out of the National Ecclesiastical Fund of Ireland. What we propose, and we think it a fair and equitable proposal, is, that, in order to give time for the free consideration of the arrangements and the construction of scales for the satisfaction of life interests, and for avoiding violent shocks and disappointments to those whose plans for life may already have been made upon the supposition of the continuance of arrangements which have so long existed, and which were solemnly made, there should be a valuation of the interest of all these grants—a life interest at a moderate scale, or at fourteen years' purchase, of the capital amount now annually voted.

[Sir S. Northcote: " The annual amount? "]

Yes, the annual amount. It is a life interest, and it is to be commuted as a life interest is commuted, upon the age of the individual. That age varies. In the case of Presbyterian ministers, as there is a large number of years, that amount is high. In the case of bishops and dignitaries it is somewhat lower. We take fourteen years as, on the whole, a fair amount of these different grants. We propose to treat them substantially as life interests, and the payment is to be analogous to that made on other life interests, and this to wind up and close all the relations between those bodies and persons and the State.

Well, now, sir, I am coming in sight of port. There are two or three points which will not take long, apart from the question of religion and matters of controversy, but which are of so much interest to gentlemen connected with Ireland and the land of Ireland, and which likewise have so innocent and beneficial a bearing on the land question of Ireland, that I must beg for a little more of the indulgence of the committee. First of all, I would proceed to explain what I fear some of my hearers will think ought to be placed in the category of financial puzzles. If they do not entirely follow me, I will ask them, without understanding me, to believe it, and I will undertake to make it good upon a future occasion. It relates to the important subject of the tithe rent-charge of Ireland. I have already said that I attach great importance to the merging of the tithe rent-charge, and for that reason the commission will step into the possession of it immediately after the passing of the act. Well, if there be here any gentlemen possessed of land in Ireland—and there are many—they will not be very grateful to me for what I am going first to state. It is that we shall give to them unconditionally the tithe rent-charge at twenty-two and one-half years' purchase. That is, of course, twenty-two and one-half years' purchase, not of the old gross £100, but of the £75 a year. We make that offer because we think there may be landlords in Ireland who will be disposed at once to wind up the arrangement with us.

But if gentlemen will listen to me they will see that we have another alternative for those who may not be disposed to purchase the tithe rent-charge out and out in money down at twenty-two and one-half years' purchase. It is this—We make to them a compulsory sale. I have not the least idea that anyone will object to that. We convey the tithe rent-charge to them under the following conditions: We charge them in our books with £2,250 for every net £100 a year of tithe rent-charge. That is to say, we sell them a tithe rent-charge at a rate to yield them four and one-half per cent. We then credit them on the other side with a loan of equal amount. We provide that they shall pay off that loan by annual instalments, with interest. But the rate of interest to be charged on the instalment is three and one-half per cent. The consequence of that is that a fund of one per cent. will remain as a sinking fund to absorb the principal. The purchaser of the tithe rent-charge in that form—except that he will get rid of the fluctuation, for we must give him a fixed amount—will not be called upon to make any addition whatever to his annual payment. He will be liable to that annual payment for forty-five years, and at the close of that term he will, under this arrangement, have the rent-charge, whatever it may be, for the residue of the time for nothing. That will be the financial effect of the arrangement, which, I think, will not be bad for the Irish landlord. I perceive by the buzz around me that this subject is not without some interest to a great many honorable members. I may here say that in dealing with this question I have ventured to lament the necessity under which Parliament has found itself on a former occasion of wasting the property of the Irish Church in order to prevent its being so great in its magnitude as too much to shock the public mind. We have not proceeded on that principle of wasting. We have not sought to work down the residue that will remain to be disposed of; but we have endeavored to make the most economical arrangement for the interest of that fund of which the equity of the case admits. And the committee will the more readily give me credit for what I have to say on this subject when I add that while in this manner we shall give twenty-two and one-half years' purchase for the tithe rent-charge of Ireland, the average rate at which that charge sells in the market is very little, if at all, more than sixteen or seventeen years' purchase. On the other hand, it is not a bad arrangement for the public, because it may be safely taken as a general rule that the public, in arrangements reaching over a long period of time, are perfectly safe in undertaking to lend at three and one-half per cent.

There is another point which need not detain us more than a moment. It relates to what will be in the recollection of Irish gentlemen—but there are very few still here who were in the House at the period of the Irish Church Temporalities Act—as the Perpetuity Purchase Clauses. They were clauses of an arrangement somewhat doubtful for the interest of the national ecclesiastical property of Ireland. We feel that under this bill equity requires that the persons who are now possessed of a title to purchase under these clauses should not be suddenly deprived of that title. But we also feel it to be impossible, in a measure of disestablishment and disendowment, to keep those clauses permanently in existence, in consequence of the highly anomalous and inconvenient confusion of interests which they create. We therefore propose that the power to purchase, now in the hands of the tenant, shall remain in existence for three years from January 1, 1871, and if not made use of in that interval, it shall then finally lapse and determine.

Another question of great and universal interest arises here. The commissioners to be appointed under this bill, or some body which may succeed them, after the difficult and onerous part of the arrangement shall be disposed of, will, as I think, be the holders of a considerable amount of property. The question is in what investment shall that be held. The perpetuity purchase rents now in existence appear to form, as far as they go, a very eligible description of investment, because they have the certainty of landed income without the incidents of fluctuation, or any of those difficult administrative questions which attach to the character of the landlord. The committee will, however, agree with me that it is not desirable either that this commission which we now propose to appoint, or any State authority in its place, should continue permanently to hold the Church land which will necessarily come into its possession. Such a commission is not and cannot be permanently a good landlord, and it is far better that it should discharge itself as soon as may be of duties it cannot properly fulfil.

What we propose, then, is that in selling the proprietary rights of these estates, the power of preëmption should be provided for the tenants, and, what is more—indeed, without this addition, I do not think I could claim for this provision credit for anything more than good intentions—we further propose that in such sales three-fourths of the purchase-money may be left upon the security of the land, and that the charge so remaining shall be liquidated by instalments, upon the principle adopted in the Drainage Act, by which we make the whole repayable in twenty-two years. Now, the nature of this proposal the committee thoroughly comprehend, and I trust it will meet with their approval. It does not place the land in the market in an anomalous character; it does not make the State responsible for duties that it cannot fulfil, and the permanent retention of which is alien from its nature. And it will have the economical effect of materially improving the price that we shall get for the land, and by this means we shall try the experiment on a limited scale of breaking up properties in a manner which I believe to be perfectly safe, easy, and unexceptionable.

I will now, sir, give to the committee the financial result of these operations in a very few words. With respect to the income of the Irish Church I shall say little, for I have great difficulty in making out what it is. The Church Commission labored assiduously between 1867 and the end of 1868, and they have reported as the result of their inquiries that the income of the Irish Church is £616,000 a year. I must say, with very great respect for their sixteen months of toil, that I humbly dissent from the conclusion at which the commission arrived. It seems to me that they placed the revenue too low. I find that one of the commissioners, Colonel Adair, who is known to have taken an active part in their labors, has within the last fortnight published a statement in which he puts the income of the Irish Church as high as £839,000 a year. I do not place it quite so high as Colonel Adair, nor quite so low as the Irish Church Commission. I believe it to be about £700,000 a year.

So much for the income of the Irish Church. But what we have more to do with is the capital. I have taken the tithe rent-charge at the rate of purchase I propose, and I find that the tithe rent-charge will yield £9,000,000. I have taken the land of all kinds—Episcopal and chapter lands, those belonging to glebes, etc., and putting on them the fairest valuation that a very competent person by whom we are assisted in Dublin can make, I find that the whole undivided value of the lands and of the perpetuity rents, if sold, would be £250,000. Besides that, there is money of one kind or another in stocks and banks to the amount of £750,000. I have not attempted to value the fabrics of churches, nor the fabrics of the glebe houses, because after what I have stated of how they stand in the tenement valuation and the charge upon them, I consider it would be idle to include them in this statement as an item of any considerable amount. The result, without taking into account the glebe houses and churches, is that the whole value of the Church property in Ireland, reduced and cut down as it has been—first by the almost unbounded waste of life tenants, and second by the wisdom or unwisdom of well-intending Parliaments—the remaining value is not less than £16,000,000—an amount more considerable than I had ventured to anticipate, when, with smaller means of information, I endeavored to form an estimate of it last year.

I now come to a delicate part of the case, and here the figures must be considered as taken with rather a broad margin. Yet, on the whole, I think they will be found very near the mark, so far as the total is concerned. The life interests of incumbents of all kinds in the Church—bishops, dignitaries, and parochial clergy—will amount, I think, to say £4,900,000; and if that appears to anyone a large sum he should recollect that when divided by the large number of persons—two thousand—among whom the whole has to be apportioned, it represents a very slender acknowledgment for the labors, expectations, and costly education of those gentlemen, and for the anxieties and honest and good service by which their respective situations have been attended. The compensation of the curates, deducted from that of the incumbents, will come to £800,000. The lay compensations are not inconsiderable. They will come to £900,000. Of that something over £300,000, it is supposed, will be the value of the advowsons; but it is very difficult in Ireland to obtain fixed, clear, and definite rules for estimating their value. The transfer of them in Ireland is comparatively rare, and they are subject to a variety of contingencies which very much impair the means of judgment. It is not a large matter. We put it at about £300,000.

The other lay compensations embrace a class of persons who do not much enter into the view, looking at this subject generally; but the largest part will be absorbed by the parish clerks and sextons in Ireland, of whom the bulk, I believe, like the incumbents, have freehold offices, and must be dealt with on the very same principle as the incumbents. Then there are the officers of cathedrals, of the ecclesiastical courts, and the functionaries connected with the present Ecclesiastical Commission. These will bring up the amount of the lay compensations to about £900,000. The charge of private endowments on the fund is about £500,000, and in that, I may say in passing, will

not be included the result of a recent act of Parliament passed
by Sir Joseph Napier as to endowments of a particular class,
which it is not necessary to bring into this bill. The building
charges on the glebe houses represent £250,000. The sum necessary to clear off our engagements upon the moderate footing
we propose with respect to the Presbyterians and Maynooth will
be £1,100,000; and of that sum I ought to say two-thirds will
go to the Presbyterians, and no more than one-third to Maynooth. I must also supply two small claims I had omitted.
The Presbyterians claim, and I think it is not an unreasonable
claim, that as we admit an educational establishment to require
a little more time for maintaining it on the old system, we should
give them some consideration in the shape of money in respect
of the buildings they have raised in Belfast to meet the parliamentary grant, which we shall be prepared to concede, subject
to the maximum of £15,000. The other is a claim, not made
by the Roman Catholics, but it is our opinion it ought to be
made spontaneously, and that, I think, will be the universal opinion of the House. When the Act of 1845 was passed it was
known to be the intention that the buildings of Maynooth should
be kept in repair at the public charge. The House of Commons
modified its views shortly after. The college had no means of
meeting the necessary expense except by borrowing, and they
have gone in debt to the Board of Works to the extent of £20,-
000. I think we should feel that that debt incurred in past
time on account of these repairs, and in consequence of a change
of view on the part of Parliament, ought at once to be remitted.
I estimate the expense of this commission during the ten years
of its continuance at £200,000, and that makes my total charge
against the property of the Church amount to £8,500,000. So
that the property will be divided—for I confess I have some
faith in the moderation of my estimate—into two nearly equal
parts; or, to be quite safe, I may call it £16,000,000; and as the
charges upon it will come to between £8,000,000 and £9,000,000,
the sum at the disposal of Parliament will not be less than between £7,000,000 and £8,000,000.

I have now, sir, done with my first and second dates, but there
is one financial item which, through infirmity of memory, I
have omitted. The committee will naturally ask how we are
to pay the heavy charge that may be entailed by the commuta-

tions, because if the commutations are made, and we have every desire they should be made immediately or as soon as possible after disestablishment, they will require, between Episcopalians and Presbyterians, from £6,000,000 to £7,000,000. My answer is that, fortunately, the banking resources of my right honorable friend the Chancellor of the Exchequer are such, with respect to the deposits of the public, as to cause no serious difficulty on that part of the case; and, as a matter of prudence, we have taken power in the bill to fix the payment of commutation money in eight instalments extending over four years.

And now supposing that all the arrangements which I have so imperfectly detailed, and which the committee have listened to with so much patience—supposing that we have reached the moment when these arrangements are all completed—that is, so far completed that provision is made for all they can possibly require—I now come to the third date to which I pointed at the commencement, and I ask a question which will reawaken the flagging interest of the committee—how we are to dispose of the residue? I will first state the conditions which appear to me necessary to be combined in a good plan for the disposal of such a fund. The first two are already fixed, written, I may say, in letters of iron. It is written that the money is to be applied to Irish purposes; and it is written that it is to be applied to purposes not ecclesiastical—not for any Church, not for any clergy, not or any teaching of religion, and I hope the committee will see that in thus broadly stating what I conceive to be the obligations we have come under, I am showing a disposition not to shrink from the fulfilment of those obligations.

But there are other requisites that it is most important to combine in any plan for the application of this residue. In the first place I think there are feelings much to be respected in a large portion of the community—of those who say that the time has come when the application of this money must be dissociated from the teaching of religion, but who at the same time would desire that its future application should, if possible, bear upon it some of those legible marks of Christian character, which would be as it were a witness to its first origin and its long-continued use, being applied as nearly as circumstances admit in conformity with what is usually the *cyprès* doctrine of courts of equity. Another condition of a good plan is that it must not

drag us from one controversy into another. We must not make
this great controversy the mere doorway to another set of conflicts and disputes, perhaps equally embarrassing. One condition of a good plan is that, the question being Irish and wholly
Irish, the plan must be equal in its application to all parties,
and, as far as may be, to the whole community in Ireland. One
condition more I will mention, to which I attach the highest
value: the plan must embody the final application of the money.
The money must be so disposed as that the day may never come
when any member on either side of the House should suggest,
seeing that there was a sum of money to dispose of, some scheme
for its application, which would lead us back into all the em-
barrassments from which we are now at length vigorously struggling to free ourselves.

I will mention some of the modes suggested for the application of the money. The division of the fund among Churches
only was out of the question, because such a measure would be
in conflict with the sentiments of the people, the opinions of
this House, and the pledges which we have given and which
must be redeemed. Its application to education would not fall
so directly under the same ban, but it might give rise to the
suspicion in Ireland that it was an endeavor to get rid of the
annual grant, and might launch us into the controversies connected with the system of national education in that country. It
has been proposed by some that the fund should be applied to
public works in Ireland.

Those who have followed the history of the great attempt we
made at public works in Ireland in reference to the Shannon
drainage, will admit that the prospect opened by such a proposal is not very inviting. In the first place, it is a project which
would lead to jobbery, and in the next place it would set every
part of Ireland at variance with every other part in the scramble
to obtain the largest possible portion of the money. In the third
place, do what you could to promote equality, the application of
the money must be unequal, because more would be given to
certain districts than to others; and if the money were applied
in the way of loan, the arrangement would lead to great improvi-
dence, because when one public work was ended the money
would flow back and become again available, and it would be
impossible to make the fund a permanent foundation for loans

without encountering difficulties of an objectionable character. In the same way reasons may be adduced against the application of the fund to railways, and, besides, it is impossible for us to connect the question of Irish railways with the question of the Irish Church. I know the interest which exists for railways in Ireland; but I also know that it is a question of great difficulty and complexity; and it is our duty in laying before you a measure for which we claim the merit of finality to make some proposal obvious and clear in character, and which does not involve you in any difficult inquiries. It will be the duty of the Government to give a careful consideration to all proposals in regard to Irish railways, without connecting them with the present matter.

It has next been proposed that the money should be applied to the poor-rates. Such an application, it appears to me, would be a great mistake. I am not in the least inclined to deny that the land and the landlords of Ireland may derive some considerable benefit in the long run from any mode in which the money might be applied for the benefit of Ireland; but when a system of legal obligation has been there constituted to satisfy a primary want—an obligation recognized in all quarters as incumbent on the property of the country—I do not think it necessary that this fund should be applied in relief of that legal obligation on property. I think we should be guilty of a great breach of duty in so applying it. The people of Ireland are, generally speaking, Roman Catholics, and I am ashamed to think how exceedingly small a portion of public money has fallen to their share as Roman Catholics. The mass of the people of Ireland are, therefore, entitled to be made, as far as possible, the principal recipients in the applications of the fund. I will venture to read to the committee the preamble of the bill, which I hope will be in the hands of members to-morrow night. It says: " Whereas it is expedient that the union created by act of Parliament between the Churches of England and Ireland, as by law established, should be dissolved, and that the Church of Ireland, as so separated, should cease to be established by law, and that after satisfying, so far as possible, upon principles of equality as between the several religious denominations in Ireland, all just and equitable claims, the property of the said Church of Ireland, or the proceeds thereof, should be held and applied for the advantage of the Irish people, but not for the maintenance of any Church or clergy or other ministry, nor for the teaching of religion; and it is further expedient that the said property, or the proceeds thereof, should be appropriated mainly to the relief of unavoidable calamity and suffering, yet so as not to cancel or impair the obligations now attached to property under the act for the relief of the poor." It is the latter part of the passage which defines the application of the money. There is in every country a region of want and suffering lying between the independent part of the community, on the one hand, and the purely pauperized population on the other. For this region of want and suffering it is very hard to make adequate provision by the poor-law, which is almost intended to be niggard in its operations, because, if it were made liberal and large, the risk would then be run of doing the greatest possible injury to the independent laborer struggling to maintain himself. The want and suffering I now speak of are partly relieved, not through the medium of the poor-law, but through the medium of the county cess—a heavy and increasing tax—not divided, as in the case of the poor-rate, between owner and occupier, but paid only by the occupier. The burden of this tax is not limited, like the poor-rate, to occupations above £4 in value, but descends to the most miserable tenements, the holders of which are required to pay for a class of suffering which in every Christian country should be relieved by a large and liberal expenditure.

Take, first of all, the lunatic asylums. The care of lunatics is one of the great duties of the community, and in Ireland, though the provision for them has as yet by no means overtaken the whole country, the cost on this head is already from £120,000 to £140,000, and will ultimately rise to £200,000. This expenditure is defrayed by the county cess, collected from the class of occupiers I have described. The case of the deaf and dumb and of the blind is the next melancholy topic I will refer to. The alleviation of the condition of the deaf, the dumb, and the blind, scarcely comes within the province of the poor-law, because it is a very costly matter. You will keep a pauper in a workhouse, and keep him decently, in Ireland, for some £7 or £8 a year; but you will not keep these classes—you will not give to the deaf and dumb and the blind the most precious boon you

can give them—that is, training and instruction—under, perhaps, £30 or £40 per head per year. It is no common act to train
these people and to convey to them, through the beneficial channels that the Almighty has given us, the blessings of knowledge
and the faculty of applying their bodily powers to their own
support. This description of want and suffering is marked out
by every feature that can recommend it for the application of
any funds like these. There are those who say these funds
should not be secularized. I respect the feelings of those who
are against the secularization of such funds; but I say that if
we go back to the history of ecclesiastical property in Europe
the suggested application is not to be condemned and denounced
as secularization. The property of the Church was divisible
into four parts. One of these was consecrated to the use of the
poor; and, of all the poor, the afflicted cases I have named make
the strongest appeal to human compassion. At the same time,
when I know the condition of the Irish peasant, when I see that
the charge through the medium of the county cess is to be laid
mainly upon him, in the first instance, and wholly upon him
by the present machinery of the law, I hail the occasion this
gives us of at once effecting a great improvement in relieving
the Irish occupier, and especially the poor occupier, from an
important portion of his burden, and of providing a more ample,
a more uniform, and a better regulated source of income for
the relief of the very sorest of human afflictions.

The general framework of this plan will be developed when
the third of the days I have described is arrived at. It will be
the duty of the commission to report to the Queen that provision is made for all the purposes contemplated in the act,
and it will be their duty also to report what is the amount of
surplus revenue available for these ulterior purposes, the whole
of which will be enumerated in the bill. I will not trouble the
committee now by reading them. I will not say whether or not
it might be necessary to resort to further legislation; but these
sums would be administered, not under any system wholly new,
but they would be administered upon principles and according
to rules which are already in partial and imperfect operation in
Ireland. We shall escape altogether the religious difficulty,
because we only purpose to stand upon ground the firmness
and solidity of which we have ascertained by experience, and to

make these sums available for their destined application, probably in most cases through the medium, and in all cases under
the control—and that we provide in the bill—of the Poor-Law
Commissioners for Ireland. I have mentioned lunatics first because the provision to be made for lunatics is the largest of all.
Next to these in order is the making a satisfactory provision
for the training and instruction of the deaf and dumb and the
blind. I beg the committee to understand I am not now speaking of institutions in which the deaf, the dumb, and the blind,
are to be mewed up for life, but simply of schools in which they
may receive that kind of instruction that they are capable of
receiving for their own benefit; then to go out again into the
world and play their part, so far as Providence permits, as useful
members of society. We believe that a good system in aid of
the poor-law may be provided for that class of persons at an
expense of about £30,000 a year, and the ultimate expense of
the provision for lunatics would be £185,000 a year. The provision for other forms of mental weakness besides that I have
named—that is, for idiots and others—might cost about £20,000
a year.

There is a provision urgently needed in Ireland, and that
is a supply of properly trained nurses for the use of paupers
and for the poor who are above the paupers. The Irish medical
men are known for their skill, but they are scattered over the
country much more thinly than in England. The unions are
large, and the public medical officer cannot be in two places at
once. I am sorry to be informed upon good authority that the
injuries to health, and even to life, which result from the want
of skilled nurses, especially for women in labor, are grievous.
The Poor-Law Guardians shrink from incurring the necessary
expense, and make the requisite provision in very few cases;
but for a sum of £15,000 nurses might be provided all over Ireland. Reformatories and industrial schools languish in Ireland; they receive parliamentary grants; but between parliamentary grants and private benevolence they are inadequately
supported. We shall propose to the committee that they also
be included as recipients of £10,000 of these funds.

There is another charge, and that is for county infirmaries, to
which I must call the particular attention of Irish members.
The infirmary system of Ireland is at present charged upon the

county cess, and is a burden on the poorest occupiers of the land. It is very imperfect in two particulars. In the first place, it often happens that the infirmary of the county, though in the capital of the county, is not central; and, although it is supported by taxes levied from the whole county, it is really a benefit only to a very small portion of it. In the second place, the government of these infirmaries is wholly antiquated and unsuitable, and needs to be reformed. The sum to be claimed by the county infirmaries, hospitals, etc., may be put down at £51,000 a year. The general financial result is that I have pointed to a fund of between seven and eight millions, and the charges which will be most likely to occur under these heads, and which may be assumed from time to time as we are provided with the means, amount to £311,000 a year.

With the provision of all these requirements I think we should be able to combine very great reforms; we shall be able to apply strict principles of economy and good administration to all these departments; we shall be able to redivide Ireland into districts around county infirmaries, well managed and governed, and so disposed as greatly to increase facility of access to them. Lastly, I have to mention that to which I confess I attach very great value and importance. It should be known that the state of things I have pointed out with regard to the county cess has attracted the attention of Irish members, and the attention of a committee of this House, which has recommended that the county cess be put upon the same footing as the poor-rate, that the poorer occupiers be relieved, and that the payment be divided between the landlord and the tenant. We certainly shall be in a better condition for inviting the Irish landlord to accede to that change when we are able to offer, as we shall offer by this plan, a considerable diminution of the burdens of the county cess. This is, in general terms, the mode in which we propose to apply the residue, and I am certain I am justified in inviting the serious attention of the House to the plan, and in expressing my confident expectation and belief that the more it is examined, the more will members find, passing over the objections they may have to disestablishment and disendowment, that it is a good and solid plan, full of public advantage.

I believe I have now gone through the chief of the almost

endless arrangements, and I have laid as well as I am able the plans of the Government before the committee. I will not venture to anticipate the judgment of the committee, but I trust the committee will be of opinion it is a plan at any rate loyal to the expectations we held out on a former occasion, and loyal to the people of England who believed our promises. I hope also the members of the committee may think that the best pains we could give have been applied in order to develop and mature the measure, and I say that with great submission to the judgment of gentlemen on this and on the other side of the House. It is a subject of legislation so exceedingly complex and varied that I have no doubt there must be errors, there must be omissions, and there may be many possible improvements; and we shall welcome from every side, quite irrespective of differences of opinion on the outlines of the measure, suggestions which, when those outlines are decided upon, may tend to secure a more beneficial application of these funds to the welfare of the people of Ireland. I trust, sir, that although its operation be stringent, and although we have not thought it either politic or allowable to attempt to diminish its stringency by making it incomplete, the spirit towards the Church of Ireland as a religious communion, in which this measure has been considered and prepared by my colleagues and myself, has not been a spirit of unkindness.

Perhaps at this time it would be too much to expect to obtain full credit for any declaration of that kind. We are undoubtedly asking an educated, highly respected, and generally pious and zealous body of clergymen to undergo a great transition; we are asking a powerful and intelligent minority of the laity in Ireland, in connection with the Established Church, to abate a great part of the exceptional privileges they have enjoyed; but I do not feel that in making this demand upon them we are seeking to inflict an injury. I do not believe they are exclusively or even mainly responsible for the errors of English policy towards Ireland; I am quite certain that in many vital respects they have suffered by it; I believe that the free air they will breathe under a system of equality and justice, giving scope for the development of their great energies, with all the powers of property and intelligence they will bring to bear, will make that Ireland which they love a country for them not less enviable and not less beloved in the future than it has been in the past. As respects the Church, I admit it is a case almost without exception. I do not know in what country so great a change, so great a transition, has been proposed, and has been embodied in a legislative provision, by which the ministers of a religious communion that have enjoyed during so many ages the favored position of an established church, will no longer remain in that position. I can well understand that to many among them such a change appears to be nothing less than ruin and destruction. From the height on which they now stand to the apparent abyss into which they think they will have to descend there is something that recalls the words used in " King Lear," when Edgar endeavors to persuade Gloucester that he has fallen—from the cliffs of Dover. He says:

> " Ten masts at each make not the altitude
> Which thou hast perpendicularly fallen ;
> Thy life's a miracle."

And yet but a little after the old man rallies from his delusion, and finds that he has not fallen at all. And so I venture to trust that when, stripped of the fictitious and adventitious aid upon which we have too long taught the Irish Establishment to lean, it shall come to place its trust in its own resources, in its own secret wisdom, in all that can draw forth the energies of its ministers and its members, and the high hopes and promises of the gospel that it teaches, it will find that it has entered upon a new era of its existence, an era fraught with hope and promise. At any rate, I think the day has certainly come when an end has finally to be put to the union, not between the Church as a religious association, but between the Establishment and the State, which was commenced under circumstances little auspicious, and which has continued to bear fruits of unhappiness to Ireland, and of discredit and scandal to England.

Sir, there is more to say. This measure is in every sense a great measure—great in its principle, great in the multitude not merely of its technical but of its important, weighty, and interesting provisions. It is not a great measure only, but it is a testing measure. It is a measure which will show to one and all of us of what metal we are made. Upon us all it brings a great responsibility—first and foremost undoubtedly upon us

who occupy this bench. We are deeply chargeable—we are
deeply guilty, if we have either dishonestly, as some think, or if
we have even prematurely or unwisely, challenged so gigantic
an issue. I know well the punishments that are due to rashness
in public men; and that ought to fall upon those men who with
hands unequal to the task attempt to guide the chariot of the
sun. But our responsibility, though heavy, is not exclusive. It
passes on from us to every man who has to take part in the discussion and in the decision of this question. Every man who
proceeds to the discussion is under the most solemn obligation
to raise the level of his vision, and to expand its scope in proportion to the greatness of the object. The working of our
constitutional government itself is upon its trial, for I do not
believe there ever was a time when the whole of the legislative
machinery was set in motion under the conditions of peace and
order and constitutional regularity, to deal with a question
graver or more profound. And more especially is the credit
and fame of this great assembly involved. This assembly, which
has inherited from so many long ages accumulated honor from
numberless triumphs of peaceful but courageous legislation, is
now called upon to address itself to a task which would indeed
have demanded all the best energies of the very best of your
fathers and your ancestors. I believe it will prove to be worthy
of the task. Should it fail, even the fame of the House of Commons will suffer no disparagement; should it succeed, even that
fame, I venture to say, will receive no small nor insensible addition. I must not ask gentlemen opposite to concur in these
few sentences, grateful as I am to them for the kindness with
which they have heard the statement which I have made. But I
beg and pray them to bear with me for a moment while, for myself and my colleagues, I say that we are sanguine of the issue.
We believe this controversy is near its end, and, for my part,
I am deeply convinced that, when the day of final consummation
shall arise, and when the words are spoken that give the force
of law to the work embodied in this measure—a work of peace
and justice—those words will be echoed from every shore where
the name of Ireland and the name of Great Britain have been
heard; and the answer to them will come back in the approving
verdict of civilized mankind.

PEACE AND WAR

—

BY

JOHN BRIGHT

JOHN BRIGHT

1811—1889

The friends of peace in modern civilized countries have always had the regard and respect of the people; though these sentiments are generally accompanied by an intimation of kindly scepticism as to the practical result of their labors. The condition of the world is still so far from perfect, and the abuses which exist are so firmly established in most cases, that the average man of the world feels inclined to disbelieve that any remedy except the old one of force will suffice to remove them. External peace, in other words, cannot be brought about while war exists internally; or if it could, its best blessing would be lost. While we are kindly disposed towards the apostles of peace, therefore, we incline to regard them as impracticable enthusiasts, and to listen to their exhortations with a smile.

But when a man like John Bright uplifts his voice in support of the peace men, and urges his views with eloquent arguments, and a long life of devotion, we cannot choose but listen, and profit by what we hear. For after all, the way to universal peace is by individual unselfishness; and the utterances of men like Bright tend to show us how to be unselfish, and demonstrate the enormous benefits that would accrue from a practical application in society of the principles of Christianity. We listen to a disciple who is himself an illustration of the doctrine he preaches; why should we not become his fellow disciple, and use our influence to win other supporters? Thus there is no estimating how much Bright and others of his creed have done or may do towards hastening the advent of the millennium.

John Bright was born in 1811, the son of a rich manufacturer, and was himself always a man of large wealth. He early formed a friendship with Cobden, and supported him in his advocacy of free trade. He entered Parliament in 1843; in 1868 he became President of the Board of Trade; was afterwards chancellor of the duchy of Lancaster, and in 1883 was elected Rector of Glasgow University. The individuality of his opinions, and his strict conscientiousness, constantly compelled him to oppose the policy of the existing Government, whatever party was in control. He was compelled even to abandon his old friend, Gladstone, when the latter, as Prime Minister, permitted the bombardment of Alexandria. That part of his career which produced the most useful and tangible practical results, was during the time that he was making speeches against the Corn Laws. He rivalled Cobden himself in the conviction which he produced upon his hearers, and in the instruction he insinuated into their minds. There was a luminousness and elevation about Bright's oratory which was unlike the style of any other public man of his time; and the fascination of his address is irresistible. His personal appearance and manner were grave and winning, and his voice was the fitting and flexible vehicle of his thoughts. He died on March 27, 1889. His speech on " Peace and War " is a good example of his style.

PEACE AND WAR

Delivered at Llandudno, November 22, 1876, at the close of a lecture on "International Arbitration," by the Rev. W. Glover.

I T gave me great pleasure two or three days ago to see on the walls of your town a placard announcing that Mr. Glover was about to come amongst you to deliver a lecture upon the momentous question of peace and war, and I received—I don't know whether it was a deputation or not—but I had an interview with three of your townsmen, much respected and influential amongst you, who did me the honor of asking me to attend this meeting, and to add whatever I might be able to add to the arguments which would be brought before you by the lecturer. I could not well resist the urgent invitation which was offered me. I am not, as you know, what is called a resident of Llandudno, but I have been here almost every year for more than twenty years past, and I felt that I had something like a special interest in the people amongst whom I had spent so much time during many months in the year. I was laboring under serious and prolonged illness during one visit which my family paid to this place; we were struck by a very heavy and grievous affliction. These things dwell in memory, and they strengthen and deepen the interest which they feel, and which I feel, for everything connected with the interests of this town. And I may say that I have watched its growth and its increasing prosperity with as much interest as if I had been settled permanently amongst you. And when I look at the position of our town and its beautiful bay, when I look around and see the beauties of our locality, when I remember how near you are to all the finest scenery of this glorious North Wales, and when I observe and enjoy the beauty of our climate, which in winter, I believe, is not surpassed by that of any other place in the

United Kingdom, and when I remember all the courtesy and all the kind attention which I have met, I am free to say that I have great faith in your future, and I hope and believe that your growth and prosperity will be continued, and will be lasting.

The lecture which we have heard—and which, I am afraid, the modesty of Mr. Glover has induced him, because I was to follow him, to cut shorter than he would have otherwise done— is one which has interested me very much, and I think it is well timed. For there could scarcely be a period within our recol- lection—not more than one or two, I think—when questions of greater, importance were stirring the minds of the people from one end of the kingdom to the other. It is to me astound- ing when I look back and see what has been the error and the folly into which the people of this country have been led in time past upon the question of war. We live in two considerable islands—Great Britain and Ireland. We are separated from the Continent by a sea passage, which in itself is a great de- fence, and we have been for about three hundred years unas- sailed, and believe, with our population, and our wealth, and our means, and our freedom, we are practically more unassailable than almost any other kingdom in the world. And yet, not- withstanding all that, we have spent, probably, in a period that does not go back beyond the lifetime of persons now living, two thousand millions of money in war, all of which, I believe, might with honor have been avoided, and in needless or excessive armaments in preparing for war. Mr. Glover has referred to the fifty millions which we are spending every year—one half of it paying the interest of money bor- rowed to carry on wars in past time, and the other half spent an- nually on the army and navy for the purposes of supposed events, or for purposes of war in which we may be hereafter in- volved. Mr. Glover quoted an expression of Lord Russell's, that he doubted whether there had been any war during the last hundred years that might not have been avoided without any sacrifice of the interests or honor of this country, by those rea- sonable concessions which we are constantly making amongst . each other as individuals, and which would be in no degree in- jurious or dishonorable if made between nations.

A hundred years ago—just a hundred years ago this very year—this country was engaged in a war with the colonies now forming the United States of America. What happened when that war was over? A change of opinion extraordinary—no, not extraordinary, for it always takes place—but a change of opinion very remarkable. Whilst the war was going on people in many parts of the country were in favor of it, and the King and his ministers were doggedly determined to continue the war. But a few years after it was over everybody condemned it, and now, probably, there is no single man in this country, of any political party, however benighted, however ignorant, however positive, however unteachable, who would not condemn the folly and wickedness of that war with the American colonies. Well, but that war was supposed to have cost this country close upon one hundred millions of money, and it left between the inahıbtants of these colonies—grown now to be a great nation, even greater in numbers than this, so far as the population of Great Britain and Ireland may be counted—it left feelings of anger and bitterness which are now only slowly passing away from amongst us. But after the American War was over only a few years we engaged in another and still greater and more prolonged struggle with the republic of France; and the reason we went into war with France was because France was a republic, and held opinions supposed to be dangerous to the monarchy and aristocracy of this country; and that war was continued afterwards for the overthrow of the Emperor Napoleon, and concluded, after about twenty-two years' existence. The cost to this country, I dare say, all told, was a thousand millions sterling; and yet now everybody—nobody more than Lord Russell—everybody, or almost everybody, condemns that war; and I believe that by greater moderation and greater wisdom on the part of the government and the press and the people of this country it might have been avoided. It left us with five hundred millions of debt, accumulated, in addition to the previous debts, during the continuance of that one single but prolonged struggle. We condemned, as I said, the American War a few years after it was over; I mean that your forefathers did. Our fathers condemned the French war not long after it was over; and since then we have had another war of great magnitude, but not of very long continuance, to which Mr. Glover has referred, which generally goes by the name of the Crimean War—war with Russia—the main portion of the struggle taking place in the Crimea. But now, as far as I can judge, everybody—perhaps I ought not to say " everybody," because, perhaps, Her Majesty's ministers would not agree with me, but nearly everybody condemns that war; and I think every single man who knows anything about it would admit that we gained absolutely nothing but discredit and loss—loss of life and increased debt—from the struggle which this country carried on with Russia twenty-two years ago. In the placard to which I have referred calling this meeting there is a statement of how much is spent every year in armaments and matters connected with wars past or to come—how much a month, how much a week, how much a day, how much an hour, and I don't know whether it is not my duty to say how much per minute. But now take another illustration. You can form some idea of an estate of two thousand acres of the best land in your Welsh counties, and you will perhaps be surprised when I tell you that our expenditure of fifty millions per year for past wars and for present military expenses is equal to the swallowing up every day for the six working days of every week during the year of an estate of that magnitude. Now, can it be possible that anything like this is necessary? It seems to me that the whole world is wrong; that everything is wrong in the creation and arrangement of the conditions under which men live on this earth, if man himself is not very wrong, having brought matters to this dreadful condition.

Take the last great case that I have referred to—the case of the Russian or Crimean War. At the time when it was being waged there was not one man in twenty who really knew anything about it. At this moment I don't believe you could find one man in a hundred throughout England who could give you any clear account of the war—the progress of negotiations, the difficulties which were met with, and which were not overcome, and, finally, of the state of things which precipitated the catastrophe and brought on that lamentable and most inglorious struggle. But now look back to the passions which were exhibited at that time. You see what a change has come. Like as it was with the American War, that was condemned; as it was after the French War, that was condemned; so it is now after the Russian War, that is all but universally condemned, so that we have come—I believe the nation has come mainly and by a

vast majority—to the conclusion that the object was unworthy
of our efforts, and that the result was absolute and entire failure.
But leaving for a moment the question of expense, I will ask
you to consider the question of the loss of life. Mr. Glover
has told you not one-twentieth of the loss of life in that war. A
most minute and careful history of the war has been written by
a gentleman with whom I am acquainted, who was in Parliament for several years, very near where I sat—Mr. Kinglake—
who has paid most scrupulous attention to every fact with regard to the war, and I see it quoted from his book that he believes, first and last, that not less than one million of men lost
their lives in connection with that struggle. Remember who
were concerned. The chief were Russia, Turkey, England,
France, and the kingdom of Sardinia, which is now the kingdom of Italy. The French lost more men, I believe, than we
did, the Turks possibly more than either of them; the loss of
Russia is not to be counted; and we stand now in this lamentable and terrible condition, that we were the country that went
rashly and violently and passionately into the war. We have
not a single thing of the slightest value to show for it, but on the
other side we have that vast loss of treasure, and sacrifice and
slaughter of a million of human beings.

Some people think that the loss of life in war is a very common thing, and that it is not worth talking about. They think a
soldier takes his wages and stands his chance. I recollect being
disgusted during the time of the war by the observation of a
gentleman at the dinner of a person of high rank in this country,
and of the party by whom the war was originated. He said:
" As for the men that are killed, I think nothing of that. A
man can only die once, and it does not matter very much where
he dies or how he dies." Now I think it matters a good deal.
It matters a good deal to widows and orphans, and sisters and
friends. It matters a good deal to thousands, scores of thousands, and hundreds of thousands of men who are cut off in the
very flower of their youth, that they should be thrust with the
passionate thrust of a bayonet, or rent asunder by shot and shell
—killed it may be at once, or left lingering on the field or in hos-
pital, dying of intense and inconceivable agonies. What is it
that is so valuable as life? What happens if some unfortunate
visitor to this place, or unfortunate and helpless boatman is

drowned in your bay? Does it not make a sensation in your community? Is there not a feeling of grief that passes from heart to heart until there is not one man, woman, or child amongst you that did not feel that a calamity has happened in your neighborhood? And what if there be a wreck? I was in this neighborhood two or three days after the wreck of the " Rothesay Castle," forty-five or forty-six years ago, and I suppose nearly a hundred men and women were drowned on that occasion. I was down at the scene of the wreck of the " Royal Charter " only a few years ago, when nearly four hundred persons were drowned. Did it matter nothing? I saw a poor, gray-headed man there wandering along the beach, as he wandered day after day in hope, not that he might find his son alive, but that he might find even the dead body of his son, that he might be comforted by giving it a fitting burial. These things gave a shock to the whole district, to the whole nation, and rightly and inevitably so. Look, again, to the accidents on railways. Take the sad accident in this county—the most appalling that has ever happened on any railway in this kingdom —I mean the accident at Abergele, when men were destroyed in a moment, apparently, without a moment's warning. Take the terrible accidents that happen from time to time in the collieries in various parts of the country. See what woe is caused by them, and remember, as you must remember, how every family in the country is stirred and filled with grief at the narrative of the disasters that have occurred. Well, now, take other things that happen that distress us connected with the loss of life. Take the private murders that are committed throughout the kingdom, and hangings that take place of the criminals who have been guilty of these murders. All these things fill us at times with sorrow, and cover our feelings and our hearts with gloom; and now take together all the accidents from boats that you have ever heard of, all the accidents from shipwrecks that have ever been recorded; take all the accidents on railways since railways were first made, and all the accidents in mines since the bowels of the earth were penetrated to obtain coal for the use of man; and besides these take all the lamentable private murders which have been caused by passion, or cupidity, or vengeance; and take all the hangings of all the criminals— and there have been far too many under the law of this country

—more brutal in this matter, I believe, in past times than even now, and than the laws of any other Christian country—I say take all these phases of destruction of human life, add them all together, and bring them into one, bring them all into one great sum, and what are they in comparison with the millions of human beings who have been destroyed and slaughtered in a single Russian war? And the war only lasted two years, and the French war lasted more than twenty years. Almost half the time from the accession of William III in this country up to 1875—almost if not more than half that time—this Christian country was engaged in sanguinary struggles with some other so-called Christian nations on the Continent of Europe. Now, seeing what was paid for the Russian War, and seeing what an entire failure it turned out with regard to the pretended objects which it was supposed likely to secure—the people of England did not go into war in their passionate moments without some idea that some good is to follow—seeing how much we have lost, and how great was the crime we committed, is it not astounding there should be any man, much more than that man should be in the lofty position of Prime Minister—ruler of this nation—who should by unadvised, unwise speaking invite the nation to involve itself in another war that may be no less prolonged, that may cause equal loss and equal slaughter, and that undoubtedly will result in a total failure, as the war twenty-two years ago which we had.

And it is the old story now just as it was in those days—that Russia is an aggressive power. I am afraid almost all powers, as opportunity offers, have been aggressive; but he would be a most ingenious calculator who could show that there was any power in the wide world that during the last hundred years has been more aggressive than that power of which we in this meeting form a humble and small party. It is said now, as it was said then, that Russia was aggressive, and that Russia intended to conquer Turkey, and capture and hold Constantinople, and to dominate alike over Europe and over Asia. There was not the slightest proof of it. All the proof was the other way. Russia from the beginning of these disturbances has made the most distinct and frank offers to the English government as to the terms in which the Russian government and people believe that peace might be made, to the enormous and permanent advantage of the Christian subjects of the Porte. It is said—it was said then—that Turkey was the only safe keeper of the straits of the Bosphorus and the Dardanelles—that is, the straits which lead from the Black Sea to the Mediterranean. There was no proof that Turkey is the safe keeper of those straits. The Porte held those straits for three hundred years, and would not allow any mercantile ship to pass through them, and it was only by the power of Russia, and by a treaty with Russia, after the war with Russia, that these straits were opened to the navigation of the mercantile ships of the world. And no doubt the time will come, and must come, when these straits will be opened, not only to mercantile ships, but to the ships of the navies of all nations of the world. Now and at a former time it was said, too, that England's interests were at stake—interests in India and interests in the Levant. There was no proof of it then; there is no proof of it now. Of all the speakers in public, of all the writers in the press who have written against Russia in this matter and in favor of Turkey, and in favor of war, there is not one of them who has been able to lay down accurately and distinctly any kind of proof that the interests or honor of England were concerned in the course we have taken with regard to this great Eastern question. Why, if you were some poor and hapless criminal brought to trial before one of your courts, and before a jury, if liberty only is at stake, there is more care still. You have advocates on each side, you have witnesses for the prosecution and for the defence, you have an impartial jury, and the judge is careful that nothing shall be said against the prisoner that is not proved, and he warns the jury against being actuated by prejudice, and to put away what they have heard before the trial comes on, and he entreats them, if there be any feature in the case which can leave a doubt on the mind of any one of them as to the guilt of the poor wretch at the bar, that they shall give their verdict in his favor. But here you go into a great transaction, a great war, you spend your millions of money, you send your brothers and sons to the slaughter, and you condemn to death, it may be, as in the last case, a million of human beings, and you have not got a single definite or proved fact to justify the course you have taken.

I deny altogether that there is anything in the aggressive

character of Russia, or anything with regard to the guardian-
ship of the straits, or anything with which the honor and the
interests of England is concerned, to justify us in the course we
are taking with regard to this matter, or that justified us twenty
years ago in that war, or would justify us now if the government
were to involve the country in another struggle. Look at the
map of Europe and measure the distance from London, or if
you like from the Land's End, round by Gibraltar, the whole
length of the Mediterranean, through the Sea of Marmora to
Constantinople, you will find that we are close upon three
thousand miles away. Does any man believe that the honor
and interests of England are so involved in the question of territory or of conquest in that part of the world, that it can justify us in vast, tremendous, and incalculable sacrifices for a war
of this nature? The nations that are nearer to Russia are not
afraid of her. Germany is a powerful country, and Austria
is powerful, though less powerful than Germany; but both of
them have interests as direct and as clear as any interest that
we can pretend to have, and yet they can be tranquil. They do
not get into a passion. Their Prime Ministers do not speak—
what shall I call it?—rhodomontade and balderdash. They do
not blow the trumpet and call the nations to arms for purely
fancied causes, like those in which—I say it with as much sincerity as ever I have said anything in my life—in which we
have as much interest as would justify us in sending one
single man to slaughter. But I hope and I believe that out
of this matter there will not be war. The statements that are
offered to us in the newspapers this morning appear to me as
likely very much to soothe anxieties which we sometimes feel
upon this matter. There is a conversation which has taken
place between the English minister to Russia and the Emperor
of Russia. I believe no man in the world who knows anything
about the Emperor of Russia doubted for a moment that he
at least is as anxious for peace as any of the statesmen of either
party in this country—and I think the explicit declarations
which he has made are immensely to his credit—not merely the
opinions which he holds and which he has declared; but in his
position he has condescended to make these expressive declarations with a view to appeal to the common-sense and good-
sense, the peaceful feeling if you like, the Christian and human

feeling, of the population of England. Now, the public, notwithstanding what I say, are not wholly free from terror and from
suspicion of the Russian power, but their conscience has been
touched by some knowledge of the past, and by the horrors
committed by the Turks, of which, bad as they are, only
a faint outline has been fully narrated to us even by the corre-
spondents of the London papers. But they hesitate still, and I
believe they will not be dragged into war at the bidding of any
minister. If public opinion be right, the government, I think,
in this matter will not go wrong.

There is one point with regard to this question, not with
regard to the Eastern question, but rather with regard to the
question which was specially brought before us by Mr. Glover
in his interesting speech, on which I would like to make two or
three observations. I think we ought to begin to ask ourselves
how it is that Christian nations should be involved in so many
wars? If one may presume to ask one's self what, in the eye
of the Supreme Ruler, is the greatest crime which His creatures
commit, I think we may almost with certainty conclude that it
is the crime of war. Someone has described it as the sum
of all villanies. It has been the cause of sufferings, misery, and
slaughter which neither tongue nor pen can ever describe, and
all this has been going on for eighteen hundred years after men
have adopted the religion whose founder and whose head is de-
nominated the Prince of Peace It was announced as a religion
which was intended to bring " peace on earth, and good-will
toward men "; and yet, after all these years, peace on earth has
not come, and the good-will among men is only partially and
occasionally exhibited, and amongst nations we find almost no
trace of it century after century. Now, in this country we have
a great institution called the Established Church. I suppose
that great institution numbers 20,000 or more places of worship,
churches in various parts of the kingdom. I think this does
not include what there are in Scotland and Ireland. With these
20,000 churches there are at least 20,000 men, educated and for
the most part Christian men, anxious to do their duty as teachers of the religion of peace; and besides these there are 20,000
other churches which are not connected with the established
institution, but have been built and are maintained by that
portion of the people who go generally under the name of Dis-

senters or Nonconformists, and they have other 20,000 ministers also—men as well educated in the bulk, as much Christian
and devoted men, as the others, and they are at work continually, from day to day, and they preach from Sabbath to Sabbath what they believe to be the doctrines of the Prince of
Peace; and yet, notwithstanding all that, war, profligate war,
is either just behind us or it is just before us, and we have twenty-five or twenty-six millions a year spent in sustaining armies
and navies in view of wars which may suddenly and soon take
place. Now, why is it, I should like to ask, if there be any
clergyman of the Church of England, or any minister of a Non-
conformist body here, and if my words should go from this
platform to a wider circle than can now hear me, I would ask
all these ministers of these churches—on this point there can
be no difference between church and chapel, for all these teachers and preachers profess to be the servants of the Most High
God, and teachers of the doctrines of His Divine Son—and
being such, may I not appeal to them and say: What have you
40,000 or 50,000 men, with such vast influences, what have you
been doing with this great question during all the years that
you have ministered and called yourselves ministers of the
Prince of Peace? And I would not confine my appeal to them
only, but to the devout men of every church and every chapel
who surround the minister and uphold his hand, who did in
many things his bidding, and who join him heartily and conscientiously in his work. I say: What are they doing? Why
is it that there has never been a combination of all religious
and Christian teachers of the country with the view of teaching
the people what is true, what is Christian, upon this subject? I
believe it has been within the power of the churches to do far
more than statesmen can do in matters of this kind. I believe
they might so bring this question home to the hearts and consciences of the Christian and good men of their congregations that a great combination of public opinion might be
created which would wholly change the aspect of this question
in this country and before the world, and would bring to the
minds of statesmen that they are not the rulers of colonists
of Greece, or of the marauding hordes of ancient Rome, but
that they are, or ought to be, the Christian rulers of a Christian
people.

And now I have said all that is necessary on this occasion. I ought to say I only engaged with my friends who called upon me to make a few observations which might arise out of the lecture which we expected would be delivered, and which to-night we have heard with so much pleasure. It is not to be supposed, of course, that a small town, just as it were new-born into the family of towns like Llandudno, should have a powerful influence upon public opinion, and upon government. You represent a small town with a small population; you cannot control or terrify a feeble, or unwise, or unprincipled administration, but you can add to the great volume of sound opinion throughout the country, whose mandate such administration dare not in the long run disobey.

In Wales there is much that Welshmen have to be proud of. There is no part of the country, I believe, where, for the population, there are so few offences committed against the law; there is no part of the country in which the people by voluntary effort have done so much for education and for the teaching of the Christian religion; there is no part of the country to which Englishmen can come with so much pleasure to behold all that is beautiful in nature, and all that the inhabitants of this district have so much reason to love and to be proud of. May I ask you then to do what you can—you are not asked to do more, but whoever you may come in contact with, whenever you may have the opportunity of discussing this great question, to go to the kernel of it, stripped of all the husk by which statesmen and the press succeed so often in misleading the people; go to the kernel of the matter, and ask yourself the question: Can it be your duty to send out your sons and brothers three thousand miles to the slaughter—it may be of the Russians or any other people—can it be your duty to do this? Ask your consciences within the sight of Heaven if it can be your duty; and if you cannot find an answer in the affirmative, then, I say, have nothing to do with the accursed system, and wherever your influence extends, let it be honestly and earnestly in favor of Christianity and peace.

FUNERAL ORATION ON LORD PALMERSTON

—

BY

DEAN STANLEY
(Arthur Penrhyn Stanley)

ARTHUR PENRHYN STANLEY, DEAN STANLEY

1815—1881

Arthur Penrhyn Stanley, the second son of Edward Stanley, Bishop of Norwich, was born at Alderley while his father was rector of that parish, on December 13, 1815. He entered Rugby in January, 1829, where Dr. Arnold had been installed as head-master the previous summer. During the three years or more spent under the care of that eminent man Stanley's respect for his teacher "ripened into an affection that rose to veneration" Arnold's influence was the "load-star" of his life, as he expressed himself, and there can be no doubt that it guided him in his conduct through the turmoil and animosity of religious factions which he soon was to encounter at Oxford during a critical period of his life.

Stanley went to Balliol College as an exhibitioner from Rugby and became distinguished for his scholarship throughout his college career. In 1838 he was chosen a fellow of University College, and in December of the following year he was ordained by the Bishop of Oxford

In 1840 Stanley set out for a tour of Italy, Switzerland, and Greece, and scarcely a year passed after that without his making some extensive trip to the Continent, Asia, America, or other parts of the world. The appointment of Arnold to the chair of modern history at Oxford in 1841 gave extreme satisfaction to Stanley. He had hoped his influence would restore a healthier tone to university life, and his disappointment was therefore great when Arnold died, June 12, 1842. The life of Arnold by Dean Stanley, which was published two years later, secured for him a recognized position in the world of letters. During the religious controversies agitating Oxford at this time, Stanley did not sympathize with the views of either faction As a tutor his efforts met with the greatest success, so much that his college rose to a high rank in the university In his sermons " On the Apostolic Age," delivered during the years 1846 and 1847, he expounded views divergent from those of both parties and defended the cause of free inquiry as applied to Biblical study. In July, 1851, after the death of his father, Stanley was appointed a canon of Canterbury and left Oxford. The next five years were a period of great literary activity, interrupted only by tours abroad

A larger sphere of activity presented itself to Stanley when, in December, 1856, he was appointed professor of ecclesiastical history at Oxford Here, through his lectures and through the pulpit, he exercised a remarkable influence on the young men with whom he came in contact, while his passion for justice plunged him into many controversies He was invited to accompany the Prince of Wales on a tour in the East, and on his return married Lady Augusta Bruce, on December 23, 1863. In January of the following year he was installed as Dean of the Abbey in succession to Trench, who became Archbishop of Dublin. In his new capacity Dean Stanley soon became prominent. In literature, in the official duties of his office, and in the pulpit, his labors were fruitful of the best and most far-reaching results He was a firm advocate and upholder of the established law governing the relations of the Church and State and was opposed to every attempt to loosen the ties between them.

Stanley's was a mind marked by the breadth of its charity and his attitude of toleration towards those of other religious beliefs. He insisted that the essence and vitality of Christianity lay not in dogmas, forms, and institutions, but in the true Christian character. Stanley died July 18, 1881. His fine oration on Lord Palmerston is one of numerous funeral orations he delivered during his career.

FUNERAL ORATION ON LORD PALMERSTON

Delivered October 29, 1865, on the Sunday following Lord Palmerston's burial in Westminster Abbey

SEE that ye walk circumspectly . . . redeeming the time . . . understanding what the will of the Lord is.[1] So spoke the Apostle in the epistle of this day. He tells his readers to " walk circumspectly "—that is, with a keen, critical observance of all they see; to " redeem the time "— that is, to make the most of every opportunity that is thrown in their way, not to let any part of it escape them; to make every effort of mind and heart to " understand what the will of the Lord is "—that is, to understand what is the special intention of God, wrapped up in the different dispensations of joy and sorrow which come across them. It is this very thing which we are called upon to do this day—to look hard into the essential lessons of the great solemnity at which, on Friday last, so many of us assisted; to redeem, and make the most of, for our instruction, the opportunity of serious thought, thus afforded to us; to understand, so far as we can, what is the will of the Lord concerning us, in the national homage then paid to the illustrious dead.

It is one of the most instructive parts of solemnities of this kind that each has its own peculiar lesson to convey. Of all the great men who are laid within these walls, every single one, probably, is laid there for a separate and distinct reason, which could not apply to anyone else. That grand truth which was read in our ears in the funeral lesson, from the apostolic epistle, has its special force on every such occasion here—" There is one glory of the sun, and another glory of the moon, and another glory of the stars; for one star differeth from another star in glory."

[1] Ephesians, v. 15, 16, 17.

349

In the chambers of the dead, in the temple of fame, no less than in the house of our heavenly Father, there are indeed " many mansions," many stages, many degrees. Each human soul that is gifted above its fellows, leaves, as it passes out of the world, a light of its own, that no other soul, whether more or less greatly gifted, could give equally. As each lofty peak in some mountain is illuminated with a different hue of its own, by the setting sun, so, also, each of the higher summits of human society is lit up by the sunset of life with a different color, derived, it may be, from the materials of which it is composed, or from the relative position which it occupies, but each, to those who can discern it rightly, conveying a new and separate lesson of truth, of duty, of wisdom, and of hope.

What, then, are the special lessons which we may learn from the character of the remarkable man who has been taken away, and from the tribute paid to his memory? I leave altogether the questions of political and religious parties, which have no place here, and confine myself entirely to those direct, practical lessons which may be applied to all, of whatever opinions, equally. I leave, also, altogether, those questions of the unseen world which are known to God only. I leave them, as our Church leaves them, to that holy and merciful Saviour, whose mighty working is able to subdue all things to Himself, who sees as man sees not, but who, we cannot doubt, commends to our admiration whatsoever there is good and true in every one of His servants, that from each we may understand the more fully what the will of the Lord is, what the whole counsel of God is towards us.

First, then, there was this singular peculiarity, that the gifts by which the eminence of the departed statesman was achieved were such as are far more within the reach of all of us than is usually the case with those who occupy a position like his. It has been said of Judas Maccabæus, that of all military chiefs, he was the one who accomplished the greatest victories with the smallest amount of external resources. It may be said of our late chief, that of all political leaders, he accomplished the greatest success by the most homely and the most ordinary means. It is this which makes his life, in many respects, an example and an encouragement to all. The persevering devotion of his days and nights to the public service, the toil and en-

durance of more than half a century in the various high stations in which he was employed—these are qualities which
might be imitated by every single person, from the highest to
the lowest amongst you. You, whoever you may be, who are
disposed, as so many young man are, to give yourselves up to
ease and self-indulgence, who think everything that costs you
any trouble a reason for putting work aside, remember that not
by such faint-hearted, idle carelessness can God or man be
served, or the end of any human soul be attained, in this life
or the next. You, whoever you be, who are working on zealously, humbly, honestly, in your different stations, work on the
more zealously and the more faithfully, from this day forward,
with the feeling that, in the honors paid to me who was, in
these respects, but a fellow-laborer with you, the nation, as
in the sight of God, has set its seal on the value of work, on
the nobleness of toil, on the grandeur of long, laborious days,
on the splendor of plodding, persevering diligence.

Again, he won his way, as we have been told a hundred times,
not so much by eloquence, or genius, or far-sighted wisdom, as
by the lesser graces of cheerfulness, good humor, gayety, and
kindness of heart, tact, and readiness—lesser graces, doubtless,
graces of which some of the highest characters have been almost destitute, yet graces which are assuredly not less the gifts
of God—graces which, even in the house of God, we do well to
reverence and admire. Those who may think it a matter of
little moment to take offence at the slightest affront; those who
by their presence throw a dark chill over whatever society they
take part in; those who make the lives of those around them
miserable, by recklessly trampling on their tenderest feelings,
and wounding them in their weakest point; those who poison
discussion and embitter controversy by pushing particular views
to their extremest consequences, by widening differences between man and man; those who think it a duty to make the
worst of everyone from whom they dissent, and to maintain
a never-ending protest against those who have ever done them
a wrong, or from whom they have ever differed—such as these
may have higher pretensions and, it may be, higher claims on
our respect; yet if they would understand what the will of the
Lord is, a silent rebuke will rise to them from yonder grave,
such as God designs for their special benefit. The statesman

who had always a soft word ready to turn away wrath; who, if
at times he attacked or was attacked justly, yet never bore
lasting malice towards his enemies; who was able to see, even
in those who opposed him, the true worth and value of their
essential characters—from him, and from the honor paid to
him, many an eager partisan, many a hard polemic, many an
austere moralist, may learn a lesson that nothing else could
teach them. How many, by praising him, have condemned
themselves! How many, by making much of him, have made
much of the very graces which, in all other times and persons,
they have been unwilling even to acknowledge!

Yet again, the long life which has just closed was an enduring witness to the greatness of that gift which even heathens
recognized, of hope, unfailing, elastic hope. " Never despair! "
so the vicissitudes of the octogenarian chief seemed to say to
us. From a youth of comparative obscurity, from a middle-
age of constant struggle with opposition, through a shifting
career of many changes and many falls, was attained at last that
serene and bright old age, that calm and honored death, which,
in its measure, is within the reach of all of us, if God should so
prolong our years, and if we should not despair of ourselves.
Never be dispirited; never say, " It is too late "; never think
that your day is past; never lose heart under opposition; hold
on to the end, and you may at last be victorious and successful,
even as he was—it may be in still nobler causes, and with still
more lasting results. Nor let us shut out the encouragement
which this is designed to give us, by saying that it was, after
all, only the natural result of a buoyant and vigorous constitution. To a great degree, no doubt, it was so; yet it also
rested in large measure on the deeper ground of a quiet conviction that the fitting course for a man was to do what is
good for the moment, without vainly forecasting the future—
to do the present duty, and to leave the results to God. " I do
not understand," so he once said to one who knew him well—
" I do not understand what is meant by the anxiety of responsibility. I take every pains to do what is for the best, and
having done that, I am perfectly at ease, and leave the consequences altogether alone." That strain, indeed, is of a higher
mood: it is the strain of the inspired wisdom of ancient days
—" Whatsoever thy hand findeth to do, do it with all thy

might." It is the strain, also, may we not say, of true Christain humility and courage, which may well calm many a care, and nourish many a hope, and strengthen many a faith, beside, and beyond, and above the care, and the hope, and the faith of a mere political career.

And this leads me to another and a wider view of the subject, in which, nevertheless, all, even the humblest of us, may take an interest. If any were asked what was the thought or belief which, from first to last, most distinctly guided his policy and sustained his spirit, they would say his unfailing trust in, and concern for, the greatness of England. He was an Englishman even to excess. It was England, rather than any special party in England—it was the honor and interests of England, rather than even the constitution, or the State, or the Church of England, that fired his imagination, and stimulated his efforts, and secured his fame. For this it was that his name was known throughout the world, in the most secluded villages of Calabria, on the wild shores of the Caspian, in the monastic solitudes of Thibet. To England, and to no lesser interest, the vast length of that laborious life, with whatsoever shortcomings, was in all simplicity and faithfulness devoted. My brethren, I know well that when I thus speak there are considerations far greater than these by which the human soul must be stayed in life and death, by which the world and Church are guided on their appointed course; but on this occasion this is the thought which presses most forcibly upon us; this is the framework in which those higher considerations present themselves; this is the special opportunity which we are to redeem, and out of which the will of the Lord will make itself clear. In this great historic building, on the disappearance from amongst us of one of our chief historic names in the sight of all that was highest and noblest in our national life gathered round that open vault, it is the very mission of the preacher to ask you to reflect on what should be our Christian duty towards that kingly commonwealth of which we, no less than he, are members—of which we, no less than he, are proud—for which we, no less than he, are bound in the sight of God to lay down our lives and to spend our latest breath.

" England, we love thee better than we know! "

It was surely an allowable feeling which caused one whose
voice has often been heard from this place thus to describe the
thrill of joy and exultation with which, in a foreign land, he—

> ". . . heard again thy martial music blow,
> And saw thy gallant children to and fro
> Pace, keeping ward at one of those huge gates
> Which, like twin giants, watch the Herculean straits."[2]

Some such feeling of pride as this it was which was roused by
the awe awakened in many a distant and many a suffering nation at the sound of the powerful name now to be inscribed
within these walls.

But it is with loftier thoughts than pride or even thankfulness that our spirits mount upwards when we reflect on what
is really involved in that idea which so inspired the long career
which has just closed—England, and a citizen of England.
Think of our marvellous history, slowly evolved out of our
marvellous situation. Think of that fusion of hostile races and
hostile institutions within the same narrow limits, Think of
the long, bright, continuous line of our literature such as is unknown in any other country. Think of our refuge for freedom
and for justice. Think of our temperate monarchy and constitution, so fearfully and wonderfully wrought out through
the toil and conflict of so many centuries. Think of our pure
domestic homes. Think of the English prayers and the English
Bible woven into our inmost and earliest recollections. Think
of the liberty of conscience and the liberty of speech which give
to conscience and to speech a double, treble weight and value.
Think of the sober religious faith which shows itself amongst
us in so many diverse forms, each supplying what the other
wants. These are some of the elements which go to make up
the whole idea that is conjured up by the sacred name of England for which our statesman lived and died.

And then remember that what England is, or will be, depends
in great measure on her own individual sons and daughters.
Nations are the schools in which individual souls are trained.
The virtues and the sins of a nation are the virtues and the
sins of each one of its citizens, on a larger scale and written
in gigantic letters. To be a citizen of England, according to

[2] " Gibraltar ": a sonnet, by R. C. Trench, Archbishop of Dublin.

our lost chief, was the greatest boast, the greatest claim on protection and influence, that a man could show in any part of the world. To be a citizen of England in the fullest sense, worthy of all that England has been and might be, worthy of our noble birthright, worthy of our boundless opportunities, this is, indeed, a thought which should rouse every one of us, not in presumptuous confidence, but in all Christian humility, to redeem the time that is still before us, and to labor to understand what the will of the Lord is for ourselves and for our children. When, two days ago, we stood amidst the deepening gloom round the grave of the aged statesman, it was impossible not to feel that we were witnessing not only the flight of an individual spirit into the unseen world, but the close of one generation, one stage of our history, and the beginning of another. We had climbed to the height of one of those ridges which part the past from the future. We were on the water-shed of the dividing streams. We saw the last thread of the waters which belonged to the earlier epoch amongst the remains of which the ashes of the dead were laid; we were on the turning-point whence, henceforward, the springs of political and national life will flow in another direction, taking their rise from another range, destined to commingle with other seas, and to fertilize other climes. Even the oldest of living statesmen, compared with him who has gone, belongs to a newer age, and has to face a newer world. On this eminence, so to speak, we stand to-day. To this new start in our pilgrimage we have each one of us to look forward. It is not in England as in other countries, where the national will is but little felt compared with the will of a single ruler. Here, for good or for evil, the mind, the wishes, the character of the people are almost everything. That public opinion, of which we hear so much, which was believed to be the guiding star of the sagacious mind which has just gone from us—that public opinion is moulded by everyone who has a will, or heart, or head, or conscience of his own, throughout this vast empire. On you, on me, on old and young, on rich and poor, it more or less depends, whether that public opinion be elevating or depressing, just or unjust, pure or impure, Christian or un-Christian. If it be true, as some think, that to follow and not to lead public opinion must henceforth be the course of our statesmen, then our responsibility and the responsibility of the nation is deepened further still. The very creation of the character of our public men must then devolve in a manner upon those below them and around them. They may inspire us, but we must also inspire them. We must strive with all our strength to be that in our stations which we would wish them to be in theirs. We must act as those act in a beleaguered city, where every sentinel knows that on his single courage and fidelity may depend the fate of all. A single resolute mind, loving the truth, and the truth only, has ere now brought the whole mind of a nation round to himself. A single pure spirit has, by its own pure and holy aspirations, breathed a new spirit into the corrupt mass of a whole national literature. A single voice raised constantly in behalf of honesty, and justice, and mercy, and freedom, has rendered forever impossible practises which were once universal.

"Brethren," so says the Apostle in the chapter which you have just heard in this evening's service, "Brethren, forgetting those things which are behind, and reaching forth unto those things which are before, I press towards the mark, for the prize of the high calling of God in Christ Jesus." So let me call upon you, in the presence of that grave which has been so lately closed; in the prospect of the changes and trials, whatsoever they may be, which are now before us; in the midst of those mighty memories by which we are surrounded; in the face of that mighty future to which we are all advancing, forget those things which are behind. Forget in him who is gone all that was of the earth and earthy; reach forward in his character to all that is immortal—the kindness, the perseverance, the freedom from party spirit, the hope, the self-devotion, which can never pass away, and which are still before each one of us. Forget, too, in the past and the present generation, all that is behind, all that is behind the best spirit of our age, all that is behind the true spirit of the gospel, all that is behind the requirements of the most enlightened and the most Christian conscience; and reach forward, one and all, towards those great things which we may trust are still before us—the great problems which our age, if any, may solve, the great tasks which our nation alone can accomplish, the great doctrines of our common faith, which we may have the opportunity of grasping with a firmer hold than ever before, the great reconciliation of things old with things new, of things common with things sacred, of class with class, of man with man, of nation with nation, of church with church, of all with God. This is the high calling of England, this is the high calling of an English statesman, this is the high calling of every English citizen, this is the high calling of the nineteenth century, this is the will of the Lord concerning us ; this, and nothing less than this, is " the prize of the high calling of God in Christ Jesus " our Lord.

ONE-MAN POWER

—

BY

LORD SALISBURY

(Robert Arthur Talbot Gascoyne Cecil)

ROBERT ARTHUR TALBOT GASCOYNE CECIL,
LORD SALISBURY

Robert Arthur Talbot Gascoyne Cecil was born at Hatfield in 1830. He is the eldest surviving son of the second Marquis of Salisbury, and succeeded in 1868, after the demise of his elder brother in 1865, to the title and estates of the family. Lord Salisbury was educated at Eton and later at Christ Church, Oxford. He was elected fellow of All Souls' College, and in the same year entered Parliament as a member for Stamford, which seat he held for many years in the Conservative interests. In Lord Derby's third administration Lord Salisbury was appointed Secretary of State for India, but soon resigned on account of the discordant views on the Reform Bill prevalent in the Cabinet. When Disraeli returned to power in 1874 he was again appointed to the same office. In November, 1876, Lord Salisbury was sent as special ambassador to Constantinople to assist in adjusting the difficulties respecting the Christian subjects of the Sultan, but the proposals of the great powers were rejected by the Turkish government

In April of the following year Salisbury succeeded the Earl of Derby as Secretary of State for Foreign Affairs, and soon after joined the Earl of Beaconsfield as representative of Great Britain at the Congress of Berlin. The successes achieved for their country by the two British statesmen, incidental to the new division of the Sultan's dominions, mark, perhaps, the period of the greatest triumphs in the lives of both men.

After the death of Lord Beaconsfield in 1881 Lord Salisbury became the leader of the Conservatives in the Upper House. Since then his career has been most intimately connected with the successes and reverses of that party. Lord Salisbury was a vigorous opponent of Gladstone on the Irish Home Rule bill, and on the defeat of Gladstone in 1886 Lord Salisbury became once more Prime Minister. His party remained in power for six years, Salisbury assuming the portfolio of foreign affairs in 1888, when a reconstruction of the ministry was made necessary by the resignation of Lord Randolph Churchill from the Cabinet The present government, in which Lord Salisbury holds the portfolio of Foreign Affairs and is Prime Minister, was returned to power in 1895

Lord Salisbury is a man of science and a scholar as well as a statesman. Though not endowed with any great oratorical powers, his public speeches, like the one on "One-Man Power," given here, are masterpieces of exposition and style.

ONE-MAN POWER

Delivered at Dumfries, October 22, 1884

I N rising to thank Lord Galloway, the Conservative Associa-
tions, and you, for the kind reception which has been
accorded to me, I cannot in the first instance forbear
from noting the melancholy fact that if I had addressed you
here from this platform a year ago it is probable that the chair
would have been occupied by another person. I cannot welcome my noble friend the Duke of Buccleuch to his new honors
and the vast position of influence which they give him without
recalling the memory of that splendid Scotchman and patriot
who has passed away. He passed a life far longer in that position than an ordinary life. In the discharge, in the sedulous
and unfailing discharge, of the highest duties of a subject he
never permitted the privileges and enjoyment which his position gave him to induce him for a moment to forget the obligations under which he lay towards his fellow-subjects, or the
duties which his position imposed upon him. He passed a life
of unflagging exertion in the discharge of social duties of no
common importance, and he leaves behind him a memory of
sagacity, of patriotism, of public spirit, of equable and calm
judgment, which no Scotchman within our experience has surpassed or equalled.

Gentlemen, I approach the task of addressing you to-night
with the somewhat consoling feeling that we are standing on
the verge of the close of this autumn campaign. It has been
one of considerable exertion, not only for the speakers, but for
the hearers, and my impression is that when it passes into history those who have passed through it will dismiss it with the
hope that the like of it may never occur again. But from a political point of view I cannot say that it has left upon my mind
a shade of regret for the course which the House of Lords

and the Conservative party have thought it their duty to take. It appears to me that it has left the Conservative party more united than ever it was before, and it has given to the country an opportunity of discussing questions deeply affecting the constitutional working of our Government—an opportunity of hearing both sides of the question, and of forming their deliberate judgment thereupon.   From all I see and all I hear I do not believe that that judgment is unfavorable to the existing constitution of the country.   Some people on the other side are constantly telling us that we have not pursued the right course for the benefit of the Tory party.   I am always struck with the singular perception which our adversaries have of that which the Tory party in its own interests ought to do, and they have not been tired of impressing upon us that we have made a great mistake in not attacking them in their own way—that we have drawn attention to matters which we had better not have noticed, and that we have committed the great impolicy of bringing in the first place the question of the House of Lords before the country; and, in the second place, that we have distracted the minds of the people of this country from the other blunders of the Government.   Now, I accept with thankfulness that admission on the part of our opponents that there are considerable blunders of the Government to notice, but I do not in the least admit the error which they impute to us, because the imputation of that error rests upon the assumption that the people of this country must be treated rather like lunatics, and that it is dangerous to mention any matter in their hearing lest it should set up a perilous and destructive line of thought.   I do not believe in the policy of plastering over difficulties and trying to avoid dangers by reticence.   The only chance we have in this country is fair, free, open discussion; and if I am told that we have brought before the attention of the country subjects which but for us would not have been brought before them I say all the better.   The sooner that they discuss them the better they will be able to judge upon them.   The only thing that we have to fear is a hasty, uninformed judgment, and the longer they are able to discuss them the more thoroughly these questions are agitated in their view, with the more perfect confidence may we assure ourselves of the sound judgment that will ultimately be arrived at.

Now, as we approach the close of this campaign, let us try to impose our experience, let us try to trace what are the tendencies, what the prospects which the progress and character of this agitation have disclosed before us. I think, if you will examine all that is new in the character of this agitation, you will find that the indications point in one particular direction. You will find that there is a tendency, beyond anything that our fathers have experienced before, to give the power to the ministry of the day, and especially to the Prime Minister who is at their head; and in all the arguments that have been urged and the new doctrines that have been impressed upon us that is the tendency, that is the object to which our opponents seem to direct their efforts, and in my judgment that is the course of events which it most concerns the people of this country to prevent. Now, if you will look at the state of this controversy, which has been thrashed out before you during the last three months, you will see that we stand at this point. The Government have summoned an early session. They want to pass, so they tell us, the franchise bill and a redistribution bill. According to all former precedent, according to the ordinary practice of Parliament, what they would do would be to introduce those two bills together, and to pass them through as quickly as they can. They have an unusually long session in which to do it, because they have begun six weeks earlier than the ordinary session, and therefore it is presumable that even within the time they have before next August they would be able, if they try, to accomplish this object. But they are not limited to next August. There is nothing which it is more important to remember, when they tell you they have no time to pass these bills, that the amount of time they will take is absolutely a matter of their own discretion. They can continue the session; they have no need to prorogue Parliament, for they can continue it as long as they like; and, therefore, if they do not get time enough to pass these two bills, which they profess their desire to pass, and which they have called us at this early period for passing, it must be entirely their own decision or their own fault. Well, you may ask me, why do not the Government take advantage of this? Why did they not introduce these two bills at once and pass them together? They tell us they cannot pass these bills unless they can put the Houses of Parliament under compulsion—I am not using my own words, that was precisely the word used by Lord Hartington—unless they could put the Houses of Parliament under compulsion they say that they will not be able to pass these two bills.   I need not tell you that this is an entirely new pretension in our constitutional history.   Never before has a minister of the Crown assumed to have the right to exercise compulsion upon the free decision of the two Houses of Parliament.   They are repeatedly trying to impress upon you that this is a conflict with the House of Lords, but this idea of compulsion points to the House of Commons, because it would be just as easy to agitate against the House of Lords upon the question of redistribution as upon the question of franchise. Therefore, it is the House of Commons which they aim at when they say that they must be armed with a power of compulsion which they do not now possess—that is to say, they must be able to say to the House of Commons, "Unless you pass this bill which we present to you, this redistribution bill, you will have to submit to the franchise without redistribution, which we know you will regard as a horrible alternative."   Well, I said just now that the reticence principle rather made you think they were treating the people of England as lunatics, but this idea makes me think they are treating the people of England as if they were babies in arms.   Those who have domestic experience may know that the way of making a baby take medicine is to pinch its nose and to insert a drenching-spoon into its mouth, and in that way the baby is made to take the medicine to which it would otherwise object.   That is precisely the process Her Majesty's Government propose to apply to the House of Commons.   They propose, by means of this parliamentary drenching-spoon, to force down the throats of the House of Commons the medicine which they know very well if the House of Commons had the opportunity of unbiassed judgment it would decline to accept.

I think we have in some of the revelations that have recently been made an explanation why the ordinary mode of taking medicine is to be abandoned, and why the drenching-spoon is to be resorted to.   I dare say you have read the clear, forcible, and vigorous exposition of the defects of the redistribution bill which appeared in the "Standard" from the mouth of Lord

Randolph Churchill. I need not repeat his demonstration, I should only spoil it by doing so; but it seems to be substantially just and fair. There is one feature of it which I cannot forbear to notice. About ten days ago Lord Hartington, speaking at Rawtenstall, spoke to us with pitying contempt of our unworthy desire to cast up how many we should gain or how many we should lose by any redistribution bill. Well, it seemed to me at the time a very dignified appeal, and I was much struck that a day or two afterwards appeared this bill, which had been prepared by a committee of the Cabinet. From that it appeared that somewhat strange things had been done in Lord Hartington's own county. A certain town called Accrington has 60,000 inhabitants, and, as you know, according to strict numeral calculations 54,000 inhabitants is enough to qualify for a member, but the town of Accrington was not to have a member. And why? Because it was in Lord Hartington's county, and because the urban voters in the town of Accrington, who vote for Lord Hartington, would be made county voters instead of urban voters by that arrangement. Well, when that appeared I thought there was something exquisitely humorous in Lord Hartington's deprecation of our unworthy conduct in casting up the amount of seats we should gain or lose. I do not for a moment accuse Lord Hartington of being conscious of what his friends are doing, but no doubt the moment he saw that scheme appear in the " Standard " he took a cab and dashed down to the office and insisted that Accrington should have a member. The point that I have ventured to bring before you is that all these proceedings go in the direction that I have indicated to you. It is effected by that tendency to give excessive power to the ministry which I ventured to signalize to you as the great danger of our day. The ministry recommend for their own reasons and purposes some scheme to the House of Commons. They are afraid that the House of Commons will not, according to the ordinary practice, pass it, and they require, for the first time in our history, powers of compulsion. They require to be able to put the House of Commons under a penalty unless it will pass a redistribution scheme which suits their purpose. If they were not actuated by party motives it would involve the most intolerable annoyance, for it would involve the assumption that they are capable of dictating to the

Houses of Parliament that which the Houses of Parliament ought to accept, and that their judgment is superior to any that the Houses of Parliament can exercise.

Take another point. Mr. Chamberlain has been good enough to say, with singular reiteration, that this is a contest between the House of Lords and the people, and he goes into a great many heroics about the duty of some people to resist this intolerable aristocratic tyranny. My impression is, if there is any aristocratic tyranny, a very small portion of this free people would know how to get rid of it at once; but the truth is that there is no conflict whatever between the House of Peers and the people. What the House of Lords desire to know is what the people think. They desire to know it in the authorized and regular way. They wish to know it by the counting of opinions at the polls. That is the only way in which it can be really ascertained. I have no doubt that Mr. Chamberlain would wish us to believe that the hired ruffians who were sent to break into Aston Hall the other day represented the people; but we decline to accept that species of indication of popular opinion. As for the demonstrations, I can say two things of them. In the first place, one side or the other, I do not believe they have affected two per cent. of the population; and, in the second place, as far as any fair return of them will give indication, it seems to me that opinion is as much in the Conservative as in the Radical direction. But if they dispute our view the simple resource—a resource of which they are marvellously afraid—is to consult the people. They tell us they are delighted with this agitation, and that the whole public opinion is on their side. My impression is that if they were so delighted they would not be so mortally afraid of the possibility of an appeal to it. You know, those who can remember elections as they were some ten or eleven years ago, that the form was that first a show of hands was taken, and if anybody objected to the show of hands and demanded a poll, then a poll was taken; but I never heard anybody say that because you objected to a show of hands, and demanded a poll, therefore you were repudiating the authority of the constituency. The House of Lords is in that position. It does not think that the show of hands is any clear indication that the people have decided against the course which they have pursued, and they demand a poll;

and if a poll is not granted to them now they have no wish, according to the common phrase, to force a dissolution. A dissolution will come soon enough. According to the constitutional doctrine laid down by Mr. Gladstone himself there must be a dissolution within fifteen or sixteen months, and the House of Lords are perfectly content to wait for that time. They have no wish to force a dissolution, but they will not accept a show of hands decided by not an impartial authority; and they insist that this great issue can only be decided by the great national poll.

But now the point I want to observe is the doctrine that is held on the other side upon this subject. We are told that it is an intolerable thing that the House of Lords should have the power to force a dissolution. As I have said to you, the House of Lords has never pretended to do anything of the kind. All it has pretended to do is to put by a certain question until a dissolution can be had. But who is to have this power of dissolution? Is it the Crown? No Mr. Gladstone was very careful in his last speech to point out that the Crown in his view meant nothing but the decision of the Prime Minister. I do not agree with him. I do not admit that to be the constitutional law. In my view, whatever else is surrendered to the discretion of the Prime Minister, this question of dissolution never can be disconnected from the initiative and the will of the Crown. And I will tell you why. A dissolution is the only appeal the people have against a Prime Minister who is not acting according to their wish. That the Prime Minister should have a right of advising an appeal to the people I do not deny for a moment, but I do deny that he has a right to interpose his will and say, The people may storm and object; they may think that my course is wrong, but so long as I can control the majority in the House of Commons, elected under my auspices, controlled by my machinery, so long I will not permit an appeal to be made to the people against myself. That does not seem to me to be true constitutional law. But whether it is true or not, what I wish to point out to you is the tendency of all these new doctrines that are started, not to centre all power into the hands of the Prime Minister alone. Mr. Chamberlain insists that the majority shall have all power, and that the minority shall have no rights, and he says that if the majority abuse the power they shall soon become a minority. Aye, but there are seven long years to run before the majority becomes a minority. There are seven long years to run before any abuse of power can be punished, and during that time blows may be dealt against the institutions of the country which it will be impossible afterwards to repair. In his zeal to control the power of the people against the House of Lords Mr. Chamberlain has introduced a new way of expressing the opinion of the people. But, as you know, or at least as his friends have thought, the best way to express the opinions of the people is by attacking a meeting at which so moderate and careful a statesman as Sir Stafford Northcote was to express his opinions—by dint of bludgeons and chair-backs to make the expression of opinion impossible. Mr. Chamberlain has been pleased to say that this riot at Birmingham was due to some observations which I made. The observations which I made were that if he incited to a riot I hoped that he would head the riot, when I was pretty confident that his head would get broken. If Mr. Chamberlain means to say that a minister of the Crown who incites a riot ought not to have his head broken I differ from Mr. Chamberlain. To incite to disorder is a grave offence on the part of anybody, but on the part of a Cabinet Minister, on the part of one of those who are charged with the peace and order of the vast industrial communities in which we live, it is one of the greatest offences that a man could commit. But I do not wish to argue the point with Mr. Chamberlain if he thinks that the penalty of having his head broken for such an offence is too severe. For the sake of argument I am willing to put the question aside. Let us leave Mr. Chamberlain's head alone, and assume that some milder chastisement would be appropriate to the supposed offence. What I want to point out to you is that they all fall into the same groove, which I have already pointed out to you as the groove in which Liberal opinion is fitting itself. It all implies that despotic imposition of the opinion of the majority, which happens to be Liberal, upon their opponents, and the use of any means, no matter how repulsive or atrocious, which may seem likely to compass the results at which he aims. In this country of Scotland you have had some people who have even improved upon Mr. Chamberlain's lessons. Sir George Campbell, who in his time was charged with the government of sixty-four millions of people, and would have disposed of anybody who had incited to disorder with extreme rapidity, is reported to have said: " I entreat you now to be content with lawful proceedings "—these were his words— " but if the House of Lords does not pass the franchise bill, why then we will take stronger measures." That is to say, stronger measures than lawful proceedings. That is the kind of result which Liberal doctrine, as preached by Mr. Chamberlain, is producing in this country.

Now, there are other indications of the same tendency—a tendency against which I think all good citizens should watch; and there are indications which show at once what danger attends this one-man power. In 1881, as you are aware, there were a series of actions terminating in an action on Majuba Hill, and there were a series of negotiations terminating in a convention which the Boers have not observed, and which the English ministry again and again has consented to revise. Well, what was our constitutional majority doing during that time? Why was it the House of Commons did not interpose to stop proceedings so much at variance with all the traditions of this country? The House of Commons was blameless in the matter. Again and again Sir Michael Hicks-Beach urged upon the Government that some opportunity should be given of discussing the affairs of the Transvaal. Again and again the Prime Minister, contrary to all precedent, refused to give any opportunity for reviewing the conduct of his own Government. Again and again his power over the majority of the House of Commons was used to prevent any such discussion. And it was not till the middle of the month of August, till the House was empty and everyone exhausted, and, what is more, till the false steps had been irrevocably taken, it was not till then that a full discussion was obtained of the policy to which the Government were committing the country. Again, what happened this year? You know what is the state of things in Egypt. I do not know where to begin in the list of Government blunders, because it goes so far back; but after the destruction of poor General Hicks the Government, in a moment of singular ill-advisedness, announced their intention to all the tribes, friendly and otherwise, that they were about to abandon Gordon. It was the first piece of practice to which they ever committed themselves. The result was, of course, the tribes, who always worship the rising sun, turned against us, and the lives of many garrisons to which we were in honor committed became endangered. Well, then the Government conceived the extraordinary idea of sending one man, without forces of any kind, to try and save the lives of those garrisons. It is needless to say that one man did not succeed, and that the garrisons got their throats cut, but that was not all. The one man, the heroic General Gordon, of whose character and efforts it is impossible to speak in language of too high encomium, he in his efforts to do the strange and impossible duty which the Government had imposed upon him, placed himself in a position of imminent danger from which he could not rescue himself. And now that the garrisons have had their throats cut, and General Hicks has been butchered, at an enormous cost, something like, I believe, £150,000 or £160,000 a week, we are fitting out a great expedition for the purpose of rescuing the man whom we ought not to have sent on a task which it was impossible for him to perform, in order to save the lives of garrisons who have long ago been butchered, and to attain no other object whatever but in this way to remedy the pile of blunders which one upon another the Government have committed. This is one very serious matter. We are committed, in a time of increasing distress and declining trade, to a tremendous expedition which, when it has succeeded, will only result in putting us in the same position in which we were two years ago, and in which we might have remained if the Government had had ordinary common-sense. But that is not all. The Government, which have always been so proud of the concert of Europe, have contrived by an act of illegality— to which they have added features unnecessarily harsh and repulsive—by an act of illegality they have contrived to unite Europe against them, and cannot now count on the countenance of any European power in solving this difficult problem which they have made for themselves in Egypt.

Again, I ask, where was the constitutional machine? Why did not the House of Commons interfere to prevent this great absurdity? The answer is the same. Against all former precedent the Government used its majority to prevent the House of Commons having an opportunity of discussion, and the mode in which the Government used its majority was so peculiar that I must venture to dwell for a moment upon it. It was agreed—they seemed to think that they could not in decency refuse to agree—to give a day for the discussion of the policy upon which the late conference was initiated, which would have given an opportunity for an explanation of the whole Egyptian policy. The Government had given the day; the day came; the mover was there with his motion; all the speakers were ready; all the forces were assembled for a division, when there arose a gentleman—and the Government and the gentleman tell us that it was by accident—there arose Mr. Goschen, whose word we are bound to believe, to move that it was not expedient that this discussion should take place, and the Government thereupon took up his motion in the strangest possible way. They did not honestly vote with him; they voted against him; but there suddenly spread through their ranks an inconceivable and perfectly unprecedented paroxysm of disobedience. All the most devoted followers of the Government on that occasion voted against them. It was told to me—it has been denied since, but I suspect there was something in it—that some of those who ordinarily marshalled the forces of the Government stood in the door, and by signs not easily mistakable showed which way their preference lay. At all events, that strange result was produced that son was set against father and brother against brother on that strange and monstrous occasion. Mr. Gladstone's son voted against him. Lord Northbrook's son voted against him. Lord Spencer's brother voted against him It was a fearful moment for the dominion of the evil powers The discussion did not take place. The controlling power of the House of Commons was paralyzed. No supervision of the Government's efforts was made, and the result is that hopeless imbroglio in Egypt, diplomatic and military, upon which, with so much apprehension, the people of this island are now looking. Again, I say, you see here what is the result of departing from your old constitutional rules. You see what is the result of leaving to the Government of the day this despotic, unquestioned power which they claim as the result of Liberal principles. You see now what is the result of this strange and monstrous conversion which makes the party that professed to defend freedom and progress the champions of the power of the man and the advocates of unlimited submission.

I wish before I sit down to turn for a short time from this subject, because I confess I feel, and I have felt in this autumn campaign, that the result of the argumentative contest to which the Government has challenged us was that a question of importance, comparatively secondary, was obscuring matters of far greater moment to the country. I will not refer on the present occasion to the great dangers and difficulties which threaten us in connection with foreign affairs, but I will only say this—that it is not by any act of ours if those matters have been pushed back into the second distance, and if the attention of the constituencies and of the people has been concentrated on a matter that is not, speaking comparatively, of primary importance. Lord Hartington reproaches us that in the midst of the dangers which we point out to the Empire we have agitated this question. Our answer is, in the first place, that it was not by our advice that in this particular crisis this question was brought forward at all; and, in the second place, this Government have chosen to desert the road which all former Governments in dealing with the reform of the representation had uniformly trodden; and that if evil results have come from this abandonment of precedent with them and not with us, who point them out, the responsibility must lie. But the matter to which I wish to call your attention—I hardly need to do so—is the condition at this moment in which industries of the country find themselves, and the necessity that your attention and the attention of all who give themselves to politics, of all who exercise any influence, however humble, upon the management of affairs, should be concentrated at this crisis. You know that for years back there has been depression, and that it seems to be going on from bad to worse. You know, no one better, what it is in agriculture. It used to be thought, the Duke of Richmond's commission thought so, that there was nothing but the sun to blame, and that when a good harvest came back agricultural prosperity would return with it; but we have had a year which I imagine is as good as any we can expect to have. We shall not have many such years as we have had last year, and yet I have been told by those to whom the matter is familiar that the agricultural prospect in many parts of the country was never

more gloomy than it is at the present moment. Why is that?
First, because your prices have failed. And why have your
prices failed? Because your buyers are no longer numerous or
keen. And why are your buyers no longer numerous or keen?
Because trade and industry no longer give them the material
wherewith to purchase. Therefore your inland market is destroyed. I know that outside agriculture a cry of distress is
rising from one after another of the great industries by which
this great country is supported. We have heard terrible accounts from Sunderland of 30,000 to 40,000 being out of work.
When I was in Glasgow they told me there were as many as
50,000 people out of work there. I believe that in Newcastle
the distress is assuming graver and graver proportions every
day. For some reason or other the great mechanism by which
the trade and industry of this country have hitherto been
worked seems to have failed at some points, and we only ask,
What is the cause, and how far is it possible that, by powers
which Government possess, by the action of any political force,
any mitigation of this evil can be brought about.

Do not let me seem to hold out a hope which I do not myself
entertain, that any action of the Government can wholly mitigate the distress under which we suffer. I know that it is not
so, that there are causes outside the power of any political machinery which impose upon us the suffering which is now present, and which is, I fear, in the immediate future. But though
we may not be able to prevent we may be able to palliate and to
mitigate, and we must ask ourselves, Is there anything in the
political conduct of our Government which aggravates or has
aggravated this evil? Is there any change of policy by which
these disasters can be mitigated or averted? There is one
thing that I have always been anxious to urge upon all assem-
blies of my countrymen—I feel that it is not sufficiently recognized in the legislation of recent years—and that is that industry
cannot flow unless capital is confident, and capital will not be
confident as long as it fears that Parliament may meddle with it,
and balk it of its profits. There is no question of this, that of
recent years Parliament has been singularly meddlesome. I do
not say that it is from a bad motive; on the contrary, usually the
motive has been philanthropy—possibly in some cases of ill-
guided philanthropy—but always pure and humane motives

have been at the bottom of this meddlesome legislation, but the effect has been not to interfere with periods of prosperity, but in periods of difficulty to make capital shrink from exposing itself to unknown dangers and to deprive the workman's industry of the only food by which it can be nourished.   In acting thus men do not think much of the action of Parliament.   They think that, happen what may, be the restrictions what they may, they can at all events secure profit enough to pay them for the risk and trouble they incur.   But when bad times come, and when the question in every man's mind arises whether he shall invest his capital in an industry or not, there comes up the doubt, Had I not better desist, seeing the temper that prevails in Parliament?   I know they have passed act after act, with whatever motive, that has diminished our profits hitherto.   How can I know that they will not pass acts of the same character in future?   And this tendency becomes much more dangerous when the policy of Parliament approaches, if ever so small a degree, to the character of confiscation.   If there is in the legislation a tendency dishonestly to interfere with the rights of men for the purpose of gaining Parliamentary or electioneering strength, the evil is not confined to the number of people whom their conduct injures   The evil spreads throughout the community.   A feeling of fear attaches itself to all enterprises upon which the capitalist is invited to embark, and many more industries suffer than those which are affected by the particular legislation to which I refer.

Now, I will give you an example.   There has been a good deal of legislation about land.   I do not wish in the least to discuss its character, but it has had the effect of frightening the owners of land   What has been the result?   I heard in this neighborhood, in this county, of a very great industrial proposal, which would have given employment to a vast number of men; it was laid before wealthy men, who were interested in it as territorial proprietors, but the answer was: " At ordinary times we might have been glad to look upon this undertaking.   It might have added to our property and have promoted the welfare of the community.   But with the tendency that has shown itself in Parliament we dare not risk any large sums of money and sink them in improvements which would take many years to realize, because we do not know how far the doctrines which now prevail may operate hereafter to prevent us reaping the profits to which we are entitled." I want you, if possible, to put aside all consideration of the owners of land altogether. Do not think whether it is just to them or not. What I want you to think of is whether it is good for a community, and what I say is that this feeling of doubt and apprehension is the most dangerous disease by which the industry of a community could be affected. It affects a community precisely as cattle disease has affected the industry of cattle-breeding in this country. The foot-and-mouth disease was only in a few localities by itself, it did not do an enormous amount of harm, but it filled every man's mind with apprehension, it limited the investment of capital, and as the investment of capital was limited employment was restricted, wages ceased to flow, and distressed populations had to appeal to the sympathy of the public for their support. That is one serious evil of the tendency which recent Parliaments have shown which I should be wrong if I did not impress upon you.

There is another matter—a much more serious matter, and one which you must carefully consider—and that is the condition of the markets of the world. I am not speaking now of foreign policy. No doubt it is very disappointing that a ministry which came in on principles of peace should have so conducted its foreign policy that at every step it seems to dry up a market by which the produce of the industry of this country might be absorbed Egypt, the Cape of Good Hope, China—all these are names familiar to the markets of this country. In all these the operations which have taken place, the political events which have developed themselves under the auspices of the present Government, have diminished the purchasing power, have restricted the exportation, and have consequently added to the volume of distress which threatens us in the approaching winter. But there is another and much more serious question. It is a question which politicians do not like to deal with, but which will grow from year to year, and which invites the attention of the people of this country—I mean the effect which obstructive and hostile tariffs have upon the interests of this country. We have undergone as great a disappointment in this respect When free trade was adopted we hoped that free trade would spread through the world, but we are almost the only converts after nearly half a century has passed. It is not only so, but matters seem to be getting worse rather than better. I do not know if you have noticed the fact that in the French Chambers the French Minister has recently announced his intention of putting a duty upon corn and a fresh duty upon cattle. I do not quote it as a case of a tariff which interferes with the exports of this country. I quote it to show you that the anticipations which were entertained years and years ago that all nations, when we once set the example, would follow in our footsteps in free trade, have, most unhappily, not been realized. Mr. Bright is very fond of referring to the achievements of free trade as one that entitles him forever to the gratitude of his countrymen. I do not differ as to the value of free trade, but I differ very much as to the value of Mr. Bright's services. When free trade was pressed upon Lord Melbourne just at the close of his administration in 1840—and Lord Melbourne, as you know, was a Liberal minister—his answer was: " I admire free trade exceedingly, but it seems to me absurd to introduce it without some communication with the other nations of the world; because if we do so we sacrifice the only bribe that we have to offer them when we admit their produce free to induce them to do the same." That was the opinion of Lord Melbourne. About that time Mr. Bright came into the controversy. He did not deal with it as a matter of scientific discussion, as a question to be argued out before the tribunal of the people; he dealt with it as an opportunity of setting class against class. He seized upon that one question of the corn laws, and he tried, and with his friends he was successful in his efforts, to persuade them that the only obstacle, the only objection, to free trade was the greed which he imputed to the owners and the occupiers of the land. What was the result of this turn to the controversy given by Mr. Bright? He has always loved to treat every political discussion as material for sowing dissension between the classes of which this community is composed. He raised a formidable agitation, and Sir Robert Peel, rightly or wrongly, was of opinion that it was necessary for the interests of the country that that agitation should be closed. Without waiting for any negotiations with foreign powers he introduced the system of free trade, which Mr. Gladstone has carried further, and the consequence is that we have now no motive by which we can prevail upon foreign powers to lower tariffs or open their markets to our industries, which sorely need them. Do not understand me to be blaming Sir Robert Peel. He acted under great difficulties, and there is much to be said for what he did, but that the result of that one-sided policy of free trade has been unfortunate I, for one, cannot doubt. It puts us in the position that though we gain by the free importation of corn and other materials, so that the prices of them are low to the consumers, we do not gain all that we might have gained. We do not gain an issue for the industry of our own community or for the exportation of goods that we produce. We do not gain an issue to those industries, and therefore those industries languish. Therefore employment is becoming scarcer, wages are becoming smaller, and the distress of the population is becoming larger, and the blessings of free trade, which ought to have been enormous, have been robbed of half their value, owing to the precipitate and the improvident manner in which the position of this country as regards other countries was sacrificed.

Well now, I have pressed this point upon you precisely because in all this matter of free trade there is a habit on the part of ministerial advocates of what I may call browbeating. They treat this question of free trade as if it were some revelation from heaven which it would be blasphemy to inquire into. If you suggest that some particular working of it should be examined, if you ask for an inquiry into the effect on some particular industry, if you say that, owing to some miscalculation, it has not produced all that was expected of it, they cried out, " Oh! you are a mere protectionist; all your protestations are of no avail; we will not listen to you for a moment." I protest against dealing in that spirit with any question which affects the industry and the livelihood of vast masses of our countrymen. Politics is not an exact science, and if those formulas of free trade in which they trust are not producing the results which they anticipated, and which they promised to us, we, at least, without incurring the imputation of any economic heresy, may press for an inquiry to examine where is the defect, where the shortcoming to which our misfortunes point. I am anxious, in speaking the words which I believe will close the autumn controversy, to urge upon you that you should not allow the matters that we have discussed, however important they are, to obscure in your sight the far more momentous questions which surround the industry, the employment, the social well-being of the people. It seems a mere derision to tell men who are starving in Sunderland and Glasgow that we are fighting for the question as to how they shall exercise their privilege at the ballot-box; to offer to men who are without employment, who have muscles to labor, but who cannot with their best will compass the limits of their daily need—to offer to them some extension of the franchise or arrangement of seats is like offering a stone to those who are asking for bread. I entreat you not to allow these questions to be banished from your minds by the din of the controversy which is now passing away. I do not say that I can put into any formula that can be placed at a meeting like this the remedy that may be required. What I ask is that the best intellect of the country shall be applied to the discovery of what is the cost of the most terrible evil by which the country can be afflicted. I know there are complicated difficulties. I know that by diplomatic instruments we, in the full confidence in our political orthodoxy, have been winding band after band round our own limbs, so that in many cases we are not free to move. I know that such a position involves relations unprecedented in the history of the world with our self-governed colonies; I know it involves our imperial relations with far-distant lands. I do not ask for a simple remedy or profess to have any compact or ready nostrum by which our difficulties can be dispelled. All I propose to you is, do not allow yourselves to be driven off from the consideration of this momentous question by being told that you are protectionists in disguise, or by being told that this is a thing which has been decided many years ago, and that if you venture to inquire into it you will suggest doubts of the soundness of the opinions you entertain. The interests that are involved are far too large, far too deep, too pathetic, and too perilous for arguments of that kind. This agitation which has taken place during the autumn is in many respects highly beneficial to the country. I think it has brought before the minds of the people of the country questions with which they must grapple, facts which they must learn to understand, if they are to be our rulers. I desire nothing better than that they should be thoroughly and perfectly informed. I think the agitation has had a tendency to strengthen the

House of Lords in the opinion of the people of this country. But the only reason for which I could possibly regret it would be if it should have the effect of diverting your minds and the minds of the constituencies of this country from the far graver and more important questions which are approaching us in the immediate future. I should regret it deeply if it blinded your eyes to the dark and black clouds which are surrounding our horizon. I should regret it deeply if it diverted your attention from the problems which you as governors of this country must grapple with and must solve. I should regret it deeply if it induces us for a moment to forget that the first function of government, its most vital and imperative duty, is to care for the industry, the vast industry, whose prosperity or depression means the difference between well-being and misery, between health and disease, between a life of hope and a life of despair to millions of our toiling fellow-countrymen.

FUNERAL ORATION ON GENERAL GRANT

—

BY

CANON FARRAR
(Frederic William Farrar)

FREDERIC WILLIAM FARRAR, CANON FARRAR

Frederic William Farrar was born at Bombay, India, August 7, 1831. He was educated at King William's College, in the Isle of Man, and later at King's College, London. He graduated from Trinity College, Cambridge, in 1854, with the highest honors, was made fellow of Trinity two years later, became a master of arts in 1857, and was admitted into priest's orders the same year.

For many years, from 1855 to 1871, Farrar was one of the assistant masters at Harrow, first under Dr Vaughan and later under Dr Butler. For the succeeding five years, from 1871 to 1876, he held the head-mastership at Marlborough He has been repeatedly one of the select preachers at Cambridge and chosen to deliver special lectures at both universities. He was appointed chaplain-in-ordinary to the Queen in 1873 and, in April, 1876, to a canonry in Westminster Abbey and to the rector-ship of St Margaret's. Made Archdeacon of Westminster in 1883, he accepted the chaplaincy of the House of Commons in 1890 To this uninterrupted series of preferments we must add his latest appointment as Dean of Canterbury and Deputy Clerk to the closet of the Queen in 1895.

As an author Canon Farrar has gained some distinction in three distinct fields of labor. He is the author of some works of fiction, in which he depicts school and college life from his own experience; they have retained their popularity with the readers for whom they were intended. His practical work at school led him to undertake philological researches, the results of which, embodied in several works, while not of the highest scientific value, have done much to make the subjects popular and to stimulate others to further inquiry. He has also written much on public education, and done much to enlarge the ideas on this subject in England.

The greater number of works of Canon Farrar have, however, been produced by him as a theologian and a religious writer, among these his " Life of Christ " is undoubtedly the best known and most widely read, reaching its twelfth edition in a single year. Being of a speculative turn of mind, yet in close touch with the tendencies and aspirations of the times, he is one of those men who thoroughly appreciate the difficulties which the Christian Church encounters from materialistic philosophy and the unsparing criticism of the day.

On his visit to America in 1885 Canon Farrar was received everywhere with a hearty welcome from all classes Of late years he has become an advocate of the entire suppression of the traffic in liquor.

The many distinctions he had conferred upon him give ample proof of his great powers in the pulpit His thoughts are always clear, logical, and well arranged, while the style in his sermons, as in his books, is invariably brilliant and rhetorical. His " Funeral Oration on General Grant," delivered in London simultaneously with General Grant's funeral in America, is a beautiful and touching eulogy.

FUNERAL ORATION ON GENERAL GRANT

Delivered in Westminster Abbey, London, August 4, 1885.

EIGHT years have not passed since the Dean of Westminster, whom Americans so much loved and honored, was walking round this Abbey with General Grant, and explaining to him its wealth of great memorials. Neither of them had attained the allotted span of human life, and for both we might have hoped that many years would elapse before they went down to the grave, full of years and honors. But this is already the fourth summer since the dean fell asleep, and to-day we are assembled at the obsequies of the great soldier whose sun has gone down while it yet was day, and at whose funeral service in America tens of thousands are assembled at this moment to mourn with his widow, family, and friends. Yes; life at the best is but as a vapor that passeth away. The glories of our birth and state are shadows, not substantial things. But when death comes, what nobler epitaph can any man have than this, that, having served his generation, by the will of God he fell asleep? Little can the living do for the dead. The pomps and ceremonies of earthly grandeur have lost their significance, but when our soul shall leave its dwelling the story of one fair and virtuous action is above all the escutcheons on our tombs or silken banners over us. I would desire to speak simply and directly, and, if with generous appreciation, yet with no idle flattery of him whose death has made a nation mourn. His private life, the faults and failings of his character, whatever they may have been, belong in no sense to the world. They are for the judgment of God, whose merciful forgiveness is necessary for the best of what we do and are. We touch only on his public actions and services, the record of his strength, his magnanimity, his self-control, his generous deeds. His life falls into four marked divisions, of which each has its own lesson for us. He touched on them himself in part when he said:

" Bury me either at West Point, where I was trained as a youth; or in Illinois, which gave me my first commission; or in New York, which sympathized with me in my misfortunes."

His wish has been respected, and on the cliff overhanging the Hudson his monument will stand, to recall to the memory of future generations those dark days of a nation's history which he did so much to close. First came the early years of growth and training, of poverty and obscurity, of struggle and self-denial. Poor and humbly born, he had to make his own way in the world. God's unseen providence, which men nickname chance, directed his boyhood. A cadetship was given him at the military academy of West Point, and after a brief period of service in the Mexican War, in which he was three times mentioned in despatches, seeing no opening for a soldier in what seemed likely to be days of unbroken peace, he settled down to a humble life in a provincial town. Citizens of St. Louis will remember the rough backwoodsman who sold cord wood from door to door, and who afterwards became a leather-seller in the obscure town of Galena. Those who knew him in those days have said that if anyone had predicted that the silent, unprosperous, unambitious man, whose chief aim was to get a plank road from his shop to the railway depot, would become twice President of the United States, and one of the foremost men of his day, the prophecy would have seemed extravagantly ridiculous. But such careers are the glory of the American continent. They show that the people have a sovereign insight into intrinsic force. If Rome told with pride how her dictators came from the plough-tail, America, too, may record the answer of the President who, on being asked what would be his coat-of-arms, answered, proudly mindful of his early struggles, " A pair of shirt sleeves." The answer showed a noble sense of the dignity of labor, the noble superiority to the vanities of feudalism, a strong conviction that men are to be honored simply as men and not for the prizes of birth and accident, which are without them. You have of late years had two martyr Presidents, both men, sons of the people. One was the homely man, who at the age of seven was a farm lad, at seventeen a rail-splitter, at twenty a boatman on the Mississippi, and who in manhood proved to be one of the most honest and God-fearing of modern rulers. The other grew up from a shoeless child in a log-hut on the prairies, round which the wolves prowled in the winter snow, to be a humble teacher in Hiram Institute. With these Presidents America need not blush to name also the leather-seller of Galena. Every true man derived his patent of nobleness direct from God.

Did not God choose David from the sheepfold, from following the ewes great with young ones, to make him the ruler of his people Israel? Was not the Lord of Life and all the worlds for thirty years a carpenter at Nazareth? Do not such things illustrate the prophecy of Solomon:

" Seest thou a man diligent in his business? he shall stand before kings; he shall not stand before mean men."

When Abraham Lincoln sat, book in hand, day after day, under the tree, moving round it as the shadow crossed, absorbed in mastering his tasks; when James Garfield rang the bell at Hiram Institute on the very stroke of the hour, and swept the school-room as faithfully as he mastered his Greek lesson; when Ulysses Grant, sent with his team to meet some men who came to load his cart with logs, and, finding no men, loaded the cart with his own boy's strength—they showed in the conscientious performance of duty the qualities which were to raise them to become kings of men. When John Adams was told that his son, John Quincy Adams, had been elected President of the United States, he said: " He has always been laborious, child and man, from infancy."

But the youth was not destined to die in the deep valley of obscurity and toil, in which it is the lot—and perhaps the happy lot—of most of us to spend our little lives. The hour came; the man was needed. In 1861 there broke out that most terrible war of modern days Grant received a commission as colonel of volunteers, and in four years the struggling toiler had been raised to the chief command of a vaster army than had ever been handled by any mortal man. Who could have imagined that four years would make that enormous difference? But it is often so. The great men needed for such tremendous crises have stepped often, as it were, out of a door in the wall which no man had noticed; and, unannounced, unheralded, without prestige, have made their way silently and single-handed to the front. And there was no luck in it. It was a work of inflexible faithfulness, of indomitable resolution, of sleepless energy, and iron purpose and tenacity. In the campaigns of Fort Donelson; in the desperate battle at Shiloh; in the siege of Corinth; in the successful assaults at Pittsburg; in battle after battle, in siege after siege; whatever Grant had to do, he did it with his might. Other generals might fail—he would not fail. He showed what a man could do whose will was strong. He undertook, as General Sherman said of him, what no one else would have ventured, and his very soldiers began to reflect something of his indominable determination. His sayings revealed the man. " I have nothing to do with opinions," he said, at the outset, " and shall only deal with armed rebellion." " In riding over the field," he said at Shiloh, " I saw that either side was ready to give way, if the other showed a bold front. I took the opportunity, and ordered an advance along the whole line." " No terms," he wrote to General Buckner at Fort Donelson (and it is pleasant to know that General Buckner stood as a warm friend beside his dying bed); " no terms other than unconditional surrender can be accepted." " My headquarters," he wrote from Vicksburg, " will be on the field." With a military genius which embraced the vastest plans while attending to the smallest details, he defeated, one after another, every great general of the Confederates, except General Stonewall Jackson. The Southerners felt that he held them as in the grasp of a vise; that this man could neither be arrested nor avoided. For all this he has been severely blamed. He ought not to be blamed. He has been called a butcher, which is grossly unjust. He loved peace; he hated bloodshed; his heart was generous and kind. His orders were to save lives, to save treasure, but at all costs to save his country—and he did save his country. His army cheerfully accepted the sacrifice, wrote its farewells, buckled its belts, and stood ready. The struggle was not for victory; it was for existence. It was not for glory; it was for life and death. Grant had not only to defeat armies, but to annihilate their forces; to leave no choice but destruction or submission. He saw that the brief ravage of the hurricane is infinitely less ruinous than the interminable malignity of the pestilence, and in the colossal struggle, victory, swift, decisive, overwhelming, was the truest mercy. In silence and with determination, and with clearness of insight, he was like your Washington and our Wellington. He was like them also in this, that the word " cannot " did not exist in a soldier's dictionary, and what he achieved was achieved without bluster. In the hottest fury of all his battles, his speech was never known to be more than " yea, yea," and " nay, nay." He met General Lee at Appomattox. He received his surrender with faultless delicacy. He immediately issued an order that the Confederates should be supplied with rations. Immediately his enemies surrendered, he gave them terms as simple and as generous as a brother could have given them— terms which healed differences; terms of which they freely acknowledged the magnanimity. Not even entering the capital, avoiding all ostentation, unelated by triumph, as unruffled by adversity, he hurried back to stop recruits and to curtail the vast expenses of the country. After the surrender at Appomattox Court House the war was over. He had put his hand to the plough and had looked not back. He had made blow after blow, each following where the last had struck; he had wielded like a hammer the gigantic forces at his disposal, and had smitten opposition into the dust. It was a mighty work, and he had done it well. Surely history has shown that for the future destinies of a mighty nation it was a necessary and blessed work! The Church utters her most indignant anathema at an unrighteous war, but she has never refused to honor the faithful soldiers who fight in the cause of their country and God. The gentlest and most Christian of modern poets has used tremendous thought:

> " God's most dreaded instrument
> In working out a pure intent
> Is man arrayed for mutual slaughter,
> Yea, carnage is his daughter ! "

We shudder even as we quote the words, but yet the cause for which General Grant fought—the honor of a great people, and the freedom of a whole race of mankind—was a great and noble cause. And the South has accepted that desperate and bloody arbitrament. Two of the Southern generals, we rejoice to hear, will bear General Grant's funeral pall. The rancor and ill-feeling of the past are buried in oblivion; true friends

had been made out of brave foemen. Americans are no longer
Northerners and Southerners, Federals and Confederates, but
they are Americans. " Do not teach your children to hate,"
said General Lee, to an American lady ; " teach them that they
are Americans. I thought that we were better off as one nation
than as two, and I think so now." " The war is over," said
Grant, " and the best sign of rejoicing after victory will be to
abstain from all demonstrations in the field." " Let us have
peace," were the memorable words with which he ended his
inaugural address as President. On the rest of the great soldier's life, we will only touch in very few words. As Wellington
became Prime Minister of England, and lived to be hooted in
the streets of London, so Grant, more than half against his will,
became President, and for a time lost much of his popularity.
He foresaw it all, but it is not for a man to choose; it is for a man
to accept his destiny. What verdict history may pronounce on
him as a politician I know not ; but here, and now, the voice
of censure, deserved or undeserved, is silent. When the great
Duke of Marlborough died and one began to · speak of his
avarice, " He was so great a man," said Bolingbroke, " I have
forgotten that he had that fault."

It was a fine and delicate rebuke, and we do not intend to
rake up a man's faults and errors. Those errors, whatever they
may have been, we leave to the mercy of the Merciful, and the
atoning blood of his Saviour. Beside the open grave, we speak
only in gratitude of his great achievements. Let us record his
virtue in brass, for men's example ; but let his faults, whatever
they may have been, be writ in water. Some may think that
it would have been well for Grant if he had died in 1865, when
steeples clanged and cities were illuminated and congregations
rose in his honor. Many and dark clouds overshadowed the
last of his days—the blow of financial ruin ; the dread that men
should suppose that he had a tarnished reputation ; the terrible
agony of an incurable disease. But God's ways are not our
ways. To bear that sudden ruin, that speechless agony, required a courage nobler and greater than that of the 'battle-
field, and human courage grows magnificently to the height of
human need. " I am a man," said Frederick the Great, " and
therefore born to suffer." On the long agonizing death-bed,
Grant showed himself every inch a hero, bearing his agonies

and trials without a murmur, with rugged stoicism, in un-flinching fortitude; yes, and we believe in a Christian's pa-tience and a Christian's prayers. Which of us can tell whether those hours of torture and misery may not have been blessings in disguise; whether God may not have been refining the gold from the brass, and the strong man had been truly purified by the strong agony? We are gathered here in England to do honor to his memory and to show our sympathy with the sor-row of a great sister nation. Could we be gathered in a more fitting place? We do not lack here memorials to recall the his-tory of your country. There is the grave of André; there is the monument raised by grateful Massachusetts to the gallant Howe; there is a temporary resting-place of George Peabody; there is the bust of Longfellow; over the dean's there is the faint semblance of Boston Harbor. We add another memory to-day. Whatever there may have been between the two na-tions to forget and forgive, it is forgotten and forgiven. " I will not speak of them as two peoples," said General Grant at Newcastle in 1877, " because, in fact, we are one people, with a common destiny, and that destiny will be brilliant in pro-portion to the friendship and coöperation of the brethren dwelling on each side of the Atlantic," Oh ! if the two peoples, which are one people, be true to their duty, and true to their God, who can doubt that in their hands are the destinies of the world? Can anything short of dementation ever thwart a des-tiny so manifest? Your founders were our sons; it was from our past that your present grew. The monument of Sir Walter Raleigh is not that nameless grave in St. Margaret's; it is the State of Virginia   Yours and ours alike are the memories of Captain John Smith and of the Pilgrim Fathers, of General Oglethorpe's strong benevolence of soul, of the apostolic holi-ness of Berkeley, and the burning zeal of Wesley and White-field. Yours and ours alike are the plays of Shakespeare and the poems of Milton; ours and yours alike are all that you have accomplished in literature or in history—the songs of Longfellow and Bryant, the genius of Hawthorne and of Irving, the fame of Washington, Lee, and Grant. But great memories imply great responsibilities.

It was not for nothing that God has made England what she is; not for nothing that the free individualism of a busy multitude, the humble traders of a fugitive people, snatching the New World from feudalism and bigotry, from Philip II and Louis XIV, from Menendez and Montcalm, from the Jesuit and the Inquisition, from Torquemada, and from Richelieu, to make it the land of the Reformation and the republic of Christianity and of peace. " Let us auspicate all our proceedings in America," said Edmund Burke, " with the old Church cry, *Sursum corda*." But it is for America to live up to this spirit of such words, not merely to quote them with proud enthusiasm. We have heard of—

> "New times, new climes, new lands, new men, but still
> The same old tears, old crimes, and oldest ill."

It is for America to falsify the cynical foreboding. Let her take her place side by side with England in the very van of freedom and of progress, united by a common language, by common blood, by common measures, by common interest, by a common history, by common hopes; united by the common glory of great men, of which this great temple of silence and reconciliation is the richest shrine. Be it the steadfast purpose of the true peoples who are one people to show all the world not only the magnificent spectacle of human happiness, but the still more magnificent spectacle of two peoples which are one people, loving righteousness and hating iniquity, inflexibly faithful to the principles of eternal justice which are the unchanging laws of God.

THE SUBSTANCE OF SERMONS

—

BY

CHARLES HADDON SPURGEON

CHARLES HADDON SPURGEON

1834—1892

Spurgeon was one of the great natural orators of the pulpit: a phe-
nomenon hardly explicable upon any scientific theory; for there was
nothing in the antecedents, or in the early personal experience of the
humble usher in a Cambridge private school that can serve to explain
the mighty preacher who, when hardly twenty years of age, was already
drawing vast and excited audiences to listen to what he might have
to say on the relations between God and man What should the homely,
coarse-looking, crude Essex country boy know of those relations? By
what charter was he entitled to counsel and exhort his generation on
the highest of human duties, and to interpret to them the profound and
eternal wisdom conveyed in the Book of God's Word? His figure was
squat and awkward, his face fat and clumsy, with heavy mouth, snub
nose, and pale eyes; there was in him no form nor comeliness Even
his voice had none of the exquisite modulations, the tones of pathos and
spiritual exaltation, which might rouse a drugged soul or spur self-
complacent ungodliness to purge itself of sin And yet Charles Haddon
Spurgeon was heard, during his ministry, by millions of men and women,
who found in him the chief incitement of their lives to virtue and charity, to the patient endurance of pain, and to steadfast faith in God and
immortality The words he uttered week after week in that Newington
Tabernacle, built especially to seat the large and enthusiastic crowds
that flocked each Sabbath to hear him, were taken down, and printed,
and scattered broadcast over the English-speaking world, to serve as
moral and religious nourishment to countless homes in England and
America

The biographical facts of his career are few and simple. He was born
at Kelvedon, Essex, June 19, 1834 After a school education at Colchester and Maidstone, he became usher of a private school in Cambridge, and in 1851 pastor of a Baptist church near Cambridge; whence
he removed with his congregation to Southwark in 1853, and to the
Tabernacle in 1861 During his ministration he found time to found
an orphanage, a college for pastors, and various schools and alms-
houses He edited a magazine, "The Sword and Trowel," and wrote
numerous books of religious exhortation and counsel He died, worn
out in body, but full of spiritual vitality to the last, in 1892, at the
age of fifty-eight The "Substance of Sermons," given here, is filled
with advice to young ministers. It is characteristic of Spurgeon's best
style, being concise, thoughtful, and penetrating to the heart of the
subject.

THE SUBSTANCE OF SERMONS

WE must throw all our strength of judgment, memory, imagination, and eloquence, into the delivery of the gospel; and not give to the preaching of the cross our random thoughts while wayside topics engross our deeper meditations. Depend upon it, if we brought the intellect of a Locke or a Newton, and the eloquence of a Cicero, to bear upon the simple doctrine of "believe and live," we should find no surplus strength. Brethren, first and above all things, keep to plain evangelical doctrines; whatever else you do or do not preach, be sure incessantly to bring forth the soul-saving truth of Christ and Him crucified. I know a minister whose shoe-latchet I am unworthy to unloose, whose preaching is often little better than sacred miniature painting—I might also say holy trifling. He is great upon the ten toes of the beast, the four faces of the cherubim, the mystical meaning of badgers' skins, and the typical bearings of the staves of the ark, and the windows of Solomon's temple; but the sins of business men, the temptations of the times, and the needs of the age, he scarcely ever touches upon. Such preaching reminds me of a lion engaged in mouse hunting, or a man-of-war cruising after a lost water-butt. Topics scarcely in importance equal to what Peter calls " old wives' fables," are made great matters of by those microscopic divines to whom the nicety of a point is more attractive than the saving of souls. You will have read in Todd's " Student's Manual " that Harcatius, King of Persia, was a notable mole-catcher; and Briantes, King of Lydia, was equally *au fait* at filing needles; but these trivialities by no means prove them to have been great kings; it is much the same in the ministry; there is such a thing as meanness of mental occupation unbecoming the rank of an ambassador of heaven.

Among a certain order of minds at this time the Athenian desire of telling or hearing some new thing appears to be predominant. They boast of new light, and claim a species of inspiration which warrants them in condemning all who are out of their brotherhood, and yet their grand revelation relates to a mere circumstantial of worship, or to an obscure interpretation of prophecy; so that, at sight of their great fuss and loud cry concerning so little, we are reminded of

> " Ocean into tempest tossed
> To waft a feather or to drown a fly."

Worse still are those who waste time in insinuating doubts concerning the authenticity of texts, or the correctness of Biblical statements concerning natural phenomena. Painfully do I call to mind hearing one Sabbath evening a deliverance called a sermon, of which the theme was a clever inquiry as to whether an angel did actually descend and stir the pool at Bethesda, or whether it was an intermitting spring, concerning which Jewish superstition had invented a legend. Dying men and women were assembled to hear the way of salvation, and they were put off with such vanity as this! They came for bread, and received a stone; the sheep looked up to the shepherd, and were not fed. Seldom do I hear a sermon, and when I do I am grievously unfortunate, for one of the last I was entertained with was intended to be a justification of Joshua for destroying the Canaanites, and another went to prove that it was not good for man to be alone. How many souls were converted in answer to the prayers before the sermons I have never been able to ascertain, but I shrewdly suspect that no unusual rejoicing disturbed the serenity of the golden streets.

Believing my next remark to be almost universally unneeded, I bring it forward with diffidence—do not overload a sermon with too much matter. All truth is not to be comprised in one discourse. Sermons are not to be bodies of divinity. There is such a thing as having too much to say, and saying it till hearers are sent home loathing rather than longing. An old minister walking with a young preacher pointed to a cornfield and observed, " Your last sermon had too much in it, and it was not clear enough, or sufficiently well arranged; it was like that field of wheat, it contained much crude food, but none fit for use. You should make your sermons like a loaf of bread, fit for eating, and in convenient form." It is to be feared that human heads (speaking phrenologically) are not so capacious for theology as they once were, for our forefathers rejoiced in sixteen ounces of divinity, undiluted and unadorned, and could continue receiving it for three or four hours at a stretch, but our more degenerate, or perhaps more busy, generation requires about an ounce of doctrine at a time, and that must be the concentrated extract or essential oil, rather than the entire substance of divinity. We must in these times say a great deal in a few words, but not too much, nor with too much amplification. One thought fixed on the mind will be better than fifty thoughts made to flit across the ear. One tenpenny nail driven home and clenched will be more useful than a score of tin-tacks loosely fixed, to be pulled out again in an hour.

Our matter should be well arranged according to the true rules of mental architecture. Not practical inferences at the basis and doctrines as the topstones; not metaphors in the foundations, and propositions at the summit; not the more important truths first and the minor teachings last, after the manner of an anti-climax; but the thought must climb and ascend; one stair of teaching leading to another; one door of reasoning conducting to another, and the whole elevating the hearer to a chamber from whose windows truth is seen gleaming in the light of God. In preaching, have a place for everything, and everything in its place. Never suffer truths to fall from you pell-mell. Do not let your thoughts rush as a mob, but make them march as a troop of soldiery. Order, which is heaven's first law, must not be neglected by heaven's ambassadors.

Your doctrinal teaching should be clear and unmistakable. To be so it must first of all be clear to yourself. Some men think in smoke and preach in a cloud. Your people do not want a luminous haze, but the solid *terra firma* of truth. Philosophical speculations put certain minds into a semi-intoxicated condition, in which they either see everything double, or see nothing at all. The head of a certain college in Oxford was years ago asked by a stranger what was the motto of the arms of that university. He told him that it was "*Dominus illuminatio mea.*" But he also candidly informed the stranger that, in his private opinion, a motto more appropriate might be, "*Aristoteles tenebræ meæ.*" Sensational writers have half crazed many honest men who have conscientiously read their lucubrations out of a notion that they ought to be abreast of the age, as if such a necessity might not also require us to attend the theatres in order to be able to judge the new plays, or frequent the turf that we might not be too bigoted in our opinions upon racing and gambling. For my part, I believe that the chief readers of heterodox books are ministers, and that if they would not notice them they would fall still-born from the press. Let a minister keep clear of mystifying himself, and then he is on the road to becoming intelligible to his people. No man can hope to be felt who cannot make himself understood. If we give our people refined truth, pure scriptural doctrine, and all so worded as to have no needless obscurity about it, we shall be true shepherds of the sheep, and the profiting of our people will soon be apparent.

Endeavor to keep the matter of your sermonizing as fresh as you can. Do not rehearse five or six doctrines with unvarying monotony of repetition. Buy a theological barrel-organ, brethren, with five tunes accurately adjusted, and you will be qualified to practise as an ultra-Calvinistic preacher at Zoar and Jireh, if you also purchase at some vinegar factory a good supply of bitter, acrid abuse of Arminians, and duty-faith men. Brains and grace are optional, but the organ and the wormwood are indispensable. It is ours to perceive and rejoice in a wider range of truth. All that these good men hold of grace and sovereignty we maintain as firmly and boldly as they; but we dare not shut our eyes to other teachings of the Word, and we feel bound to make full proof of our ministry, by declaring the whole counsel of God. With abundant themes diligently illustrated by fresh metaphors and experiences, we shall not weary, but, under God's hand, shall win our hearers' ears and hearts.

Let your teachings grow and advance; let them deepen with your experience, and rise with your soul-progress. I do not mean preach new truths; for, on the contrary, I hold that man happy who is so well taught from the first that, after fifty years of ministry, he has never had to recant a doctrine or to mourn an important omission; but I mean let our depth and insight continually increase, and where there is spiritual advance it will be so. Timothy could not preach like Paul. Our earlier productions must be surpassed by those of our riper years; we must never make these our models; they will be best burned, or only preserved to be mourned over because of their superficial character. It were ill, indeed, if we knew no more, after being many years in Christ's school; our progress may be slow, but progress there must be, or there will be cause to suspect that the inner life is lacking or sadly unhealthy. Set it before you as most certain that you have not yet attained, and may grace be given you to press forward towards that which is yet beyond. May you all become able ministers of the New Testament, and not a whit behind the very chief of preachers, though in yourselves you will still be nothing.

The word " sermon " is said to signify a thrust, and, therefore, in sermonizing it must be our aim to use the subject in hand with energy and effect, and the subject must be capable of such employment. To choose mere moral themes will be to use a wooden dagger; but the great truths of revelation are as sharp swords. Keep to doctrines which stir the conscience and the heart. Remain unwaveringly the champions of a soul-winning gospel. God's truth is adapted to man, and God's grace adapts man to it. There is a key which, under God, can wind up the musical box of man's nature; get it, and use it daily. Hence I urge you to keep to the old-fashioned gospel, and to that only, for assuredly it is the power of God unto salvation.

Of all I would wish to say this is the sum; my brethren, preach Christ, always and evermore. He is the whole gospel. His person, offices, and work must be our one great, all-comprehending theme. The world needs still to be told of its Saviour, and the way to reach Him. Justification by faith should be far more than it is the daily testimony of Protestant pulpits; and if with this master truth there should be more generally associated the other great doctrines of grace, the better for our churches and our age. If with the zeal of Methodists we can preach the doctrine of Puritans a great future is before us. The fire of Wesley, and the fuel of Whitefield, will cause a burning which shall set the forests of error on fire, and warm the very soul of this cold earth. We are not called to proclaim philosophy and metaphysics, but the simple gospel. Man's fall, his need of a new birth, forgiveness through an atonement, and salvation as the result of faith, these are our battle-axe and weapons of war. We have enough to do to learn and teach these great truths, and accursed be that learning which shall divert us from our mission, or that wilful ignorance which shall cripple us in its pursuit. More and more am I jealous lest any views upon prophecy, church government, politics, or even systematic theology, should withdraw one of us from glorying in the cross of Christ. Salvation is a theme for which I would fain enlist every holy tongue. I am greedy after witnesses for the glorious gospel of the blessed God. O that Christ crucified were the universal burden of men of God. Your guess at the number of the beast, your Napoleonic speculations, your conjectures concerning a personal Antichrist—forgive me, I count them but mere bones for dogs; while men are dying, and hell is filling, it seems to me the veriest drivel to be muttering about an Armageddon at Sebastopol or Sadowa or Sedan, and peeping between the folded leaves of destiny to discover the fate of Germany. Blessed are they who read and hear the words of the prophecy of the Revelation, but the like blessing has evidently not fallen on those who pretend to expound it, for generation after generation of them have been proved to be in error by the mere lapse of time, and the present race will follow to the same inglorious sepulchre. I would sooner pluck one single brand from the burning than explain all mysteries. To win a soul from going down into the pit is a more glorious achievement than to be crowned in the arena of theological controversy as Doctor Sufficientissimus; to have faithfully unveiled the glory of God in the face of Jesus Christ will be in the final judgment accounted worthier service than to have solved the problems of the religious Sphinx, or to have cut the Gordian knot of apocalyptic difficulty. Blessed is that ministry of which Christ is all.

THE FUTURE OF THE BRITISH EMPIRE

EMPIRE

—

BY

JOSEPH CHAMBERLAIN

JOSEPH CHAMBERLAIN

Joseph Chamberlain was born in London in July, 1836. He was educated at University College, and in early life became a member of a manufacturing firm in Birmingham which his father had founded in 1854 He retired from this firm early in the seventies with independent means. Mr. Chamberlain had by this time gained a considerable local reputation on account of his radical opinions and a fluency of speech with which he expounded his views in public In 1868 he had been appointed chairman of the first executive committee of the Education League, and in this capacity he conducted a movement that led to the passing of the Elementary Education Act in 1870 In 1873 he became chairman of the Birmingham school board, to which he had been elected three years before. The transfer to the city authorities of the gas and water works was largely due to his energy

During this time Chamberlain, a liberal in politics, became widely known as an advocate of ultra-radical measures, and gained great popularity with the masses As the motto for his party he would have: Free church, free land, free schools, and free labor Elected alderman in 1873, he was three times in succession elected mayor of Birmingham. He was defeated as a candidate for Parliament from Sheffield at the general election in 1874, but was returned unopposed for Birmingham two years later. In 1880, when the Liberals returned to power, Chamberlain was nominated President of the Board of Trade and admitted to a seat in the Cabinet. His influence within and without Parliament had been steadily increasing in the mean time, and he now came to be regarded as the leader of the radical wing of the Liberal party.

He became President of the Local Government Board after the election of 1886, but resigned in March of the same year, owing to his strong objection to Gladstone's Home Rule Bill From this time dates the formation of the Liberal-Unionist party, henceforth closely allied with the Conservatives, of which Chamberlain became the leader in the House of Commons. Chamberlain's hostile attitude to Gladstone, his secession from his old party, and his affiliation with the Conservative interests brought upon him much unfavorable criticism

When the Conservatives returned to power in 1895 Chamberlain took the portfolio of Colonial Secretary The so-called Ashantee War was an incident of his first year's tenure of that office He effectually cleared himself before a Parliamentary committee of any implication imputed to him in the Jameson raid in 1896 His management of the Transvaal affair, especially the manner in which he conducted the negotiations that led to the war with the two South African republics, is a matter of contemporaneous history. He was elected lord rector of Glasgow University in 1896.

THE FUTURE OF THE BRITISH EMPIRE

Delivered at a dinner given to celebrate the completion of the Natal Railway, London, November 6, 1895*

I THANK you sincerely for the hearty reception you have given to this toast. I appreciate very much the warmth of your welcome, and I see in it confirmation of the evidence which is afforded by the cordial and graceful telegram from the premier of Natal, which has been read by your chairman, and by other public and private communications that I have received, that any man who makes it his first duty, as I did, to draw closer together the different portions of the British Empire will meet with hearty sympathy, encouragement, and support. I thank my old friend and colleague, Sir Charles Tupper, for the kind manner in which he has spoken of me. He has said much, no doubt, that transcends my merits, but that is a circumstance so unusual in the life of a politician that I do not feel it in my heart to complain. I remember that Dr. Oliver Wendell Holmes, who was certainly one of the most genial Americans who ever visited these shores, said that when he was young he liked his praise in teaspoonfuls, that when he got older he preferred it in tablespoonfuls, and that in advanced years he was content to receive it in ladles. I confess that I am arriving at the period when I sympathize with Dr. Oliver Wendell Holmes.

Gentlemen, the occasion which has brought us together is an extremely interesting one. We are here to congratulate Natal, its government, and its people, and to congratulate ourselves on the completion of a great work of commercial enterprise and civilization, which one of our colonies, which happens

* This dinner was the first public occasion on which Mr. Chamberlain appeared in his official capacity as Secretary of State for the Colonies. His speech is in reply to the toast "The Right Honorable Joseph Chamberlain, Secretary of State for the Colonies," which was proposed by Sir Charles Tupper, High Commissioner of Canada.

to be the last to have been included in the great circle of self-governing communities, has brought to a successful conclusion, giving once more a proof of the vigor and the resolution which have distinguished all nations that have sprung from the parent British stock.

This occasion has been honored by the presence of the representatives of sister colonies, who are here to offer words of sympathy and encouragement; and, in view of the representative character of the gathering, I think, perhaps, I may be permitted, especially as this is the first occasion upon which I have publicly appeared in my capacity as Minister for the Colonies, to offer a few words of a general application.

I think it will not be disputed that we are approaching a critical state in the history of the relations between ourselves and the self-governing colonies. We are entering upon a chapter of our colonial history, the whole of which will probably be written in the next few years, certainly in the lifetime of the next generation, and which will be one of the most important in our colonial annals, since upon the events and policy which it describes will depend the future of the British Empire. That empire, gentlemen, that world-wide dominion to which no Englishman can allude without a thrill of enthusiasm and patriotism, which has been the admiration and perhaps the envy of foreign nations, hangs together by a thread so slender that it may well seem that even a breath would sever it.

There have been periods in our history, not so very far distant, when leading statesmen, despairing of the possibility of maintaining anything in the nature of a permanent union, have looked forward to the time when the vigorous communities to which they rightly entrusted the control of their own destinies would grow strong and independent, would assert their independence, and would claim entire separation from the parent stem. The time to which they look forward has arrived sooner than they expected. The conditions to which they refer have been more than fulfilled; and now these great communities, which have within them every element of national life, have taken their rank amongst the nations of the world; and I do not suppose that anyone would consider the idea of compelling them to remain within the empire as within the region of intelligent speculation. Yet, although, as I have said, the time has come, and the conditions have been fulfilled, the results which these statesmen anticipated have not followed. They felt, perhaps, overwhelmed by the growing burdens of the vast dominions of the British Crown. They may well have shrunk from the responsibilities and obligations which they involved; and so it happened that some of them looked forward not only without alarm, but with hopeful expectation to a severance of the union which now exists.

But if such feelings were ever entertained they are entertained no longer. As the possibility of separation has become greater, the desire for separation has become less. While we on our part are prepared to take our share of responsibility, and to do all that may fairly be expected from the mother country, and while we should look upon a separation as the greatest calamity that could befall us—our fellow-subjects on their part see to what a great inheritance they have come by mere virtue of their citizenship; and they must feel that no separate existence, however splendid, could compare with that which they enjoy equally with ourselves as joint heirs of all the traditions of the past, and as joint partakers of all the influence, resources, and power of the British Empire.

I rejoice at the change that has taken place. I rejoice at the wider patriotism, no longer confined to this small island, which embraces the whole of Greater Britain and which has carried to every clime British institutions and the best characteristics of the British race. How could it be otherwise? We have a common origin, we have a common history, a common language, a common literature, and a common love of liberty and law. We have common principles to assert, we have common interests to maintain. I said it was a slender thread that binds us together. I remember on one occasion having been shown a wire so fine and delicate that a blow might break it; yet I was told that it was capable of transmitting an electrical energy that would set powerful machinery in motion. May it not be the same with the relations which exist between the colonies and ourselves; and may not that thread of union be capable of carrying a force of sentiment and of sympathy which will yet be a potent factor in the history of the world?

There is a word which I am almost afraid to mention, lest at the very outset of my career I should lose my character as a practical statesman. I am told on every hand that imperial federation is a vain and empty dream. I will not contest that judgment, but I will say this: "That man must be blind indeed who does not see that it is a dream which has vividly impressed itself on the mind of the English-speaking race, and who does not admit that dreams of that kind, which have so powerful an influence upon the imagination of men, have somehow or another an unaccountable way of being realized in their own time." If it be a dream, it is a dream that appeals to the highest sentiments of patriotism, as well as to our material interests. It is a dream which is calculated to stimulate and to inspire everyone who cares for the future of the Anglo-Saxon people. I think myself that the spirit of the time is, at all events, in the direction of such a movement. How far it will carry us no man can tell, but, believe me, upon the temper and the tone in which we approached the solution of the problems which are now coming upon us depend the security and the maintenance of that world-wide dominion, that edifice of imperial rule which has been so ably built for us by those who have gone before.

Gentlemen, I admit that I have strayed somewhat widely from the toast which your chairman has committed to my charge. The toast is "The Prosperity of South Africa and the Natal and Transvaal Railway." As to South Africa, there can be no doubt as to its prosperity. We have witnessed in our own time a development of natural and mineral wealth in that country altogether beyond precedent or human knowledge; and what we have seen in the past, and what we see in the present, is bound to be far surpassed in the near future. The product of the mines, great as it is at present, is certain to be multiplied many fold, and before many years are over the mines of the Transvaal may be rivalled by the mines of Mashonaland or Matabeleland; and in the train of this great, exceptional, and wonderful prosperity, in the train of the diamond-digger and of the miner, will come a demand for labor which no man can measure—a demand for all the products of agriculture and of manufacture, in which not South Africa alone, but all the colonies and the mother-country itself must have a share.

The climate and soil leave nothing to be desired, and there is only one thing wanted—that is, a complete union and identity of sentiment and interest between the different States existing in South Africa. Gentlemen, I have no doubt that that union will be forthcoming—although it may not be immediately established. I do not shut my eyes to differences amongst friends which have unfortunately already arisen and which have not yet been arranged. I think these differences, if you look below the surface, will be found to be due principally to the fact that we have not yet achieved in South Africa that local federation which is the necessary preface to any serious consideration of the question of imperial federation. But, gentlemen, in these differences, my position, of course, renders it absolutely necessary that I should take no side. I pronounce no opinion, and it would not become me to offer any advice; although, if the good offices of my department were at any time invoked by those who are now separated, all I can say is that they would be heartily placed at their service.

Gentlemen, I wish success to the Natal Railway, and to every railway in South Africa. There is room for all. There is prosperity for all—enough to make the mouth of an English director positively water. There is success for all, if only they will not waste their resources in internecine conflict. I have seen with pleasure that a conference is being held in order to discuss, and I hope to settle, these differences. I trust that they may be satisfactorily arranged. In the mean time I congratulate our chairman, as representing this prosperous colony, upon the enterprise they have displayed, upon the difficulties they have surmounted, and on the success they have already achieved. And I hope for them—confidently hope—the fullest share in that prosperity which I predict without hesitation for the whole of South Africa.

ORATION ON ROBERT BURNS

—

BY

LORD ROSEBERY
(Archibald Philip Primrose)

ARCHIBALD PHILIP PRIMROSE, LORD ROSEBERY

Archibald Philip Primrose, Earl of Rosebery, was born in London May 7, 1847, and succeeded to the title on the death of his grandfather in 1868. He was educated at Eton and at Christ Church, Oxford. He made his first speech in Parliament in 1870, when Gladstone selected him to second the address to the speech from the throne. The first ten years of his public career are devoid of any notable incidents, though he took during all this time an active interest in the movements for social and educational reforms. He was elected Lord Rector of the University of Aberdeen in 1880. Lord Rosebery's public career as a Liberal statesman begins with his appointment as Under-Secretary of State for the Home Department in August, 1881 He became First Commissioner of Works in November, 1884. In Gladstone's next administration Rosebery was assigned the important post of Secretary of State for Foreign Affairs and won general approval for the tact and skill he displayed in settling the difficulties growing out of the Servo-Bulgarian war and the Greek claims for territorial indemnity.

Lord Rosebery remained a firm supporter of his chief when Gladstone brought forward his first Home Rule for Ireland Bill, when many political followers deserted their chief and the Liberal party. On Gladstone's return to power Lord Rosebery was appointed Foreign Minister a second time, and on the former's retirement from public life he was offered the Premiership by the Queen. The passing by of some of the older leaders of the Liberal party caused for a time a good deal of dissatisfaction and lack of support in the party. Rosebery was obliged to work with a small majority and had the misfortune to follow a leader of such great prestige as Mr. Gladstone. The Liberal majority gradually dwindled down and Lord Rosebery placed his resignation in the hands of the Queen

Lord Rosebery has long been and remains one of the most popular of the public men of England He is a man of broad views and is ever interested in movements to promote the betterment of the condition of the laboring classes As a public speaker he is in great demand and his public utterances are always received with consideration and respect. He is the author of the well-known monograph on the younger Pitt and a recognized authority on Robert Burns. His oration on the Scotch poet is given here.

ORATION ON ROBERT BURNS

Delivered before the tomb of Robert Burns, at Dumfries, Scotland, July 21, 1896.

L ADIES AND GENTLEMEN: I come here as a loyal burgess of Dumfries, to do honor to the greatest burgess of Dumfries. You, Mr. Provost, have laid upon me a great distinction but a great burden. Your most illustrious burgess obtained privileges for his children in respect of his burgess-ship, but you impose on your youngest burgess an honor that might well break anybody's back—that of attempting to do justice in any shape or fashion to the hero of to-day's ceremony. But we citizens of Dumfries have a special claim to be considered on this day. We are surrounded by the choicest and the most sacred haunts of the poet. You have in this town the house in which he died, the "Globe" where we could have wished that some phonograph had then existed which could have communicated to us some of his wise and witty and wayward talk. You have the street commemorated in M'Culloch's tragic anecdote when Burns was shunned by his former friends, and you have the paths by the Nith which are associated with some of his greatest work. You have near you the room in which the whistle was contended for, and in which, if mere legend is to be trusted, the immortal Dr. Gregory was summoned to administer his first powders to the survivors of that memorable debauch. You have the stack-yard in which, lying on his back and contemplating—

> "Thou lingering star, with lessening ray,
> That lov'st to greet the early morn,"

he wrote the lines " To Mary in Heaven "—perhaps the most pathetic of his poems. You have near you the walk to the river, where, in this transport, he passed his wife and children

without seeing them, " his brow flushed and his eyes shining "
with the lustre of "Tam o' Shanter." "I wish you had but
seen him," said his wife; " he was in such ecstasy that the
tears were happing down his cheeks." That is why we are
in Dumfries to-day. We come to honor Burns among these
immortal haunts of his.

But it is not to Dumfries alone that he is commemorated
to-day; for all Scotland will pay her tribute. And this, surely,
is but right. Mankind owes him a general debt. But the debt
of Scotland is special. For Burns exalted our race, he hal-
lowed Scotland and the Scottish tongue. Before his time we
had for a long period been scarcely recognized; we had been
falling out of the recollection of the world. From the time of
the union of the crowns, and still more from the time of the
legislative union, Scotland had lapsed into obscurity. Except
for an occasional riot or a Jacobite rising, her existence was
almost forgotten. She had, indeed, her Robertsons and her
Humes writing history to general admiration, but no trace of
Scottish authorship was discoverable in their works; indeed,
every flavor of national idiom was carefully excluded. The
Scottish dialect, as Burns called it, was in danger of perishing.
Burns seemed at this juncture to start to his feet and reassert
Scotland's claim to national existence; his Scottish notes rang
through the world, and he thus preserved the Scottish language
forever; for mankind will never allow to die that idiom in
which his songs and poems are enshrined. That is a part of
Scotland's debt to Burns.

But this is much more than a Scottish demonstration; it is a
collection of representatives from all quarters of the globe to
own a common allegiance and a common faith. It is not only
Scotsmen honoring the greatest of Scotsmen—we stretch far
beyond a kingdom or a race—we are rather a sort of poetical
Mohammedans gathered at a sort of poetical Mecca.

And yet we are assembled in our high enthusiasm under circumstances which are somewhat paradoxical. For with all the
appearance of joy, we celebrate not a festival, but a tragedy.
It is not the sunrise but the sunset that we commemorate. It
is not the birth of a new power into the world, the subtle germ
of a fame that is to survive and inspire the generations of men;
but it is perhaps more fitting that we celebrate the end and not

the beginning. For the coming of these figures is silent; it is their disappearance that we know. At this instant that I speak there may be born into the world the equal of a Newton or a Cæsar, but half of us would be dead before he had revealed himself. Their death is different. It may be gloomy and disastrous; it may come at a moment of shame or neglect; but by that time the man has carved his name somewhere on the temple of fame. There are exceptions, of course; cases where the end comes before the slightest, or any but the slightest, recognition—Chatterton choking in his garret, hunger of body and soul all unsatisfied; Millet selling his pictures for a song; nay, Shakespeare himself. But, as a rule, death in the case of genius closes the first act of a public drama; criticism and analysis may then begin their unbiassed work free from jealousy or friendship or personal consideration for the living. Then comes the third act, if third act there be.

No, it is a death, not a birth, that we celebrate. This day a century ago, in poverty, delirium, and distress, there was passing the soul of Robert Burns. To him death comes in clouds and darkness, the end of a long agony of body and soul; he is harassed with debt, his bodily constitution is ruined, his spirit is broken, his wife is daily expecting her confinement. He has lost almost all that rendered his life happy—much of friendship, credit, and esteem. Some score years before, one of the most charming of English writers, as he lay dying, was asked if his mind was at ease, and with his last breath Oliver Goldsmith owned that it was not. So it was with Robert Burns. His delirium dwelt on the horrors of a jail; he uttered curses on the tradesman who was pursuing him for debt. "What business," said he to his physician in a moment of consciousness, "what business has a physician to waste his time upon me? I am a poor pigeon not worth plucking. Alas! I have not feathers enough to carry me to my grave." For a year or more his health had been failing. He had a poet's body as well as a poet's mind; nervous, feverish, impressionable; and his constitution, which, if nursed and regulated, might have carried him to the limit of life, was unequal to the storm and stress of dissipation and a preying mind. In the previous autumn he had been seized with a rheumatic attack; his digestion had given way; he was sunk in melancholy and gloom. In his last April

he wrote to his friend Thomson, " By Babel's streams I've sate
and wept almost ever since I saw you last; I have only known
existence by the pressure of the heavy hand of sickness, and
have counted time by the repercussions of pain. Rheumatism,
cold, and fever have formed to me a terrible combination. I
close my eyes in misery, and open them without hope." It
was sought to revive him by sea-bathing, and he went to stay at
Brow-well. There he remained three weeks, but was under
no delusion as to his state.

" Well, madam," he said to Mrs. Riddell on arriving, " have
you any commands for the other world?" He sat that evening
with his old friend, and spoke manfully of his approaching
death, of the fate of his children, and his fame; sometimes in-
dulging in bitter-sweet pleasantry, but never losing the consciousness of his condition. In three weeks he wearied of the
fruitless hunt for health, and he returned home to die. He
was only just in time   When he re-entered his home on the
eighteenth he could no longer stand; he was soon delirious;
in three days he was dead. " On the fourth day," we are told,
" when his attendant held a cordial to his lips, he swallowed it
eagerly, rose almost wholly up, spread out his hands, sprang
forward nigh the whole length of the bed, fell on his face, and
expired."

I suppose there are many who can read the account of
these last months with composure. They are more fortunate
than I. There is nothing much more melancholy in all biog-
raphy. The brilliant poet, the delight of all society, from the
highest to the lowest, sits brooding in silence over the drama
of his spent life; the early innocent home, the plough and the
savor of fresh-turned earth, the silent communion with nature
and his own heart, the brief hour of splendor, the dark
hour of neglect, the mad struggle for forgetfulness, the bitterness of vanished homage, the gnawing doubt of fame, the dis-
tressful future of his wife and children—an endless witch-dance
of thought without clew or remedy, all perplexing, all soon to
end while he is yet young, as men reckon youth; though none
know so well as he that his youth is gone, his race is run, his
message delivered.

His death revived the flagging interest and pride that had
been felt for him. As usual, men began to realize what they

had lost when it was too late.   When it was known that he was dying the townspeople had shown anxiety and distress.   They recalled his fame and forgot his fall.   One man was heard to ask, with a touch of quaint simplicity, " Who do you think will be our poet now? "   The district set itself to prepare a public funeral for the poet who died penniless among them.   A vast concourse followed him to his grave.   The awkward squad, as he had foreseen and deprecated, fired volleys over his coffin. The streets were lined with soldiers, among them one who, within sixteen years, was to be Prime Minister.   And while the procession wended its gloomy way as if no element of tragedy were to be wanting, his widow's hour of travail arrived and she gave birth to the hapless child that had caused the father so much misgiving.   In this place and on this day it all seems present to us—the house of anguish, the thronged churchyard, the weeping neighbors.   We feel ourselves part of the mourning crowd.   We hear those dropping volleys and that muffled drum; we bow our heads as the coffin passes, and acknowledge with tears the inevitable doom.   Pass, heavy hearse, with thy weary freight of shattered hopes and exhausted frame; pass, with thy simple pomp of fatherless brains and sad moralizing friends; pass, with the sting of death to the victory of the grave; pass, with the perishable, and leave us the eternal.

It is rare to be fortunate in life; it is infinitely rarer to be fortunate in death.   " Happy in the occasion of his death," as Tacitus said of Agricola, is not a common epitaph.   It is comparatively easy to know how to live, but it is beyond all option and choice to compass the more difficult art of knowing when and how to die.   We can generally, by looking back, choose a moment in a man's life when he had been fortunate had he dropped down dead.   And so the question arises naturally to-day, Was Burns fortunate in his death—that death which we commemorate?   There can, I fancy, be only one answer; it was well that he died when he did; it might even been better for himself had he died a little earlier.   The terrible letters that he wrote two years before to Mrs. Riddell and Mr. Cunningham betoken a spirit mortally wounded.   In those last two years the cloud settles, never to be lifted.   " My constitution and frame were *ab origine* blasted with a deep incurable taint of hypochondria which poisons my existence."   He found perhaps

some pleasure in the composition of his songs, some occasional
relief in the society of boon companions; but the world was
fading before him.

There is an awful expression in Scotland which one never
hears without a pang, " So-and-so is done," meaning that he is
physically worn out.   Burns was " done."   He was struggling
on like a wounded deer to his death.   He had often faced the
end, and not unwillingly.   " Can it be possible," he once wrote
to Mrs. Dunlop, " that when I resign this frail, feverish being
I shall still find myself in conscious existence?   When the last
gasp of agony has announced that I am no more to those who
know me and the few who love me; when the cold, unconscious
corse is resigned to the earth to be the prey of reptiles and
become a trodden clod, shall I be yet warm in life, enjoying or
enjoyed?"   Surely that reads as if he foresaw this day and
would fain be with us—as indeed he may be.   Twelve years
before he had faced death in a less morbid spirit:

> " Why [he asked] am I loath to leave this earthly scene?
>   Have I so found it full of pleasing charms?
> Some days of joy, with draughts of ill between,
>   Some gleams of sunshine, 'mid renewing storms."

He had, perhaps, never enjoyed life so much as is supposed,
though he had turned to it a brave, cheerful, unflinching face,
and the last years had been years of misery.   " God have mercy
on me," he wrote years before the end, " a poor damned, incau-
tious, duped, unfortunate fool!   The sport, the miserable victim of rebellious pride, hypochondriac imagination, agonizing
sensibility, and bedlam passions."   There was truth in this out-
burst.   At any rate, his most devoted friends—and to be an ad-
mirer of Burns is to be his friend—may wish that he had not
lived to write the letter to Mr. Clark, piteously pleading that a
harmless toast may not be visited hardly upon him; or that to
Mrs. Riddell, beginning—" I write you from the regions of
hell and the horrors of the damned "; or to be harried by his
official superiors as a political suspect; shunned by his fashion-
able friends for the same reason; wandering like a neglected
ghost in Dumfries, avoided and ignored.   " That's all over
now, my young friend," he said, speaking of his reign in society, " and werena my heart licht I wad dee."   All this was in

1794. Had he died before then, it might have been happier for himself, and we should have lost some parts of his life which we would rather forget; but posterity could not have spared him; we could not have lost the exquisite songs which we owe to those years; but, above all, the supreme creed and comfort which he bequeathed to the world—

"A man's a man for a' that,"

would have remained undelivered.

One may, perhaps, go further and say that poets—or those whom the gods love—should die young. This is a hard saying, but it will not greatly affect the bills of mortality. And it applies only to poets of the first rank; while even here it has its exceptions, and illustrious exceptions they are. But surely the best poetry is produced before middle age, before the morning and its illusions have faded, before the heaviness of noon and the baleful cool of evening. Few men, too, can bear the strain of a poet's temperament through many years. At any rate, we may feel sure of this, that Burns had produced his best, that he would never again have produced a " Tam o' Shanter," or a " Cottar's Saturday Night," or a " Jolly Beggars "; and that long before his death, though he could still write lines affluent with tenderness and grace, "the hand of pain and sorrow and care," to use his own words, "had lain heavy upon" him.

And this leads to another point. To-day is not merely the melancholy anniversary of death, but the rich and incomparable fulfilment of prophecy. For this is the moment to which Burns looked when he said to his wife, " Don't be afraid; I'll be more respected a hundred years after I am dead than I am at present! " To-day the hundred years are completed, and we can judge of the prediction. On that point we must all be unanimous. Burns had honor in his lifetime, but his fame has rolled like a snowball since his death, and it rolls on. There is, indeed, no parallel to it in the world; it sets the calculations of compound interest at defiance. He is not merely the watchword of a nation that carries and implants Burns-worship all over the globe as birds carry seeds, but he has become the champion and patron saint of democracy. He bears the banner of the essential equality of man. His birthday is celebrated —137 years after its occurrence—more universally than that of any human being. He reigns over a greater dominion than any empire that the world has ever seen. Nor does the ardor of his devotees decrease. Ayr and Ellisland, Mauchline and Dumfries, are the shrines of countless pilgrims. Burns statues are a hardy annual. The production of Burns manuscripts was a lucrative branch of industry until it was checked by untimely intervention. The editions of Burns are as the sands of the sea. No canonized name in the calendar excites so blind and enthusiastic a worship. Whatever Burns may have contemplated in his prediction, whatever dream he may have fondled in the wildest moments of elation, must have fallen utterly short of the reality. And it is all spontaneous. There is no puff, no advertisement, no manipulation. Intellectual cosmetics of that kind are frail and fugitive; they rarely survive their subject; they would not have availed here. Not was there any glamour attached to the poet; rather the reverse. He has stood by himself; he has grown by himself. It is himself and no other that we honor.

But what had Burns in his mind when he made this prediction? It might be whimsically urged that he was conscious that the world had not yet seen his masterpiece, for the " Jolly Beggars " was not published till some time after his death. But that would not be sufficient, for he had probably forgotten its existence. Nor do I think he spoke at haphazard. What were perhaps present to his mind were the fickleness of his contemporaries towards him, his conviction of the essential splendor of his work, the consciousness that the incidents of his later years had unjustly obscured him, and that his true figure would be perceived as these fell away into forgetfulness or were measured at their true value. If so, he was right in his judgment, for his true life began with his death; with the body passed all that was gross and impure; the clear spirit stood revealed, and soared at once to its accepted place among the fixed stars, in the firmament of the rare immortals.

THE DESERTION OF GENERAL GORDON

—

BY

LORD CHURCHILL

(Randolph Henry Spencer Churchill)

RANDOLPH HENRY SPENCER CHURCHILL, LORD CHURCHILL

1849—1895

Randolph Henry Spencer Churchill, Lord Churchill, was the second son of the sixth Duke of Marlborough, and was born February 13, 1849 He was educated at Merton's College, Oxford In 1874 Churchill was returned to Parliament for Woodstock, which seat he held till 1885 The same year he married a daughter of Leonard Jerome, of New York

Little was heard of Lord Churchill during the first years of his parliamentary career From 1880 onward he became conspicuous both in the House of Commons and on public platforms for the violence with which he attacked the Liberal party He was, for some time during this period, the leader of the so-called fourth party, consisting of a coterie of ultra-conservative members in the House.

On the accession of the Conservatives to power in 1885 he filled the office of Secretary of State for India, where his short tenure of office was marked by the annexation of Upper Burmah It was during this time that Churchill's career gave the brightest promise for the future He was beginning to be regarded as the Tory leader, and it was commonly said that the mantle of Lord Beaconsfield had fallen on the young, able and untiring chief of the Tory democracy

After the defeat of the Conservatives in 1885 and their return to power after six months, in the same year, Lord Churchill filled the office of Chancellor of the Exchequer and became leader of his party in the House of Commons His resignation in the same year was a surprise to both his political followers as well as his opponents; but it is not unlikely that ill-health, brought on by over-exertion, was responsible for this step In a letter conveying his resignation he wrote to Lord Salisbury that he was resolved to sacrifice himself on the altar of thrift and economy. His attacks on the disbursing departments of the government were henceforth sharp and incisive, but he spoke and voted steadfastly on the side of the Conservatives His speech on the "Desertion of General Gordon" made a great sensation at the time of its delivery. Lord Churchill died in 1895.

THE DESERTION OF GENERAL GORDON

Delivered in the House of Commons, May 13, 1884

I DO not think that it is necessary to debate this question with any great amount of heat, or with set oratorical phrases, or with great warmth of invective or vitupera-tion. The question itself is as simple a question as ever pre-sented itself to Parliament. The motion before the House is couched in terms of extreme moderation. The Prime Minis-ter said that it was not a manly or courageous motion; I doubt whether the Prime Minister or any one of his colleagues is a judge of what is manly or courageous. Those adjectives rep-resent qualities in which Her Majesty's Government have proved themselves conspicuously deficient. But I think that it was a strange criticism on the part of the Prime Minister. What is the motion of the right honorable baronet? It is a motion expressing regret that the efforts of General Gordon have not been properly seconded by the acts of the Government at home, and expressing a determination to provide now for the safety of General Gordon. I myself can see nothing unmanly or wanting in courage in such a motion as that; but I am bound to say that I can see a great deal that is wanting in courage in the Prime Minister's speech last night. I wonder whether the Prime Minister recollects an incident which took place in 1830. The right honorable gentleman would have been about twenty years of age, and I have no doubt was well acquainted with the political incidents of that day. The Duke of Wellington made a speech on the subject of parliamentary reform. When he sat down there were buzzings and whisperings and evident con-sternation on his own side; so much so that the Duke asked what was the cause of it, and the reply was, " Your Grace has announced the fall of your Government, that is all." If the Prime Minister had had the advantage of occupying the posi-

419

tion which I occupy, and had been able to see the deepening gloom which settled down on his followers as he proceeded with his remarks, and the blank dismay that overspread their faces, and if he had heard the buzzings and whisperings and consternation in the lobby, and had asked the noble lord, the member for Flintshire, what was the cause of it, if the noble lord, the member for Flintshire, was an intelligent and able noble lord, he would have replied, " Sir, you have annnounced the fall of your Government."

What was that speech? It was an announcement in the most solemn manner on the part of Her Majesty's Government, by their chief representative, of the final and definite abandonment of General Gordon. Of that there can be absolutely no doubt whatever in the mind of anyone who listened to him or who has read the report of his speech. That speech reminded me of the conduct of a Roman governor of eighteen hundred years ago, who washed his hands in the face of the multitude. That speech announced in the most open and unmistakable manner the abandonment of General Gordon. This is a course which I am certain the country is not prepared to ratify, and which I think Parliament is not prepared to adopt.

What was the mission of General Gordon? What was its nature? The mission, to my mind, was in theory and intention one of the noblest ever undertaken. The object of the mission was twofold. It was to rescue the garrisons in the Soudan, numbering something like 30,000, exclusive of women and children, and it was to restore freedom and tranquillity to harassed and oppressed tribes. The whole nation acquiesced in that mission, as, I believe, it acquiesced in the abandonment of the Soudan. I do not think it could be asserted for one moment that any person on the Opposition side of the House has ever advocated the re-conquest of the Soudan, and I may say that I have never heard anybody who is responsible on this side of the House censure the abandonment of the Soudan. But, although the nation and the Opposition acquiesced in the abandonment of the Soudan, the nation felt deeply the solemn and high duties which that abandonment imposed upon them, and the nation hailed with pleasure, and I may almost say with rapture, the mission of General Gordon, and was prepared to condone many an error because the Government had entrusted those duties to be discharged by so generous, so gallant, and so noble an officer as General Gordon. I do not believe that any mission which ever left this country had ever created so much interest; but the very intensity of the interest excited is the measure of the responsibility imposed upon the Government to do their part in assisting General Gordon to carry his dangerous mission to a successful conclusion. The Prime Minister said last night that the Government had discharged their responsibility to the utmost. I take leave to traverse the right honorable gentleman's statement, and say that the Government have not discharged one bit of that responsibility. I assert that, as it was the duty of the Government to have seconded to the very utmost the mission of General Gordon, they ought, at the outset, to have considerably increased their force in Egypt, and to have moved British troops up the Nile. The first appearance of General Gordon in Upper Egypt prevented disturbances. He found a state of semi-order, and he pacified it completely. There can be no doubt that if it had been known that the British force had been increased, and that British troops had been moved up the Nile, the first effect of the mission, instead of being transient, would have been permanent. More than that, the season was exceptionally favorable for the movement of troops, and that movement would have been perfectly consistent with the pacific character of the mission of General Gordon. Material support is not out of character with a mission which is essentially pacific; and if any supporter or member of the Government should deny that assertion, I have only to point to the conduct of the Government with respect to Suakin completely to make out my case. The conduct of the Government in that case was to give material support to the efforts to restore order in that part of the Soudan—and why should material support have been limited to Suakin? I submit that that was the first failure of the Government to recognize their responsibility to General Gordon. Then the Government had another warning Soon after General Gordon arrived at Khartoum he made an urgent appeal to the. Government to send him Zebehr Pacha I have never been one of those who have been disposed to blame the Government for not acceding to that request. I think not only that Zebehr is a man with whom no British Government ought to have any connection, but I believe that he would have done his best to assassinate General Gordon when he got to Khartoum. But the Prime Minister, curiously enough, told the House last night that he thought General Gordon was right in asking for Zebehr, and said he had been disposed to go almost any length to meet the request, and gave an extraordinary reason for not doing what he said was right, and what he was prepared to go almost any length to do. He said, " I did not do what I thought I should do, because I feared I might be placed in a minority."

[Mr Gladstone: The noble lord has represented what I said with perfect inaccuracy I did not say that I should in any case have sent Zebehr, but I said that, whereas the arguments for sending Zebehr might have been very nearly balanced, and, in the minds of some, might have preponderated, the one argument that was conclusive against it was not that the Government would have been placed in a minority, but that the sending of Zebehr would have been stopped by a vote in the House of Commons.]

Lord Churchill: That is exactly the same thing. If the Prime Minister had come down to the House and proposed to send Zebehr, and a vote had been taken against him, does anyone think that he would have retained office? It would have been a vote of censure on the Government. My contention, therefore was right. I feel that that is a fair construction to put upon the words of the Prime Minister. It is in accordance with former acts of the right honorable gentleman, because I recollect that he once said he did not restore order in Ireland when he might have done so, because he was not certain whether at that time he should have obtained a majority of the House of Commons. But what I wonder at is, that the Government, knowing the character of General Gordon, his love of the Soudanese, and his low opinion of this abandoned ruffian Zebehr, and seeing that General Gordon had made an appeal for him to be sent to his assistance, did not have their eyes opened to the fact that General Gordon's position at Khartoum had become untenable, that his mission was far more desperate than had been imagined, and that his position was one of imminent peril. I wonder, and shall wonder forever, that the Government at that time did not take measures to provide for the safety of General Gordon—to increase the British forces at Cairo, and to move British troops up the Nile. It was on February 27th that the Government refused to allow Zebehr to go to Khartoum, and certainly at that time a movement of troops might have been carried on without the slightest risk. That is the second conspicuous, undeniable failure of the Government to provide for the relief of General Gordon. The Prime Minister taunted the Opposition because they cheered him when he announced the expedition to Suakin. We cheered that announcement, not because we were in love with the dangers of the expedition, and not because we did not see them, but because it occurred to us that the dangers were far outweighed by the advantages which would obviously result from the expedition. The object of that expedition was threefold. It was to preserve the safety of the ports of the Red Sea, to relieve Tokar, and to open up a route to Berber. On those grounds alone did we cheer the announcement of the Government; but when we found, to our disgust and dismay, that not one of those objects had been in any part obtained, we lost no time in condemning the expedition to Suakin, and supporting the motion of the honorable member for Northampton. That was a clear and consistent course of conduct   General Gordon was not in favor of that expedition; but I can quite understand that, under the circumstances in which he was placed, he would not like to put an absolute negative upon it. General Gordon, however, did not imagine that the Government would have allowed the troops to fight two bloody and unprovoked battles, and then sail away without having effected anything.

Let me compare the Government's treatment of Suakin with their treatment of General Gordon. What is Suakin? Suakin is a dirty, wretched, plague-stricken port on the Red Sea, of no value to Egypt, or to anyone but the Soudanese tribes. What is General Gordon? The Prime Minister told us last night that General Gordon is " a great personality "; more than that, he is the envoy of the Queen; more than that, Gordon's life is invaluable to his country, because a nation does not turn out Gordons by the dozen every day. The Prime Minister was angry with the right honorable gentleman last night because he said that the Government ought to have given material sup-

port to General Gordon.   But why was it wrong to do that for
General Gordon, a great personality, the envoy of the Queen,
a man invaluable to his country, which you did so lavishly and
so uselessly for this dirty port on the Red Sea?   For this port
the Government shed blood in torrents, they poured out money
like water; but for Gordon they refused to advance one British
soldier one single step, or to provide him with one single half-
penny of money.   In comparing the treatment of Suakin by the
Government with the treatment of General Gordon, the logic
of facts is hopelessly fatal to their position.   As I listened to
the Prime Minister last night a curious idea came into my head.
I thought of the singularly different—the inexplicably different
—manner in which different individuals appeal to his sympathies.   I compared his efforts in the cause of General Gordon
with his efforts in the cause of Mr. Bradlaugh.   I remembered the courage, the perseverance, the eloquence, he displayed and the amount of time of the House of Commons which
was consumed by the Government in their desperate adherence
to that man.   If the hundredth part of those invaluable moral
qualities bestowed upon Mr. Bradlaugh had been given to the
support of a Christian hero, the success of General Gordon's
mission would have been at this time assured.   And this struck
me as most remarkable when the Prime Minister sat down—
that the finest speech he ever delivered in the House of Commons was in support of Mr. Bradlaugh, and the worst speech
he ever delivered, was, by common consent, in the cause of the
Christian hero.   That is an instructive historical contrast.
The Prime Minister made a most extraordinary remark last
night which reveals the incapacity of the present Government
for dealing with those difficult commotions abroad.   He said,
in reply to the right honorable gentleman who questioned the
wisdom of the Government in not sending troops to Berber,
" What would be the use of sending a few British troops?"
Well, for fifty years the Prime Minister has been more or less
in the service of the Crown, and has been identified with some
of the most glorious exploits of British valor, and after all that
experience he gets up and asks the House of Commons what
would be the value of a few hundred British soldiers?   Surely,
when he asked this question he must have been thinking, not
of the early and military glories with which he was connected,

but of the unfortunate events of Laing's Nek and Majuba Hill. For my part, I think the value of a few hundred soldiers at Berber would have been great. They would in the first place have opened up the road across the desert. Their very passing across the desert would have produced an effect; it would have confirmed the wavering, given hope to the fugitives, and saved the garrisons. It would have been very apparent to everyone in that part of the world that those British troops were merely the precursors of others, and it would have prevented the present isolation of General Gordon. The troops were ready and anxious to go; General Graham was anxious to go. I do not know whether the Prime Minister is aware of it, because in his exalted position he may be denied the knowledge open to humbler men—but the feeling of the troops coming away from Suakin was one of utter and intense disgust. Because those brave men, who whenever they perform deeds of fame are exposed to the jeers and jibes of honorable gentlemen opposite—these brave men were filled with the conviction that all their bravery had gone for nothing, and, more than that, that they had slaughtered brave and gallant foes for no purpose whatever. The whole of that force was only too anxious, too desirous, by opening up the road to Berber, to place something tangible on record as the result of their exertions. The Prime Minister argued in a most extraordinary manner that he and his colleagues had no longer any duties to perform toward the Soudan garrison. He sent General Gordon to get the garrisons out; General Gordon had failed; and, really, he and his colleagues cannot any further be bothered with the matter. That was the whole drift of his speech, because the House noticed how he descended upon the right honorable baronet, and asked which garrisons were to be rescued—that of Gondola, Bahr Gazelle, or what others? Your duty is to recognize the claims of every one of them. They were recognized by a unanimous House of Commons when General Gordon was sent out. I adhere to that assertion. It was the duty of General Gordon to rescue them when you sent him out, and the duty of rescuing them lies heavily upon this country, that placed them in peril by abandoning the Soudan. At any rate, there is one duty, and that is the duty of England to support her envoy. The position of an envoy is sacred not so much to the country to which he is sent, because that may be an uncivilized country, but sacred to the country which sends him out, and essentially sacred when that envoy is placed in a position of peril in a distant land. The fear to go to war in support of an envoy is a certain indication of a decaying empire, and the abandonment of an envoy by a British Government, with the sanction of a British Parliament, is the sure sign of a falling state.

The right honorable gentleman says that in October he would consider this question again—a very reasonable allowance of time to procure the information of which the Government stands in need; and he imagines that by October, having obtained that information, the Government will be able to devote their attention to the rescue of General Gordon. Does he think that England will wait till October to hear what he is going to do? If so, how low an estimate must the Prime Minister have formed of the countrymen who so long have worshipped and put their trust in him! Such is their reward for the devotion of many years! If the Prime Minister thinks that the British people will wait till the month of October, does he think that the Mahdi will wait till then? Because, whatever may be the qualities of the British people, the Mahdi has shown qualities which will enable us to calculate the rate of his advance. Does not the right honorable gentleman propose to take any steps to guard the inhabitants of Lower Egypt against the incursion of the Mahdi until the time when he says climatic influences will not endanger the health of the troops? If the right honorable gentleman does not propose to take any steps for that purpose, I cannot believe that the decision of the Government will be indorsed by the House of Commons. Very little would be necessary now to arrest the Madhi—a slight movement of troops, a slight movement of ships, a little more energy, a little more common-sense, a little more consistency in your foreign despatches, and the thing would be done. But now the Prime Minister is going to meet the powers of Europe in conference. He is going to meet after this debate—if he survives it—he is going to meet in conference on the Egyptian question powers represented by standing armies numbering millions of men. I like conferences, and advocate them under certain conditions. But I will illustrate my meaning. Compare the position which Lord Beaconsfield occupied at the Congress of Berlin with the position which the Prime Minister will occupy at the conference which is now to take place. The one, by a mere movement of the fleet, and by movement of troops, had arrested the advance of the Russian army at the very threshold of the goal to which for a century they had been approaching; the other appears before the conference as having been afraid, and as having stated his fear in this House, to arrest the march of a barbarian and to rescue an English envoy I should like to know whether the Government can appear on terms of equality with the other powers in such circumstances as these. The Government go to the conference having done a dishonorable act. The conference will not be so much a conference for the consideration of European affairs, of powers meeting on terms of equality, as a tribunal called together to pronounce judgment on the crimes of a delinquent and recreant nation. The Government denounce the motives of those who bring forward this vote of censure, and say that it is dictated not by a love of country, but by a spirit of party. The Prime Minister has had fifty years of parliamentary experience, and I ask him to tell us, from motives of intelligent curiosity, whether he ever knew a vote of censure which had not for its object and for its end a transference of power, and, if that is the general character of a vote of censure, why is the particular vote of censure which has been moved by the right honorable gentleman on the front Opposition bench so vile? The right honorable gentleman says that the Opposition is ambitious and unjust. I should like to know, when the Prime Minister conducted in 1877 that agitation which electrified the country, whether he was not ambitious and whether he was not unjust? Were not these adjectives applicable to him when he boasted at Oxford that for a considerable time he had rested neither night nor day in his endeavors to thwart the policy of the Government of that time? What does this transference of power mean which the Prime Minister says is so mischievous and pernicious? So far as I can make out, it means the immediate rescue of Gordon, as opposed to the autumnal and uncertain rescue of Gordon in six months' time; it means the restoration of order in Egypt, as opposed to the continuance of anarchy; it means the repulse of the Mahdi, as opposed to a general Mahommedan rising; it means, I believe, taking Egypt under

English protection, and extending the might of Britain over
that disturbed land for a time. That is what I believe the transference of power means in regard to Egypt. May I ask what
it means at home? For the Whigs it means a cessation of voting day after day that black is white. What does it mean to
the Radical party? It means that, after abandoning for four
years every principle on which they came into power, they
will at length be able to reconcile their principles with their
votes. But we are told that there must not be a transference of
power because it is necessary to pass the reform bill. Well,
reform is no longer a party question, and a treatment of the
question by the Opposition proves that it would be dealt with
by them on a more complete and larger basis. The object of
this vote of censure is a transference of power, and the sooner
that comes the better for the country. The Government, when
they went to Egypt, abandoned every atom of principle which
they possessed, and Egypt has been their Nemesis, and I believe will be their ruin. But the whole question is at last,
thank God, presented to us in an intelligible form: Will you
or will you not rescue Gordon now? Answer, " Ay " or " No."
The people of England and Scotland and of Ireland also say
" Ay." The Prime Minister and a few Radical fanatics alone
say " No "; but, great as is the Prime Minister's power, long
as has been his career, dazzling as is his eloquence, and undoubtedly glorious as is his name, on a question such as this
the odds are so overwhelmingly great that even the Prime
Minister himself must either submit or resign.

THE GREATEST THING IN THE WORLD

BY

HENRY DRUMMOND

HENRY DRUMMOND

1851—1897

Henry Drummond was especially the product of an era in which the most extreme doctrines of scientific agnosticism had become popularized, and by being popularized had often been misunderstood to a degree that was in danger of destroying faith in Christianity, if not in all religious theories, commonly so called. He was born in Stirling, Scotland, in 1851, and was educated for the ministry, taking university courses at Edinburgh and Tübingen, and subsequently passing through the Free Church Divinity Hall On his ordination to the ministry, his mind was widened during his incumbency of a Presbyterian mission in the island of Malta He became lecturer and afterwards Professor of Biology in the Free Church College at Glasgow, in 1878, and subsequently travelled through the United States, Africa, and Australia, lecturing on the sociological, scientific, and moral aspects of Christian religion His religious enthusiasm and charming personality made many friends and admirers, and his influence among young and earnest men was remarkable.

His study of biology had naturally made him fully acquainted with the theories of Darwin and Huxley, and his wish to reconcile evolution with a notion of psychology that would not militate against the assumptions of Christianity prompted his work, "Natural Law in the Spiritual World," which, while it did not meet with the assent of the scientific world, was undoubtedly of much use in strengthening in their religious belief many of the readers to whom the volume was addressed. The popularity of this treatise is proved by the fact that it has been translated, after passing through many English editions, into French, German, Dutch, and Norwegian. There can, however, be no doubt that Drummond was on much safer ground when he produced his inimitable treatise, "The Greatest Thing in the World." This work is a most acute and practical enlargement of St. Paul's celebrated chapter on charity, or rather love. Clearness and simplicity of style, glowing devotion, and a certain strain of intense enthusiasm, which sometimes rises into eloquence, characterize this essay or address, which appeals to mankind at large, without distinction of nationality, intellectual prepossession, or religious sect It is a work which must be accepted without challenge as a clear and vivid expression of humanitarian sentiment, perfectly in harmony with the highest Christian idealism.

Drummond had early associated himself with the evangelists, Moody and Sankey, who induced him to accompany them from time to time on their preaching circuits. While he lectured on strictly scientific subjects during the week, he addressed large audiences, principally of workingmen, on Sundays, when he dealt with themes undoubtedly nearer to his heart. One fruit of his travels was his volume "Tropical Africa," but he returned to his religio-scientific line of thought in his "Ascent of Man" His last work was "Pax Vobiscum." He died in 1897, in his forty-sixth year, of consumption. His early death, due doubtless, in some measure, to his indefatigable labors, was deeply deplored through the length and breadth of Christendom.

THE GREATEST THING IN THE WORLD

EVERYONE has asked himself the great question of antiquity as of the modern world: What is the *summum bonum*—the supreme good? You have life before you Once only you can live it. What is the noblest object of desire, the supreme gift to covet?

We have been accustomed to be told that the greatest thing in the religious world is faith. That great word has been the keynote for centuries of the popular religion; and we have easily learned to look upon it as the greatest thing in the world. Well, we are wrong. If we have been told that, we may miss the mark. I have taken you, in the chapter which I have just read, to Christianity at its source; and there we have seen, " The greatest of these is love." It is not an oversight. Paul was speaking of faith just a moment before. He says, " If I have all faith, so that I can remove mountains, and have not love, I am nothing." So far from forgetting, he deliberately contrasts them, " Now abideth faith, hope, love," and without a moment's hesitation the decision falls, " The greatest of these is love."

And it is not prejudice. A man is apt to recommend to others his own strong point. Love was not Paul's strong point. The observing student can detect a beautiful tenderness growing and ripening all through his character as Paul gets old; but the hand that wrote, " The greatest of these is love," when we meet it first, is stained with blood.

Nor is this letter to the Corinthians peculiar in singling out love as the *summum bonum*. The masterpieces of Christianity are agreed about it. Peter says, " Above all things have fervent love among yourselves." Above all things. And John goes further, " God is love." And you remember the profound remark which Paul makes elsewhere, " Love is the fulfilling of the law." Did you ever think what he meant by that? In

those days men were working their passage to heaven by keeping the Ten Commandments, and the hundred and ten other
commandments which they had manufactured out of them.
Christ said, I will show you a more simple way. If you do one
thing, you will do these hundred and ten things, without ever
thinking about them. If you love, you will unconsciously fulfil the whole law. And you can readily see for yourselves how
that must be so. Take any of the commandments. "Thou
shalt have no other gods before Me." If a man love God, you
will not require to tell him that. Love is the fulfilling of that
law. "Take not His name in vain." Would he ever dream of
taking His name in vain if he loved Him? "Remember the
Sabbath day to keep it holy." Would he not be too glad to have
one day in seven to dedicate more exclusively to the object of
his affection? Love would fulfil all these laws regarding God.
And so, if he loved man, you would never think of telling him
to honor his father and mother. He could not do anything else.
It would be preposterous to tell him not to kill. You could only
insult him if you suggested that he should not steal—how could
he steal from those he loved? It would be superfluous to beg
him not to bear false witness against his neighbor. If he loved
him it would be the last thing he would do. And you would
never dream of urging him not to covet what his neighbors had.
He would rather they possessed it than himself. In this way
"Love is the fulfilling of the law."

It is the rule for fulfilling all rules, the new commandment
for keeping all the old commandments, Christ's one secret of
the Christian life.

Now Paul had learned that; and in this noble eulogy he has
given us the most wonderful and original account extant of
the *summum bonum*. We may divide it into three parts. In
the beginning of the short chapter, we have love constrasted;
in the heart of it we have love analyzed; towards the end, we
have love defended as the supreme gift.

THE CONTRAST.—Paul begins by contrasting love with other
things that men in those days thought much of. I shall not
attempt to go over those things in detail. Their inferiority is
already obvious.

He contrasts it with eloquence. And what a noble gift it is,
the power of playing upon the souls and wills of men, and

rousing them to lofty purposes and holy deeds. Paul says, "If I speak with the tongues of men and of angels, and have not love, I am become as sounding brass, or a tinkling cymbal." And we all know why. We have all felt the brazenness of words without emotion, the hollowness, the unaccountable unpersuasiveness of eloquence behind which lies no love.

He contrasts it with prophecy. He contrasts it with mysteries. He contrasts it with faith He contrasts it with charity. Why is love greater than faith? Because the end is greater than the means. And why is it greater than charity? Because the whole is greater than the part. Love is greater than faith, because the end is greater than the means. What is the use of having faith? It is to connect the soul with God. And what is the object of connecting man with God? That he may become like God. But God is love. Hence faith, the means, is in order to love, the end. Love, therefore, obviously is greater than faith. It is greater than charity, again, because the whole is greater than a part. Charity is only a little bit of love, one of the innumerable avenues of love, and there may even be, and there is, a great deal of charity without love. It is a very easy thing to toss a copper to a beggar on the street; it is generally an easier thing than not to do it. Yet love is just as often in the withholding.

We purchase relief from the sympathetic feelings roused by the spectacle of misery, at the copper's cost. It is too cheap for us, and often too dear for the beggar. If we really loved him we would either do more for him, or less.

Then Paul contrasts it with sacrifice and martyrdom. And I beg the little band of would-be missionaries—and I have the honor to call some of you by this name for the first time—to remember that though you give your bodies to be burned, and have not love, it profits nothing! You can take nothing greater to the heathen world than the impress and reflection of the love of God upon your own character. That is the universal language. It will take you years to speak in Chinese, or in the dialects of India. From the day you land, that language of love, understood by all, will be pouring forth its unconscious eloquence It is the man who is the missionary, it is not his words. His character is his message. In the heart of Africa, among the great lakes, I have come across black men and women who remembered the only white man they ever saw before—David Livingstone; and as you cross his footsteps in that dark continent, men's faces light up as they speak of the kind doctor who passed there years ago. They could not understand him; but they felt the love that beat in his heart. Take into your new sphere of labor, where you also mean to lay down your life, that simple charm, and your lifework must succeed. You can take nothing greater, you need take nothing less. It is not worth while going if you take anything else. You may take every accomplishment; you may be braced for every sacrifice; but if you give your body to be burned, and have not love, it will profit you and the cause of Christ nothing.

THE ANALYSIS.—After contrasting love with these things, Paul, in three verses, very short, gives us an amazing analysis of what this supreme thing is. I ask you to look at it. It is a compound thing, he tells us It is like light. As you have seen a man of science take a beam of light and pass it through a crystal prism, as you have seen it come out on the other side of the prism broken up into its component colors—red, and blue, and yellow, and violet, and orange, and all the colors of the rainbow—so Paul passes this thing, love, through the magnificent prism of his inspired intellect, and it comes out on the other side broken up into its elements And in these few words we have what one might call the spectrum of love, the analysis of love. Will you observe what its elements are? Will you notice that they have common names; that they are virtues which we hear about every day; that they are things which can be practised by every man in every place in life, and how, by a multitude of small things and ordinary virtues, the supreme things, the *summum bonum*, is made up? The spectrum of love has nine ingredients:

Patience—" Love suffereth long."
Kindness—" And is kind."
Generosity—" Love envieth not."
Humility—" Love vaunteth not itself, and is not puffed up."
Courtesy—" Doth not behave itself unseemly."
Unselfishness—" Seeketh not her own."
Good Temper—" Is not easily provoked."
Guilelessness—" Thinketh no evil."

Sincerity—" Rejoiceth not in iniquity, but rejoiceth in the truth."

Patience; kindness; generosity; humility; courtesy; unselfishness; good temper; guilelessness; sincerity—these make up the supreme gift, the stature of the perfect man. You will observe that all are in relation to men, in relation to life, in relation to the known to-day and the near to-morrow, and not to the unknown eternity. We hear much of love to God; Christ spoke much of love to man. We make a great deal of peace with heaven; Christ made much of peace on earth. Religion is not a strange or added thing, but the inspiration of the secular life, the breathing of an eternal spirit through this temporal world. The supreme thing, in short, is not a thing at all, but the giving of a further finish to the multitudinous words and acts which make up the sum of every common day.

There is no time to do more than make a passing note upon each of these ingredients. Love is patience. This is the normal attitude of love, love passive, love waiting to begin; not in a hurry; calm; ready to do its work when the summons comes, but meantime wearing the ornament of a meek and quiet spirit. Love suffers long; beareth all things; believeth all things; hopeth all things. For love understands, and therefore waits.

Kindness   Love active. Have you ever noticed how much of Christ's life was spent in doing kind things—in merely doing kind things? Run over it with that in view, and you will find that He spent a great proportion of His time simply in making people happy, in doing good turns to people. There is only one thing greater than happiness in the world, and that is holiness; and it is not in our keeping; but what God has put in our power is the happiness of those about us, and that is largely to be secured by our being kind to them.

" The greatest thing," says some one, " a man can do for his Heavenly Father is to be kind to some of His other children." I wonder why it is that we are not all kinder than we are? How much the world needs it. How easily it is done. How instantaneously it acts. How infallibly it is remembered. How superabundantly it pays itself back—for there is no debtor in the world so honorable, so superbly honorable, as love. " Love never faileth." Love is success, love is happiness, love is life. " Love," I say, with Browning, " is energy of life."

> " For life, with all it yields of joy or woe
>   And hope and fear,
>   Is just our chance o' the prize of learning love—
>   How love might be, hath been indeed, and is."

Where love is, God is. He that dwelleth in love dwelleth in God. God is love.

Therefore love. Without distinction, without calculating, without procrastination, love. Lavish it upon the poor, where it is very easy; especially upon the rich, who often need it most; most of all upon our equals, where it is very difficult, and for whom perhaps we each do least of all. There is a difference between trying to please and giving pleasure.

Always give pleasure. Lose no chance of giving pleasure. For that is the ceaseless and anonymous triumph of a truly loving spirit. " I shall pass through this world but once. Any good thing, therefore, that I can do, or any kindness that I can show to any human being, let me do it now. Let me not defer it or neglect it, for I shall not pass this way again."

Generosity. " Love envieth not." This is love in competition with others. Whenever you attempt a good work you will find other men doing the same kind of work, and probably doing it better. Envy them not. Envy is a feeling of ill-will to those who are in the same line as ourselves, a spirit of covetousness and detraction. How little Christian work even is a protection against un-Christian feeling That most despicable of all the unworthy moods which cloud a Christian's soul assuredly waits for us on the threshold of every work, unless we are fortified with this grace of magnanimity. Only one thing truly need the Christian envy, the large, rich, generous soul which " envieth not."

And then, after having learned all that, you have to learn this further thing, Humility—to put a seal upon your lips and forget what you have done. After you have been kind, after love has stolen forth into the world and done its beautiful work, go back into the shade again and say nothing about it. Love hides even from itself Love waives even self-satisfaction. " Love vaunteth not itself, is not puffed up "

The fifth ingredient is a somewhat strange one to find in this *summum bonum·* Courtesy. This is love in society, love in relation to etiquette: " Love doth not behave itself unseemly."

Politeness has been defined as love in trifles. Courtesy is said
to be love in little things. And the one secret of politeness is to
love. Love cannot behave itself unseemly. You can put the
most untutored persons into the highest society, and if they
have a reservoir of love in their heart, they will not behave
themselves unseemly. They simply cannot do it. Carlyle said
of Robert Burns that there was no truer gentleman in Europe
than the ploughman-poet. It was because he loved everything
—the mouse, and the daisy, and all the things, great and small,
that God had made   So with this simple passport he could
mingle with any society, and enter courts and palaces from his
little cottage on the banks of the Ayr. You know the meaning
of the word " gentleman." It means a gentle man—a man
who does things gently with love. And that is the whole art
and mystery of it. The gentle man cannot in the nature of
things do an ungentle, an ungentlemanly thing   The ungentle
soul, the inconsiderate, unsympathetic nature cannot do anything else. " Love doth not behave itself unseemly."

Unselfishness. " Love seeketh not her own." Observe:
Sceketh not even that which is her own. In Britain the Englishman is devoted, and rightly, to his rights. But there come
times when a man may exercise even the higher right of giving
up his rights. Yet Paul does not summon us to give up our
rights. Love strikes much deeper. It would have us not seek
them at all, ignore them, eliminate the personal element altogether from our calculations. It is not hard to give up our
rights. They are often external. The difficult thing is to give
up ourselves. The more difficult thing still is not to seek things
for ourselves at all. After we have sought them, bought them,
won them, deserved them, we have taken the cream off them
for ourselves already   Little cross then perhaps to give them
up. But not to seek them, to look every man not on his own
things, but on the things of others—*id opus est.* " Seekest thou
great things for thyself? " said the prophet; " seek them not."
Why? Because there is no greatness in things. Things cannot
be great. The only greatness is unselfish love. Even self-denial
in itself is nothing, is almost a mistake. Only a great purpose
or a mightier love can justify the waste. It is more difficult, I
have said, not to seek our own at all, than having sought it, to
give it up. I must take that back. It is only true of a partly

selfish heart. Nothing is a hardship to love, and nothing is hard. I believe that Christ's yoke is easy. Christ's "yoke" is just His way of taking life. And I believe it is an easier way than any other. I believe it is a happier way than any other. The most obvious lesson in Christ's teaching is that there is no happiness in having and getting anything, but only in giving. I repeat, there is no happiness in having or in getting, but only in giving. And half the world is on the wrong scent in the pursuit of happiness. They think it consists in having and getting, and in being served by others. It consists in giving, and in serving others. He that would be great among you, said Christ, let him serve. He that would be happy, let him remember that there is but one way—it is more blessed, it is more happy, to give than to receive.

The next ingredient is a very remarkable one: good temper. "Love is not easily provoked." Nothing could be more striking than to find this here.

We are inclined to look upon bad temper as a very harmless weakness. We speak of it as a mere infirmity of nature, a family failing, a matter of temperament, not a thing to take into very serious account in estimating a man's character. And yet here, right in the heart of this analysis of love, it finds a place; and the Bible again and again returns to condemn it as one of the most destructive elements in human nature

The peculiarity of ill-temper is that it is the vice of the virtuous. It is often the one blot on an otherwise noble character. You know men who are all but perfect, and women who would be entirely perfect, but for an easily ruffled, quick-tempered, or "touchy" disposition. This compatibility of ill-temper with high moral character is one of the strangest and saddest problems of ethics. The truth is, there are to great classes of sin—sins of the body, and sins of the disposition The "prodigal son" may be taken as a type of the first, the "elder brother" of the second. Now society has no doubt whatever as to which of these is the worse. Its brand falls without a challenge, upon the prodigal. But are we right? We have no balance to weigh one another's sins, and coarser and finer are but human words; but faults in the higher nature may be less venial than those in the lower, and to the eye of Him who is love, a sin against love may seem a hundred times more base. No form of vice, not worldliness, not greed of gold, not drunkenness itself, does more to un-Christianize society than evil temper. For imbittering life, for breaking up communities, for destroying the most sacred relationships, for devastating homes, for withering up men and women, for taking the bloom off childhood, in short, for sheer gratuitous misery producing power, this influence stands alone. Look at the elder brother, moral, hardworking, patient, dutiful—let him get all credit for his virtues —look at this man, this baby, sulking outside his own father's door. "He was angry," we read, "and would not go in." Look at the effect upon the father, upon the servants, upon the happiness of the guests. Judge of the effect upon the prodigal —and how many prodigals are kept out of the kingdom of God by the unlovely character of those who profess to be inside? Analyze, as a study in temper, the thundercloud itself as it gathers upon the elder brother's brow. What is it made of? Jealousy, anger, pride, uncharity, cruelty, self-righteousness, touchiness, doggedness, sullenness—these are the ingredients of this dark and loveless soul. In varying proportions, also, these are the ingredients of all ill-temper. Judge if such sins of the disposition are not worse to live in, and for others to live with, than the sins of the body. Did Christ indeed not answer the question Himself when He said, "I say unto you that the publicans and the harlots go into the kingdom of heaven before you." There is really no place in heaven for a disposition like this A man with such a mood could only make heaven miserable for all the people in it Except, therefore, such a man be born again, he cannot, he simply cannot, enter the kingdom of heaven. For it is perfectly certain—and you will not misunderstand me—that to enter heaven a man must take it with him

You will see then why temper is significant. It is not in what it is alone, but in what it reveals. This is why I take the liberty now of speaking of it with such unusual plainness It is a test for love, a symptom, a revelation of an unloving nature at bottom. It is the intermittent fever which bespeaks unintermittent disease within; the occasional bubble escaping to the surface which betrays some rottenness underneath; a sample of the most hidden products of the soul dropped involuntarily when off one's guard; in a word, the lightning form of a hundred hideous and un-Christian sins. For a want of patience, a want of kindness, a want of generosity, a want of courtesy, a want of unselfishness, are all instantaneously symbolized in one flash of temper.

Hence it is not enough to deal with the temper. We must go to the source, and change the inmost nature, and the angry humors will die away of themselves. Souls are made sweet not by taking the acid fluids out, but by putting something in—a great love, a new spirit, the spirit of Christ. Christ, the spirit of Christ, interpenetrating ours, sweetens, purifies, transforms all. This only can eradicate what is wrong, work a chemical change, renovate and regenerate, and rehabilitate the inner man. Will power does not change man. Time does not change man. Christ does. Therefore, " Let that mind be in you which was also in Christ Jesus." Some of us have not much time to lose. Remember once more, that this is a matter of life or death. I cannot help speaking urgently, for myself, for yourselves. " Whoso shall offend one of these little ones, which believe in me, it were better for him that a mill-stone were hanged about his neck, and that he were drowned in the depth of the sea." That is to say, it is the deliberate verdict of the Lord Jesus that it is better not to live than not to love. It is better not to live than not to love.

Guilelessness and sincerity may be dismissed almost with a word. Guilelessness is the grace for suspicious people. And the possession of it is the great secret of personal influence. You will find, if you think for a moment, that the people who influence you are people who believe in you. In an atmosphere of suspicion men shrivel up; but in that atmosphere they expand, and find encouragement and educative fellowship. It is a wonderful thing that here and there in this hard, uncharitable world there should still be left a few rare souls who think no evil. This is the great unworldliness. Love " thinketh no evil," imputes no motive, sees the bright side, puts the best construction on every action What a delightful state of mind to live in! What a stimulus and benediction even to meet with it for a day! To be trusted is to be saved. And if we try to influence or elevate others, we shall soon see that success is in proportion to their belief of our belief in them For the respect of another is the first restoration of the self-respect a man has lost;

our ideal of what he is becomes to him the hope and pattern of what he may become.

"Love rejoiceth not in iniquity, but rejoiceth in the truth." I have called this sincerity from the words rendered in the Authorized Version by "rejoiceth in the truth." And, certainly, were this the real translation, nothing could be more just. For he who loves will love truth not less than men. He will rejoice in the truth—rejoice not in what he has been taught to believe; not in this church's doctrine or in that; not in this ism or in that ism; but "in the truth." He will accept only what is real; he will strive to get at facts; he will search for truth with an humble and unbiassed mind, and cherish whatever he finds at any sacrifice. But the more literal translation of the Revised Version calls for just such a sacrifice for truth's sake here. For what Paul really meant is, as we there read, "Rejoiceth not in unrighteousness, but rejoiceth with the truth," a quality which probably no one English word—and certainly not sincerity—adequately defines. It includes, perhaps more strictly, the self-restraint which refuses to make capital out of others' faults; the charity which delights not in exposing the weakness of others, but "covereth all things"; the sincerity of purpose which endeavors to see things as they are, and rejoices to find them better than suspicion feared or calumny denounced.

So much for the analysis of love. Now the business of our lives is to have these things fitted into our characters   That is the supreme work to which we need to address ourselves in this world, to learn love   Is life not full of opportunities for learning love?   Every man and woman every day has a thousand of them. The world is not a playground; it is a schoolroom. Life is not a holiday, but an education. And the one eternal lesson for us all is how better we can love. What makes a man a good cricketer? Practice. What makes a man a good artist, a good sculptor, a good musician? Practice. What makes a man a good linguist, a good stenographer? Practice. What makes a man a good man? Practice. Nothing else   There is nothing capricious about religion. We do not get the soul in different ways, under different laws, from those in which we get the body and the mind. If a man does not exercise his arm he develops no biceps muscle; and if a man does not exercise his soul, he acquires no muscle in his soul, no strength of character, no vigor of moral fibre, nor beauty of spiritual growth. Love is not a thing of enthusiastic emotion. It is a rich, strong, manly, vigorous expression of the whole round Christian character—the Christ-like nature in its fullest development. And the constituents of this great character are only to be built up by a ceaseless practice

What was Christ doing in the carpenter's shop? Practising. Though perfect, we read that He learned obedience, He increased in wisdom and in favor with God and man. Do not quarrel, therefore, with your lot in life. Do not complain of its never-ceasing cares, its petty environment, the vexations you have to stand, the small and sordid souls you have to live and work with. Above all, do not resent temptation; do not be perplexed because it seems to thicken round you more and more, and ceases neither for effort nor for agony nor prayer. That is the practice which God appoints you; and it is having its work in making you patient, and humble, and generous, and unselfish, and kind, and courteous. Do not grudge the hand that is moulding the still too shapeless image within you It is growing more beautiful, though you see it not, and every touch of temptation may add to its perfection. Therefore, keep in the midst of life. Do not isolate yourself. Be among men, and among things, and among troubles, and difficulties, and obstacles. You remember Goethe's words: *Es bildet ein Talent sich in der Stille, Doch ein Character in dem Strom der Welt.* " Talent develops itself in solitude; character in the stream of life "

Talent develops itself in solitude—the talent of prayer, of faith, of meditation, of seeing the unseen; character grows in the stream of the world's life. That chiefly is where men are to learn love

How? Now, how? To make it easier, I have named a few of the elements of love. But these are only elements. Love itself can never be defined. Light is a something more than the sum of its ingredients—a glowing, dazzling, tremulous ether. And love is something more than all its elements—a palpitating, quivering, sensitive, living thing. By synthesis of all the colors, men can make whiteness, they cannot make light. By synthesis of all the virtues, men can make virtue, they cannot make love. How then are we to have this transcendent living whole conveyed into ours souls? We brace our wills to secure it. We try to copy those who have it. We lay down rules about it We watch. We pray. But these things alone will not bring love into our nature Love is an effect And only as we fulfil the right condition can we have the effect produced Shall I tell you what the cause is?

If you turn to the Revised Version of the First Epistle of John you will find these words: "We love because He first loved us." "We love," not "We love Him." That is the way the old version has it, and it is quite wrong.

"We love—because He first loved us" Look at that word "because" It is the cause of which I have spoken. "Because He first loved us," the effect follows that we love, we love Him, we love all men. We cannot help it Because He loved us, we love, we love everybody. Our heart is slowly changed. Contemplate the love of Christ, and you will love. Stand before that mirror, reflect Christ's character, and you will be changed into the same image from tenderness to tenderness. There is no other way You cannot love to order You can only look at the lovely object, and fall in love with it, and grow into likeness to it. And so look at this perfect character, this perfect life Look at the great sacrifice as He laid down Himself, all through life, and upon the cross of Calvary; and you must love Him. And loving Him, you must become like Him Love begets love. It is a process of induction Put a piece of iron in the presence of an electrified body, and that piece of iron for a time becomes electrified. It is changed into a temporary magnet, in the presence of a permanent magnet, and as long as you leave the two side by side, they are both magnets alike. Remain side by side with Him who loved us, and gave Himself for us, and you too will become a permanent magnet, a permanently attractive force; and like Him you will draw all men unto you, like Him you will be drawn unto all men. That is the inevitable effect of love. Any man who fulfils that cause must have that effect produced in him Try to give up the idea that religion comes to us by chance, or by mystery, or by caprice It comes to us by natural law, or by supernatural law, for all law is divine Edward Irving went to see a dying boy once, and when he entered the room he just put his hand on the sufferer's head, and said, "My boy, God loves you," and went away And the boy started

DRUMMOND

from his bed, and called out to the people in the house, " God loves me! God loves me! " It changed that boy. The sense that God loved him overpowered him, melted him down, and began the creating of a new heart in him. And that is how the love of God melts down the unlovely heart in man, and begets in him the new creature, who is patient and humble and gentle and unselfish. And there is no other way to get it. There is no mystery about it. We love others, we love everybody, we love our enemies, because He first loved us.

THE DEFENCE.—Now I have a closing sentence or two to add about Paul's reason for singling out love as the supreme possession. It is a very remarkable reason. In a single word it is this: it lasts. " Love," urges Paul, " never faileth." Then he begins again one of his marvellous lists of the great things of the day, and exposes them one by one. He runs over the things that men thought were going to last, and shows that they are all fleeting, temporary, passing away.

" Whether there be prophecies, they shall fail." It was the mother's ambition for her boy in those days that he should become a prophet. For hundreds of years God had never spoken by means of any prophet, and at that time the prophet was greater than the king. Men waited wistfully for another messenger to come, and hung upon his lips when he appeared as upon the very voice of God. Paul says, " Whether there be prophecies, they shall fail " This book is full of prophecies. One by one they have " failed "; that is, having been fulfilled, their work is finished; they have nothing more to do now in the world except to feed a devout man's faith.

Then Paul talks about tongues. That was another thing that was greatly coveted. " Whether there be tongues, they shall cease." As we all know, many, many centuries have passed since tongues have been known in this world They have ceased. Take it in any sense you like. Take it, for illustration merely, as languages in general—a sense which was not in Paul's mind at all, and which, though it cannot give us the specific lesson, will point the general truth. Consider the words in which these chapters were written—Greek. It has gone. Take the Latin— the other great tongue of those days. It ceased long ago. Look at the Indian language. It is ceasing. The language of Wales, of Ireland, of the Scottish Highlands is dying before our eyes.

The most popular book in the English tongue at the present time, except the Bible, is one of Dickens's works, his " Pick-wick Papers " It is largely written in the language of London street life , and experts assure us that in fifty years it will be un-intelligible to the average English reader.

Then Paul goes further and with even greater boldness adds, " Whether there be knowledge, it shall vanish away " The wisdom of the ancients, where is it? It is wholly gone. A schoolboy to-day knows more than Sir Isaac Newton knew His knowledge has vanished away. You put yesterday's news-paper in the fire. Its knowledge has vanished away. You buy the old editions of the great encyclopedias for a few pence Their knowledge has vanished away. Look how the coach has been superseded by the use of steam. Look how electricity has superseded that, and swept a hundred almost new inven-tions into oblivion. One of the greatest living authorities, Sir William Thompson, said the other day, " The steam engine is passing away." Whether there be knowledge, it shall vanish away " At every workshop you will see, in the back yard, a heap of old iron, a few wheels, a few levers, a few cranks, broken and eaten with rust. Twenty years ago that was the pride of the city. Men flocked in from the country to see the great in-vention; now it is superseded, its day is done And all the boasted science and philosophy of this day will soon be old But yesterday, in the University of Edinburgh, the greatest figure in the faculty was Sir James Simpson, the discoverer of chloroform The other day his successor and nephew, Profes-sor Simpson, was asked by the librarian of the university to go to the library and pick out the books on his subject that were no longer needed. And his reply to the librarian was this: " Take every text-book that is more than ten years old, and put it down in the cellar " Sir James Simpson was a great author-ity only a few years ago: men came from all parts of the earth to consult him; and almost the whole teaching of that time is consigned by the science of to-day to oblivion And in every branch of science it is the same. " Now we know in part. We see through a glass, darkly."

Can you tell me anything that is going to last? Many things Paul did not condescend to name. He did not mention money, fortune, fame; but he picked out the great things of his time, the things the best men thought had something in them, and brushed them peremptorily aside. Paul had no charge against these things in themselves. All he said about them was that they would not last. They were great things, but not supreme things. There were things beyond them. What we are stretches past what we do, beyond what we possess. Many things that men denounce as sins are not sins; but they are temporary. And that is a favorite argument of the New Testament John says of the world, not that it is wrong, but simply that it " passeth away." There is a great deal in the world that is delightful and beautiful; there is a great deal in it that is great and engrossing; but it will not last. All that is in the world, the lust of the eye, the lust of the flesh, and the pride of life, are but for a little while. Love not the world, therefore. Nothing that it contains is worth the life and consecration of an immortal soul. The immortal soul must give itself to something that is immortal. And the only immortal things are these: " Now abideth faith, hope, love, but the greatest of these is love."

Some think the time may come when two of these three things will also pass away—faith into sight, hope into fruition. Paul does not say so. We know but little now about the conditions of the life that is to come But what is certain is that love must last. God, the eternal God, is love. Covet, therefore, that everlasting gift, that one thing which it is certain is going to stand, that one coinage which will be current in the universe when all the other coinages of all the nations of the world shall be useless and unhonored You will give yourselves to many things; give yourselves first to love. Hold things in their proportion *Hold things in their proportion* Let at least the first great object of our lives be to achieve the character defended in these words, the character—and it is the character of Christ—which is built round love.

I have said this thing is eternal. Did you ever notice how continually John associates love and faith with eternal life? I was not told when I was a boy that " God so loved the world that He gave His only begotten Son, that whosoever believeth in Him should have everlasting life " What I was told, I remember, was, that God so loved the world that, if I trusted in Him, I was to have a thing called peace, or I was to have rest, or I was to have joy, or I was to have safety. But I had to find out for myself that whosoever trusteth in Him—that is, whosoever loveth Him—for trust is only the avenue to love—hath everlasting life. The gospel offers a man life. Never offer men a thimbleful of gospel. Do not offer them merely joy, or merely peace, or merely rest, or merely safety; tell them how Christ came to give men a more abundant life than they have, a life abundant in love, and therefore abundant in salvation for themselves, and large in enterprise for the alleviation and redemption of the world. Then only can the gospel take hold of the whole of a man, body, soul, and spirit, and give to each part of his nature its exercise and reward. Many of the current gospels are addressed only to a part of man's nature. They offer peace, not life; faith, not love; justification, not regeneration. And men slip back again from such religion because it has never really held them. Their nature was not all in it. It offered no deeper and gladder life-current than the life that was lived before. Surely it stands to reason that only a fuller love can compete with the love of the world.

To love abundantly is to live abundantly, and to love forever is to live forever. Hence, eternal life is inextricably bound up with love. We want to live forever for the same reason that we want to live to-morrow. Why do you want to live to-morrow? It is because there is someone who loves you, and whom you want to see to-morrow, and be with, and love back. There is no other reason why we should live on than that we love and are beloved. It is when a man has no one to love him that he commits suicide. So long as he has friends, those who love him and whom he loves, he will live; because to live is to love. Be it but the love of a dog, it will keep him in life; but let that go and he has no contact with life, no reason to live. He dies by his own hand. Eternal life also is to know God, and God is love. This is Christ's own definition. Ponder it. " This is life eternal, that they might know Thee the only true God, and Jesus Christ whom Thou hast sent." Love must be eternal. It is what God is. On the last analysis, then, love is life. Love never faileth, and life never faileth, so long as there is love. That is the philosophy of what Paul is showing us; the reason why in the nature of things love should be the supreme thing—because it is going to last; because in the nature of things it is an eternal life. It is a thing that we are living now, not that we get when we die, that we shall have a poor chance of getting when we die unless we are living now   No worse fate can befall a man in this world than to live and grow old alone, unloving, and un-loved.   To be lost is to live in an unregenerate condition, love-less and unloved, and to be saved is to love; and he that dwell-eth in love dwelleth already in God   For God is love.

Now I have all but finished. How many of you will join me in reading this chapter once a week for the next three months? A man did that once and it changed his whole life. Will you do it? It is for the greatest thing in the world. You might begin by reading it every day, especially the verses which describe the perfect character.   " Love suffereth long and is kind, love en-vieth not; love vaunteth not itself."   Get these ingredients into your life   Then everything that you do is eternal   It is worth doing.   It is worth giving time to   No man can become a saint in his sleep; and to fulfil the condition required demands a certain amount of prayer and meditation and time, just as im-provement in any direction, bodily or mental, requires prepara-tion and care.   Address yourselves to that one thing, at any cost have this transcendent character exchanged for yours. You will find as you look back upon your life that the moments that stand out, the moments when you have really lived, are the moments when you have done things in a spirit of love   As memory scans the past, above and beyond all the transitory pleasures of life, there leap forward those supreme hours when you have been enabled to do unnoticed kindnesses to those round about you, things too trifling to speak about, but which you feel have entered into your eternal life. I have seen almost all the beautiful things God has made; I have enjoyed almost every pleasure that He has planned for man; and yet as I look back I see standing out above all the life that has gone, four or five short experiences when the love of God reflected it-self in some poor imitation, some small act of love of mine, and these seem to be the things which alone of all one's life abide. Everything else in all our lives is transitory.   Every other good is visionary.   But the acts of love which no man knows about, or can ever know about—they never fail.   In the book of Mat-thew, where the judgment day is depicted for us in the imagery of One seated upon a throne and dividing the sheep from the goats, the test of a man then is not, " How have I believed?"

but " How have I loved? " The test of religion, the final test of religion, is not religiousness, but love. I say the final test of religion at that great day is not religiousness, but love; not what I have done, not what I have believed, not what I have achieved, but how I have discharged the common charities of life. Sins of commission in that awful indictment are not even referred to. By what we have not done, by sins of omission, we are judged. It could not be otherwise. For the withholding of love is the negation of the spirit of Christ, the proof that we never knew Him, that for us He lived in vain. It means that He suggested nothing in all our thoughts, that He inspired nothing in all our lives, that we were not once near enough to Him to be seized with the spell of His compassion for the world. It means that:

> " I lived for myself, I thought for myself,
>   For myself, and none beside—
> Just as if Jesus had never lived,
>   As if He had never died."

It is the Son of Man before whom the nations of the world shall be gathered. It is in the presence of humanity that we shall be charged. And the spectacle itself, the mere sight of it, will silently judge each one. Those will be there whom we have met and helped; or there, the unpitied multitude whom we neglected or despised. No other witness need be summoned. No other charge than lovelessness shall be preferred. Be not deceived. The words which all of us shall one day hear sound not of theology, but of life, not of churches and saints, but of the hungry and the poor; not of creeds and doctrines, but of shelter and clothing; not of Bibles and prayer-books, but of cups of cold water in the name of Christ. Thank God the Christianity of to-day is coming nearer the world's need. Live to help that on. Thank God men know better, by a hair's-breadth, what religion is, what God is, who Christ is, where Christ is. Who is Christ? He who fed the hungry, clothed the naked, visited the sick. And where is Christ? Where?—whoso shall receive a little child in My name receiveth Me. And who are Christs? Everyone that loveth is born of God.

www.ingramcontent.com/pod-product-compliance
Lightning Source LLC
Chambersburg PA
CBHW020922020726
47495CB00002B/301